Alfonso María de Liguori, Eugene Grimm

The Passion and the Death of Jesus Christ

Alfonso Maria de Liguori, Eugene Grimm

The Passion and the Death of Jesus Christ

ISBN/EAN: 9783742814524

Manufactured in Europe, USA, Canada, Australia, Japa

Cover: Foto ©Thomas Meinert / pixelio.de

Manufactured and distributed by brebook publishing software
(www.brebook.com)

Alfonso Maria de Liguori, Eugene Grimm

The Passion and the Death of Jesus Christ

𝕿𝖍𝖊 𝕮𝖊𝖓𝖙𝖊𝖓𝖆𝖗𝖞 𝕰𝖉𝖎𝖙𝖎𝖔𝖓.

THE
PASSION AND THE DEATH
OF JESUS CHRIST.

BY

St. ALPHONSUS DE LIGUORI,
Doctor of the Church.

EDITED BY

REV. EUGENE GRIMM,
Priest of the Congregation of the Most Holy Redeemer.

NEW YORK, CINCINNATI, AND ST. LOUIS:
BENZIGER BROTHERS,
Printers to the Holy Apostolic See.

R. WASHBOURNE,　　　　　　　　M. H. GILL & SON,
18 PATERNOSTER ROW, LONDON.　　50 UPPER O'CONNELL STREET, DUBLIN.
1887.

APPROBATION.

By virtue of the authority granted me by the Most Rev. Nicholas Mauron, Superior General of the Congregation of the Most Holy Redeemer, I hereby sanction the publication of the work entitled "The Passion and the Death of Jesus Christ," which is Vol. V. of the new and complete edition in English of the works of Saint Alphonsus de Liguori, called "The Centenary Edition."

ELIAS FRED. SCHAUER,

Sup. Prov. Baltimorensis.

BALTIMORE, MD., *October* 15, 1886.

CONTENTS.

SIMPLE EXPOSITION OF THE CIRCUMSTANCES OF THE PASSION OF JESUS CHRIST.

ACCORDING TO THE NARRATION OF THE HOLY EVANGELISTS.

WITH SOME REFLECTIONS AND AFFECTIONS.

CONSIDERATIONS ON THE PASSION OF JESUS CHRIST.

Contents.

MEDITATIONS ON THE PASSION OF JESUS CHRIST

FOR EACH DAY OF THE WEEK.

MEDITATIONS DRAWN FROM THE CONSIDERATIONS.

MEDITATIONS FOR THE LAST FIFTEEN DAYS OF LENT.

MEDITATIONS FOR THE EASTER FESTIVAL.

VARIOUS EXERCISES.

THE fifth volume of the Ascetical Works is entirely devoted to the Passion of Jesus Christ. It consists of five parts, namely: 1. Reflections on the Passion. 2. The Simple Exposition of the Passion. 3. Considerations. 4. Meditations. 5. Other Exercises of Piety.

A short treatise on the Passion has been given in. Volume II. The "Darts of Fire" has been inserted in Volume IV.—ED.

INVOCATION

OF JESUS AND MARY.

O Saviour of the world, O Love of souls, O Lord most lovely of all beings! Thou by Thy Passion didst come to win to Thyself our hearts, by showing us the immense love that Thou didst bear to us in accomplishing a redemption which has brought to us a sea of benedictions, and which cost Thee a sea of pains and ignominies. It was principally for this end that Thou didst institute the Most Holy Sacrament of the Altar, in order that we might have a perpetual memorial of Thy Passion: " That we might have forever a perpetual memorial of so great a benefit," says St. Thomas, " He gives his body to be the food of the faithful,"[1] which St. Paul had already said. *As often as you shall eat this bread, you shall show the death of the Lord.*[2] Oh, how many holy souls hast Thou persuaded by these prodigies of love, consumed by the flames of Thy love, to renounce all earthly goods, in order to dedicate themselves entirely to loving Thee alone, O most amiable Saviour! O my Jesus! I pray Thee make me always remember Thy Passion; and grant that I also, a miserable sinner, overcome at last by so many loving devices, may return to love Thee, and to show Thee, by my poor love, some mark of gratitude for the excessive love which Thou, my God and my Saviour, hast borne to

[1] " Ut autem tanti beneficii jugis in nobis maneret memoria, corpus suum in cibum fidelibus dereliquit."—*Off Corp. Chr.* l. 2.

[2] " Quotiescumque enim manducabitis panem hunc, et calicem bibetis, mortem Domini annuntiabitis."—1 *Cor.* xi. 26.

me. Remember, my Jesus, that I am one of those sheep of Thine, to save which Thou didst come down on the earth and didst sacrifice Thy divine life. I know that, after having redeemed me by Thy death, Thou hast not ceased to love me, and that Thou dost still bear to me the same love that Thou hadst for me when Thou didst die for my sake. Oh, permit me no longer to lead a life of ingratitude towards Thee, my God, who dost so much deserve to be loved, and hast done so much to be loved by me!

And thou, O most holy Virgin Mary, who didst take so great a part in the Passion of thy Son, obtain for me, I beseech thee, through the merits of thy sorrows, the grace to experience a taste of that compassion which thou didst so sensibly feel at the death of Jesus, and obtain for me also a spark of that love which wrought all the martyrdom of thy afflicted heart. Amen.

" Let my mind, O Lord Jesus Christ, I beseech Thee, be absorbed in the fiery and honeyed sweetness of Thy love, that I may die for love of the love of Thee, who wert pleased to die for love of the love of me."[1]

[1] " Absorbeat, quæso, Domine Jesu Christe, mentem meam ignita et melliflua vis amoris tui, ut amore amoris tui moriar, qui amore amoris mei dignatus es mori."—*Prayer of St. Francis Assisi.*

TO THE READER.

In my book on the *Glories of Mary*, I promised to write for you another that should treat of the love of Jesus Christ; but on account of my corporal infirmities, my Director would not permit me to keep my promise. I have been scarcely able to publish these short Reflections on the Passion of Jesus Christ. These Reflections, however, contain the gist of what I had gathered for my subject, withholding only what had reference to the Incarnation and birth of our Saviour, as I intended to compose from it a little work for the Novena of Christmas, which I shall afterwards publish, if I obtain permission. Nevertheless, I hope that the little work that I offer you to-day will be pleasing to you, especially since it will put before you, in regular order, the passages of Holy Scripture referring to the love that Jesus Christ showed us in his death; for there is nothing more apt to stimulate a Christian to the love of God than the word of God itself that is drawn from Holy Writ.

Let us, therefore, love Jesus Christ, who is our Saviour, our God, and our supreme good. This is the reason why I invite you to cast a glance at the Passion; for you will find therein all the motives that we can have to hope for eternal life and to love God; and in this our salvation consists.

All the saints cherished a tender devotion towards Jesus Christ in his Passion; this is the only means by which they sanctified themselves. Father Balthasar Alvarez, as we read in his life, used to say that one should not think of having done anything so long as one has not succeeded in constantly keeping in one's heart Jesus crucified. His method of prayer consisted in placing himself at the feet of Jesus crucified, by meditating especially on his poverty, his humiliations, sorrows, and by listening to the lesson that our Lord made him hear from the height of the cross. You may also hope to sanctify yourself if you continue in like manner to consider what your divine Redeemer has done and suffered for you.

Ask him, without ceasing, to give you his love; and this grace you should never weary to ask from your Queen, the Blessed Virgin, who is called the Mother of beautiful love. And when you ask this great gift for yourself, ask it also for me, who have desired to contribute to your sanctification in offering you this little work. I promise to do the same thing for you in order that, one day, in paradise, we may embrace each other in a holy charity, and may recognize each other as devoted servants of our most amiable Saviour, finding ourselves united there in the society of the elect to see forever, face to face, and love for all eternity, Jesus, our Saviour and our love.   Amen.

INTRODUCTION.

HOW USEFUL IT IS TO MEDITATE ON THE PASSION OF JESUS CHRIST.

The lover of souls, our most loving Redeemer, declared that he had no other motive in coming down upon earth to become man than to enkindle in the hearts of men the fire of his holy love: *I am come to cast fire on earth; and what will I but that it be kindled?*[1] And, oh, what beautiful flames of love has he not enkindled in so many souls, especially by the pains that he chose to suffer in his death, in order to prove to us the immeasurable love which he still bears to us!

Oh, how many souls, happy in the wounds of Jesus, as in burning furnaces of love, have been so inflamed with his love that they have not refused to consecrate to him their goods, their lives, and their whole selves, surmounting with great courage all the difficulties which they had to encounter in the observance of the divine law, for the love of that Lord who, being God, chose to suffer so much for the love of them! This was just the counsel that the Apostle gave us, in order that we might not fail, but make great advances in the way of salvation: *Think diligently upon Him who endureth such opposition from sinners against Himself, that you be not wearied, fainting in your minds.*[2]

Wherefore St. Augustine, all inflamed with love at the sight of Jesus nailed on the cross, prayed thus sweetly:

[1] " Ignem veni mittere in terram; et quid volo, nisi ut accendatur?"
—*Luke*, xii. 49.
[2] " Recogitate enim eum, qui talem sustinuit a peccatoribus adversum semetipsum contradictionem, ut ne fatigemini, animis vestris deficientes."—*Heb.* xii. 3.

2

"Imprint, O Lord, Thy wounds in my heart, that I may read therein suffering and love: suffering, that I may endure for Thee all suffering; love, that I may despise for Thee all love.[1] Write, he said, my most loving Saviour, write on my heart Thy wounds, in order that I may always behold therein Thy sufferings and Thy love. Yes, because, having before my eyes the great sufferings that Thou, my God, didst endure for me, I may bear in silence all the sufferings that it may fall to my lot to endure; and at the sight of the love which Thou didst exhibit for me on the cross, I may never love or be able to love any other than Thee.

And from what source did the saints draw courage and strength to suffer torments, martyrdom, and death, if not from the sufferings of Jesus crucified? St. Joseph of Leonessa, a Capuchin, on seeing that they were going to bind him with cords, for a painful incision that the surgeon was to make in his body, took into his hands his crucifix and said, "Why these cords? why these cords? Behold, these are my chains—my Saviour nailed to the cross for love of me. He, through his sufferings, constrains me to bear every trial for his sake." And thus he suffered the amputation without a complaint; looking upon Jesus, who, *as a lamb before his shearers, was dumb, and did not open His mouth.*[2]

Who, then, can ever complain that he suffers wrongfully, when he considers Jesus, who was *bruised for our sins?*[3] Who can refuse to obey, on account of some inconvenience, when Jesus *became obedient unto death?*[4] Who can refuse ignominies, when they behold Jesus treated as a fool, as a mock king, as a disorderly person; struck,

[1] "Scribe, Domine, vulnera tua in corde meo, ut in eis legam dolorem et amorem: dolorem, ad sustinendum pro te omnem dolorem; amorem, ad contemnendum pro te omnem amorem.
[2] "Et non aperuit os suum."—*Isa.* liii. 7.
[3] "Attritus propter scelera nostra."—*Isa.* liii. 5.
[4] "Factus obediens usque ad mortem."—*Phil.* ii. 8.

spit upon on his face, and suspended upon an infamous gibbet?

Who could love any other object besides Jesus when they see him dying in the midst of so many sufferings and insults, in order to captivate our love? A certain devout solitary prayed to God to teach him what he could do in order to love him perfectly. Our Lord revealed to him that there was no more efficient way to arrive at the perfect love of him than to meditate constantly on his Passion. St. Teresa lamented and complained of certain books which had taught her to leave off meditating on the Passion of Jesus Christ, because this might be an impediment to the contemplation of his divinity; and the saint exclaimed, "O Lord of my soul, O my Jesus crucified, my treasure! I never remember this opinion without thinking that I have been guilty of great treachery. And is it possible that Thou, my Lord, couldst be an obstacle to me in the way of a greater good? Whence, then, do all good things come to me, but from Thee?" And she then added, "I have seen that, in order to please God, and to induce him to grant us great graces, he wills that they should all pass through the hands of this most sacred humanity, in which his divine majesty declared that he took pleasure." [1]

For this reason, Father Balthasar Alvarez said that ignorance of the treasures that we possess in Jesus was the ruin of Christians ; and therefore his most favorite and usual meditation was on the Passion of Jesus Christ. He meditated especially on three of the sufferings of Jesus,—his poverty, contempt, and pain; and he exhorted his penitents to meditate frequently on the Passion of our Redeemer, telling them that they should not consider that they had done anything at all, until they had arrived at retaining Jesus crucified continually present in their hearts.

[1] Life, chap. 22.

"He who desires," says St. Bonaventure, "to go on advancing from virtue to virtue, from grace to grace, should meditate continually on the Passion of Jesus."[1] And he adds that "there is no practice more profitable for the entire sanctification of the soul than the frequent meditation of the sufferings of Jesus Christ."[2]

St. Augustine also said that a single tear shed at the remembrance of the Passion of Jesus is worth more than a pilgrimage to Jerusalem, or a year of fasting on bread and water. Yes, because it was for this end that our Saviour suffered so much, in order that we should think of his sufferings; because if we think on them, it is impossible not to be inflamed with divine love: *The charity of Christ presseth us*,[3] says St. Paul. Jesus is loved by few, because few consider the pains he has suffered for us; but he that frequently considers them cannot live without loving Jesus. "The charity of Christ presseth us." He will feel himself so constrained by his love that he will not find it possible to refrain from loving a God so full of love, who has suffered so much to make us love him.

Therefore the Apostle said that he desired to know nothing but Jesus, and Jesus crucified; that is, the love that he has shown us on the cross: *I judged not myself to know anything among you but Jesus Christ, and Him crucified*.[4] And, in truth, from what books can we better learn the science of the saints—that is, the science of loving God—than from Jesus crucified? That great servant of God, Brother Bernard of Corlione, the Capu-

---

[1] "Si vis, homo, de virtute in virtutem, de gratia in gratiam proficere, quotidie mediteris Domini passionem."

[2] "Nihil enim in anima ita operatur universalem sanctificationem, sicut meditatio passionis Christi."

[3] "Charitas enim Christi urget nos."—2 *Cor.* v. 14.

[4] "Non enim judicavi me scire aliquid inter vos, nisi Jesum Christum, et hunc crucifixum."—1 *Cor.* ii. 2.

chin, not being able to read, his brother religious wanted to teach him, upon which he went to consult his crucifix; but Jesus answered him from the cross, "What is reading? what are books? Behold, I am the book wherein thou mayst continually read the love I have borne thee." O great subject to be considered during our whole life and during all eternity! A God dead for the love of us! a God dead for the love of us! O wonderful subject!

St. Thomas Aquinas was one day paying a visit to St. Bonaventure, and asked him from what book he had drawn all the beautiful lessons he had written. St. Bonaventure showed him the image of the Crucified, which was completely blackened by all the kisses that he had given it, and said, "This is my book whence I receive everything that I write; and it has taught me whatever little I know."

In short, all the saints have learned the art of loving God from the study of the crucifix. Brother John of Alvernia, every time that he beheld Jesus wounded, could not restrain his tears. Brother James of Tuderto, when he heard the Passion of our Redeemer read, not only wept bitterly, but broke out into loud sobs, overcome with the love with which he was inflamed toward his beloved Lord.

It was this sweet study of the crucifix which made St. Francis become a great seraph. He wept so continually in meditating on the sufferings of Jesus Christ, that he almost entirely lost his sight. On one occasion, being found crying out and weeping, he was asked what was the matter with him. "What ails me?" answered the saint. "I weep over the sorrows and insults inflicted on my Lord; and my sorrow is increased when I think of those ungrateful men who do not love him, but live without any thought of him." Every time that he heard the bleating of a lamb, he felt himself touched with compassion at the thought of the death of Jesus, the Immaculate Lamb, drained of every drop of blood upon the cross for the sins of the world. And therefore this loving saint could find no subject on which he exhorted his brethren with greater eagerness than the constant remembrance of the Passion of Jesus.

This, then, is the book—Jesus crucified—which, if we constantly read it, will teach us, on the one hand, to have a lively fear of sin, and, on the other hand, will inflame us with love for a God so full of love for us; while we read in these wounds the great malice of sin, which reduced a God to suffer so bitter a death in order to satisfy the divine justice, and the love which our Saviour has shown us in choosing to suffer so much in order to prove to us how much he loved us.

Let us beseech the divine Mother Mary to obtain for us from her Son the grace that we also may enter into these furnaces of love, in which so many loving hearts are consumed, in order that, our earthly affections being there burned away, we also may burn with those blessed flames, which render souls holy on earth and blessed in heaven. Amen.

REFLECTIONS AND AFFECTIONS

PASSION OF JESUS CHRIST.

CHAPTER I.

THE LOVE OF JESUS CHRIST IN BEING WILLING TO SATISFY THE DIVINE JUSTICE FOR OUR SINS.

I.

We read in history of a proof of love so prodigious that it will be the admiration of all ages.

There was once a king, lord of many kingdoms, who had one only son, so beautiful, so holy, so amiable, that he was the delight of his father, who loved him as much as himself. This young prince had a great affection for one of his slaves; so much so that, the slave having committed a crime for which he had been condemned to death, the prince offered himself to die for the slave; the father, being jealous of justice, was satisfied to condemn his beloved son to death, in order that the slave might remain free from the punishment that he deserved: and thus the son died a malefactor's death, and the slave was freed from punishment.

This fact, the like of which has never happened in this world, and never will happen, is related in the Gospels, where we read that the Son of God, the Lord of the universe, seeing that man was condemned to eternal death in punishment of his sins, chose to take upon himself human flesh, and thus to pay by his death the penalty due to man: *He was offered because it was His own will.*[1] And his Eternal Father caused him to die upon the cross to save us miserable sinners: *He spared not His own Son, but delivered Him up for us all.*[2] What dost thou think, O devout soul, of this love of the Son and of the Father?

Thou didst, then, O my beloved Redeemer, choose by Thy death to sacrifice Thyself in order to obtain the pardon of my sins. And what return of gratitude shall I then make to Thee? Thou hast done too much to oblige me to love Thee; I should indeed be most ungrateful to Thee if I did not love Thee with my whole heart. Thou hast given for me Thy divine life; I, miserable sinner that I am, give Thee my own life. Yes, I will at least spend that period of life that remains to me only in loving Thee, obeying Thee, and pleasing Thee.

II.

O men, men! let us love this our Redeemer, who, being God, has not disdained to take upon himself our sins, in order to satisfy by his sufferings for the chastisement which we have deserved: *Surely He hath borne our infirmities, and carried our sorrows.*[3]

St. Augustine says that our Lord in creating us formed us by virtue of his power, but in redeeming us he has saved us from death by means of his sufferings : "He created us in his strength ; he sought us back in his weakness."[4]

[1] " Oblatus est, quia ipse voluit."—*Isa.* liii. 7.
[2] " Proprio Filio suo non pepercit, sed pro nobis omnibus tradidit illum."—*Rom.* viii. 32.
[3] " Vere languores nostros ipse tulit, et dolores nostros ipse portavit."—*Isa.* liii. 4.
[4] " Condidit nos fortitudine sua, quæsivit nos infirmitate sua."—*In Jo. tr.* 15.

How much do I not owe Thee, O Jesus my Saviour! Oh, if I were to give my blood a thousand times over,—if I were to spend a thousand lives for Thee,—it would yet be nothing. Oh, how could any one that meditated much on the love which Thou hast shown him in Thy Passion, love anything else but Thee? Through the love with which Thou didst love us on the cross, grant me the grace to love Thee with my whole heart. I love Thee, infinite Goodness; I love Thee above every other good; and I ask nothing more of Thee but Thy holy love.

"But how is this?" continues St. Augustine. How is it possible, O Saviour of the world, that Thy love has arrived at such a height that when I had committed the crime, Thou shouldst have to pay the penalty? "Whither has Thy love reached? I have sinned; Thou art punished." [1]

And what could it then signify to Thee, adds St. Bernard, that we should lose ourselves and be chastised, as we well deserved to be; that Thou shouldst choose to satisfy with Thy innocent flesh for our sins, and to die in order to deliver us from death! "O good Jesus, what doest Thou? We ought to have died, and it is Thou who diest. We have sinned and Thou sufferest. A deed without precedent, grace without merit, charity without measure." [2] O deed which never has had and never will have its match! O grace which we could never merit! O love which can never be understood!

III.

Isaias had already foretold that our blessed Redeemer should be condemned to death, and as an innocent lamb

[1] "Quo tuus attigit amor? Ego inique egi, tu pœna mulctaris."—*Medit.* c. 7.

[2] "O bone Jesu! quid tibi est? Mori nos debuimus, et tu solvis? Nos peccavimus, et tu luis?—Opus sine exemplo, gratia sine merito, charitas sine modo."—*Apud Lohn. Bibl.* tit. 110, § 3.

brought to the sacrifice : *He shall be led as a sheep to the slaughter.*' What a cause of wonder it must have been to the angels, O my God, to behold their innocent Lord led as a victim to be sacrificed on the altar of the cross for the love of man ! And what a cause of horror to heaven and to hell, the sight of a God extended as an infamous criminal on a shameful gibbet for the sins of his creatures !

Christ hath redeemed us from the curse of the law, being made a curse for us (for it is written, Cursed is every one that hangeth on a tree): that the blessing of Abraham might come to the Gentiles through Jesus Christ.' "He was made a curse upon the cross," says St. Ambrose, "that thou mightest be blessed in the kingdom of God."'

O my dearest Saviour ! Thou wert, then, content, in order to obtain for me the blessing of God, to embrace the dishonor of appearing upon the cross accursed in the sight of the whole world, and even forsaken in Thy sufferings by Thy Eternal Father,—a suffering which made Thee cry out with a loud voice, *My God, My God, why hast Thou forsaken Me ?*' Yes, observes Simon of Cassia, it was for this end that Jesus was abandoned in his Passion in order that we might not remain abandoned in the sins which we have committed : "Therefore Christ was abandoned in his sufferings that we might not be abandoned in our guilt."' O prodigy of compassion ! O excess of love of God towards men ! And how can there

---

[1] "Sicut ovis ad occisionem ducetur."—*Isa.* liii. 7.

[2] "Christus nos redemit de maledicto legis, factus pro nobis maledictum, quia scriptum est : Maledictus omnis qui pendet in ligno ; ut in gentibus benedictio Abrahæ fieret in Christo Jesu."—*Gal.* iii. 13.

[3] "Ille maledictum in cruce factus est, ut tu benedictus esses in Dei regno."—*Epist.* 47.

[4] "Deus meus ! Deus meus ! ut quid dereliquisti me ?"—*Matt.* xxvii. 46.

[5] "Ideo Christus derelictus est in pœnis, ne nos derelinquamur in culpis."—*Lib.* xiii. *de Pass. D.*

be a soul who believes this, O my Jesus, and yet loves
Thee not?

IV.

*He hath loved us, and washed us from our sins in His own
blood.*' Behold, O men, how far the love of Jesus for us
has carried him, in order to cleanse us from the filthiness
of our sins. He has even shed every drop of his blood
that he might prepare for us in this his own blood a bath
of salvation : "He offers his own blood," says a learned
writer, "speaking better than the blood of Abel : for
that cried for justice ; the blood of Christ for mercy." *
Whereupon St. Bonaventure exclaims, "O good Jesus,
what hast Thou done?"* O my Saviour, what indeed
hast Thou done? How far hath Thy love carried
Thee? What hast Thou seen in me which hath made
Thee love me so much? "Wherefore hast Thou loved
me so much? Why, Lord, why? What am I?"* Wherefore didst Thou choose to suffer so much for me? Who
am I that Thou wouldst win to Thyself my love at so
dear a price? Oh, it was entirely the work of Thy infinite love! Be Thou eternally praised and blessed for
it.

*O all ye that pass by the way, attend and see if there be any
sorrow like to My sorrow.*' The same seraphic Doctor,
considering these words of Jeremias as spoken of our
blessed Redeemer while he was hanging on the cross

' " Dilexit nos, et lavit nos a peccatis nostris in sanguine suo."—
Apoc. i. 5.

* " Offert sanguinem melius clamantem quam Abel; quia iste justitiam, sanguis Christi misericordiam interpellabat."—*Contens.* l. 10, d.
4. c. 1, *sp.* 1.

* " O bone Jesu ! quid fecisti ?"

* " Quid me tantum amasti ? quare, Domine, quare? quid sum ego?"
—*Stim. div. am.* p. 1, c. 13.

* " O vos omnes qui transitis per viam I attendite, et videte si est
dolor sicut dolor meus."—*Lam.* i. 12.

dying for the love of us, says, "Yes, Lord, I will attend and see if there be any love like unto Thy love."[1] By which he means, I do indeed see and understand, O my most loving Redeemer, how much Thou didst suffer upon that infamous tree ; but what most constrains me to love Thee is the thought of the affection which Thou hast shown me in suffering so much, in order that I might love Thee.

V.

That which most inflamed St. Paul with the love of Jesus was the thought that he chose to die, not only for all men, but for him in particular : *He loved me, and delivered Himself up for me.*[1] Yes, he has loved me, said he, and for my sake he gave himself up to die. And thus ought every one of us to say ; for St. John Chrysostom asserts that God has loved every individual man with the same love with which he has loved the world : "He loves each man separately with the same measure of charity with which he loves the whole world."[1] So that each one of us is under as great obligation to Jesus Christ for having suffered for every one, as if he had suffered for him alone.

For supposing, my brother, Jesus Christ had died to save you alone, leaving all others to their original ruin, what a debt of gratitude you would owe to him ! But you ought to feel that you owe him a greater obligation still for having died for the salvation of all. For if he had died for you alone, what sorrow would it not have caused you to think that your neighbors, parents, brothers, and friends would be damned, and that you would, when this life was over, be forever separated from them ? If

[1] "Imo, Domine, attendam, et videbo si est amor sicut amor tuus."
[2] "Dilexit me, et tradidit semetipsum pro me."—*Gal.* ii. 20.
[4] "Adeo singulum quemque hominum pari charitatis modo diligit, quo diligit universum orbem."—*In Gal.* ii. 20.

you and your family had been slaves, and some one came
to rescue you alone, how would you not entreat of him
to save your parents and brothers together with yourself! And how much would you thank him if he did
this to please you! Say, therefore, to Jesus :

O my sweetest Redeemer! Thou hast done this for me
without my having asked Thee; Thou hast not only
saved me from death at the price of Thy blood, but also
my parents and friends, so that I may have a good hope
that we may all together enjoy Thy presence forever in
paradise. O Lord! I thank Thee, and I love Thee, and I
hope to thank Thee for it, and to love Thee forever in
that blessed country.

VI.

Who could ever, says St. Laurence Justinian, explain
the love which the divine Word bears to each one of us,
since it surpasses the love of every son towards his
mother, and of every mother for her son? "The intense
charity of the Word of God surpasses all maternal and
filial love ; neither can human words express how great
his love is to each one of us !"[1] So much so, that our Lord
revealed to St. Gertrude that he would be ready to die
as many times as there were souls damned, if they were
yet capable of redemption : "I would die as many deaths
as there are souls in hell."[2]

O Jesus, O treasure more worthy of love than all
others! why is it that men love Thee so little? Oh! do
Thou make known what Thou hast suffered for each of
them, the love that Thou bearest them, the desire Thou
hast to be loved by them, and how worthy Thou art of

---

[1] "Præcellit omnem maternum ac filialem affectum Verbi Dei im-
mensa charitas; neque humano valet explicare eloquio, quo circa
unumquemque moveatur amore."—*De Tr. Chr. Ag.* c. 5.

[2] "Toties morerer, quot sunt animæ in inferno."—*Rev.* l. 7, c. 19.

being loved.   Make Thyself known, O my Jesus, make
Thyself loved.

VII.

I am the good shepherd, said our Redeemer ; *the good
shepherd gives his life for his sheep.*[1]   But, O my Lord,
where are there in the world shepherds like unto Thee?
Other shepherds will slay their sheep in order to preserve their own life.   Thou, O too loving Shepherd,
didst give Thy divine life in order to save the life of Thy
beloved sheep.   And of these sheep, I, O most amiable
Shepherd, have the happiness to be one.   What obligation, then, am I not under to love Thee, and to spend my
life for Thee, since Thou hast died for the love of me in
particular !   And what confidence ought I not to have
in Thy blood, knowing that it has been shed to pay the
debt of my sins !   *And thou shalt say in that day, I will
give thanks to Thee, O Lord.   Behold, God is my Saviour;
I will deal confidently, and will not fear.*[2]   And how can I
any longer mistrust Thy mercy, O my Lord, when I
behold Thy wounds?   Come, then, O sinners, and let us
have recourse to Jesus, who hangs upon that cross as it
were upon a throne of mercy.   He has appeased the
divine justice, which we had insulted.   If we have
offended God, he has done penance for us ; all that is
required for us is contrition for our sins.   O my dearest
Saviour, to what have Thy pity and love for me reduced
Thee ?   The slave sins, and Thou, Lord, payest the
penalty for him.   If, therefore, I think of my sins, the
thought of the punishment I deserve must make me
tremble ; but when I think of Thy death, I find I have

---

[1] " Ego sum Pastor bonus.   Bonus Pastor animam suam dat pro
ovibus suis."—*John,* x. 11.

[2] " Et dices in die illa : Confitebor tibi, Domine ! . . . Ecce Deus
Salvator meus ; fiducialiter agam, et non timebo."—*Isa.* xii. 1.

more reason to hope than to fear. O blood of Jesus!
thou art all my hope.

VIII.

But this blood, as it inspires us with confidence, also
obliges us to give ourselves entirely to our Blessed Redeemer. The Apostle exclaims, *Know you not that you
are not your own? For you are bought with a great price.*[1]
Therefore, O my Jesus, I cannot any longer, without
injustice, dispose of myself, or of my own concerns, since
Thou hast made me Thine by purchasing me through
Thy death.   My body, my soul, my life are no longer
mine; they are Thine, and entirely Thine. In Thee
alone, therefore, will I hope. O my God, crucified and
dead for me, I have nothing else to offer Thee but this
soul, which Thou hast bought with Thy blood; to Thee
do I offer it. Accept of my love, for I desire nothing
but Thee, my Saviour, my God, my love, my all.   Hitherto I have shown much gratitude towards men; to Thee
alone have I, alas! been most ungrateful. But now I
love Thee, and I have no greater cause of sorrow than
my having offended Thee. O my Jesus, give me confidence in Thy Passion; root out of my heart every affection that belongs not to Thee. I will love Thee alone,
who dost deserve all my love, and who hast given me so
much reason to love Thee. And who, indeed, could refuse to love Thee, when they see Thee, who art the
beloved of the Eternal Father, dying so bitter and cruel
a death for our sake? O Mary, O Mother of fair love, I
pray thee, through the merits of thy burning heart, obtain for me the grace to live only in order to love thy
Son, who, being in himself worthy of an infinite love,
has chosen at so great a cost to acquire to himself the

[1] "An nescitis quoniam . . . non estis vestri? Empti enim estis
pretio magno."—1 *Cor.* vi. 19.

love of a miserable sinner like me.   O love of souls, O
my Jesus! I love Thee, I love Thee, I love Thee; but still
I love Thee too little.   Oh, give me more love, give me
flames that may make me live always burning with Thy
love!   I do not myself deserve it; but Thou dost well
deserve it, O infinite Goodness.   Amen.   This I hope,
so may it be.

CHAPTER II.

JESUS CHOSE TO SUFFER SO MUCH FOR US, IN ORDER THAT
WE MAY UNDERSTAND THE GREAT LOVE HE HAS FOR US.

I.

"Two things," says Cicero, " make us know a lover—
that he does good to his beloved, and that he suffers torments for him; and this last is the greatest sign of true
love."[1]   God has indeed already shown his love to man
by many benefits bestowed upon him; but his love
would not have been satisfied by only doing good to
man, as says St. Peter Chrysologus, if he had not found
the means to prove to him how much he loved him by
also suffering and dying for him, as he did by taking
upon him human flesh: " But he held it to be little if he
showed his love without suffering;"[2] and what greater
means could God have discovered to prove to us the
immense love which he bears us than by making himself
man and suffering for us?   " In no other way could the
love of God towards us be shown,"[3] writes St. Gregory
Nazianzen.

[1] " Duo sunt, quæ amantem produnt: amato benefacere, et pro
amato cruciatus ferre; et hoc est majus."

[2] " Sed parum esse credidit, si affectum suum erga nos non etiam
adversa sustinendo monstraret."—*Serm.* 69.

[3] " Non aliter Dei amor erga nos declarari poterat."

My beloved Jesus, how much hast Thou labored to show me Thy love, and to make me enamoured of Thy goodness! Great indeed, then, would be the injury I should do Thee if I were to love Thee but little, or to love anything else but Thee.

II.

Ah, when he showed himself to us, a God, wounded, crucified, and dying, did he not indeed (says Cornelius à Lapide) give us the greatest proofs of the love that he bears us? " God showed his utmost love on the cross." [1] And before him St. Bernard said that Jesus, in his Passion, showed us that his love towards us could not be greater than it was: "In the shame of the Passion is shown the greatest and incomparable love." [2] The Apostle writes that when Jesus Christ chose to die for our salvation, then appeared how far the love of God extended towards us miserable creatures: *The goodness and kindness of God our Saviour appeared.* [3]

O my most loving Saviour! I feel indeed that all Thy wounds speak to me of the love that Thou bearest me. And who that had so many proofs of Thy love could resist loving Thee in return? St. Teresa was indeed right O most amiable Jesus, when she said that he who loves Thee not gives a proof that he does not know Thee.

III.

Jesus Christ could easily have obtained for us salvation without suffering, and in leading a life of ease and delight; but no, St. Paul says, *having joy set before Him, He endured the cross.* [4] He refused the riches, the delights,

[1] " Summum Deus in cruce nobis ostendit amorem!"—*In* 1 *Cor.* i. 25.

[2] " In passionis rubore maxima et incomparabilis ostenditur charitas."—*De Pass.* c. 41.

[3] " Benignitas et humanitas apparuit Salvatoris nostri Dei."—*Tit.* iii. 4.

[4] " Proposito sibi gaudio, sustinuit crucem."—*Heb.* xii. 2.

the honors of the world, and chose for himself a life of poverty, and a death full of suffering and ignominy. And wherefore? Would it not have sufficed for him to have offered to his eternal Father one single prayer for the pardon of man? for this prayer, being of infinite value, would have been sufficient to save the world, and infinite worlds besides. Why, then, did he choose for himself so much suffering, and a death so cruel, that an author has said very truly, that through mere pain the soul of Jesus separated itself from his body?[1] To what purpose so much cost in order to save man? St. John Chrysostom answers, a single prayer of Jesus would indeed have sufficed to redeem us; but it was not sufficient to show us the love that our God has borne us: "That which sufficed to redeem us was not sufficient for love."[2] And St. Thomas confirms this when he says, "Christ, in suffering from love, offered to God more than the expiation of the offence of the human race demanded."[3] Because Jesus loved us so much, he desired to be loved very much by us; and therefore he did everything that he could, even unto suffering for us, in order to conciliate our love, and to show that there was nothing more that he could do to make us love him: "He endured much weariness," says St. Bernard, "that he might bind man to love him much."[4]

IV.

And what greater proof of love, says our Saviour himself, can a friend show towards the person he loves than

---

[1] "Inter agones purus dolor animam a corpore disjunxit."—*Contens.* l. 10, d. 4, c. 1, *sp.* 1.

[2] "Quod sufficiebat redemptioni, non sufficiebat amori."

[3] "Christus, ex charitate patiendo, majus aliquid Deo exhibuit, quam exigeret recompensatio offensæ humani generis."—P. 3, q. 48, a. 2.

[4] "Multum fatigationis assumpsit, quo multæ dilectionis hominem debitorem teneret."—*In Cant.* s. 11.

to give his life for his sake? *Greater love than this no man hath, that a man lay down his life for his friends.*[1] But Thou, O most loving Jesus, says St. Bernard, hast done more than this, since Thou hast given Thy life for us, who were not Thy friends, but Thy enemies, and rebels against Thee: "Thou hast a greater charity, Lord, in giving Thy life for Thy enemies."[2] And this is what the Apostle observes when he writes, *He commendeth His charity towards us, because when as yet we were sinners, according to the time Christ died for us.*[3]

Thou wouldst then die for me, Thy enemy, O my Jesus; and yet can I resist so much love? Behold, here I am; since Thou dost so anxiously desire that I should love Thee, I will drive away every other love from my breast, and will love Thee alone.

V.

St. John Chrysostom says that the principal end Jesus had in his Passion was to discover to us his love, and thus to draw our hearts to himself by the remembrance of the pains that he has endured for us: "This was the principal cause of the Passion of our Lord; he wished it to be known how great was the love of God for man,— of God, who would rather be loved than feared."[4] St. Thomas adds that we may, through the Passion of Jesus, know the greatness of the love that God bears to man: "By this man understands the greatness of the love of

---

[1] "Majorem hac dilectionem nemo habet, ut animam suam ponat quis pro amicis suis."—*John*, xv. 13.

[2] "Tu majorem habuisti, Domine, charitatem, ponens animam etiam pro inimicis."—*S. de Pass. D.*

[3] "Commendat autem charitatem suam Deus in nobis, quoniam, cum adhuc peccatores essemus, secundum tempus Christus pro nobis mortuus est."—*Rom.* v. 8.

[4] "Hæc prima causa passionis Domini, quia sciri voluit quantum amaret hominem Deus, qui plus amari voluit, quam timeri."—*De Pass.* s. 6.

God to man." [1]   And St. John had said before, *In this we have known the charity of God, because He hath laid down his life for us.* [2]

O my Jesus, Immaculate Lamb sacrificed on the cross for me! let not all that Thou hast suffered for me be lost, but accomplish in me the object of. Thy great sufferings! [3] Oh, bind me entirely with the sweet chains of Thy love, in order that I may not leave Thee, and that I may never-more be separated from Thee: "Most sweet Jesus, suffer me not to be separated from Thee; suffer me not to be separated from Thee." [4]

VI.

St. Luke relates that Moses and Elias on Mount Tabor, speaking of the Passion of Jesus Christ, called it an excess: *And they spoke of his excess that he should accomplish in Jerusalem.* [5] "Yes," says St. Bonaventure, and rightly was the Passion of Jesus called an excess; for "it was an excess of suffering and an excess of love." [6] And a devout author adds, "What more could he suffer that he has not endured? The excess of his love reached the highest point." [7] Yes, indeed; for the divine law imposes on men no other obligation than that of loving their neighbors as themselves; but Jesus has loved man more than himself: "He loved these more than himself," [8] says St. Cyril.

---

[1] "Per hoc homo cognoscit quantum Deus hominem diligat."— P. 3, q. 46, a. 3.

[2] "In hoc cognovimus charitatem Dei, quoniam ille animam suam pro nobis posuit."—1 *Jo.* iii. 16.

[3] "Tantus labor non sit cassus."

[4] "Jesu dulcissime! ne permittas me separari a te, ne permittas me separari a te."

[5] "Dicebant Excessum ejus, quem completurus erat in Jerusalem." —*Luke,* ix. 31.

[6] "Excessus doloris, excessus amoris."

[7] "Quid ultra pati potuit, et non pertulit? ad summum pervenit summus amoris excessus."—*Contens.* l. 10, d. 4, c. 1, *sp.* 1.

[8] "Magis hos quam seipsum amavit."

Thou didst, then, O my beloved Redeemer,—I will say to Thee with St. Augustine,—love me more than Thyself, since to save me Thou wouldst lose Thy divine life,—a life infinitely more precious than the lives of all men and angels put together. Thou didst love me more than Thyself, because Thou wert willing to die for me.[1]

O infinite God! exclaims the Abbot Guerric, Thou hast for the love of men (if it is lawful to say so) become prodigal of Thyself.[2] "Yes, indeed," he adds, "since Thou hast not been satisfied with bestowing Thy gifts, but Thou hast also given Thyself to recover lost man."[3] O prodigy, O excess of love, worthy only of infinite goodness!

"And who," says St. Thomas of Villanova, "will ever be able, Lord, to understand even in the slightest degree the immensity of Thy love in having loved us miserable worms so much that Thou didst choose to die, even upon a cross, for us?"[4]   "Oh, how this love," continues the same saint, "exceeds all measure, all understanding!"[5]

VII.

It is a pleasing thing to see a person beloved by some great man; and more so if the latter has the power of raising him to some great fortune; but how much more sweet and pleasing must it be to us to see ourselves beloved by God, who can raise us up to an eternity of happiness? Under the old law men might have doubted

[1] "Dilexisti me plus quam te, quia mori voluisti pro me."—*Sol. an. ad D. c. xiii.*

[2] "O Deum, si fas est dici, prodigum sui præ desiderio hominis!"

[3] "An non prodigum sui, qui, non solum sua, sed seipsum impendit, ut hominem recuperaret?"—*In Pent. s. 1.*

[4] "Quis amoris tui vim cognosceret, quis vel suspicari posset a longe charitatis ardorem, quod sic amares, ut teipsum cruci et morti exponeres pro vermiculis?"

[5] "Excedit hæc charitas omnem scientiam, omnem sensum."—*In Nat. D. conc. 3.*

whether God loved them with a tender love; but after having seen him shed his blood on an infamous gibbet and die for us, how can we doubt his loving us with infinite tenderness and affection? O my soul, behold now thy Jesus, hanging from the cross all covered with wounds! behold how, by these wounds, he proves to thee the love of his enamoured heart: " The secrets of his heart are revealed through the wounds. of his body," [1] says St. Bernard.

My dearest Jesus, it does indeed afflict me to see Thee dying with so dreadful sufferings upon an ignominious tree; but at the same time I am greatly consoled and inflamed with love for Thee, when I see by means of these wounds the love that Thou bearest me. O heavenly seraphs, what do you think of the love of my God, *who loved me and delivered Himself for me?*" [2]

VIII.

St. Paul says that when the Gentiles heard it preached that Jesus was crucified for the love of men, they thought it such nonsense that they could not believe it. *But we preach Christ crucified, unto the Jews, indeed, a stumbling-block, and unto the Gentiles foolishness.* [3] And how is it possible, said they. to believe that an omnipotent God, who wants nothing in order to be perfectly happy as he is, would choose to become man and die on a cross to save men? This would be the same, said they, as to believe that a God had become mad for love of men : *But unto the Gentiles foolishness.* [4] And thus they refused to believe it. But faith teaches us that Jesus has really undertaken and accomplished this great work of redemp-

---

[1] " Patet arcanum cordis per foramina corporis."—*In Cant.* s. 61.
[2] "Qui dilexit me, et tradidit semetipsum pro me."—*Gal.* ii. 20.
[3] "Nos autem prædicamus Christum crucifixum, Judæis quidem scandalum, Gentibus autem stultitiam."—1 *Cor.* i. 23.
[4] " Gentibus autem stultitiam."

tion which the Gentiles esteemed and called folly. "We have seen," says St. Laurence Justinian, "Eternal Wisdom, the only-begotten of God, become as it were a fool through the excessive love he bears man." [1] Yes, adds Cardinal Hugo, for it seemed nothing but a folly that a God should choose to die for men: "It seemed a folly that God should die for the salvation of men." [2]

The Blessed Giacopone, who in this world had been a man of letters, and afterwards became a Franciscan, seemed to have become mad through the love that he bore to Jesus Christ. One day Jesus appeared to him and said, Giacopone, why do you commit these follies? "Why," he answered, because Thou hast taught them me. If I am mad," said he; "Thou hast been more mad than I, in that Thou hast died for me. I am a fool, for Thou hast been a greater fool." [3]

Thus, also, St. Mary Magdalen of Pazzi, being in an ecstasy, exclaimed, "O God of love! O God of love! The love that Thou bearest to creatures, O my Jesus, is too great indeed." And one day, when quite enraptured, she took an image of the Crucified, and began running about the monastery, crying, "O Love! Love! I shall never rest, my God, from calling Thee Love." Then turning to the religious, she said, "Do you not know, my dear sisters, that Jesus Christ is nothing but love? He is even mad with love, and I will go on saying it continually." And she added that she wished she could be heard by the whole universe when she called Jesus "Love," in order that the love of Jesus might be known and loved by all. And she sometimes even began to ring the bell, in order that all the people in the world should come

---

[1] "Agnovimus Sapientiam amoris nimietate infatuatam."—*Serm. de Nat. Dom.*

[2] "Stultitia videtur, quod mortuus fuerit Deus propter salutem hominum."—*In* 1 *Cor.* iv.

[3] "Stultus sum, quia stultior me fuisti."

(as she desired, if it had been possible) to love her Jesus.

Yes, my sweetest Redeemer, permit me to say so, this Thy spouse was indeed right when she called Thee mad with love. And does it not indeed seem a folly that Thou shouldst. choose to die for love of me, for so ungrateful a worm as I am, and whose offences Thou didst foresee, as well as the infidelities of which I should be guilty ? But if Thou, my God, art thus become mad, as it were, for the love of me, how is it that I do not become mad for the love of a God ? When I have seen Thee crucified and dead for me, how is it that I can think of any other than Thee? Yes, O my Lord, my sovereign good, more worthy of love than every other good, I love Thee more than myself. I promise for the future to love none other but Thee, and to think constantly on the love Thou hast shown me by dying in the midst of so many sufferings for me. O scourges, O thorns, O nails, O cross, O wounds, O sufferings, O death of my Saviour! you irresistibly constrain me to love him who has so much loved me. O Incarnate Word, O loving God! my soul is enamoured with Thee. I would fain love Thee so much that I should find no pleasure but in pleasing Thee, my most sweet Lord; and since Thou dost so earnestly desire my love, I protest that I will only live for Thee. I desire to do whatever Thou willest of me. O my Jesus! I pray Thee, help me, and grant that I may please Thee entirely and continually in time and in eternity. Mary, my Mother, entreat Jesus for me, in order that he may grant me his holy love; for I desire nothing else in this world and in the next but to love Jesus. Amen.

CHAPTER III.

JESUS, FOR LOVE OF US, CHOSE TO SUFFER THE PAINS OF HIS PASSION, EVEN FROM THE BEGINNING OF HIS LIFE.

I.

The divine Word came into the world and took upon him human flesh in order to make himself loved of man, and therefore he came with such a longing to suffer for our sake, that he would not lose a moment in beginning to torment himself, at least by apprehension. Hardly was he conceived in the womb of Mary, when he represented to his mind all the sufferings of his Passion; and, in order to obtain for us pardon and divine grace, he offered himself to his eternal Father to satisfy for us through his dolors all the chastisements due to our sins; and from that moment he began to suffer everything that he afterwards endured in his most bitter death.

O my most loving Redeemer! what have I hitherto done or suffered for Thee? If I could for a thousand years endure for Thy sake all the torments that all the martyrs have suffered, they would yet be nothing compared with that one first moment in which Thou didst offer Thyself and begin to suffer for me.

II.

The martyrs did indeed suffer great pains and ignominy; but they only endured them at the time of their martyrdom. Jesus even from the first instant of his life continually suffered all the torments of his Passion; for, from the first moment, he had before his eyes all the horrid scene of torments and insults which he was to receive from men. Wherefore he said by the mouth of

the prophet, *My sorrow is continually before me.*[1] O my
Jesus! Thou hast been so desirous to suffer for my sake
that Thou wouldst even endure Thy sufferings before
the time; and yet I am so desirous after the pleasures of
this world. How many times have I offended Thee in
order to please my body! O my Lord! through the
merits of Thy sufferings, take away from me, I beseech
Thee, all affection for earthly pleasures. For Thy love
I desire to abstain from this satisfaction. [*Mention it.*]

III.

God, in his compassion for us, does not generally re-
veal to us the trials that await us before the time when
we are destined to endure them. If a criminal who is
executed on a gibbet had had revealed to him from the
first use of his reason the torture that awaited him,
could he even have been capable of joy? If Saul from
the beginning of his reign had had present to his mind the
sword that was to pierce him, if Judas had foreseen the
cord that was to suffocate him,—how bitter would their
life have been!

Our kind Redeemer, even from the first instant of his
life, had always present before him the scourges, the
thorns, the cross, the outrages of his Passion, the desolate death that awaited him. When he beheld the victims which were sacrificed in the temple, he well knew
that they were figures of the sacrifice which he, the Immaculate Lamb, would one day consummate on the altar
of the cross. When he beheld the city of Jerusalem, he
well knew that he was there to lose his life in a sea of
sorrows and reproaches. When he saw his dear Mother,
he already imagined that he saw her in an agony of suffering at the foot of the cross, near his dying self.

So that, O my Jesus, the horrible sight of all these

---

[1] "Dolor meus in conspectu meo semper."—*Ps.* xxxvii. 18.

evils kept Thee during the whole of Thy life continually tormented and afflicted before the time of Thy death. And Thou didst accept and suffer everything for my sake. O my agonizing Lord! the sight alone of all the sins of the world, especially of mine, by which Thou didst already foresee I should offend Thee, rendered Thy life more afflicted and painfnl than all the lives that ever have been or ever will be. But, O my God, in what barbarous law is it written that a God should have so great love for a creature, and yet that creature should live without loving his God, or rather should offend and displease him? O my Lord, make me know the greatness of Thy love, in order that I may no longer be ungrateful to Thee. Oh, if I but loved Thee, my Jesus,—if I really loved Thee,—how sweet it would be to me to suffer for Thee!

IV.

Jesus appeared one day on the cross to Sister Magdalen Orsini, who had been suffering for some time from some great affliction, and animated her to suffer it in peace. The servant of God answered, "But, Lord, Thou didst only hang on the cross for three hours, whereas I have gone on suffering this pain for several years." Jesus Christ then said to her reproachingly, "O ignorant that thou art, what dost thou mean? From the first moment that I was in my Mother's womb, I suffered in my heart all that I afterwards endured on the cross."

And I, my dear Redeemer, how can I, at the sight of such' great sufferings which Thou didst endure for my sake, during Thy whole life, complain of those crosses which Thou dost send me for my good. I thank Thee for having redeemed me with so much love and such sufferings. In order to animate me to suffer with patience the pains of this life, Thou didst take upon Thyself all our evils. O my Lord, grant that Thy sorrows may be ever present

to my mind, in order that I may always accept and desire to suffer for Thy love.

V.

Great as the sea is Thy destruction.[1] As the waters of
the sea are all salt and bitter, so the life of Jesus Christ
was full of bitterness and void of all consolation, as he
himself declared to St. Margaret of Cortona. Moreover,
as all the waters of the earth unite in the sea, so did all
the sufferings of men unite in Jesus Christ; wherefore
he said by the mouth of the Psalmist, *Save me, O God,
for the waters are come in even unto my soul. I am come into
the depth of the sea, and a tempest hath overwhelmed Me.*[2]
Save me, O God, for sorrows have entered even the in-
most parts of my soul, and I am left submerged in a
tempest of ignominy and of sufferings, both interior and
exterior.

O my dearest Jesus, my love, my life, my all, if I behold from without Thy sacred body, I see nothing else
but wounds. But if I enter into Thy desolate heart, I
find nothing but bitterness and sorrows, which made
Thee suffer the agonies of death. O my Lord, and who
but Thee, who art infinite goodness, would ever suffer
so much, and die for one of Thy creatures? But because
Thou art God, Thou dost love as a God alone can love,
with a love which cannot be equalled by any other love.

VI.

St. Bernard says, "In order to redeem the slave, the
Father did not spare his own Son, nor did the Son spare
himself."[3] O infinite love of God! On the one hand

---

[1] " Magna est enim velut mare contritio tua."—*Lam.* ii. 13.

[2] " Salvum me fac, Deus, quoniam intraverunt aquæ usque ad animam meam ; veni in altudinem maris, et tempestas demersit me."—
Ps. lxviii. 2.

[3] " Ut servum redimeret, nec Pater Filio, nec sibi Filius ipse pepercit."—*S. de Pass. D.*

the eternal Father required of Jesus Christ to satisfy for all the sins of men: *The Lord hath laid on Him the iniquity of us all.*' On the other hand, Jesus, in order to save men in the most loving way that he could, chose to take upon himself the utmost penalty due to divine justice for our sins. Wherefore, as St. Thomas asserts, he took upon himself in the highest degree all the sufferings and outrages that ever were borne.' It was on this account that Isaias called him *a man of sorrows, despised, and the most abject of men.*' And with reason; for Jesus was tormented in all the members and senses of his body, and was still more bitterly afflicted in all the powers of his soul; so that the internal pains which he endured infinitely surpassed his external sufferings. Behold him, then, torn, bloodless; treated as an impostor, as a sorcerer, a madman, abandoned even by his friends, and finally persecuted by all, until he finished his life upon an infamous gibbet. *Know you what I have done to you?*'

O my Lord! I do indeed know how much Thou hast done and suffered for my sake; but Thou knowest, alas! that I have hitherto done nothing for Thee. My Jesus, help me to suffer something for Thy love before death overtakes me. I am ashamed of appearing before Thee; but . I will no longer be ungrateful, as I have been so many years towards Thee. Thou hast deprived Thyself of every pleasure for me; I will for the love of Thee renounce all the pleasures of the senses. Thou hast suffered so many pains for me; I will for Thy sake suffer all the pains of my life and of my death as it shall best please Thee. Thou hast been forsaken; I will be con-

---

¹ "Posuit Dominus in eo iniquitatem omnium nostrum."—*Isa.* liii. 6.

² "Assumpsit dolorem in summo, vituperationem in summo."

³ "Despectum, et novissimum virorum, virum dolorum."—*Isa.* liii. 3.

⁴ "Scitis quid fecerim vobis?"—*John*, xiii. 12.

tent that all should forsake me, provided Thou dost not forsake me, O my only and sovereign good! Thou hast been persecuted; I accept whatever persecution may befall me. Finally, Thou hast died for me; I will die for Thee. O my Jesus, my Treasure, my love, my all! I love Thee. Oh, give me more love! Amen.

CHAPTER IV.

THE GREAT DESIRE WHICH JESUS HAD TO SUFFER AND TO DIE FOR LOVE OF US.

I.

Oh, how exceedingly tender, loving, and constraining was that declaration of our Blessed Redeemer concerning his coming into the world, when he said that he had come to kindle in souls the fire of divine love, and that his only desire was that this holy flame should be enkindled in the hearts of men : *I am come to cast fire upon the earth; and what will I but that it should be kindled ?* [1] He continued immediately to say that he was expecting to be baptized with the baptism of his own blood—not, indeed, to wash out his own sins, since he was incapable of sinning, but to wash out our sins, which he had come to satisfy by his sufferings : " The Passion of Christ is called baptism, because we are purified in his blood." [2] And therefore our loving Jesus, in order to make us understand how ardent was his desire to die for us, added, with sweetest expression of his love, that he felt an immense longing for the time of his Passion, so great was

[1] " Ignem veni mittere in terram; et quid volo, nisi ut accendatur?" —*Luke* xii. 49.

[2] " Passio Christi dicitur Baptismus, quia in ejus sanguine purificamur."

his desire to suffer for our sake. These are his loving words : *I have a baptism wherewith I am to be baptized ; and how am I straitened until it be accomplished?* [1]

O God, the lover of men, what more couldst Thou have said or done in order to put me under the necessity of loving Thee? And what good could my love ever do Thee, that Thou didst choose to die, and didst so much desire death in order to obtain it? If a servant of mine had only desired to die for me, he would have attracted my love; and can I then live without loving Thee with all my heart, my king and God, who didst die for me, and who hadst such a longing for death in order to acquire to Thyself my love?

II.

Jesus, knowing that His hour was come that He should pass out of the world to the Father, having loved His own, . . . He loved them unto the end.[2] St. John says that Jesus called the hour of his Passion *his* hour; because, as a devout commentator writes, this was the time for which our Redeemer had most sighed during his whole life; because by suffering and dying for men, he desired to make them understand the immense love that he bore to them: "That is the hour of the lover, in which he suffers for the object beloved:"[3] because suffering for the beloved is the most fit way of discovering the love of the lover, and of captivating to ourself the love of the beloved.

O my dearest Jesus, in order to show me the great

[1] "Baptismo babeo baptizari; et quomodo coarctor, usquedum perficiatur?"
[2] "Sciens Jesus quia venit hora ejus, ut transeat ex hoc mundo ad Patrem, cum dilexisset suos . . ., in finem dilexit eos."—*John*, xiii. 1.
[3] "Amantis hora illa est, qua pro amico patitur."—*Barrad.* T. iv. l. 2, c. 5.

love Thou bearest me, Thou wouldst not commit the work of my redemption to any other than Thyself. Was my love, then, of such consequence to Thee that Thou wouldst suffer so much in order to gain it? Oh, what more couldst Thou have done if Thou hadst had to gain to Thyself the love of Thy divine Father? What more could a servant endure to acquire to himself the affections of his master than what Thou hast suffered in order that Thou mayest be loved by me, a vile, ungrateful slave?

III.

But behold our loving Jesus already on the point of being sacrificed on the Altar of the Cross for our salvation, in that blessed night which preceded his Passion. Let us hear him saying to his disciples, in the last supper that he makes with them, *With desire have I desired to eat this pasch with you.*[1] St. Laurence Justinian, considering these words, asserts that they were all words of love: "With desire have I desired; this is the voice of love."[2] As if our loving Redeemer had said, O men, know that this night, in which my Passion will begin, has been the time most longed after by me during the whole of my life; because I shall now make known to you, through my sufferings and my bitter death, how much I love you, and shall thereby oblige you to love me in the strongest way it is possible for me to do. A certain author says that in the Passion of Jesus Christ the divine omnipotence united itself to love,—love sought to love man to the utmost extent that omnipotence could arrive at; and omnipotence sought to satisfy love as far as its desire could reach.

[1] " Desiderio desideravi hoc Pascha manducare vobiscum."—*Luke,* xxii. 15.

[2] " Desiderio desideravi; charitatis est vox hæc."—*De Tr. Chr. Ag.* c. 2.

O sovereign God! Thou hast given Thyself entirely
to me; and how, then, shall I not love Thee with my
whole self? I believe,—yes, I believe Thou hast died for
me; and how can I, then, love Thee so little as constantly to forget Thee, and all that Thou hast suffered
for me? And why, Lord, when I think on Thy Passion,
am I not quite inflamed with Thy love, and do I not become entirely Thine, like so many holy souls who, after
meditating on Thy sufferings, have remained the happy
prey of Thy love, and have given themselves entirely to
Thee?

IV.

The spouse in the Canticles said that whenever her
Spouse introduced her into the sacred cellar of his Passion, she saw herself so assaulted on all sides by divine
love that, all languishing with love, she was constrained
to seek for relief to her wounded heart: *The king brought
me into the cellar of wine, he set in order charity in me. Stay
me up with flowers, compass me about with apples; because I
languish with love.*[1] And how is it possible for a soul to
enter upon the meditation of the Passion of Jesus Christ
without being wounded, as by so many darts of love, by
those sufferings and agonies which so greatly afflicted
the body and soul of our loving Lord, and without being
sweetly constrained to love him who loved her so much?

O Immaculate Lamb, thus lacerated, covered with
blood, and disfigured, as I behold Thee on this cross,
how beautiful and how worthy of love dost Thou yet
appear to me! Yes, because all these wounds that I behold in Thee are to me signs and proofs of the great
love that Thou bearest to me. Oh, if all men did but
contemplate Thee often in that state in which Thou wert

---

[1] "Introduxit me in cellam vinariam, ordinavit in me charitatem.
Fulcite me floribus, stipate me malis; quia amore langueo."—*Cant.*
ii. 4.

4

one day made a spectacle to all Jerusalem, who could help being seized with Thy love? O my beloved Lord, accept me to love Thee, since I give Thee all my senses and all my will. And how can I refuse Thee anything, if Thou hast not refused me Thy blood, Thy life, and all Thyself?

V.

So great was the desire of Jesus to suffer for us, that in the night preceding his death he not only went of his own will into the garden, where he knew that the Jews would come and take him, but, knowing that Judas the traitor was already near at hand with the company of soldiers, he said to his disciples, *Arise, let us go; behold he that will betray Me is at hand.*[1] He would even go himself to meet them, as if they came to conduct him, not to the punishment of death, but to the crown of a great kingdom.

O my sweet Saviour, Thou dost, then, go to meet Thy death with such a longing to die, through the desire that Thou hast to be loved by me! And shall I not have a desire to die for Thee, my God, in order to prove to Thee the love that I bear Thee? Yes, my Jesus, who hast died for me, I do also desire to die for Thee. Behold, my blood, my life, I offer all to Thee. I am ready to die for Thee as Thou wilt, and when Thou wilt. Accept this miserable sacrifice which a miserable sinner offers to Thee, who once offended Thee, but now loves Thee more than himself.

VI.

St. Laurence Justinian, in considering this word "I thirst,"[2] which Jesus pronounced on the cross when he was expiring, says that this thirst was not a thirst which

---

[1] "Surgite, eamus; ecce, qui me tradet, prope est."—*Mark,* xiv. 42.
[2] "Sitio."

proceeded from dryness, but one that arose from the ardor of the love that Jesus had for us: " This thirst springs from the fever of his love." [1] Because by this word our Redeemer intended to declare to us, more than the thirst of the body, the desire that he had of suffering for us, by showing us his love : and the immense desire that he had of being loved by us, by the many sufferings that he endured for us: " This thirst proceeds from the fever of his love." And St. Thomas says, " By this ' I thirst ' is shown the ardent desire for the salvation of the human race." [2]

O God, enamoured of souls, is it possible that such an excess of goodness can remain without correspondence on our part ? It is said that love must be repaid by love; but by what love can Thy love ever be repaid ? It would be necessary for another God to die for Thee, in order to compensate for the love that Thou hast borne us in dying for us. And how, then, couldst Thou, O my Lord, say that Thy delight was to dwell with men, if Thou dost receive from them nothing but injuries and ill-treatment ? Love made Thee, then, change into delights the sufferings and the insults that Thou hast endured for us. O my Redeemer, most worthy of love, I will no longer resist the stratagems of Thy love ; I give Thee from henceforth my whole love. Thou art and shalt be always the only beloved one of my soul. Thou didst become man in order that Thou mayest have a life to devote to me; I would fain have a thousand lives, in order that I may sacrifice them all for Thee. I love Thee, O infinite goodness, and I will love Thee with all my strength. I will do all that lies in my power to please Thee. Thou, being innocent, hast suffered for me; I a

[1] " Sitis hæc de ardore nascitur charitatis."—*De Tr. Chr. Ag.* c. 19.

[2] " Per hoc *Sitio!* ostenditur ejus ardens desiderium de salute generis humani."—*In Jo.* xix. *lect.* 5.

sinner, who have deserved hell, desire to suffer for **Thee**
as much as Thou willest. O my Jesus! assist, I pray
Thee, by Thy merits, this desire which Thou dost Thyself give me. O infinite God, I believe in Thee, I hope
in Thee, I love Thee. Mary, my Mother, intercede for
me. Amen.

CHAPTER V.

THE LOVE OF JESUS IN LEAVING HIMSELF FOR OUR FOOD BEFORE HIS DEATH.

I.

*Jesus, knowing that His hour was come that He should
pass out of this world to the Father, having loved His own who
were in the world, He loved them to the end.*[1] Our most
loving Redeemer, on the last night of his life, knowing
that the much-longed-for time had arrived on which he
should die for the love of man, had not the heart to leave
us alone in this valley of tears; but in order that he
might not be separated from us even by death, he would
leave us his whole self as food in the Sacrament of the
Altar; giving us to understand by this that, having
given us this gift of infinite worth, he could give us
nothing further to prove to us his love: *He loved them unto
the end.*[2] Cornelius à Lapide, with St. Chrysostom and
Theophylact, interprets the words "unto the end" according to the Greek text, and writes thus: "He loved
them with an excessive and supreme love."[3] Jesus in

---

[1] "Sciens Jesus quia venit hora ejus, ut transeat ex hoc mundo ad
Patrem, cum dilexisset suos . . ., in finem dilexit eos."—*John,*
xiii. 1.

[2] "In finem dilexit eos."

[3] "Quasi dicat: Extremo amore et summe dilexit eos."

this sacrament made his last effort of love towards men, as the Abbot Guerric says : " He poured out the whole power of his love upon his friends." [1]

This was still better expressed by the holy Council of Trent, which, in speaking of the Sacrament of the Altar, says that our Blessed Saviour " poured out of himself in it, as it were, all the riches of his love towards us." [2] The angelical St. Thomas was therefore right in calling this Sacrament "a Sacrament of love, and a token of the greatest love that a God could give us." [3] And St. Bernard called it "the love of loves." [4] And St. Mary Magdalen of Pazzi said that a soul, after having communicated, might say, " It is consummated;" [5] that is to say, My God, having given himself to me in this Holy Communion, has nothing more to give me. This saint, one day asked one of her novices what she had been thinking of after Communion; she answered, "Of the *love of Jesus*." "Yes," replied the saint; "when we think of this love, we cannot pass on to other thoughts, but must stop upon love."

O Saviour of the world, what dost Thou expect from men, that Thou hast been induced even to give them Thyself in food? And what can there be left to Thee to give us after this Sacrament, in order to oblige us to love Thee? Ah, my most loving God, enlighten me that I may know what an excess of goodness this has been of Thine, to reduce Thyself unto becoming my food in Holy Communion! If Thou hast, therefore, given Thyself entirely to me, it is just that I also should give my-self wholly to Thee. Yes, my Jesus, I give myself en-

---

[1] "Omnem vim amoris effudit amicis."—*Serm. de Asc. D.*
[2] "Divitias sui erga homines amoris velut effudit."—*Sess.* xlii. *cap.* 2.
[3] " Sacramentum charitatis, summæ charitatis Christi pignus est."
[4] "Amor amorum."
[5] "Consummatum est!"

tirely to Thee. I love Thee above every good, and I
desire to receive Thee in order to love Thee more.
Come, therefore, and come often, into my soul, and
make it entirely Thine. Oh that I could truly say to
Thee, as the loving St. Philip Neri said to Thee when
he received Thee in the Viaticum, " Behold my love, behold my love ; give me my love."

II.

*He that eateth My flesh, and drinketh My blood, abideth
in Me, and I in him.*' St. Denis, the Areopagite, says
that love always tends towards union with the object
beloved. And because food becomes one thing with
him who eats it, therefore our Lord would reduce himself to food, in order that, receiving him in Holy Communion, we might become of one substance with him :
Take ye and eat, said Jesus ; *this is My body.*' As if he
had said, remarks St. John Chrysostom, " Eat Me, that
the highest union may take place."' O man, feed thyself on Me, in order that thou and I may become one
substance. In the same way, says St. Cyril of Alexandria, as two pieces of melted wax unite together, so a
soul that communicates is so thoroughly united to Jesus
that Jesus remains in it, and it in Jesus. O my beloved
Redeemer, exclaims, therefore, St. Laurence Justinian,
how couldst Thou ever come to love us so much that
Thou wouldst unite Thyself to us in such a way that Thy
heart and ours should become but one heart? "Oh,
how admirable is Thy love, O Lord Jesus, who wouldst
incorporate us in such a manner with Thy body, that we
should have but one heart with Thee."'

' "Qui manducat meam carnem et bibit meum sanguinem, in me
manet, et ego in illo."—*John*, vi. 57
' " Accipite et comedite ; hoc est corpus meum."—*Matt.* xxvi. 26.
' "Me comede, ut summa unio fiat."—*In.* 1 *Tim. hom.* 15.
' "O quam mirabilis est dilectio tua, Domine Jesu, qui tuo corpori
taliter nos incorporare voluisti, ut tecum unum cor haberemus !"—
De Inc. div. cm. c. 5.

Well did St. Francis de Sales say, in speaking of Holy Communion : "In no action does our Saviour show himself more loving or more tender than in this one, in which, as it were, he annihilates himself and reduces himself to food in order to penetrate our souls, and unite himself to the hearts of his faithful ones." So that, says St. John Chrysostom, "To that Lord on whom the angels even dare not fix their eyes, to him we unite ourselves, and we are made one body, one flesh."[1] "But what shepherd," adds the saint, "feeds the sheep with his own blood? Even mothers give their children to nurses to feed them ; but Jesus in the Blessed Sacrament feeds us with his own blood, and unites us to himself. What shepherd feeds his sheep with his own blood? And why do I say shepherd? There are many mothers who give their children to others to nurse ; but this he has not done, but feeds us with his own blood."[2] In short, says the saint, because he loves us so ardently, he chose to make himself one with us by becoming our food. "He mixed himself with us, that we might be one ; this they do whose love is ardent."[3]

O infinite love, worthy of infinite love, when shall I love Thee, my Jesus, as Thou hast loved me? O divine food, Sacrament of love, when wilt Thou draw me entirely to Thyself? Thou hast nothing left to do in order to make Thyself loved by me. I am constantly intending to begin to love Thee, I constantly promise Thee to do so ; but I never begin. I will from this day begin to love Thee in earnest. Oh, do Thou enable me to do so. Enlighten me, inflame me, detach me from earth, and

[1] " Huic nos unimur, et facti sumus unum corpus, una caro."

[2] " Quis pastor oves proprio pascit cruore ? Et quid dico, Pastor? Matres multæ sunt quæ filios aliis tradunt nutricibus. Hoc autem ipse non est passus, sed ipse nos proprio sanguine pascit."—*Ad pop. Ant. hom.* 60.

[3] " Semetipsum nobis immiscuit, ut unum quid simus ; ardenter enim amantium hoc est."—*Ibid. hom.* 61.

permit me not any longer to resist so many enticements of Thy love. I love Thee with my whole heart, and I will therefore leave everything in order to please Thee, my life, my love, my all. I will constantly unite myself to Thee in this Holy Sacrament, in order to detach myself from everything, and to love Thee only, my God. I hope, through Thy gracious assistance, to be enabled to do so.

III.

St. Laurence Justinian says, "We have seen the All-wise made foolish by excess of love." [1] We have seen a God who is wisdom itself become a fool through the love he has borne to man. And is it not so? Does it not seem, exclaims St. Augustine, a folly of love, that a God should give himself as food to his creatures? "Does it not seem madness to say, Eat my flesh, drink my blood?" [2] And what more could a creature have said to his Creator? "Shall I make bold to say that the Creator of all things was beside himself through the excess of his loving goodness?" [3] Thus St. Denis speaks, and says, that God through the greatness of his love has almost gone out of himself; for, being God, he has gone so far as to become man, and even to make himself the food of men. But, O Lord, such an excess was not becoming Thy majesty. No, but love, answers St. John Chrysostom for Jesus, does not go about looking for reasons when it desires to do good and to make itself known to the object beloved; it goes, not where it is becoming, but where it is carried by its desire. "Love is

[1] "Vidimus Sapientiam amoris nimietate infatuatam."—*Serm. de Nat. D.*

[2] "Nonne videtur insania: Manducate meam carnem, bibite meum sanguinem?"—*In Ps.* 33, *en.* 1.

[3] "Audebimus et loqui, quod auctor omnium, præ amatoriæ bonitatis magnitudine, extra se sit?"—*De Div. Nom.* c. 4.

unreasoning, and goes as it is led, and not as it ought." [1]

O my Jesus, how ought I not to be covered with shame when I consider that, having Thee before me, who art the infinite Good and lovely above every good, and so full of love for my soul, I have yet turned back to love vile and contemptible things, and for their sake have forsaken Thee. O my God, I beseech Thee, discover to me every day more and more the greatness of Thy goodness, in order that I may every day be more and more enamoured of Thee, and may labor more and more to please Thee. Ah, my Lord, what object more beautiful, more good, more holy, more amiable can I love besides Thee? I love Thee, infinite goodness, I love Thee more than myself, and I desire to live only that I may love Thee, who dost deserve all my love.

IV.

St. Paul remarks also on the time which Jesus chooses to make us this gift of the most Holy Sacrament ; a gift which surpasses all the other gifts which an Almighty God could make ; as St. Clement says, "A gift surpassing all fulness." [2] And St. Augustine says, "Although omnipotent, he could give no more." [3] The Apostle remarks that *The Lord Jesus, the same night in which He was betrayed, took bread, and, giving thanks, broke and said, Take ye and eat ; this is my body which shall be delivered for you.* [4] In that same night, then, when men were thinking of preparing torments and death for Jesus, our beloved Re-

---

[1] "Amor ratione caret, et vadit quo ducitur, non quo debeat."— *Serm.* 147.

[2] "Donum transcendens omnem plenitudinem."

[3] "Cum esset omnipotens plus dare non potuit."

[4] "Dominus Jesus, in qua nocte tradebatur, accepit panem, et gratias agens fregit, et dixit : Accipite et manducate ; hoc est corpus meum, quod pro vobis tradetur."—1 *Cor.* xi. 23.

deemer thought of leaving them himself in the Blessed Sacrament ; giving us thereby to understand that his love was so great that, instead of being cooled by so many injuries, it was then more than ever yearning towards us. O most loving Saviour, how couldst Thou have so great love for men as to choose to remain with them on this earth to be their food, after they had driven Thee away from it with so much ingratitude !

Let us also remark the immense desire which Jesus had during all his life for the arrival of that night in which he had determined to leave us this great pledge of his love. For at the moment of his instituting this most sweet sacrament he said, *With desire I have desired to eat this pasch with you* ;' words which discover to us the ardent desire which he had to unite himself to us in Communion through the love which he bore us : " This is the voice of most burning charity," ' says St. Laurence Justinian. And Jesus still retains at the present time the same desire towards all the souls that love him. There is not a bee, said he one day to St. Matilda, that throws itself with such eagerness upon the flowers in order to suck out the honey, as I, through the violence of my love, hasten to the soul that desires me. '

O lover, too full of love, there are no greater proofs left for Thee to give me in order to persuade me that Thou dost love me. I bless Thy goodness for it. O my Jesus, I beseech Thee, draw me entirely to Thyself. Make me love Thee henceforth with all the affections and tenderness of which I am capable. Let it suffice to others to love Thee with a love only appreciative and predominant, for I know that Thou wilt be satisfied with it ; but I shall not be satisfied until I see that I love

---

¹ " Desiderio desideravi hoc Pascha manducare vobiscum."—*Luke*, xxii. 15.

' " Flagrantissimæ charitatis est vox hæc."—*De Tr. Chr. Ag.* c. 2.

³ " *Spir. Grat.* l. 2, c. 3.

Thee also with all the tenderness of my heart, more than friend, more than brother, more than father, and more than spouse. And where indeed shall I find a friend, a brother, a father, a spouse, who will love me as much as Thou hast loved me, my Creator, my Redeemer, and my God? who for the love of me hast spent Thy blood and Thy life; and, not content with that, dost give Thyself entirely to me in this Sacrament of love. I love Thee, then, O my Jesus, with all the affections of my soul; I love Thee more than myself. Oh, help me to love Thee; I ask nothing more of Thee.

V.

St. Bernard says that God loves us for no other reason than that he may be loved by us: "God only loved that he might be loved."[1] And therefore our Saviour protested that he had come upon earth in order to make himself loved: *I am come to send a fire upon the earth.*[2] And oh, what flames of holy love does Jesus kindle in souls in this most divine Sacrament! The Venerable Father Francis Olimpio, a Theatine, said that nothing was so fit to excite our hearts to love the sovereign good as the most Holy Communion. Hesychius called Jesus in the Sacrament a "divine fire."[3] And St. Catharine of Sienna, one day perceiving, in the hands of a priest, Jesus in the Sacrament under the appearance of a furnace of love, was full of astonishment that the whole world was not consumed by the fire. The Abbot Rupert, and St. Gregory of Nyssa said that the altar itself was the wine-cellar where the espoused soul is inebriated with the love of her Lord; so much so, that, forgetful of earth, it burns and languishes with holy love: *The king brought me,* says the spouse in the Canticles, *into the*

[1] "Non ad aliud amat Deus, nisi ut ametur."—*In Cant.* s. 83.
[2] "Ignem veni mittere in terram."—*Luke*, xii. 49.
[3] "Ignis divinus."

cellar of wine; he set in order charity in me. Stay me up with flowers, compass me about with apples; because I languish with love.[1]

O love of my soul, most Holy Sacrament; oh that I could always remember Thee, to forget everything else, and that I could love Thee alone without interruption and without reserve! Ah, my Jesus, Thou hast knocked so frequently at the door of my heart, that Thou hast at last, I hope, entered therein. But since Thou hast entered there, drive away, I pray Thee, all its affections that do not tend towards Thyself. Possess Thyself so entirely of me, that I may be able with truth to say to Thee from this day forth, with the Prophet, *What have I in heaven? and besides Thee what do I desire on earth? The God of my heart, and my portion forever.*[2] Yes, O my God, what else do I desire but Thee upon earth or in heaven? Thou alone art and shalt always be the only Lord of my heart and my will; and Thou alone shalt be all my portion, all my riches, in this life and in the next.

VI.

Go, said the Prophet Isaias—go, publish everywhere the loving inventions of our God, in order to make himself loved of men: *You shall draw waters with joy out of the Saviour's fountains; and you shall say in that day, Praise ye the Lord, and call upon His name, make His inventions known among the people.*[3] And what inventions has not the love of Jesus made in order to make himself loved

---

[1] "Introduxit me in cellam vinariam, ordinavit in me charitatem. Fulcite me floribus, stipate me malis; quia amore langueo."—*Cant.* ii. 4.

[2] "Quid mihi est in cœlo? et a te quid volui super terram? Deus cordis mei, et pars mea, Deus, in æternum."—*Ps.* lxxii. 25.

[3] "Haurietis aquas in gaudio de fontibus Salvatoris; et dicetis in illa die: Confitemini Domino, et invocate nomen ejus; notas facite in populis adinventiones ejus."—*Isa.* xii. 3.

by us ? Even on the cross he has opened in his wounds so many fountains of grace, that to receive them it is sufficient to ask for them in faith. And, not satisfied with this, he has given us his whole self in the Most Holy Sacrament.

O man, says St. John Chrysostom, wherefore art thou so niggardly, and dost use so much reserve in thy love for that God who hath given his whole self to thee without any reserve ? " He gave himself wholly to thee, reserving nothing for himself."[1] This is just, says the angelic Doctor, what Jesus has done in the Sacrament of the Altar, wherein " he has given us all that he is and all that he has."[2] Behold, adds St. Bonaventure, that immense God, "whom the world cannot contain, become our prisoner and captive"[3] when we receive him into our breast in Holy Communion. Wherefore St. Bernard, transported with love when he considered this, exclaimed, My Jesus would make himself " the inseparable guest of my heart."[4] And since my God, he concludes, has chosen to " spend himself entirely for my sake,"[5] it is reasonable that I should employ all that I am in serving and loving him.

Ah, my beloved Jesus, tell me, what more is there left for Thee to invent in order to make Thyself loved ? And shall I, then, continue to live so ungrateful to Thee as I have hitherto done ? My Lord, permit it not. Thou hast said, that he who feeds on Thy flesh in Communion shall live through the virtue of Thy grace : *He that eateth Me, the same also shall live by Me.*[6] Since, then,

[1] " Totum tibi dedit, nihil sibi reliquit."
[2] " Deus in Eucharistia totum quod ipse est, et habet, in summo dedit."—*De Beat.* c. 3.
[3] " Ecce, quem mundus capere non potest, captivus noster est."— *Exp. Miss.* c. 4.
[4] " Indivisus cordis mei hospes."
[5] " Totus in meos usus expensus."—*In Circ.* s. 3.
[6] " Qui manducat me, et ipse vivet propter me."—*John*, vi. 58.

Thou dost not disdain that I should receive Thee in Holy Communion, grant that my soul may always live the true life of Thy grace. I repent, O sovereign good, of having despised it in times past; but I bless Thee that Thon dost give me time to weep over the offences that I have committed against Thee, and to love Thee in this world. During the life that remains to me, I will place all my affections in Thee, and endeavor to please Thee as much as I possibly can. Help me, O my Jesus; forsake me not, I beseech Thee. Save me by Thy merits, and let my salvation be to love Thee always in this life and in eternity. Mary, my Mother, do thou also assist me.

CHAPTER VI.

THE BLOODY SWEAT AND AGONY SUFFERED BY JESUS IN THE GARDEN.

I.

Behold, our most loving Saviour, having come to the Garden of Gethsemani, did of his own accord make a beginning of his bitter Passion by giving full liberty to the passions of fear, of weariness, and of sorrow to come and afflict him with all their torments : *He began to fear; and to be heavy,*[1] *to grow sorrowful, and to be sad.*[2]

He began, then, first to feel a great fear of death, and of the sufferings he would have soon to endure. *He began to fear ;*[3] but how? Was it not he himself that had offered himself spontaneously to endure all these torments? *He was offered because He willed it.*[4] Was it

[1] "Cœpit pavere et tædere."—*Mark,* xiv. 33.
[2] "Contristari et mœstus esse."—*Matt.* xxvi. 37.
[3] "Cœpit pavere."
[4] "Oblatus est, quia ipse voluit."—*Isa.* liii. 7.

not he who had so much desired this hour of his Passion, and who had said shortly before, *With desire have I desired to eat this Pasch with you?*[1] And yet how is it that he was seized with such a fear of death, that he even prayed his Father to deliver him from it? *My Father, if it be possible, let this chalice pass from Me.*[2] The Venerable Bede answers this, and says, "He prays that the chalice may pass from him, in order to show that he was truly man."[3] He, our loving Saviour, chose indeed to die for us in order by his death to prove to us the love that he bore us; but in order that men might not suppose that he had assumed a fantastic body (as some heretics have blasphemously asserted), or that by virtue of his divinity he had died without suffering any pain, He therefore made this prayer to his heavenly Father, not indeed with a view of being heard, but to give us to understand that he died as man, and afflicted with a great fear of death and of the sufferings which should accompany his death.

O most amiable Jesus! Thou wouldst, then, take upon Thee our fearfulness in order to give us Thy courage in suffering the trials of this life. Oh, be Thou forever blessed for Thy great mercy and love! Oh, may all our hearts love Thee as much as Thou desirest, and as much as Thou deservest!

II.

He began to be heavy.[4] He began to feel a great weariness on account of the torments that were prepared for Him. When one is weary, even pleasures are painful.

---

[1] "Desiderio desideravi hoc Pascha manducare vobiscum."—*Luke,* xxii. 15.

[2] "Pater mi! si possibile est, transeat a me calix iste."—*Matt.* xxvi. 39.

[3] "Orat transire calicem, ut ostendat quod vere homo erat."—*In Marc.* xiv.

[4] "Cœpit tædere."

Oh, what anguish united to this weariness must Jesus Christ have felt at the horrible representation which then came before his mind, of all the torments, both ex-terior and interior, which, during the short remainder of his life, were so cruelly to afflict his body and his blessed soul! Then did all the sufferings he was to endure pass distinctly before his eyes, as well as all the insults that he should endure from the Jews and from the Romans; all the injustice of which the judges of his cause would be guilty towards him; and, above all, he had before him the vision of that death of desolation which he should have to endure, forsaken by all, by men and by God, in the midst of a sea of sufferings and con-tempt. And this it was that caused him so heavy grief that he was obliged to pray for consolation to his eter-nal Father. O my Jesus! I compassionate Thee, I thank Thee, and I love Thee.

And there appeared to Him an angel, . . . *strengthening Him.*[1] Strength came, but, says the Venerable Bede, this rather increased than lightened his sufferings: "Strength did not diminish, but increased his sorrow."[2] Yes, for the angel strengthened him, that he might suffer still more for the love of men and the glory of his Father.

Oh, what sufferings did not this first combat bring Thee, my beloved Lord! During the progress of Thy Passion, the scourges, the thorns, the nails, came one after the other to torment Thee. But in the garden all the sufferings of Thy whole Passion assaulted Thee all together and tormented Thee. And Thou didst accept all for my sake and my good. O my God! how much I regret not having loved Thee in times past, and having preferred my own accursed pleasures to Thy will! I

---

[1] "Apparuit autem illi angelus de cœlo, confortans eum."—*Luke,* xxii. 43.
[2] "Confortatio dolorem non minuit, sed auxit."

detest them now above every evil, and repent of them
with my whole heart. O my Jesus ! forgive me.

III.

He began to grow sorrowful and to be sad.[1] Together
with this fear and weariness, Jesus began to feel a great
melancholy and affliction of soul. But, my Lord, art
Thou not he who didst give to Thy martyrs such a delight in suffering that they even despised their torments
and death? St. Augustine[2] said of St. Vincent that he
spoke with such joy during his martyrdom that it
seemed as if it were not the same person that suffered
and that spoke. It is related of St. Laurence that whilst
he was burning on the gridiron, such was the consolation he enjoyed in his soul that he defied the tyrant,
saying, "Turn, and eat."[3] How, then, my Jesus, didst
Thou, who gavest such great joy to Thy servants in dying, choose for Thyself such extreme sorrowfulness in
Thy death ?

O delight of paradise, Thou dost rejoice heaven and
earth with Thy gladness; why, then, do I behold Thee
so afflicted and sorrowful ? Why do I hear Thee say
that the sorrow that afflicts Thee is enough to take away
Thy life? *My soul is sorrowful even unto death.*[4] O my
Redeemer, why is this ? Ah, I understand it all. It was
less the thought of Thy sufferings in Thy bitter Passion,
than of the sins of men that afflicted Thee; and amongst
these, alas, were my sins, which caused Thee this great
dread of death.

IV.

He, the Eternal Word, as much as he loved his Father,
so much did he hate sin, of which he well knew the

[1] "Cœpit contristari et mœstus esse."
[2] *Serm.* 275, *E. B.*
[3] "Versa et manduca."
[4] "Tristis est anima mea usque ad mortem."—*Mark,* xiv. 34.

malice; wherefore, in order to deliver the world from sin, and that he might no longer behold his beloved Father offended, he had come upon earth, and had made himself Man, and had undertaken to suffer so painful a death and Passion. But when he saw that, notwithstanding all his sufferings, there would yet be so many sins committed in the world, his sorrow for this, says St. Thomas, exceeded the sorrow that any penitent has ever felt for his own sins: "It surpassed the sorrow of all contrite souls;"[1] and, indeed, it surpassed every sorrow that ever could afflict a human heart. The reason is, that all the sorrows that men feel are always mixed with some relief; but the sorrow of Jesus was pure sorrow without any relief: "He suffered pure pain without any admixture of consolation."[2]

Oh, if I loved Thee, my Jesus—if I loved Thee, the consideration of all that Thou hast suffered for me would render all sufferings, all contempt, and all vexations sweet to me. Oh, grant me, I beseech Thee, Thy love, in order that I may endure with pleasure, or at least with patience, the little Thou givest me to suffer. Oh, let me not die so ungrateful to all Thy loving-kindnesses. I desire, in all the tribulations that shall happen to me, to say constantly, My Jesus, I embrace this trial for Thy love; I will suffer it in order to please Thee.

V.

We read in history that several penitents being enlightened by divine light to see the malice of their sins, have died of pure sorrow for them. Oh, what torment, then, must not the heart of Jesus endure at the sight of all the sins of the world, of all the blasphemies, sacri-

---

[1] "Excessit omnem dolorem cujuscumque contriti."—P. 3. q. 46, a. 6.

[2] "Purum dolorem absque ulla consolationis permixtione expertus est."—*Contens.* l. 10, d. 4, c. 1, *sf.* 1.

leges, acts of impurity, and all the other crimes which should be committed by men after his death, every one of which, like a wild beast, tore his heart separately by its own malice ? Wherefore our afflicted Lord, during his agony in the garden, exclaimed, Is this, therefore, O men, the reward that you render me for my immeasurable love ? Oh, if I could only see that, grateful for my affection, you gave up sin and began to love me, with what delight should I not hasten to die for you! But to behold, after all my sufferings, so many sins ; after so much love, such ingratitude;—this is what afflicts me the most, makes me sorrowful even unto death, and makes me sweat pure blood: *And His sweat became as drops of blood trickling down upon the ground.*[1] So that, according to the Evangelist, this bloody sweat was so copious that it first bathed all the vestments of our Blessed Redeemer, and then came forth in quantity and bathed the ground.

Ah, my loving Jesus, I do not behold in this garden either scourges or thorns or nails that pierce Thee; how, then, is it that I see Thee all bathed in blood from Thy head to Thy feet? Alas, my sins were the cruel press which, by dint of affliction and sorrow, drew so much blood from Thy heart. I was, then, one of Thy most cruel executioners, who contributed the most to crucify Thee with my sins. It is certain that, if I had sinned less, Thou, my Jesus, wouldst have suffered less. As much pleasure, therefore, as I have taken in offending Thee, so much the more did I increase the sorrow of Thy heart, already full of anguish. How, then, does not this thought make me die of grief, when I see that I have repaid the love Thou hast shown me in Thy Passion by adding to Thy sorrow and suffering? I, then, have tormented this heart, so loving and so worthy of love,

---

[1] " Et factus est sudor ejus sicut guttæ sanguinis decurrentis in terram."—*Luke*, xxii. 44.

which has shown so much love to me. My Lord, since I have now no other means left of consoling Thee than to weep over my offences towards Thee, I will now, my Jesus, sorrow for them and lament over them with my whole heart. Oh, give me, I pray Thee, so great sorrow for them as may make me to my last breath weep over the displeasure I have caused Thee, my God, my Love my All.

· VI.

He fell upon His face.' Jesus, beholding himself charged with the burden of satisfying for all the sins of the world, prostrated himself, with his face on the ground, to pray for men, as if he were ashamed to raise his eyes towards heaven, loaded as he was with such iniquities.

O my Redeemer, I behold Thee pale and worn out with sorrow; Thou art in the agony of death, and Thou dost pray: *And being in an agony, He prayed the longer.*' Tell me, my Saviour, for whom dost Thou pray! Ah, Thou didst not pray so much for Thyself at that hour as for me! Thou didst offer to Thy Eternal Father Thy all-powerful prayers, united to Thy sufferings, to obtain for me, a wretched sinner, the pardon of my sins: *Who, in the days of His flesh, with a strong cry and tears, offering up prayers and supplications to Him that was able to save Him from death, was heard for His reverence.*' O my beloved Redeemer! how is it possible that Thou couldst love so much one who has so grievously offended Thee? How couldst Thou embrace such sufferings for me, foreseeing, as Thou didst, all the ingratitude of which I should be guilty towards Thee?

¹ " Procidit in faciem suam."—*Matt.* xxvi. 39.
² " Factus in agonia, prolixius orabat."—*Luke*, xxii. 43.
³ " Qui in diebus carnis suæ, preces supplicationesque, ad eum qui possit illum salvum facere a morte, cum clamore valido et lacrymis offerens, exauditus est pro sua reverentia."—*Heb.* v. 7.

O my afflicted Lord! make me share in that sorrow which Thou didst then have for my sins. I abhor them at this present moment; and I unite this my hatred to the horror that Thou didst feel for them in the garden. O my Saviour, look not upon my sins, for hell itself would not be sufficient to expiate them, but look upon the sufferings that Thou hast endured for me! O love of my Jesus, Thou art my love and my hope. O my Lord, I love Thee with my whole soul, and will always love Thee. I beseech Thee, through the merits of that weariness and sadness which Thou didst endure in the garden, give me fervor and courage in all works that may contribute to Thy glory. Through the merits of Thy agony, grant me Thy assistance to resist all the temptations of the flesh and of hell. My God, grant me the grace always to commend myself to Thee, and always to repeat to Thee, with Jesus Christ: *Not as I will, but as Thou willest.*[1] May Thy divine will, not mine, be ever done. Amen.

CHAPTER VII.

THE LOVE OF JESUS IN SUFFERING SO MUCH CONTEMPT IN HIS PASSION.

I.

Bellarmine says that to noble spirits affronts cause greater pain than sufferings of body: " Noble spirits think more of ignominy than of pains of body."[2] Because, if the former afflict the flesh, the latter afflict the soul, which, in proportion as it is more noble than the

[1] " Non quod ego volo, sed quod tu."—*Mark*, xiv. 36.

[2] " Nobiles animi pluris faciunt ignominiam, quam dolores corporis."

body, so much the more does it feel pain. But who could have ever imagined that the most noble personage in heaven and earth, the Son of God, by coming into the world to make himself Man for love of men, would have had to be treated by them with such reproaches and injuries as if he had been the lowest and most vile of all men ? *We have seen Him despised and the most abject of men.*[1] St. Anselm asserts that Jesus Christ was willing to suffer such and so great dishonors that it could not be possible for him to be more humbled than he was in his Passion: "He humbled himself so much, that he could not go beyond it."[2]

O Lord of the world, Thou art the greatest of all kings; but Thou hast willed to be despised more than all men, in order to teach me the love of contempt. Because, then, Thou hast sacrificed Thine honor for love of me, I am willing to suffer for love of Thee every affront which shall be offered to me.

II.

And what kind of affronts did not the Redeemer suffer in his Passion? He saw himself affronted by his own disciples. One of them betrays him, and sells him for thirty pieces. Another denies him many times, protesting publicly that he knows him not; and thus attesting that he was ashamed to have known him in the past. The other disciples, then, at seeing him taken and bound, all fly and abandon him: *Then His disciples leaving Him, all fled away.*[3]

O my Jesus, thus abandoned, who will ever undertake Thy defence, if, when Thou art first taken, those most

[1] "Vidimus eum . . . despectum et novissimum virorum."—*Isa.* liii. 2.

[2] "Ipse se tantum humiliavit ut ultra non posset."—*In Phil.* ii.

[3] "Tunc discipuli ejus, relinquentes eum, omnes fugerunt."—*Mark,* xiv. 50.

dear to Thee depart from and forsake Thee? But, my God, to think that this dishonor did not end with Thy Passion! How many souls, after having devoted themselves to follow Thee, and after having been favored by Thee with many graces and special signs of love, being then driven by some passion of vile interest, or human respect, or sordid pleasure, have ungratefully forsaken Thee!

Which of these ungrateful ones is found to turn and lament, saying, Ah, my dear Jesus, pardon me; for I will not leave Thee again. I will rather lose my life a thousand times than lose Thy grace, O my God, my love, my all.

III.

Behold how Judas, arriving in the garden together with the soldiers, advances, embraces his Master, and kisses him. Jesus suffers him to kiss him; but, knowing already his evil intent, could not refrain from complaining of this most unjust treachery, saying, *Judas, betrayest Thou the Son of man with a kiss!*[1] Then those insolent servants crowd around Jesus, lay hands upon him, and bind him as a villain: *The servants of the Jews apprehended Jesus, and bound Him.*[2]

Ah me! what do I see? A God bound! By whom? By men; by worms created by himself. Angels of paradise, what say ye to it? And Thou, my Jesus, why dost Thou allow Thyself to be bound? What, says St. Bernard, have the bonds of slaves and of the guilty to do with Thee, who art the Holy of Holies, the King of kings, and Lord of lords? "O King of kings and Lord of lords. what hast Thou to do with chains?"[3]

---

[1] "Juda, osculo Filium hominis tradis?"—*Luke*, xxii. 48.

[2] "Ministri Judæorum comprehenderunt Jesum, et ligaverunt eum."—*John*, xviii. 12.

[3] "O Rex regum et Dominus dominantium! quid tibi et vinculis?" —*De Pass. c. 4.*

But if men bind Thee, wherefore dost Thou not loosen and free Thyself from the torments and death which they are preparing for Thee? But I understand this. It is not, O my Lord, these ropes which bind Thee. It is only love which keeps Thee bound, and constrains Thee to suffer and die for us.

"O Charity," exclaims St. Laurence Justinian, "how strong is Thy chain, by which God was able to be bound!" [1] O divine Love, thou only wast able to bind a God, and conduct him to death for the love of men.

IV.

"Look, O man," says St. Bonaventure, "at these dogs dragging him along, and the Lamb, like a victim, meekly following without resistance. One seizes, another binds him; another drives, another strikes him." [2] They carry our sweet Saviour, thus bound, first to the house of Annas, then to that of Caiphas; where Jesus, being asked by that wicked one about his disciples and his doctrine, replied that he had not spoken in private, but in public, and that they who were standing round about well knew what he had taught. *I spoke openly; lo, these know what I said.* [3] But at this answer one of those servants, treating him as if too bold, gave him a blow on the cheek: *One of the officers standing by gave Jesus a blow, saying, Answerest Thou the high-priest thus?* [4] Here exclaims St. Jerome: "Ye angels, how is it that ye are

---

[1] "O Charitas! quam magnum est vinculum tuum, quo Deus ligari potuit!"—*Lign. Vit. de Char.* c. 6.

[2] "Intuere, homo, canes istos trahentes eum ad victimam, et illum quasi agnum mansuetissimum sine resistentia ipsos sequi: alius apprehendit, alius ligat, alius impellit, alius percutit."—*Med. Vit. Chr.* c. 75,74.

[3] "Ego palam locutus sum . . : ecce hi sciunt quæ dixerim ego."—*John*, xviii. 20.

[4] "Unus assistens ministrorum dedit alapam Jesu, dicens: Sic respondes Pontifici?"—*Ibid.* 22.

silent? How long can such patience withhold you in your astonishment?"[1]

Ah, my Jesus, how could an answer so just and modest deserve such an affront in the presence of so many people? The worthless high-priest, instead of reproving the insolence of this audacious fellow, praises him, or at least by signs approves. And Thou, my Lord, sufferest all this to compensate for the affronts which I, a wretch, have offered to the divine Majesty by my sins. My Jesus, I thank Thee for it. Eternal Father, pardon me by the merits of Jesus.

V.

Then the iniquitous high-priest asked him if he were verily the Son of God: *I adjure Thee by the living God, that Thou tell us if Thou be the Christ, the Son of God.*[2] Jesus, out of respect for the name of God, affirmed that he was so indeed; whereupon Caiphas rent his garments, saying that he had blasphemed; and all cried out that he deserved death: *But they answering said, He is guilty of death.*[3]

Yes, O my Jesus, with truth do they declare Thee guilty of death, since Thou hast willed to take upon Thee to make satisfaction for me, who deserved eternal death. But if by Thy death Thou hast acquired for me life, it is just that I should spend my life wholly, yea, and if need be lose it, for Thee. Yes, my Jesus, I will no longer live for myself; but only for Thee, and for Thy love. Succor me by Thy grace.

---

[1] "O Angeli! quomodo siletis? Ad quid attonitos vos tenet tanta patientia?"

[2] "Adjuro te per Deum vivum, ut dicas nobis si tu es Christus, Filius Dei."—*Matt.* xxvi. 63.

[3] "At illi respondentes dixerunt: Reus est mortis."—*Ibid.* 66.

VI.

Then they spat in His face and buffeted Him.[1] After
having proclaimed him guilty of death, as a man already
given over to punishment, and declared infamous, the
rabble set themselves to ill-treat him all the night
through with blows, and buffets, and kicks, with pluck-
ing out his beard, and even spitting in his face, by
mocking him as a false prophet and saying, *Prophesy to
us, O Christ, who it is that struck Thee.*[2] All this our Redeemer foretold by Isaias: *I have given My body to the
strikers, and my cheeks to them that plucked them : I have
not turned away My face from them that rebuked Me and
spit upon Me.*[3] The devout Thauler[4] relates that it is an
opinion of St. Jerome that all the pains and infirmities
which Jesus suffered on that night will be made known
only on the day of the last judgment. St. Augustine,
speaking of the ignominies suffered by Jesus Christ,
says, "If this medicine cannot cure our pride, I know
not what can."[5] Ah, my Jesus, how is it that Thou art
so humble and I so proud? O Lord, give me light,
make me know who Thou art, and who I am.

Then they spat in His face.[6] "Spat!" O God, what
greater affront can there be than to be defiled by spitting? "To be spit upon is to suffer the extreme of in-

[1] "Tunc expuerunt in faciem ejus, et colaphis eum ceciderunt."—
Ibid. 67.

[2] "Prophetiza nobis, Christe, quis est qui te percussit."—*Matt.*
xxvi. 68.

[3] "Corpus meum dedi percutientibus, et genas meas vellentibus;
faciem meam non averti ab increpantibus et conspuentibus in me."
—*Isa.* l. 6.

[4] *De Vita et Pass. Salv.* c. 17.

[5] "Hæc medicina si superbiam non curat, quid eam curet, nescio."
—*Serm.* 77. E. B.

[6] "Expuerunt in faciem ejus."

sult,"[1] says Origen. Where are we wont to spit except in the most filthy place? And didst Thou, my
Jesus, suffer Thyself to be spit upon in the face? Behold how these wretches outrage Thee with blows and
kicks, insult Thee, spit on Thy face, do with Thee just
what they will; and dost Thou not threaten nor reprove
them? *When He was reviled, He reviled not ; when He
suffered, He threatened not ;-but delivered Himself to him
that judged Him unjustly.*[2] No, but like an innocent lamb,
humble and meek, Thou didst suffer all without so
much as complaining, offering all to the Father to obtain
the pardon of our sins: *Like a lamb before the shearer, He
shall be dumb, and shall not open His mouth.*[3]

St. Gertrude one day, when meditating on the injuries
done to Jesus in his Passion, began to praise and bless
him; this was so pleasing to our Lord that he lovingly
thanked her.

Ah, my reviled Lord, Thou art the King of heaven,
the Son of the Most High; Thou surely deservest not to
be ill-treated and despised, but to be adored and loved
by all creatures. I adore Thee, I bless Thee, I thank
Thee, I love Thee with all my heart. I repent of having
offended Thee. Help me, have pity upon me.

VII.

When it was day, the Jews conduct Jesus to Pilate, to
make him condemn him to death; but Pilate declares
him to be innocent: *I find no cause in this Man.*[4] And to
free himself from the importunities of the Jews who

---

[1] "Ad extremam injuriam pertinet sputamenta accipere."—*In
Matt. tr.* 35.

[2] " Cum malediceretur, non maledicebat; cum pateretur, non comminabatur; tradebat autem judicanti se injuste."--1 *Pet.* ii. 23.

[3] " Quasi agnus coram tondente se, obmutescet, et non aperiet os
suum."—*Isa.* liii. 7.

[4] " Nihil invenio causæ in hoc homine."—*Luke*, xxiii. 4.

pressed on him, seeking the death of the Saviour, he sends him to Herod. It greatly pleased Herod to see Jesus Christ brought before him, hoping that in his presence, in order to deliver himself from death, he would have worked one of those miracles of which he had heard tell; wherefore he asked him many questions. But Jesus, because he did not wish to be delivered from death, and because that wicked one was not worthy of his answers, was silent, and answered him not. Then the proud king, with his court, offered him many insults, and making them cover him with a white robe, as if declaring him to be an ignorant and stupid fellow, sent him back to Pilate: *But Herod with his soldiers despised Him, and mocked Him, putting on Him a white robe, and sent Him back to Pilate.*[1] Cardinal Hugo, in his Commentary, says, "Mocking him as if a fool, he clothed him with a white robe."[2] And St. Bonaventure, "He despised him as if impotent, because he worked no miracle; as if ignorant because he answered him not a word; as if idiotic, because he did not defend himself."[3]

O Eternal Wisdom, O divine Word! This one other ignominy was wanting to Thee, that Thou shouldst be treated as a fool bereft of sense. So greatly does our salvation weigh on Thee, that through love of us Thou willest not only to be reviled, but to be satiated with revilings; as Jeremias had already prophesied of Thee: *He shall give His cheek to him that striketh Him; He shall be filled with reproaches.*[4] And how couldst Thou bear such love to men, from whom Thou hast received nothing but

---

[1] "Sprevit autem illum Herodes cum exercitu suo, et illusit indutum veste alba, et remisit ad Pilatum."—*Luke,* xxiii. 11.

[2] "Illudens ei, quasi fatuo, induit eum veste alba."

[3] "Sprevit illum tamquam impotentem, quia signum non fecit; tamquam ignorantem, quia verbum non respondit; tamquam stolidum, quia se non defensavit."

[4] "Dabit percutienti se maxillam, saturabitur opprobriis."—*Lam.* iii. 30.

ingratitude and slights? Alas, that I should be one of these who have outraged Thee worse than Herod! Ah, my Jesus, chastise me not, like Herod, by depriving me of Thy voice. Herod did not recognize thee for what Thou art; I confess Thee to be my God. Herod loved Thee not; I love Thee more than myself. Deny me not I beseech Thee, deny me not the voice of Thy inspiration, as I have deserved by the offences that I have committed against Thee. Tell me what Thou wilt have of me, for, by Thy grace, I am ready to do all that Thou wilt.

VIII.

When Jesus had been led back to Pilate, the governor inquired of the people whom they wished to have released at that Passover, Jesus or Barabbas, a murderer. But the people cried out, *Not this Man, but Barabbas.*[1] Then said Pilate, *What, then, shall I do with Jesus?*[2] They answered, *Let Him be crucified.*[3] But what evil hath this innocent one done? replied Pilate: *What evil hath he done?*[4] They repeated, *Let Him be crucified.*[5]

And even up to this time, O God, the greater part of mankind continue to say, *Not this Man, but Barabbas;*[6] preferring to Jesus Christ some pleasure of sense, some point of honor, some outbreak of wounded pride.

Ah, my Lord, well knowest Thou that at one time I did Thee the same injury when I preferred my accursed tastes to Thee. My Jesus, pardon me, for I repent of the past, and henceforth I prefer Thee before everything. I esteem Thee, I love Thee more than any good; and am willing a thousand times to die rather than forsake Thee. Give me holy perseverance; give me Thy love.

[1] " Non hunc, sed Barabbam."—*John*, xviii. 40.
[2] " Quid igitur faciam de Jesu ?—*Matt* xxvii. 22.
[3] " Crucifigatur !"—*Ibid.*
[4] " Quid enim mali fecit ?"—*Ibid.* 23.
[5] " Crucifigatur !"—*Ibid.*
[6] " Non hunc, sed Barabbam ?"—*John*, xviii. 40.

IX.

Presently we will speak of the other reproaches which
Jesus Christ endured, until he finally died on the cross:
He endured the cross, despising the shame.[1] In the mean
while let us consider how truly in our Redeemer was fulfilled what the Psalmist had foretold, that in his Passion
he should become the reproach of men, and the outcast
of the people: *But I am a worm, and no man; the reproach
of men, and the abject of the people;*[2] even to a death of ignominy, suffered at the hands of the executioner on a
cross, as a malefactor between two malefactors: *And he
was reputed with the wicked.*[3]

O Lord, the most high, exclaims St. Bernard, become
the lowest among men! O lofty one become vile! O
glory of angels become the reproach of men! "O lowest
and highest! O humble and sublime! O reproach of
men and glory of angels!"[4]

X.

O grace, O strength of the love of God! continues St.
Bernard. Thus did the Lord most high over all become
the most lightly esteemed of all. "O grace, O power of
love, did the highest of all thus become the lowest of all?"
And who was it (adds the saint) that did this? "Who
hath done this? Love."[5] All this hath the love which
God bears towards men done, to prove how he loves us,
and to teach us by his example how to suffer with peace
contempt and injuries: *Christ suffered for us* (writes St.

[1] "Sustinuit crucem, confessione contempta."—*Heb.* xii. 2.

[2] "Ego autem sum vermis et non homo, opprobrium hominum et
abjectio plebis."—*Ps.* xxi. 7.

[3] "Et cum sceleratis reputatus est."—*Isa.* liii. 12.

[4] "O novissimum et altissimum! O humilem et sublimem! O op.
probrium hominum et gloriam angelorum!"—*Serm. de Pass. D.*

[5] "O gratiam! O amoris vim! itane summus omnium imus factus
est omnium? Quis hoc fecit? Amor!"—*In Cant.* s. 64.

Peter), *leaving you an example, that you may follow His steps.*[1]
St. Eleazar, when asked by his wife how he came to
endure with such peace the great injuries that were done
him, answered, " I turn to look on Jesus enduring contempt, and say that my affronts are as nothing in respect
to those which he my God was willing to bear for me."

Ah, my Jesus, and how is it that, at the sight of a
God thus dishonored for love of me, I know not how to
suffer the least contempt for love of Thee? A sinner,
and proud! And whence, my Lord, can come this pride?
I pray Thee by the merits of the contempt Thou didst suffer, give me grace to suffer with patience and gladness all
affronts and injuries. From this day forth I propose by
Thy help nevermore to resent them, but to receive with
joy all the reproaches that shall be offered me. Truly
have I deserved greater contempt for having despised
Thy divine majesty, and deserved the contempt of hell.
Exceeding sweet and pleasant to me hast Thou rendered
affronts, my beloved Redeemer, by having embraced so
great contempt for love of me. Henceforth I propose,
in order to please Thee, to benefit as much as possible
whoever despises me; at least to speak well of and pray
for him. And even now I pray Thee to heap Thy
graces upon all those from whom I have received any
injury. I love Thee, O infinite good, and will ever love
Thee as much as I can. Amen.

[1] " Christus passus est pro nobis, vobis relinquens exemplum, ut se
quamiqi vestigia ejus."—I *Pet.* ii. 21.

CHAPTER VIII.

THE SCOURGING OF JESUS CHRIST.

I.

Let us enter into the prætorium of Pilate, one day made
the horrible scene of the ignominies and pains of Jesus:
let us see how unjust, how shameful, how cruel, was the
punishment there inflicted on the Saviour of the world.
Pilate, seeing that the Jews continued to make a tumult
against Jesus, as a most unjust judge condemned him to
be scourged: *Then Pilate took Jesus and scourged Him.*[1]
The iniquitous judge thought by means of this barbarity
to win for him the compassion of his enemies, and thus
to deliver him from death: *I will chastise Him* (he said)
and let Him go.[2] Scourging was the chastisement inflicted
on slaves only.   Therefore, says St. Bernard, our loving
Redeemer willed to take the form, not only of a slave, in
order to subject himself to the will of others, but even
of a bad slave in order to be chastised with scourges,
and so to pay the penalty due from man, who had made
himself the slave of sin: " Taking not only the form of a
slave, that he might submit, but even of a bad slave, that
he might be beaten and suffer the punishment of the
slave of sin."[3]

O Son of God, O Thou great lover of my soul, how
couldst Thou, the Lord of infinite majesty, thus love an
object so vile and ungrateful as I am, as to subject Thy-

---

[1] " Tunc ergo apprehendit Pilatus Jesum, et flagellavit."—*John*,
xix. 1.

[2] " Corripiam ergo illum, et dimittam."—*Luke*, xxiii. 22.

[3] " Non solum formam servi accepit, ut subesset, sed etiam mali servi,
ut vapularet; et servi peccati, ut pœnam solveret."—*Serm. de Pass. D.*

self to so much punishment, to deliver me from the punishment which was my due? A God scourged! It were a greater marvel that God should receive the lightest blow than that all men and all angels should be destroyed. Ah, my Jesus, pardon me the offences that I have committed against Thee, and then chastise me as shall please Thee. This alone is enough,—that I love Thee, and that Thou love me; and then I am content to suffer all the pains Thou willest.

II.

As soon as he had arrived at the prætorium (as was revealed to St. Bridget), our loving Saviour, at the command of the servants, stripped himself of his garments, embraced the column, and then laid on it his hands to have them bound. O God, already is begun the cruel torture! O angels of heaven, come and look on this sorrowful spectacle; and if it be not permitted you to deliver your king from this barbarous slaughter which men have prepared for him, at least come and weep for compassion. And thou, my soul, imagine thyself to be present at this horrible tearing of the flesh of Thy beloved Redeemer. Look on him, how he stands,—thy afflicted Jesus,—with his head bowed, looking on the ground, blushing all over for shame, he awaits this great torture. Behold these barbarians, like so many ravening dogs, are already with the scourges attacking this innocent lamb. See how one beats him on the breast, another strikes his shoulders, another smites his loins and his legs; even his sacred head and his beautiful face cannot escape the blows. Ah me! already flows that divine blood from every part; already with that blood are saturated the scourges, the hands of the executioners, the column, and the ground. "He is wounded," mourns St. Peter Damian, "over his whole body, torn with the scourges; now they twine round his shoulders,

now round his legs—streaks upon streaks, wounds added
to fresh wounds." ¹ Ah, cruel men, with whom are you
dealing thus? Stay—stay; know that you are mistaken.
This man whom you are torturing is innocent and holy;
it is myself who am the culprit; to me, to me, who have
sinned, are these stripes and torments due. But you regard not what I say. And how canst Thou, O Eternal
Father, bear with this great injustice? How canst Thou
behold Thy beloved Son suffering thus, and not inter-
fere in his behalf? What is the crime that he has ever
committed, to deserve so shameful and so severe a punishment?

III.

*For the wickedness of My people have I struck Him.*² I
well know, says the Eternal Father, that this my Son is
innocent; but inasmuch as he has offered himself as a
satisfaction to my justice for all the sins of mankind, it
is fitting that I should so abandon him to the rage of his
enemies.

Hast Thou, then, my adorable Saviour, in compensation for our sins, and especially for those of impurity,—
that most prevalent vice of mankind,—been willing to
have Thy most pure flesh torn in pieces? And who,
then, will not exclaim, with St. Bernard, "How unspeakable is the love of the Son of God towards sinners!"³

Ah, my Lord, smitten with the scourge, I return Thee
thanks for so great love, and I grieve that I am myself,
by reason of my sins, one of those who scourge Thee.
O my Jesus! I detest all those wicked pleasures which
have cost Thee so much pain. Oh, how many years

---

¹ "Cæditur, totoque flagris corpore dissipatur; nunc scapulas, nunc
crura cingunt; vulnera vulneribus et plagas plagis recentibus ad-
dunt."—*De Tr. Chr. Ag* c. 14.

² "Propter scelus populi mei percussi eum."—*Isa.* liii. 8.

³ "O ineffabilem Filii Dei erga peccatores charitatem!"

ought I not already to have been in the flames of hell! And why hast Thou so patiently awaited me until now? Thou hast borne with me, in order that at length, overcome by so many wiles of love, I might give myself up to love Thee, abandoning sin. O my beloved Redeemer! I will offer no further resistance to Thy loving affection; I desire to love Thee henceforth to the uttermost of my power. But Thou already knowest my weakness; Thou knowest how often I have betrayed Thee. Do Thou detach me from all earthly affections which hinder me from being all Thine own. Put me frequently in mind of the love which Thou hast borne me, and of the obligation which I am under of loving Thee. In Thee I place all my hopes, my God, my love, my all.

IV.

St. Bonaventure sorrowfully exclaims, "The royal blood is flowing; bruise is superadded to bruise, and gash to gash."[1] That divine blood was already issuing from every pore; that sacred body was already become but one perfect wound; yet those infuriated brutes did not forbear to add blow to blow, as the Prophet had foretold: *And they have added to the grief of my wounds.*[2] So that the thongs not only made the whole body one wound, but even bore away pieces of it into the air, until at length the gashes in that sacred flesh were such that the bones might have been counted: *The flesh was so torn away, that the bones could be numbered.*[3] Cornelius à Lapide says that in this torment Jesus Christ ought, naturally speaking, to have died; but he willed, by his

---

[1] "Fluit regius sanguis, superadditur livor super livorem, fractura super fracturam."—*Med. vit. Chr.* c. 76.

[2] "Et super dolorem vulnerum meorum addiderunt."—*Ps.* lxviii. 27.

[3] "Concisa fuit caro, ut ossa dinumerari possent."—*Contens.* l. 10, d. 4, c. 1, *sp.* 1.

divine power, to keep himself in life, in order to suffer
yet greater pains for love of us; and St. Laurence
Justinian had observed the same thing before: "He
evidently ought to have died. Yet he reserved himself
unto life, it being his will to endure heavier sufferings."[1]

Ah, my most loving Lord, Thou art worthy of an infinite love; Thou hast suffered so much in order that I
might love Thee. Oh, never permit me, instead of loving Thee, to offend or displease Thee more! Oh, what
place in hell should there not be set apart for me, if,
after having known the love that Thou hast borne
towards such a wretch, I should damn myself, despising
a God who had suffered scorn, smitings, and scourgings
for me ; and who had, moreover, after my having so
often offended him, so mercifully pardoned me! Ah,
my Jesus, let it not, oh, let it not be thus! O my God!
how would the love and the patience which Thou hast
shown towards me be there for me in hell, another hell
even yet more full of torments!

V.

Cruel in excess to our Redeemer was this torture of
his scourging in the first place, because of the great
number of those by whom it was inflicted; who, as was
revealed to St. Mary Magdalen of Pazzi, were not fewer
than sixty. And these, at the instigation of the devils,
and even more so of the priests, who were afraid lest
Pilate should, after this punishment, be minded to release the Lord, as he had already protested to them,
saying, *I will therefore scourge Him, and let Him go,*[2]
aimed at taking away his life by means of this scourging. Again, all theologians agree with St. Bonaventure
that, for this purpose, the sharpest implements were

[1] "Debuit plane mori; se tamen reservavit ad vitam, ut graviora
perferret."—*De Tr. Chr. Ag.* c. 14.
[2] "Corripiam ergo illum, et dimittam."—*Luke,* xxiii. 22.

selected, so that, as St. Anselm declares, every stroke produced a wound; and that the number of the strokes amounted to several thousand, the flagellation being administered, as Father Crasset says, not after the manner of the Jews, for whom the Lord had forbidden that the number of strokes should ever exceed forty: *Yet so, that they exceed not the number of forty; lest thy brother depart shamefully torn;*[1] but after the manner of the Romans, with whom there was no measure.

And so it is related by Josephus, the Jew, who lived shortly after our Lord, that Jesus was torn in his scourging to such a degree that the bones of his ribs were laid bare; as it was also revealed by the most Holy Virgin to St. Bridget, in these words: " I, who was standing by, saw his body scourged to the very ribs, so that his ribs themselves might be seen. And what was even yet more bitter still, when the scourges were drawn back, his flesh was furrowed by them."[1] To St. Teresa, Jesus revealed himself in his scourging; so that the saint wished to have him painted exactly as she had seen him, and told the painter to represent a large piece of flesh torn off, and hanging down from the left elbow; but when the painter inquired as to the shape in which he ought to paint it, he found, on turning round again to his picture, the piece of flesh already drawn.

Ah, my beloved and adored Jesus, how much hast Thou suffered for love of me! Oh, let not so many pangs, and so much blood, be lost for me !

VI.

But from the Scriptures alone it clearly appears how barbarous and inhuman was the scourging of Jesus Christ.

[1] "Quadragenarium numerum non excedant, ne fœde laceratus ante oculos tuos abeat frater tuus."—*Deut.* xxv. 3.

[1] " Ego quæ astabam, vidi corpus ejus flagellatum usque ad costas, ita ut costæ ejus viderentur. Et quod amarius erat, cum retraheren tur flagella, carnes ipsis flagellis sulcabantur."—*Rev.* l. i, c. 10.

For why was it that Pilate should, after the scourging, ever have shown him to the people, saying, *Behold the Man!*[1] were it not that our Saviour was reduced to so pitiable a condition that Pilate believed the very sight of him would have moved his enemies themselves to compassion, and hindered them from any longer demanding his death?

Why was it that in the journey which Jesus, after this, made to Calvary, the Jewish women followed him with tears and lamentations? *But there followed Him a great multitude of the people, and women, who bewailed and lamented Him.*[2] Was it, perhaps, because those women loved him and believed him to be innocent? No, the women, for the most part, agree with their husbands in opinion; so that they, too, esteemed him guilty; but the appearance of Jesus after his scourging was so shocking and pitiable as to move to tears even those who hated him; and therefore it was that the women gave vent to their tears and sighs.

Why, again, was it that in this journey the Jews took the cross from off his shoulders, and gave it the Cyrenian to carry? According to the most probable opinion, and as the words of St. Matthew clearly show, *they compelled him to bear His cross;*[3] or, as St. Luke says, *And on him they laid the cross, that he might carry it after Jesus.*[4] Was it, perhaps, that they felt pity for him and wished to lessen his pains? No, those guilty men hated him, and sought to afflict him to their uttermost. But, as the blessed Denis, the Carthusian, says, "they feared lest he should die upon the way,"[5] seeing that our Lord,

---

[1] "Ecce homo!"—*John*, xix. 5.

[2] "Sequebatur autem illum multa turba populi, et mulierum quæ plangebant et lamentabantur eum."—*Luke*, xxiii. 27.

[3] "Hunc angariaverunt ut tolleret crucem ejus."—*Matt.* xxvii. 32.

[4] "Et imposuerunt illi crucem portare post Jesum."—*Luke*, xxiii. 26.

[5] "Timebant ne moreretur in via."

after the scourging, was so drained of blood and so exhausted in strength as to be scarcely able any longer to stand, falling down as he did on his road under the cross, and faltering as he went, so to speak, at every step, as if at the point of death; therefore, in order to take him alive to Calvary and see him dead upon the cross, according to their desire, that his name might ever after be one of infamy: *Let us cut him off*, said they, as the Prophet had foretold, *from the land of the living, and let his name be remembered no more.*[1] This was the end for which they constrained the Cyrenian to bear the cross.

Ah, my Lord, great is my happiness in understanding how much Thou hast loved me, and that Thou dost even now preserve for me the same love that Thou didst bear me then, in the time of Thy Passion! But how great is my sorrow at the thought of having offended so good a God! By the merit of Thy scourging, O my Jesus, I ask Thy pardon, I repent, above every other evil, of having offended Thee; and I purpose rather to die than to offend Thee again. Pardon me all the wrongs that I have done Thee, and give me the grace ever to love Thee for the time to come.

VII.

The Prophet Isaias has described more clearly than all the pitiable state to which he foresaw our Redeemer reduced. He said that his most holy flesh would have to be not merely wounded, but altogether bruised and crushed to pieces: *But He was wounded for our iniquities, He was bruised for our transgressions.*[1] For, as the Prophet goes on to say, the Eternal Father, the more perfectly to

[1] " Eradamus eum de terra viventium, et nomen ejus non memoretur amplius."—*Jer.* xi. 19.

[1] " Ipse autem vulneratus est propter iniquitates nostras, attritus est propter scelera nostra."—*Isa.* liii. 5.

satisfy his justice, and to make mankind understand the deformity of sin, was not contented without beholding his Son pounded piecemeal, as it were, and torn to shreds by the scourges: *And the Lord willed to bruise Him in infirmity.*[1] So that the blessed body of Jesus had to become like the body of a leper, all wounds from head to foot: *And we esteemed Him as a leper, and one smitten of God.*[2]

Behold, then, O my lacerated Lord, the condition to which our iniquities have reduced Thee: "O good Jesus, it is ourselves who sinned; and dost Thou bear the penalty of it?"[3] Blessed for evermore be Thy exceeding charity; and mayest Thou be beloved as Thou dost deserve by all sinners; and, above all, by me, who have done Thee more despite than others.

VIII.

Jesus one day manifested himself under his scourging to Sister Victoria Angelini; and showing her his body one mass of wounds, said to her, "These wounds, Victoria, every one of them, ask thee for love." "Let us love the Bridegroom," said the loving St. Augustine, "and the more he is presented to us veiled under deformity, the more precious and sweet is he made to the bride."[4]

Yes, my sweet Saviour, I see Thee all covered with wounds; I look into Thy beautiful face; but, O my God, it no longer wears its beautiful appearance, but disfigured and blackened with blood, and bruises, and shameful spittings: *There is no beauty in Him, nor comeliness : and we*

[1] "Et Dominus voluit conterere eum in infirmitate."—*Is.* liii. 10.

[2] "Et nos putavimus eum quasi leprosum et percussum a Deo."—*Ibid.* 4.

[3] "O bone Jesu! nos peccavimus, et tu luis!"

[4] "Amemus Sponsum; quanto magis deformis nobis commendatur, tanto carior, tanto dulcior factus est sponsæ."—*Serm.* 44, *E. B.*

beheld *Him, and esteemed Him not.*[1] But the more I see
Thee so disfigured, O my Lord, the more beautiful and
lovely dost Thou appear to me. And what are these
disfigurements that I behold but signs of the tenderness
of that love which Thou dost bear towards me? I love
Thee, my Jesus, thus wounded and torn to pieces for me;
would that I could see myself too torn to pieces for Thee,
like so many martyrs whose portion this has been! But
if I cannot offer Thee wounds and blood, I offer Thee at
least all the pains which it will be my lot to suffer. I
offer Thee my heart; with this I desire to love Thee
more tenderly even than I am able. And who is there
that my soul should love more tenderly than a God, who
has endured scourging and been drained of his blood for
me? I love Thee, O God of love! I love Thee, O infinite goodness! I love Thee, O my love, my all! I love
Thee, and I would never cease to say, both in this life and
in the other, I love Thee, I love Thee, I love Thee.
Amen.

CHAPTER IX.

THE CROWNING WITH THORNS.

I.

As the soldiers, however, perseveringly continued their
cruel scourging of the innocent Lamb, it is related that
one of those who were standing by came forward, and,
taking courage, said to them, You have no orders to kill
this man, as you are trying to do. And, saying this, he
cut the cords wherewith the Lord was standing bound.
This was revealed to St. Bridget: "Then a certain man,

[1] "Non est species ei, neque decor ; et vidimus eum, et non erat
aspectus."—*Isa.* liii. 2.

his spirit being moved within him, demanded, Are you going to kill him in this manner, uncondemned? and forthwith he cut his bonds."[1]

But hardly was the scourging ended, when those barbarous men, urged on and bribed by the Jews with money, as St. John Chrysostom avers, inflict upon the Redeemer a fresh kind of torture: *Then the soldiers of the governor taking Jesus into the prætorium, gathered together the whole band, and stripped Him, clothed Him in a purple robe, and platting a crown of thorns, they put it upon His head, and a reed in His right hand.*[2] Behold how the soldiers strip him again; and, treating him as a mock king, place upon him a purple garment, which was nothing else but a ragged cloak, one of those that were worn by the Roman soldiers, and called a chlamys; in his hand they place a reed to represent a sceptre, and upon his head a bundle of thorns to represent a crown.

Ah, my Jesus, and art not Thou, then, true king of the universe? And how is it that Thou art now become king of sorrow and reproach? See whither love has brought Thee! O my most lovely God, when will that day arrive whereon I may so unite myself to Thee, that nothing may evermore have power to separate me from Thee, and I may no longer be able to cease to love Thee! O Lord, as long as I live in this world, I always stand in danger of turning my back upon Thee, and of refusing to Thee my love, as I have unhappily done in time past. O my Jesus, if Thou foreseest that by continuing in life I should have to suffer this greatest of all misfortunes,

[1] "Tunc unus, concitato in se spiritu, quæsivit: Numquid interficietis eum sic injudicatum? Et statim secuit vincula ejus."—*Rev.* l. 1, c. 10.

[2] "Tunc milites præsidis, suscipientes Jesum in prætorium, congregaverunt ad eum universam cohortem. Et exuentes eum, chlamydem coccineam circumdederunt ei. Et plectentes coronam de spinis, posuerunt super caput ejus, et arundinem in dextera ejus."—*Matt.* xxvii. 27-30.

let me die at this moment, while I hope that I am in Thy grace! I pray Thee, by Thy Passion, not to abandon me to so great an evil. I should indeed deserve it for my sins; but Thou dost deserve it not. Choose out any punishment for me rather than this. No, my Jesus, my Jesus, I would not see myself ever again separated from Thee.

II.

And platting a crown of thorns, they put it upon His head.[1] It was a good reflection of the devout Lanspergius,[2] that this torture of the crown of thorns was one most full of pain; inasmuch as they everywhere pierced into the sacred head of the Lord, the most sensitive part, it being from the head that all the nerves and sensations of the body diverge; while it was also that torture of his Passion which lasted the longest, as Jesus suffered from the thorns up to his death, remaining, as they did, fixed in his head. Every time that the thorns on his head were touched, the anguish was renewed afresh. And the common opinion of authors agrees with that of St. Vincent Ferrer,[3] that the crown was intertwined with several branches of thorns, and fashioned like a helmet or hat, so that it fitted upon the whole of the head, down to the middle of the forehead; according to the revelation made to St. Bridget: "The crown of thorns embraced his head most tightly, and came down as low as the middle of the forehead."[4]

And, as St. Laurence Justinian says, with St. Peter Damian, the thorns were so long that they penetrated

---

[1] "Et plectentes coronam de spinis, posuerunt super caput ejus."— *Matt.* xxvii. 29.

[2] *De Pass. hom.* 33.

[3] *Serm. in Parasc.*

[4] "Corona spinea capiti ejus arctissime imposita fuit, quæ ad medium frontis descendebat."—*Rev.* l. 4, c. 70.

even to the brain: "The thorns perforating the brain." [1]
While the gentle Lamb let himself be tormented according to their will, without speaking a word, without crying out, but compressing his eyes together through the
anguish, he frequently breathed forth, at that time,
bitter sighs, as is the wont of one undergoing a torture
which has brought him to the point of death, according
as was revealed to the Blessed Agatha of the Cross: " He
very often closed his eyes, and uttered piercing sighs,
like those of one about to die." [2]   So great was the quantity of the blood which flowed from the wounds upon
his sacred head, that upon his face there was no appearance of any other color save that of blood, according to
the revelation of St. Bridget: " So many streams of blood
rushing down over his face, and filling his hair, and eyes,
and beard, he seemed to be nothing but one mass of
blood." [3]   And St. Bonaventure adds, that the beautiful
face of the Lord was no longer seen, but it appeared
rather the face of a man who had been scarified: " Then
might be seen no longer the face of the Lord Jesus, but
that of a man who had undergone excoriation." [4]

O divine love! exclaims Salvian, I know not how to
call Thee, whether sweet or cruel; seeming, as Thou
dost, to have been at one and the same time both sweet
and cruel too : "O love! what to call Thee I know not,
sweet or cruel.   Thou seemest to be both." [5] Ah, my
Jesus, true, indeed, it is that love makes Thee sweet,
as regards us, showing Thee forth to us as so passionate

[1] " Spinæ cerebrum perforantes."—*De Tr. Chr. Ag.* c. 14.

[2] " Sæpius oculos clausit, et acuta edidit suspiria quasi morituri."

[3] " Plurimis rivis sanguinis decurrentibus per faciem ejus, et crines,
oculos, et barbam replentibus, nihil nisi sanguis totum videbatur."
—*Rev.* L 4, c. 70.

[4] " Non amplius facies Domini Jesu, sed hominis excoriati videretur."

[5] "O amor! quid te appellem nescio, dulcem an asperum : utrumque esse videris."—*Epist.* 1.

a lover of our souls; but it makes Thee pitiless towards Thyself, causing Thee to suffer such bitter torments. Thou wast willing to be crowned with thorns to obtain for us a crown of glory in heaven: "He was crowned with thorns, that we may be crowned with the crown that is to be given to the elect in heaven."[1] O my sweetest Saviour, I hope to be Thy crown in paradise, obtaining my salvation through the merits of Thy sufferings; there will I forever praise Thy love and Thy mercies: "The mercies of the Lord will I forever sing; yea, I will sing them forever."[2]

III.

Ah, cruel thorns, ungrateful creatures, wherefore do ye torment your Creator thus? But to what purpose, asks St. Augustine, dost thou find fault with the thorns? They were but innocent instruments—our sins, our evil thoughts, were the wicked thorns which afflicted the head of Jesus Christ: "What are the thorns but sinners?"[3] Jesus having one day appeared to St. Teresa crowned with thorns, the saint began to compassionate him; but the Lord made answer to her: "Teresa, compassionate me not on account of the wounds which the thorns of the Jews produced; but commiserate me on account of the wounds which the sins of Christians occasion me." Thou, too, therefore, O my soul, didst then inflict torture upon the venerable head of thy Redeemer by thy many consentings to evil: *Know thou and behold how grievous and bitter it is for thee to have left the Lord thy God.*[4]

---

[1] "Coronatus est spinis, ut nos coronemur corona danda electis in patria."—*In Jo.* 17.

[2] "Misericordias Domini in æternum cantabo, in æternum cantabo."—*Ps.* lxxxviii. 2.

[3] "Spinæ quid, nisi peccatores?"

[4] "Scito et vide quia malum et amarum est reliquisse te Dominum Deum tuum."—*Jer.* ii. 19.

Open now thine eyes, and see, and bitterly bewail all thy life long the evil that thou hast done in so ungratefully turning thy back upon thy Lord and God.

Ah, my Jesus! no, Thou hast not deserved that I should have treated Thee as I have done. I have done evil; I have been in the wrong; I am sorry for it with all my heart. Oh, pardon me, and give me a sorrow which may make me bewail all my life long the wrongs that I have done Thee. My Jesus, my Jesus, pardon me, wishing, as I do, to love Thee forever.

IV.

And bowing the knee before Him, they derided Him, saying, Hail, King of the Jews: and spitting upon Him, they took a reed, and smote Him upon the head.[1] St. John adds, *And they gave Him blows.*[2] When those barbarians had placed upon the head of Jesus that crown of torture, it was not enough for them to press it down as forcibly as they could with their hands, but they took a reed to answer the purpose of a hammer, that so they might make the thorns penetrate the more deeply. They then began to turn him into derision, as if he had been a mock king; first of all saluting him on their bended knee as King of the Jews; and then, rising up, they spit into his face, and buffeted him with shouts and jests of scorn. Ah, my Jesus, to what art Thou reduced!

Had any one happened by chance to pass that place and seen Jesus Christ so drained of blood, clad in that ragged purple garment, with that sceptre in his hand, with that crown upon his head, and so derided and ill-treated by that low rabble, what would he ever have taken him to be but the vilest and most wicked man in

[1] " Et genu flexo ante eum illudebant ei, dicentes : Ave, Rex Judæorum ! Et expuentes in eum, acceperunt arundinem, et percutiebant caput ejus."—*Matt.* xxvii. 29.
[2] " Et dabant ei alapas."—*John,* xix. 3.

the world ! Behold the Son of God become at that time
the disgrace of Jerusalem ! O men, hereupon exclaims
the Blessed Denis, the Carthusian, if we will not love
Jesus Christ because he is good, because he is God, let
us love him at least for the many pains which he has
suffered for us: "If we love him not because he is good,
because he is God, let us at least love him because he
has suffered so many things for our salvation." [1]

Ah, my dear Redeemer, take back a rebellious servant
who has run away from Thee, but who now returns to
Thee in penitence. While I was fleeing from Thee and
despising Thy love, Thou didst not cease from following
after me to draw me back to Thyself; and therefore I
cannot fear that Thou wilt drive me away now that I
seek Thee, value Thee, and love Thee above everything.
Make known to me what I have to do to please Thee ;
wishing, as I do, to do it all. O my most lovely God, I
wish to love Thee in earnest; and I desire to give Thee
no displeasure more. Aid me with Thy grace. Let me
not leave Thee more. Mary, my hope, pray to Jesus for
me. Amen.

CHAPTER X.

"ECCE HOMO"—"BEHOLD THE MAN."

I.

Pilate, seeing the Redeemer reduced to that condition,
so moving, as it was, to compassion, thought that the
mere sight of him would have softened the Jews. He
therefore led him forth into the balcony; he raised up the
purple garment, and, exhibiting to the people the body

---

[1] "Si non amamus eum, quia bonus, quia Deus, saltem amemus,
quoniam tanta pro nostra salute perpessus est."—*In Matt.* 27.

of Jesus all covered with wounds and gashes, he said to them, Behold the man: *Pilate went forth again to them, and saith to them : Behold, I am bringing Him out to you, that you may know that I find no fault in Him. Jesus, therefore, went forth, wearing the crown of thorns and the purple garment; and he saith unto them, Behold the Man.*[1] *Behold the Man!* as though he would have said, Behold the man against whom you have laid an accusation before me, and who wanted to make himself a king. I, to please you, have sentenced him, innocent although he be, to be scourged: "Behold the Man, not honored as a king, but covered with disgrace."[2] Behold him now, reduced to such a state that he wears the appearance of a man that has been flayed alive; and he can have but little life left in him. If, with all this, you want me to condemn him to death, I tell you that I cannot do so, as I find not any reason for condemning him. But the Jews on beholding Jesus thus ill-treated, waxed more fierce: *When, therefore, the chief priests and the officers saw Him, they cried out, saying, Crucify Him! crucify Him!*[3] Pilate, seeing that they could not be pacified, washed his hands in the presence of the people, saying, *I am innocent of the blood of this just Man; look you to it.*[4] And they made answer, *His blood be upon us, and upon our children.*[5]

O my beloved Saviour! Thou art the greatest of all kings; yet now I behold Thee the most reviled of all

---

[1] "Exivit iterum Pilatus foras, et dicit eis : Ecce adduco vobis eum foras, ut cognoscatis quia nullam invenio in eo causam. (Exivit ergo Jesus portans coronam spineam et purpureum vestimentum.) Et dicit eis : Ecce homo !"—*John*, xix. 4, 5.

[2] "'Ecce homo,' non clarus imperio, sed plenus opprobrio."—*St. Aug. In Jo. tr.* 116.

[3] "Cum ergo vidissent eum pontifices et ministri, clamabant, dicentes : Crucifige, crucifige eum."—*John*, xix. 6.

[4] "Innocens ego sum a sanguine justi hujus ; vos videritis !"—*Matt.* xxvii. 24.

[5] "Sanguis ejus super nos et super filios nostros."—*Ibid.* 25.

mankind. If this ungrateful people knows Thee not, I
know Thee; and I adore Thee as my true King and Lord.
I thank Thee, O my Redeemer, for all the outrages that
Thou hast suffered for me; and I pray Thee to give me
a love for contempt and pains, since Thou hast so lovingly embraced them. I blush at having in time past
loved honors and pleasures so much, that for their sake
I have often gone so far as to renounce Thy grace and
Thy love. I repent of this above every other evil. I
embrace, O Lord, all the pains and ignominies that will
come to me from Thy hands. Do Thou bestow upon
me that resignation which I need. I love Thee, my
Jesus, my love, my all.

II.

But while Pilate from the balcony was exhibiting
Jesus to that populace, at the self-same time the Eternal
Father from heaven was presenting to us his beloved
Son, saying, in like manner, *Behold the Man.* Behold
this Man, who is my only-begotten Son, whom I love
with the same love wherewith I love myself: *This is My
beloved Son, in whom I am well pleased.*[1] Behold the Man,
your Saviour, him whom I promised, and for whom you
were anxiously waiting. Behold the Man, who is nobler
than all other men, become the man of sorrows. Behold
him, and see to what a pitiable condition he has reduced
himself through the love which he has borne towards
you, and in order to be, at least out of compassion, beloved by you again. Oh, look at him, and love him; and
if his great worth move you not, at least let these sorrows and ignominies which he suffers for you move you
to love him.

Ah, my God and Father of my Redeemer! I love Thy
Son, who suffers for love of me; and I love Thee, who

[1] "Hic est Filius meus dilectus, in quo mihi complacui."—*Matt.*
iii. 17.

with so much love hast abandoned him to so many pains
for me. Oh, look not on my sins by which I have so
often offended Thee and Thy Son: *Look upon the face of
Thy Christ.*[1] Behold Thine only-begotten, all covered
with wounds and shame in satisfaction for my faults;
and for his merits pardon me, and never let me again
offend Thee. *His blood be upon us.*[2] The blood of this
man, so dear unto Thee, who prays to Thee for us, and
impetrates Thy mercy, let this descend upon our souls,
and obtain for us Thy grace. O my Lord! I hate and
abhor all that I have done that displeases Thee; and I
love Thee, O infinite goodness, more than I love myself.
For love of this Thy Son give me Thy love, to enable me to conquer every passion, and to undergo every
suffering in order to please Thee.

III

*Go forth, ye daughters of Sion, and behold King Solomon
in his crown, wherewith his mother crowned him on the day
of his espousals, and on the day of the joy of his heart.*[3] Go
forth, ye souls redeemed, ye daughters of grace, go forth
to see your gentle king, on the day of his death, the day
of his joy, for thereon he made you his spouses, giving
up his life upon the cross, crowned by the ungrateful
synagogue, his mother, with a crown; not indeed one of
honor, but one of suffering and shame: "Go forth," says
St. Bernard, "and behold your king in a crown of poverty
and misery."[4]

O most beautiful of all mankind! O greatest of all
monarchs! O most lovely of all spouses! to what a state

[1] "Respice in faciem Christi tui."—*Ps.* lxxxiii. 10.
[2] "Sanguis ejus super nos!"
[3] "Egredimini et videte, filiæ Sion, regem Salomonem in diadem-
ate, quo coronavit illum mater sua, in die desponsationis illius et in
die lætitiæ cordis ejus."—*Cant.* iii. 11.
[4] "Egredimini et videte Regem vestrum in corona paupertatis, in
corona miseriæ."—*In Epiph.* s. 2

do I see Thee reduced, covered with wounds and contempt! Thou art a spouse, but a spouse of blood: *To
me Thou art a spouse of blood ;* [1] it being by means of Thy
blood that Thou hast willed to espouse Thyself to our
souls. Thou art a king, but a king of suffering and a
king of love ; it being by sufferings that Thou hast willed
to gain our affections.

O most beloved spouse of my soul! would that I were
continually recalling to my mind how much Thou hast
suffered for me, that so I might never cease to love and
please Thee! Have compassion upon me, who have cost
Thee so much. In requital for so many sufferings endured by Thee, Thou are content if I love Thee. Yes, I
do love Thee, infinite loveliness, I love Thee above everything; yet it is but little that I love Thee. O my beloved
Jesus! give me more love, if Thou wouldst that I should
love Thee more. I desire to have a very great love for
Thee. So wretched a sinner as I am ought to have been
burning in hell ever since the moment in which I first
gravely offended Thee; but Thou hast borne with me
even until this hour, because Thou dost not wish me to
burn with that miserable fire, but with the blessed fire of
Thy love. This thought, O God of my soul, sets me all
in flame with the desire of doing all that I can to
please Thee. Help me, O my Jesus; and since Thou hast
done so much, complete the work, and make me wholly
Thine.

IV.

But the Jews going on to insult the governor, crying
out, *Away with Him! away with Him! crucify Him!* [2] Pilate
said to them, *Shall I crucify your King?* and they made
answer, *We have no king but Cæsar.* [3] The worldly-minded,

[1] " Sponsus sanguinum tu mihi es."—*Exod.* iv. 25.
[2] " Tolle, tolle, crucifige eum."—*John,* xix. 15.
[3] " Regem vestrum crucifigam? Non habemus regem, nisi Cæsarem."—*Ibid.*

who love the riches, the honors, and the pleasures of earth, refuse to have Jesus Christ for their king; because, as far as this earth is concerned, Jesus was but a king of poverty, shame, and sufferings.

But if such as these refuse Thee, O my Jesus, we choose Thee for our only king, and we make our protestation that "we have no king but Jesus."[1] Yes, most lovely Saviour, *Thou art my king;*[2] Thou art and hast forever to be my only Lord. True king, indeed, art Thou of our souls; for Thou hast created them, and redeemed them from the slavery of Satan: *Thy kingdom come.*[3] Exercise, then, Thy dominion, and reign forever in our poor hearts; may they ever serve and obey Thee! Be it for others to serve the monarchs of earth, in hope of the good things of this world. Our desire it is to serve only Thee, our afflicted and despised king, in hope only of pleasing Thee, without any earthly consolations. Dear to us, from this day forth, shall shame and sufferings be, since Thou hast been willing to endure so much of them for love of us. Oh, grant us the grace to be faithful unto Thee; and to this end bestow upon us the great gift of Thy love. If we love Thee, we shall also love the contempt and the sufferings which were so much beloved by Thee; and we shall ask Thee for nothing but that which Thy faithful and loving servant St. John of the Cross asked of Thee: "Lord, to suffer and be despised for Thee; Lord, to suffer and be despised for Thee!"[4] O Mary, my Mother, intercede for me. Amen.

[1] "Non habemus regem, nisi Jesum!"
[2] "Tu es ipse Rex meus."—*Ps.* xliii. 5.
[3] "Adveniat regnum tuum."—*Matt.* vi. 10.
[4] "Domine, pati et contemni pro te."

CHAPTER XI.

THE CONDEMNATION OF JESUS CHRIST, AND HIS JOURNEY TO CALVARY.

I.

Pilate was going on making excuses to the Jews, to the effect that he could not condemn that innocent One to death, when they worked upon his fears by telling him: *If thou lettest this Man go, thou art no friend of Cæsar's.*[1] And hence the miserable judge, blinded by the fear of losing Cæsar's favor, after having so often recognized and declared the innocence of Jesus Christ, at last condemned him to die by crucifixion: *Then he delivered Him up to them, that He might be crucified.*[2]

O my beloved Redeemer (St. Bernard hereupon bewails), what crime hast Thou committed that Thou shouldst have to be condemned to death, and that death the death of the cross? "What hast Thou done, O most innocent Saviour, that the judgment upon Thee should be such? Of what crime hast Thou been guilty?"[3] Ah, I well understand, replies the saint, the reason for Thy death; I understand what has been Thy crime: "Thy crime is Thy love."[4] Thy crime is the too great love which Thou hast borne to men; it is this, not Pilate, that condemns Thee to die. No, adds St. Bonaventure, I see no just reason for Thy death, O my Jesus, save the excess of the affection which Thou bearest to us: "I see no

[1] "Si hunc dimittis, non es amicus Cæsaris."—*John.* xix. 12.
[2] "Tunc ergo tradidit eis illum, ut crucifigeretur."—*Ibid.* 16.
[3] "Quid fecisti, innocentissime Salvator, ut sic judicareris? quid commisisti?"
[4] "Peccatum tuum est amor tuus."

cause for death but the superabundance of love." [1]   Ah, so great an excess of love, goes on St. Bernard, how strongly does it constrain us, O loving Saviour, to consecrate all the affections of our hearts unto Thee ! " Such love wholly claims for itself our love." [2]

O my dear Saviour, the mere knowledge that Thou dost love me should be sufficient to make me live detached from everything, in order to study only how to love Thee and please Thee in all things: *Love is strong as death.* [3]   If love is as strong as death, oh, by Thy merits, my Saviour, grant me such a love for Thee as shall make me hold all earthly affections in abhorrence.   Give me thoroughly to understand that all my good consists in pleasing Thee, O God, all goodness and all love! I curse that time in which I loved Thee not.   I thank Thee for that Thou dost give me time in which to love Thee.   I love Thee, O my Jesus, infinite in loveliness, and infinitely loving.   With my whole self do I love Thee, and I assure Thee that I would wish to die a thousand deaths rather than ever again cease from loving Thee.

II.

The unjust sentence of death is read over to Jesus, who stands condemned; he listens to it, and humbly accepts it.   No complaint does he make of the injustice of the judge; no appeal does he make to Cæsar, as did St. Paul, but, all gentle and resigned, he submits himself to the decree of the Eternal Father, who condemns him to the cross for our sins: *He humbled Himself, being made obedient even unto death, and that the death of the cross.* [4]   And, for

[1] " Non in te video causam mortis, nisi superabundantiam charitatis."—*Stim. div. am.* p. 1, c. 2.

[2] " Hoc omnino amorem nostrum facile vindicat totum tibi."—*In Cant.* s. 20.

[3] " Fortis est ut mors dilectio."—*Cant.* viii. 6.

[4] " Humiliavit semetipsum, factus obediens usque ad mortem, mortem autem crucis."—*Phil.* ii. 8.

the love which he bears to man, he is content to die for us: *He loved us, and gave Himself up for us.*[1]

O my merciful Saviour, how much do I thank Thee! How deeply am I obliged to Thee! I desire, O my Jesus, to die for Thee, since Thou hast so lovingly accepted of death for me. But if it is not granted me to give Thee my blood and life at the hands of the executioner, as the Martyrs have done, I, at least, accept with resignation the death which awaits me; and I accept of it in the manner, and at the time, which shall please Thee. Henceforth do I offer it up to Thee in honor of Thy Majesty, and in satisfaction for my sins. I pray Thee, by the merits of Thy death, to grant me the happiness to die in Thy grace and love.

III.

Pilate delivers over the innocent Lamb into the hands of those wolves, to do with him what they will: *But he delivered Jesus up to their will.*[2] These ministers of Satan seize hold of him fiercely; they strip him of the purple garment, as is suggested to them by the Jews, and put his own raiment again upon him: *They stripped Him of the purple garment, and clothed Him in His own raiment, and led Him away to crucify Him.*[3] And this they did, says St. Ambrose, in order that Jesus might be recognized, at least, by his apparel; his beautiful face being so much disfigured with blood and wounds, that in other apparel it would have been difficult for him to have been recognized as the person he was: "They put on him his own raiment, that he might the better be recognized by all; since, as his face was all bloody and disfigured, it would not have been an easy matter for all to have recognized

---

[1] "Dilexit nos, et tradidit semetipsum pro nobis."—*Eph.* v. 2.

[2] "Jesum vero tradidit voluntati eorum."—*Luke*, xxiii 25.

[3] "Exuerunt eum chlamyde, et induerunt eum vestimentis ejus, et duxerunt eum ut crucifigerent."—*Matt.* xxvii. 31.

him."[1]   They then take two rough beams, and of them
they quickly construct the cross, the length of which was
fifteen feet, as St. Bonaventure says, with St. Anselm, and
they lay it upon the shoulders of the Redeemer.

But Jesus did not wait, says St. Thomas of Villanova,
for the executioner to lay the cross upon him ; of his
own accord he stretched forth his hands, and eagerly
laid hold of it, and placed it upon his own wounded
shoulders : " He waited not till the soldier should lay it
upon him, but he grasped hold of it joyfully."[1]   Come,
he then said, come, my beloved cross ; it is now three-
and-thirty years that I am sighing and searching for
thee.   I embrace thee, I clasp thee to my heart, for thou
art the altar upon which it is my will to sacrifice my life
out of love for my flock.

Ah, my Lord, how couldst Thou do so much good to
one who has done Thee so much evil ?   O God, when I
think of Thy having gone so far as to die under torments
to obtain for me the divine friendship, and that I have
so often voluntarily lost it afterwards through my own
fault, I would that I could die of grief !   How often hast
Thou forgiven me, and I have gone back and offended
Thee again !   How could I ever have hoped for pardon,
were it not that I knew that Thou hast died in order to
pardon me ?   By this Thy death, then, I hope for pardon, and for perseverance in loving Thee.   I repent, O
my Redeemer, of having offended Thee.   By Thy
merits, pardon me, who promise never to displease Thee
more.   I prize and love Thy friendship more than all the
good things of this world.   Oh, let it not be my lot to
go back and lose it !   Inflict me, O Lord, with any pun-

---

[1] " Induunt eum vestibus, quo melius ab omnibus cognosceretur ;
quia cum facies ejus esset cruentata et deformata, non poterat facile
ab omnibus agnosci."

[1] " Non exspectavit ut imponeretur sibi a milite, sed lætus arri-
puit."—*De Uno Mart. conc.* 3.

ishment rather than with this. O my Jesus, I am not willing to lose Thee any more ; no, I would sooner be willing to lose my life : I wish to love Thee always.

IV.

The officers of justice come forth with the criminals condemned ; and in the midst of these also moves forward unto death the King of heaven, the only-begotten Son of God, laden with his cross : *And bearing His own cross, He went forth to that place which is called Calvary.*[1] Do ye too, O blessed Seraphim, sally forth from heaven, and come and accompany your Lord, who is going to Calvary, there to be executed, together with the malefactors, upon a gibbet of infamy.

O horrifying sight ! A God executed ! Behold that Messias who but a few days before had been proclaimed the Saviour of the world, and received with acclamations and benedictions by the people, who cried out, *Hosanna to the Son of David ; blessed be He that cometh in the name of the Lord ;*[2] and, after all, to see him as, bound, ridiculed, and execrated by all, he moves along, laden with a cross, to die the death of a villain ! A God executed for men ! And shall we find any man who loves not this God ?

O my Eternal Lover, late is it that I begin to love Thee : grant that during the remainder of my life, I may make amends for the time that I have lost. I know, indeed, that all that I can do is but little in comparison with the love which Thou hast borne me ; but it is at least my wish to love Thee with my whole heart. Too great a wrong should I be doing Thee if, after so many kindnesses, I were to divide my heart in twain, and give

[1] "Et bajulans sibi crucem, exivit in eum, qui dicitur Calvariæ. locum."—*John,* xix. 17.
[2] "Hosanna Filio David ! benedictus qui venit in nomine Domini." —*Matt.* xxi. 9.

a part of it to some object other than Thyself. From this day forth I consecrate unto Thee all my life, my will, my liberty: dispose of me as Thou pleasest. I beg paradise of Thee, that there I may love Thee with all my strength. I wish to love Thee exceedingly in this life, that I may love Thee exceedingly for all eternity Aid me by Thy grace : this I beg of Thee, and hope for, through Thy merits.

V.

Imagine to thyself, O my soul, that thou meetest Jesus as he passes along in this sorrowful journey. As a lamb borne along to the slaughter-house, so is the loving Redeemer conducted unto death : *As a lamb He is led to the slaughter.*[1] So drained of blood is he and wearied out with his torments, that for very weakness he can scarcely stand. Behold him, all torn with wounds, with that bundle of thorns upon his head, with that heavy cross upon his shoulders, and with one of those soldiers dragging him along by a rope. Look at him as he goes along, with body bent double, with knees all of a tremble, dripping with blood ; and so painful is it to him to walk, that at every step he seems ready to die.

Put the question to him : O divine lamb, hast Thou not yet had Thy fill of sufferings ? If it is by them that Thou dost aim at gaining my love, oh, let Thy sufferings end here, for I wish to love Thee as Thou dost desire. No, he replies, I am not yet content : then shall I be content when I see myself die for love of you. And whither, O my Jesus, art Thou going now ? I am going, he answers, to die for you. Hinder me not: this only do I ask of, and recommend to, you, that, when you shall see me actually dead upon the cross for you, you will keep in mind the love which I have borne you ; bear it in mind, and love me.

---

[1] " Sicut ovis ad occisionem ducetur."—*Isa.* liii. 7.

O my afflicted Lord, how dear did it cost Thee to make me comprehend the love which Thou hast had for me! But what benefit could ever have resulted to Thee from my love, that Thou hast been willing to expend Thy blood and Thy life to gain it? And how could I, after having been bound by so great love, have been able so long to live without loving Thee, and unmindful of Thy affection? I thank Thee, for that now Thou dost give me light to make me know how much Thou hast loved me. O infinite goodness I love Thee above every good. Would, too, that I had the power of offering a thousand lives in sacrifice unto Thee, willing as Thou hast been to sacrifice Thine own divine life for me. Oh, grant me those aids to love Thee which Thou hast merited for me by so many sufferings! Bestow upon me that sacred fire which Thou didst come to enkindle upon earth by dying for us. Be ever reminding me of Thy death, that I may never forget to love Thee.

VI.

His government was upon His shoulder.[1] The cross, says Tertullian,[2] was precisely the noble instrument whereby Jesus Christ made acquisition of so many souls; since, by dying thereon, he paid the penalty due to our sins, and thus rescued us from hell, and made us his own. *Who His own Self bore our sins in His body upon the tree.*[3]

If God, then, O my Jesus, burdened Thee with all the sins of men—*The Lord laid upon Him the iniquities of us all,*[4]—I, with my own sins, added to the weight of the cross that Thou didst bear to Calvary. Ah, my sweet-

---

[1] "Factus est principatus super humerum ejus."—*Isa.* ix. 6.

[2] *Adv. Jud.*

[3] "Qui peccata nostra ipse pertulit in corpore suo super lignum."—1 *Pet.* ii. 24.

[4] "Posuit Dominus in eo iniquitatem omnium nostrum."—*Isa.* liii. 6.

est Saviour, Thou didst even then foresee all the wrongs
that I should do Thee ; yet, notwithstanding, Thou didst
not cease to love me, or to prepare for me all the mercies
that Thou hast since employed towards me.   If, then,
to Thee I have been dear, most vile and ungrateful sinner as I am, who have so much offended Thee, good reason is there why Thou shouldst be dear to me,—Thou, my
God, infinite in beauty and goodness, who hast loved
me so much.   Ah, would that I had never displeased
Thee!   Now, my Jesus, do I know the wrong that I have
done Thee.   O ye accursed sins of mine, what have you
done ?   You have caused me to sadden the loving heart
of my Redeemer, that heart which has loved me so
much.   O my Jesus, forgive me, repenting, as I do, of
having done despite unto Thee.   Henceforth it is Thou
who art to be the only object of my love.   I love Thee,
O infinite loveliness, with all my heart ; and I resolve to
love none else but Thee.   Pardon me, O Lord, and give
me Thy love ; I ask Thee for nothing more : "Give me
Thy love only together with Thy grace"[1] (I say unto
Thee with St. Ignatius), "and I am rich enough."

VII.

*If any man will come after Me, let him deny himself and
follow Me.*[2]   Since, then, O my Redeemer, Thou dost
go before me with Thy cross, innocent as Thou art, and
dost invite me to follow Thee with mine, go forward, for
I will not abandon Thee.   If, in time past, I have abandoned Thee, I confess that I have done wrong.   Give
me now what Thou wilt, embracing it, as I do, whatsoever it be, and willing, as I am, to accompany Thee with
it even unto death : *Let us go forth from the camp, bear-*

---

[1] "Amorem tui solum cum gratia tua mihi dones, et dives sum
satis."

[2] "Si quis vult post me venire, abneget semetipsum, et tollat
crucem suam, et sequatur me."—*Matt.* xvi. 24.

ing His reproach.[1] And how, O Lord, can it be possible for us not, for Thy love, to love sufferings and shame, loving them so much, as Thou hast done, for our salvation? But since Thou dost invite us to follow Thee, yea, it is our wish to follow Thee and to die with Thee: give us only the strength to carry it out. This strength we ask of Thee, and hope for by Thy merits. I love Thee, O my most lovely Jesus, I love Thee with all my soul, and I will never abandon Thee more; enough for me has been the time that I have gone astray from Thee. Bind me now to Thy cross. If I have despised Thy love, I repent of it with all my heart; and I now prize it above every good.

Ah, my Jesus, and who am I that thou wishest to have me for a follower of Thine, and commandest me to love Thee, and if I will not love Thee, threatenest me with hell? And why, I will say to Thee, with St. Augustine,[2] shouldst Thou hold out to me the threat of eternal miseries? For what greater misery could befall me than that of not loving Thee, O most lovely God, my Creator, my Redeemer, my paradise, my all? I see that, as a just chastisement of my offences against Thee, I should have deserved to be condemned to the inability of ever loving Thee more; but because Thou dost still love me, Thou dost continue to command me to love Thee, evermore repeating to my heart, *Thou shalt love the Lord Thy God with all thy heart, with all thy soul, and with all thy mind.*[3] I thank Thee, O my love, for this sweet precept; and in order to obey Thee, I do love Thee with all my heart, with all my soul, and with all my mind. I repent of not having loved Thee in time past. At this moment

[1] " Exeamus igitur ad eum extra castra, improperium ejus portantes."—*Heb.* xiii. 13.

[2] *Conf. B.* 1, c. 5.

[3] " Diliges Dominum Deum tuum ex toto corde tuo, et in tota anima tua, et in tota mente tua."—*Matt.* xxii. 37.

I would rather choose to undergo every suffering than live without loving Thee, and I purpose evermore to seek Thy love.   Help me, O my Jesus, to be ever making acts of love towards Thee, and to depart out of this life while making an act of love, that so I may come to love Thee, face to face, in Paradise, where I shall ever after love Thee without imperfection and without interruption, with all my powers, for all eternity.   O Mother of God, pray for me.   Amen.

CHAPTER XII.

THE CRUCIFIXION OF JESUS.

I.

Behold, here we are at the Crucifixion, at that last torture, which brought death to Jesus Christ ; here we are at Calvary, converted into a theatre for the display of divine love, where a God departs this life in an ocean of sufferings: *And when they had come to the place which is called Calvary, they crucified Him there.*[1]   The Lord having, with great difficulty, at length reached the top of the Mount alive, they violently, for the third time, tear his clothes from off him, sticking, as they did, to the sores upon his wounded flesh, and they throw him down upon the cross.   The divine lamb stretches himself out upon that bed of torment; he reaches forth to the executioners his hands and his feet to be nailed; and raising his eyes to heaven, he offers up to his Eternal Father the great sacrifice of his life for the salvation of men.   After the nailing of one of his hands, the nerves shrink, so that they had need of main force and ropes, as was revealed

[1] "Et postquam venerunt in locum qui vocatur Calvariæ, ibi crucixerunt eum."—*Luke,* xxiii. 33.

by St. Bridget, to draw the other hand and the feet up to the places where they were to be nailed; and this occasioned so great a tension of the nerves and veins, that they broke asunder with a violent convulsion: "They drew my hands and my feet with a rope to the places of the nails, so that the nerves and veins were stretched out to the full and broke asunder;"[1] inasmuch that all his bones might have been numbered, as David had already predicted: *They pierced My hands and My feet, they numbered all My bones.*[2]

Ah, my Jesus, by what power was it that Thy hands and Thy feet were nailed to this wood, but by the love Thou didst bear to men? Thou, by the pain of Thy pierced hands, wert willing to pay the penalty due to all the sins of touch that men have committed; and, by the pain of Thy feet, Thou wert willing to pay for all the steps by which we have gone our way to offend Thee. O my crucified love, with these pierced hands give me Thy benediction! Oh, nail this ungrateful heart of mine to Thy feet, that so I may no more depart from Thee, and that this will of mine, which has so often rebelled against Thee, may remain ever steadily fixed in Thy love. Grant that nothing else but Thy love, and the desire of pleasing Thee may move me. Although I behold Thee suspended upon this gibbet, I believe Thee to be the Lord of the world, the true Son of God, and the Saviour of mankind. For pity's sake, O my Jesus, never abandon me again at any period of my life; and more especially at the hour of my death, in those last agonies and struggles with hell, do Thou assist me, and strengthen me to die in Thy love. I love Thee, my crucified love, I love Thee with all my heart.

[1] "Manus et pedes cum fune trahebant ad loca clavorum, ita ut nervi et venæ extenderentur et rumperentur."—*Rev.* l. I, c. 10.

[2] "Foderunt manus meas et pedes meos: dinumeraverunt omnia ossa mea."—*Ps.* xxi. 17.

II.

St Augustine says, there is no death more bitter than that of the cross: " Among all the different kinds of death, there was none worse." [1]   Because, as St. Thomas [2] observes, those who are crucified have their hands and their feet pierced through, parts which, being entirely composed of nerves, muscles, and veins, are the most sensitive to pain; and the very weight of the body itself, which is suspended from them, causes the pain to be continuous and ever increasing in its intensity up to the moment of death.

But the pains of Jesus were far beyond all other pains; for, as the Angelic Doctor says, the body of Jesus Christ, being perfectly constituted, was more quick and sensitive to pain—that body which was fashioned for him by the Holy Spirit, expressly with a view to his suffering, as he had foretold; as the Apostle testifies, *A body thou hast fitted to Me.* [3]   Moreover, St. Thomas says that Jesus Chiist took upon himself an amount of suffering so great as to be sufficient to satisfy for the temporal punishment merited by the sins of all mankind.   Tiepoli tells us that, in the crucifixion, there were dealt twenty-eight strokes of the hammer upon his hands, and thirty-six upon his feet.

O my soul, behold thy Lord, behold thy life, hanging upon that tree : *And thy life shall be, as it were, hanging before thee.* [4]   Behold how, on that gibbet of pain, fastened by those cruel nails, he finds no place of rest.   Now he leans his weight upon his hands, now upon his feet; but on what part soever he leans, the anguish increases He turns his afflicted head, now on one side, now on the

---

[1] " Pejus nihil fuit inter omnia genera mortium."—*In Jo. tr.* 36.
[2] " P. 3, q. 46, a. 6.
[3] " Corpus autem aptasti mihi."—*Heb.* x. 5.
[4] " Et erit vita tua quasi pendens ante te."—*Deut.* xxviii. 66.

other: if he lets it fall towards his breast, the hands, by the additional weight, are rent the more; if he lowers it towards his shoulders, the shoulders are pierced with the thorns; if he leans it back upon the cross, the thorns enter the more deeply into the head.

Ah, my Jesus, what a death of bitterness is this that Thou art enduring! O my crucified Redeemer, I adore Thee on this throne of ignominy and pain. Upon this cross I read it written that Thou art a king: *Jesus of Nazareth, King of the Jews.*[1] But apart from this title of scorn, what is the evidence that Thou dost give of being a king? Ah, these hands transfixed with nails, this head pierced with thorns, this throne of sorrow, this lacerated flesh, make me well know that Thou art king, but king of love! With humility, then, and tenderness do I draw near to kiss Thy sacred feet, transfixed for love of me; I clasp in my arms this cross, on which Thou, being made a victim of love, wast willing to offer Thyself in sacrifice for me to the divine justice: *being made obedient unto death, the death of the cross.*[2] O blessed obedience which obtained for us the pardon of our sins! And what would have become of me, O my Saviour, hadst Thou not paid the penalty for me! I thank Thee O my love, and by the merits of this sublime obedience do I pray Thee to grant me the grace of obedience in everything to the divine will. All that I desire paradise for is, that I may love Thee forever, and with all my strength.

III.

Behold the King of heaven, who, hanging on that gibbet, is now on the point of giving up the ghost. Let us, too, ask of him, with the prophet: *What are those*

---

[1] " Jesus Nazarenus, Rex Judæorum."—*John*, xix. 19.

[2] " Factus obediens usque ad mortem, mortem autem crucis."— *Phil.* ii. 8.

8

wounds in the middle of Thy hands?[1] Tell me, O my
Jesus, what are these wounds in the middle of Thy
hands? The Abbot Rupert makes answer for Jesus:
"They are the memorials of charity, the price of redemption."[2] They are tokens, says the Redeemer, of
the great love which I bear towards you; they are the
payment by which I set you free from the hands of your
enemies, and from eternal death.

Do thou, then, O faithful soul, love thy God, who hath
had such love for thee; and if thou dost at any time feel
doubtful of his love, turn thine eyes (says St. Thomas
of Villanova)—turn thine eyes to behold that cross, those
pains, and that bitter death which he has suffered for
thee; for such proofs will assuredly make thee know how
much thy Redeemer loves thee: "The cross testifies, the
pains testify, the bitter death which he had endured for
thee testifies this."[3] And St. Bernard adds that the
cross cries out, every wound of Jesus cries out, that he
loves us with a true love: "The cross proclaims, the
wounds proclaim, that he truly loves."[4]

O my Jesus! how do I behold Thee weighed down
with sorrow and sadness! Ah, too much reason hast
Thou to think that while Thou dost suffer even to die of
anguish upon this wood, there are yet so few souls that
have the heart to love Thee! O my God! how many
hearts are there at the present moment, even among
those that are consecrated to Thee, who either love Thee
not, or love Thee not enough! O beautiful flame of
love, thou that didst consume the life of a God upon the
cross, oh, consume me too; consume all the disorderly

[1] "Quid sunt plagæ istæ in medio manuum tuarum?"—*Zach.* xiii. 6.
[2] "Sunt monumenta charitatis, pretia redemptionis."
[3] "Testis crux, testes dolores, testis amara mors, quam pro te sustinuit."—*Dom.* 17 p. *Pent. conc.* 3.
[4] "Clamat crux, clamat vulnus, quod ipse vere dilexit."

affections which live in my heart, and make me live burning and sighing only for that loving Lord of mine, who, for love of me, was willing to end his life, consumed by torments, upon a gibbet of ignominy! O my beloved Jesus! I wish ever to love Thee, and Thee alone, alone; my only wish is to love my love, my God, my all.

IV.

Thine eyes shall behold thy teacher.[1] It was promised to men that with their own eyes they should see their divine Master. The whole life of Jesus was one continuous example and school of perfection; but never did he better incalculate his own most excellent virtues than from the pulpit of his cross. There what an admirable instruction does he give us on patience, more especially in time of infirmity; for with what constancy does Jesus upon the cross endure with most perfect patience the pains of his most bitter death! There, by his own example, he teaches us an exact obedience to the divine precepts, a perfect resignation to God's will; and, above all, he teaches us how we ought to love. Father Paul Segneri, the younger, wrote to one of his penitents, that she ought to keep these words written at the foot of the crucifix : "See what it is to love." It seems as though our Redeemer from the cross said to us all, "See what it is to love," whenever, in order to avoid something that is troublesome, we abandon works that are pleasing in his sight, or at times even go so far as to renounce his grace and his love. He has loved us even unto death, and came not down from the cross till after having left his life thereon.

Ah, my Jesus, Thou hast loved me, even unto dying for me; and I too wish to love Thee even unto dying for Thee. How often have I offended and betrayed Thee in time past! O my Lord, revenge Thyself upon

---

[1] "Erunt oculi tui videntes Præceptorem tuum."—*Isa.* xxx. 20.

me; but let it be the revenge of pity and love. Bestow
upon me such a sorrow for my sins as may make me live
in continual grief and affliction through pain at having
offended Thee. I protest my willingness to suffer every
evil for the time to come, rather than displease Thee.
And what greater evil could befall me than that of displeasing Thee, my God, my Redeemer, my hope, my
treasure, my all.

V.

*And I, if I be lifted up from the earth, will draw all things
to Myself. But this He said, signifying what death He
should die.*[1] Jesus Christ said that when he should have
been lifted up upon the cross, he would, by his merits,
by his example, and by the power of his love, have drawn
towards himself the affection of all souls : "He drew all
the nations of the world to his love, by the merit of his
blood, by his example, and by his love."[2] Such is the
commentary of Cornelius à Lapide. St. Peter Damian
tells us the same : "The Lord, as soon as he was suspended upon the cross, drew all men to himself through
a loving desire."[3] And who is there, Cornelius goes on
to say, that will not love Jesus, who dies for love of us?
"For who will not reciprocate the love of Christ, who
dies out of love for us?"[4] Behold, O redeemed souls
(as Holy Church exhorts us), behold your Redeemer
upon that cross, where his whole form breathes love, and
invites you to love him : his head bent downwards to

[1] "Et ego, si exaltatus fuero a terra, omnia traham ad meipsum.
(Hoc autem dicebat, significans qua morte esset moriturus)."—*John,*
xii. 32.

[2] "Omnes mundi gentes ad amorem sui traxit sanguinis sui merito,
suo exemplo et amore."

[3] "Dominus, mox ut in cruce pependit, omnes ad se per amoris
desiderium traxit."—*S. de Inv. Cruc.*

[4] "Quis enim Christum ex amore pro nobis morientem non reda-
met ?"

give us the kiss of peace, his arms stretched out to embrace us, his heart open to love us : "His whole figure" (as St. Augustine says) "breathes love, and challenges us to love him in return : his head bent downwards to kiss us, his hands stretched out to embrace us, his bosom open to love us." [1]

Ah, my beloved Jesus, how could my soul have been so dear in Thy sight, beholding, as Thou didst, the wrongs that Thou wouldst have to receive at my hands ! Thou, in order to captivate my affections, wert willing to give me the extremest proofs of love. Come, ye scourges, ye thorns, nails, and cross, which tortured the sacred flesh of my Lord, come ye, and wound my heart ; be ever reminding me that all the good that I have received, and all that I hope for, comes to me through the merits of his Passion. O Thou master of love, others teach by word of mouth, but Thou upon this bed of death dost teach by suffering ; others teach from interested motives, Thou from affection, asking no recompense excepting my salvation. Save me, O my love, and let my salvation be the bestowal of the grace ever to love and please Thee ; the love of Thee is my salvation.

VI.

While Jesus was dying upon the cross, the men who were around him never ceased to torment him with reproaches and insults. Some said to him : <i>He saved others, Himself He cannot save.</i>[2] Others : <i>If He be the King of Israel, let Him now come down from the cross.</i>[3] And Jesus, while these are outraging him, what is he

[1] "Omnis figura ejus amorem spirat, et ad redamandum provocat, caput inclinatum, manus expansæ, pectus apertum."—<i>Off. Dol. B. V. resp.</i> I.

[2] "Alios salvos fecit, seipsum non potest salvum facere."—<i>Matt.</i> xxvii. 42.

[3] "Si Rex Israel est, descendat nunc de cruce."—<i>Ibid.</i>

doing upon the cross? He is, perhaps, praying the Eternal Father to punish them? No; he is praying him to pardon them : *Father, forgive them, for they know not what they do.*[1] Yes, says St. Thomas ; to show forth the immense love which he had for men, the Redeemer asked pardon of God for his very crucifiers : "To show forth the abundance of his charity, he asked pardon for his persecutors."[2] He asked it, and obtained it; for, when they had seen him dead, they repented of their sin : *They returned smiting their breasts.*[3]

Ah, my dear Saviour, behold me at Thy feet : I have been one of the most ungrateful of Thy persecutors ; do Thou for me likewise pray Thy Father to pardon me. True, indeed, it is that the Jews and the executioners knew not what they were doing when they crucified Thee ; but I well knew that, in sinning, I was offending a God who had been crucified, and had died for me. But Thy blood and Thy death have merited, even for me, the divine mercy. I cannot feel doubtful of being pardoned, after I see Thee die to obtain pardon for me. Ah, my sweet Redeemer, turn towards me one of those looks of love wherewith Thou didst look upon me, when dying for me upon the cross! Look upon me and pardon me all the ungratefulness which I have shown to Thy love. I repent, O my Jesus, of having despised Thee. I love Thee with all my heart ; and, at the sight of Thy example, because I love Thee, I love all those likewise who have offended me. I wish them all possible good, and I purpose to serve them, and to assist them to the utmost of my power, for love of Thee, O my Lord, who hast been willing to die for me, who have so much offended Thee.

[1] "Pater! dimitte illis ; non enim sciunt quid faciunt."—*Luke,* xxiii. 34.

[2] "Ad ostendendam abundantiam charitatis suæ, veniam persecutoribus postulavit."—P. 3, q. 47, a. 4.

[3] "Percutientes pectora sua, revertebantur."—*Luke,* xxiii. 48.

VII.

Remember me,[1] said the good thief to Thee, O my Jesus ; and he had the consolation of hearing these words from Thee : *This day thou shalt be with me in paradise.*[2]

Be mindful of me, say I likewise unto Thee ; be mindful, O Lord, that I am one of those sheep for whom Thou didst give Thy life. Give me, too, the consolation of making me feel that Thou dost forgive me, vouchsafing me a great sorrow for my sins. Do Thou, O great priest, who dost sacrifice Thyself for love of Thy creatures, have compassion upon me. From this day forth do I sacrifice to Thee my will, my senses, my satisfactions, and all my desires. I believe that Thou, my God, didst die, crucified, for me. Let Thy divine blood, I pray Thee, flow also upon me ; let it wash me from my sins. Let it inflame me with holy love, and make me all Thine own. I love Thee, O my Jesus, and I wish that I could die, crucified, for Thee, who didst die, crucified, for me.

O Eternal Father, I have offended Thee ; but behold Thy Son, who, hanging upon this tree, makes satisfaction to Thee for me with the sacrifice which he offers Thee of his divine life. I offer Thee his merits, which are all mine, for he has made them over to me ; and, for love of this Thy Son, I pray Thee to have mercy upon me. The greatest mercy that I ask of Thee is, that Thou wouldst give me Thy grace, which, miserable wretch that I am, I have so often wilfully despised. I repent of having outraged Thee, and I love Thee, I love Thee, my God, my all ; and, to please Thee, I am ready to endure every shame, every pain, every sorrow, and every death.

[1] " Memento mei."—*Luke*, xxiii. 42.
[2] " Hodie mecum eris in paradiso."—*Ibid.* 43.

CHAPTER XIII.

THE LAST WORDS OF JESUS UPON HIS CROSS, AND HIS EATH.

I.

St. Laurence Justinian says that the death of Jesus was the most bitter and painful of all the deaths that men have ever died; since the Redeemer died upon the cross without any, even the slightest, alleviation : "He was crucified wholly without any alleviation of suffering." [1] In the case of other sufferers, the pain is always mitigated, at all events, by some consoling thought; but the pain and sorrow of Jesus in his sufferings were pure pain, pure sorrow, without mitigation : "The extent of the suffering of Christ appears to us from the purity of its pain and sorrow," says the Angelic Doctor.[2] And hence St. Bernard, when contemplating Jesus dying upon the cross, utters this lamentation : O my Jesus, when I behold Thee upon this tree, I find nothing in Thee from head to foot but pain and sorrow. "From the sole of Thy foot to the crown of Thy head I find nothing but pain and grief." [3]

O my sweet Redeemer, O love of my soul, wherefore wouldst Thou shed all Thy blood? wherefore sacrifice Thy divine Life for an ungrateful worm like me? O my Jesus, when shall I so unite myself to Thee as nevermore to be able to separate myself from Thee, or to cease to love Thee? Ah, Lord, as long as I live in this world I stand in danger of denying to Thee my love,

[1] "Omni carens doloris temperamento."—*De Tr. Chr. Ag. c.* 17.
[2] "Magnitudo doloris Christi potest considerari ex doloris et tristitiæ puritate."—P. 3, q. 46, a. 6.
[3] "A planta pedis usque ad verticem capitis, non invenio nisi dolorem et mœrorem."

and of losing Thy friendship, as I have done in times past. O my dearest Saviour, if, by continuing in life, I shall have to suffer this great evil, by Thy Passion, I pray Thee, let me die at this moment, while, as I hope, I am in Thy grace. I love Thee, and I wish to love Thee always.

II.

Jesus, by the mouth of the Prophet, made lamentation that, when dying upon the cross, he went in search of some one to console him, but found none : *And I looked for one that would comfort Me, and I found none.*[1] The Jews and the Romans, even while he was dying, uttered against him their execrations and blasphemies. The Most Holy Mary—yes, she stood beneath the cross, in order to afford him some relief, had it been in her power to do so ; but this afflicted and loving Mother, by the sorrow which she suffered through sympathy with his pains, only added to the affliction of this her Son, who loved her so dearly. St. Bernard says that the pains of Mary all went towards increasing the torments of the Heart of Jesus : "The Mother being filled with it, the ocean of her sorrow poured itself back upon the Son."[2] So that the Redeemer, in beholding Mary sorrowing thus, felt his soul pierced more by the sorrows of Mary than by his own ; as was revealed to St. Bridget by the Blessed Virgin herself : "He, on beholding me, grieved more for me than for himself."[3] Whence St. Bernard says, "O good Jesus, great as are Thy bodily sufferings, much more dost Thou suffer in Thy Heart through compassion for Thy Mother."[4] What

[1] "Et sustinui . . . qui consolaretur, et non inveni."—*Ps.* lxviii. 21.

[2] " Repleta Matre, ad Filium redundabat inundatio amaritudinis."

[3] "Ipse, videns me, plus dolebat de me, quam de se."

[4] "O bone Jesu! tu magna pateris in corpore, sed multo magis in corde ex compassione Matris."—"Mulier, ecce filius tuus."—*John,* xix. 26.

pangs, too, must not those loving Hearts of Jesus and Mary have felt when the moment arrived in which the Son, before breathing his last, had to take his leave of the Mother! Behold what the last words were with which Jesus took his leave in this world of Mary: "Mother, behold Thy Son;" assigning to her John, whom, in his own place, he left her for a son.

O Queen of Sorrows, things given as memorials by a beloved son at the hour of his death, how very dear they are, and never do they slip away from the memory of a mother! Oh, bear it in mind that thy Son, who loved thee so dearly, has, in the person of John, left me, a sinner, to thee for a son. For the love which thou didst bear to Jesus, have compassion on me. I ask thee not the good things of earth; I behold thy Son dying in so great pains for me; I behold thee, my innocent Mother, enduring also for me so great sufferings; and I see that I, a miserable being, who deserve hell on account of my sins, have not suffered anything for love of thee—I wish to suffer something for thee before I die. This is the grace that I ask of thee; and, with St. Bonaventure, I say to thee, that if I have offended thee, justice requires that I should have suffering as a chastisement; and if I have been serving thee, it is but reason that I should have suffering as a reward: "O Lady, if I have offended thee, wound my heart for justice' sake; if I have served thee. I ask thee for wounds as my recompense."[1] Obtain for me, O Mary, a great devotion and a continual remembrance of the Passion of thy Son; and, by that pang which Thou didst suffer on beholding him breathe his last upon the cross, obtain for me a good death. Come to my assistance, O my Queen, in that last moment; make me die, loving and pronouncing the sacred names of Jesus and of Mary.

[1] "O Domina! si te offendi, pro justitia cor meum vulnera; si tibi servivi, pro mercede peto vulnera."—*Stim. div. am.* p. 1, c. 3.

III.

Jesus, seeing that he found no one to console him upon this earth, raised his eyes and his Heart to his Father, craving relief from him. But the Eternal Father, beholding the Son clad in the garment of a sinner, replied, No, my Son, I cannot give Thee consolation, now that Thou art making satisfaction to my justice for all the sins of men ; it is fitting that I too should abandon Thee to Thy pains, and let Thee die without solace. And then it was that our Saviour, crying out with a loud voice, said, My God, my God, and why hast Thou too abandoned Me? *Jesus cried out with a loud voice, saying, My God, My God, why hast Thou forsaken Me?* [1] In his explanation of this passage, the Blessed Denis, the Carthusian, says that Jesus uttered these words with a loud cry, to make all men understand the greatness of the pain and sorrow in which he died. And it was the will of the loving Redeemer, adds St. Cyprian, to die bereft of every consolation, to give proof to us of his love, and to draw to himself all our love : " He was left in dereliction, that he might show forth his love towards us, and might attract our love towards himself." [2]

Ah, my beloved Jesus, Thou art in the wrong to make Thy lamentation, saying, My God, why hast Thou abandoned me? " Why," dost Thou say? And why, I will say to Thee, hast Thou been willing to undertake to pay our penalty? Didst Thou not know that for our sins we had already deserved to be abandoned by God ? With good reason, then, is it that Thy Father hath abandoned Thee, and leaves Thee to die in an ocean of sufferings and griefs. Ah, my Redeemer, Thy derelic-

[1] "Clamavit Jesus voce magna, dicens, . . . Deus meus ! Deus meus ! ut quid dereliquisti me ?"—*Matt.* xxvii. 46.

[2] " Derelictus est, ut amorem suum erga nos ostenderet, et amorem nostrum ad se raperet."

tion gives me both affliction and consolation: it is afflicting to me to see Thee die in such great pain ; but it is consoling, in that it encourages me to hope that, by Thy merits, I shall not remain abandoned by the divine mercy, according as I should deserve, for having myself so often abandoned Thee in order to follow my own humors. Make me understand that, if to Thee it was so hard to be deprived, even for a brief interval, of the sensible presence of God, what my pain would be if I were to be deprived of God forever. Oh, by this dereliction of Thine, suffered with so much pain, forsake me not, O my Jesus, especially at the hour of my death ! Then, when all shall have abandoned me, do not Thou abandon me, my Saviour. Ah, my Lord, who wert so left in desolation, be Thou my comfort in my desolations ! Already do I understand that, if I shall love Thee without consolation, I shall content Thy heart the more. But Thou knowest my weakness ; help me by Thy grace, and then grant me perseverance, patience, and resignation.

IV.

Jesus, drawing nigh unto death, said, " *Sitio*," I thirst. Tell me, Lord, says Leo of Ostia, for what dost Thou thirst ? Thou makest no mention of those immense pains which Thou dost suffer upon the cross ; but Thou complainest only of thirst : " Lord, what dost Thou thirst for ? Thou art silent about the cross, and criest out about the thirst."[1] " My thirst is for your salvation,"[2] is the reply which St. Augustine makes for him. O soul, says Jesus, this thirst of mine is nothing but the desire which I have for thy salvation. He, the loving Redeemer, with extremest ardor, desires our

---

[1] " Domine, quid sitis ? De cruce siles et de siti clamas !"—*S. de Pass. D.*

[2] " Sitis mea, salus vestra."

souls and therefore he panted to give himself wholly to
us by his death. This was his thirst, wrote St. Laurence
Justinian : "He thirsted for us, and desired to give
himself to us."[1] St. Basil of Seleucia says, moreover,
that Jesus Christ, in saying that he thirsted, would give
us to understand that he, for the love which he bore us,
was dying with the desire of suffering for us even more
than what he had suffered : "O that desire, greater
than the Passion !"[2]

O most lovely God ! because Thou lovest us, Thou
dost desire that we should desire Thee : "God thirsts to
be thirsted for,"[3] as St. Gregory teaches us. Ah, my
Lord, dost Thou thirst for me, a most vile worm as I am ?
and shall I not thirst for Thee, my infinite God ? Oh,
by the merits of this thirst endured upon the cross, give
me a great thirst to love Thee, and to please Thee in all
things. Thou hast promised to grant us whatever we
seek from Thee : *Ask, and ye shall receive.*[4] I ask of Thee
but this one gift—the gift of loving Thee. I am, indeed,
unworthy of it ; but in this has to be the glory of Thy
blood,—the turning of a heart into a great lover of Thee,
which has, at one time, so greatly despised Thee ; to
make a perfect flame of charity of a sinner who is altogether full of mire and of sins. Much more than this
hast Thou done in dying for me. Would that I could
love Thee, O Lord infinitely good, as much as Thou dost
deserve ! I delight in the love which is borne Thee by
the souls that are enamoured of Thee, and still more in
the love Thou bearest towards Thyself. With this I
unite my own wretched love. I love Thee, O Eternal
God ; I love Thee, O infinite loveliness. Make me ever
to increase in Thy love ; reiterating to Thee frequent

---

[1] "Sitiebat nos, et dare se nobis desiderabat."—*De Tr. Chr. Ag.* c. 19.
[2] "O desiderium passione majus !"
[3] "Sitit sitiri Deus."—*Tetr. Sent.* 37.
[4] "Petite et accipietis."—*John,* xvi. 24.

acts of love, and studying to please Thee in everything,
without intermission and without reserve. Make me,
wretched and insignificant as I may be, make me at
least to be all Thine own.

V.

Our Jesus, now on the point of expiring, in dying ac-
cents said, *It is finished.*[1] He, while uttering the afore-
said word, ran over in his mind the whole course of his
life. He beheld all the fatigues he had gone through,—
the poverty, the pains, the ignominies he had suffered ;
and he offered them all anew to his Eternal Father for
the salvation of the world. Then, turning himself back
again to us, it seems as if he repeated, "It is finished;"
as though he had said, O men, all is consummated ; all
is fulfilled ; your redemption is accomplished ; the divine
justice is satisfied ; Paradise is opened ; *and behold your
time, the time of lovers.*[2] It is time at last, O men, that
you should surrender yourselves to my love. Love me,
then ; oh, love me ; for there is nothing more that I can
do in order to be loved by you. You see what I have
done in order to gain your love. For you I have led a
life which has been but one series of tribulations. At
its close, before I died, I have been content to let myself
be drained of blood, have my face spit upon, my flesh
torn to pieces, my head crowned with thorns ; until I
suffered the pains of agony upon this cross, as you see
me now. What is there that remains? It only remains
for me to die for you. Yes, it is my will to die. Come,
O death ; I give thee leave to take away my life for the
salvation of my flock. And do you, my flock, love me,
love me ; for I can do no more in order to make myself
beloved by you.

"It is consummated" (says the Blessed Tauler): "all

[1] "Consummatum est."—*John,* xix. 30.
[2] "Et ecce tempus tuum, tempus amantium."—*Ezech.* xvi. 8.

that justice exacted, all that charity demanded, all that could have been done to give proof of love."[1]

Oh, would that I too, my beloved Jesus, could say in dying, Lord, I have fulfilled all ; I have accomplished all that Thou hast given me to do ; I have borne my cross with patience ; I have pleased Thee in all things. Ah, my God, were I now to die, I should not die content ; for nothing of this could I say with truth. But am I always to live thus ungrateful to Thy love ? Oh, grant me the grace to please Thee during the remainder of my life, that, when death shall come, I may by able to say to Thee, that from this time at least I have fulfilled Thy will. If in time past I have offended Thee, Thy death is my hope. For the future it is my wish not to betray Thee more ; but from Thee it is that I hope for my perseverance. By Thy merits, O my Jesus, I ask and hope it from Thee.

VI.

Behold Jesus, at length, actually dying. Behold him, my soul, how he is in his agony amid the last respirations of his life. Behold those dying eyes, that face so pale, that feebly palpitating heart, that body already wrapped in the arms of death, and that beautiful soul now on the point of leaving that wounded body. The sky shrouds itself in darkness ; the earth quakes ; the graves open. Alas, what portentous signs are these ! They are signs that the Maker of the world is now dying.

Behold, in the last place, how our Redeemer, after having commended his blessed soul to his Eternal Father, first breathing forth from his afflicted Heart a deep sigh, and then bowing down his head in token of his obedience, and offering up his death for the salvation of

---

[1] "Consummatum est quidquid justitia exigebat, quidquid charitas poscebat, quidquid esse poterat ad demonstrandum amorem."—*De Vit. et Pass. Salv.* c. 49.

men, at length, through the violence of the pain, expires, and delivers up his spirit into the hands of his beloved Father: *And crying out with a loud voice, He said, Father, into Thy hands I commend My Spirit ; and saying this He gave up the ghost.*[1]

Draw near, O my soul, to the foot of that holy altar whereon the Lamb of God is now lying dead, sacrificed for thy salvation. Draw near, and reflect that he is dead for the love which he has borne thee. Ask your dead Lord for what you wish, and hope for all. O Saviour of the world, O my Jesus, behold to what Thy love for men has at length reduced Thee! I thank Thee that Thou hast been willing, Thou, our God, to lose Thy life that we might not lose our souls. I thank Thee for all men, but especially for myself. And who is there more than I that has reaped the fruits of Thy death? I, through Thy merits, without even so much as knowing it, was, in the outset, by baptism, made a child of the Church ; through Thy love I have been forgiven so often since, and have received so many special graces ; through Thee I have the hope of dying in the grace of God, and of coming to love Thee in Paradise.

O my beloved Redeemer, how greatly am I obliged to Thee! Into Thy pierced hands I commend my poor soul. Make me well understand what love there must have been in a God who died for me : would that I could, O Lord, die for Thee! But what would the death of a wicked slave weigh against the death of his Lord and God? Would that I could, at least, love Thee as much as I am able ; but without Thy help, O my Jesus, I can do nothing. Oh, help me! and, through the merits of Thy death, make me die to all earthly affections, that so I may love Thee only, who dost deserve all my love. I

[1] "Et clamans voce magna, Jesus ait : Pater! in manus tuas commendo spiritum meum. Et hæc dicens, exspiravit."—*Luke,* xxiii. 46.

love Thee, O infinite goodness, I love Thee, my chief
good ; and, with St. Francis, I pray Thee : "May I die
for the love of Thy love, who didst vouchsafe to die for
the love of my love." May I die to everything, out
of gratitude, at least, for Thy great love, who hast
vouchsafed to die, through Thy love for me, and in
order to be beloved by me. O Mary, my Mother, intercede for me. Amen.

CHAPTER XIV.

THE HOPE WHICH WE HAVE IN THE DEATH OF JESUS CHRIST.

I.

Jesus is the only hope of our salvation : *There is no
salvation in any other but Him.*[1] I am the only door, says
he ; and he that shall enter in through me shall assuredly find life eternal : *I am the door ; if any one enter
by Me, he shall be saved.*[2] And what sinner would ever
have been able to hope for pardon if Jesus had not, by
his blood and by his death, made satisfaction to the divine justice for us ? *He shall bear their iniquities.*[3] It is by
this that the Apostle encourages us, saying, *If the blood
of goats and of oxen sanctify such as are defiled to the cleans-
ing of the flesh, how much more shall the Blood of Christ,
who through the Holy Ghost, offered Himself up to God,
cleanse our conscience from dead works to serve the living
God!*[4] If the blood of goats and of bulls offered up in

[1] "Non est in alio aliquo salus."—*Acts,* iv. 12.
[2] "Ego sum ostium : per me si quis introierit, salvabitur."—*John,*
x. 9.
[3] "Iniquitates eorum ipse portabit."—*Isa.* liii. 11.
[4] "Si enim sanguis hircorum et taurorum, et cinis vitulæ aspersus,
inquinatos sanctificat ad emundationem carnis ; quanto magis sanguis Christi, qui per Spiritum Sanctum semetipsum obtulit immaculatum Deo, emundabit conscientiam nostram ab operibus mortuis, ad
serviendum Deo viventi ?"—*Heb.* ix. 13.

9

sacrifice removed from the Jews the outward defilements of the body, that so they could be admitted to the worship of the sanctuary, how much more shall the blood of Jesus Christ, who for love offered himself up as a satisfaction for us, remove the sins from our souls to enable us to serve our God Most High !

Our loving Redeemer, having come into the world for no other end but that of saving sinners, and beholding the sentence of condemnation already recorded against us for our sins, what was it that he did ? He by his own death paid the penalty that was due to ourselves ; and with his own blood cancelling the sentence of condemnation, in order that the divine justice might no more seek from us the satisfaction due, he nailed it to the same cross whereon he died : *Blotting out the handwriting of the decree that was against us, which was contrary to us. And the same he took out of the way, fastening it to the cross.*[1] *Christ entered once into the holy place, having found for us eternal redemption.*[2]

Ah, my Jesus, hadst Thou not found this mode of obtaining pardon for us, who would ever have been able to find it ? It was with reason that David cried out, *Declare His ways.*[3] Make known, O ye blessed, the loving contrivances which our God has employed in order to save us. Since, then, O my sweet Saviour, Thou hast had such a love for me, cease not from exercising mercy towards me. Thou, by Thy death, hast rescued me from the hands of Lucifer: into Thy hands do I consign my soul; it is for Thee to save it: *Into Thy hands I commend my spirit; Thou hast redeemed me, O God of truth.*[4]

[1] " Delens quod adversus nos erat chirographum decreti, quod erat contrarium nobis, et ipsum tulit de medio, affigens illud cruci."— *Col.* ii. 14.

[2] " Introivit semel in Sancta, æterna redemptione inventa."—*Heb.* ix. 12.

[3] "Annuntiate inter gentes studia ejus."—*Ps.* ix. 12.

[4] "In manus tuas commendo spiritum meum; redemisti me, Domine, Deus veritatis."—*Ps.* xxx. 6.

II.

Little children, these things I write to you, that you may not sin : but if any man sin, we have an Advocate with the Father, Jesus Christ the Just, and He is the propitiation for our sins.[1] Jesus Christ did not, with his death, bring to an end his intercession for us with the Eternal Father: even at the present moment he is acting as our advocate; and it seems as if he knew not what else to do in heaven, as St. Paul writes, but be moving the Father to exercise mercy towards us: *ever living to make intercession for us.*[2] And the Apostle adds that this is the end for which our Saviour is ascended into heaven: *that He may now appear in the presence of God for us.*[3] As rebels are driven away from the presence of their king, so should we sinners have nevermore been deemed worthy of admission into the presence of our God, even so much as to ask his pardon; but Jesus, as our Redeemer, makes appearance for us in the divine presence, and, through his merits, obtains for us the grace that we had lost.

You are come to Jesus the Mediator, and to the sprinkling of blood, which speaketh better than Abel.[4] Oh, with how much greater effect does the blood of the Redeemer implore for us the divine mercy than did the blood of Abel plead for chastisement on Cain! My justice (said God to St. Mary Magdalen of Pazzi) is transformed into mercy by the vengeance taken on the innocent flesh of Jesus Christ. The blood of this my Son pleads not with me for vengeance, like the blood of Abel, but pleads

---

[1] "Filioli mei, hæc scribo vobis, ut non peccetis. Sed et si quis peccaverit, Advocatum habemus apud Patrem, Jesum Christum justum; et ipse est propitiatio pro peccatis nostris."—1 *John,* ii. 1.

[2] "Semper vivens ad interpellandum pro nobis."—*Heb.* vii. 25.

[3] "Ut appareat nunc vultui Dei pro nobis."—*Heb.* ix. 24.

[4] "Accessistis ad . . . Mediatorem Jesum, et sanguinis aspersionem melius loquentem, quam Abel."—*Heb.* xii. 22, 24.

only for mercy and pity; and at the sound of this voice my justice cannot but rest appeased. This blood so binds its hands, that, so to speak, it cannot stir to take that vengeance upon sins which it used to take before.

Be not unmindful of the kindness of thy Surety.[1] Ah, my Jesus, I was already incapable, after my sins, of making satisfaction to the divine justice, when Thou, by Thy death, wert willing to make satisfaction for me. Oh, what ingratitude would mine be now, were I to be unmindful of this Thy so great mercy ! No, my Redeemer, never will I be unmindful of it; I desire to be ever thanking Thee for it, and to show forth my thankfulness by loving. Thee, and doing all that I can to please Thee. Do Thou aid me by that grace which Thou hast, by so many sufferings, merited for me. I love Thee, my Jesus, my love, my hope !

III.

Come, O my dove, into the clefts of the rock.[2] Oh, what a safe place of refuge shall we ever find in the sacred clefts of the rock, in the wounds, that is to say, of Jesus Christ ! "The clefts of the rock," says St. Peter Damian, "are the Redeemer's wounds; in these has our soul placed its hope."[3] There shall we be set free from that feeling of distrust which the sight of the sins that we have committed may produce; there shall we find weapons wherewith to defend ourselves when we shall be tempted to sin anew: *Have confidence, my children; I have overcome the world.*[4] If you have not sufficient strength (our Saviour exhorts us) to resist the assaults of the world, that offers you its pleasures, place your confidence in me, for I have

[1] "Gratiam fidejussoris ne obliviscaris; dedit enim pro te animam suam."—*Ecclus.* xxix. 19.

[2] "Columba mea in foraminibus petræ."—*Cant.* ii. 14.

[3] "Foramina petræ sunt vulnera Redemptoris. In his fidelis anima spem suam constituit."—*De S. Matt.* s. 3.

[4] "Confidite, ego vici mundum."—*John,* xvi. 33.

overcome it; and thus shall you likewise overcome.
Pray the Eternal Father, said he, for the sake of my
merits, to give you strength, and I promise you that he
will grant you whatever you ask of him in my name:
*Amen, amen, I say unto you, if you ask anything of the Father
in My name, He will give it you.*[1] And elsewhere he confirms to us the promise, saying that whatsoever grace
we shall, for his love, ask of God, he himself, who is
one with the Father, will give it us: *Whatsoever you shall
ask of the Father in My name, that I will do: that the
Father may be glorified in the Son.*[2]

Ah, Father Eternal, trusting to the merits and to
these promises of Jesus Christ, I ask not of Thee the
good things of earth, but Thy grace alone. True it is
that, after the wrongs I have done Thee, I should not
deserve either pardon or grace; yet, if I deserve them
not, Thy Son hath merited them for me, by offering up
his blood and his life for me. For the love, then, of this
Thy Son, grant me Thy pardon. Give me a great sorrow for my sins, and a great love towards Thee. Enlighten me to know how lovely is Thy goodness, and how
great is the love which Thou hast borne me from all
eternity. Make known to me Thy will, and give me
strength to fulfil it perfectly. O Lord, I love Thee, and
desire to do all that Thou dost desire of me.

IV.

Oh, how great is the hope of salvation which the death
of Jesus Christ imparts to us: *Who is He that shall condemn? Christ Jesus who died, who also maketh intercession
for us.*[3] Who is it, asks the Apostle, that has to con-

[1] "Amen, amen, dico vobis: si quid petieritis Patrem in nomine
meo, dabit vobis."—*John*, xvi. 23.
[2] "Quodcumque petieritis Patrem in nomine meo, hoc faciam, ut
glorificetur Pater in Filio."—*Ibid.* xiv. 13.
[3] "Quis est qui condemnat? Christus Jesus, qui mortuus est . . . ,
qui etiam interpellat pro nobis."—*Rom.* viii. 34.

demn us? It is that same Redeemer who, in order not to condemn us to eternal death, condemned himself to a cruel death upon a cross. From this St. Thomas of Villanova encourages us, saying, What dost thou fear, sinner, if thou art willing to leave off thy sin? How should that Lord condemn thee, who died in order not to condemn thee? How should he drive thee away when thou returnest to his feet, he who came from heaven to seek thee when thou wert fleeing from him? "What art thou afraid of, sinner? How shall he condemn thee penitent, who dies that thou mayst not be condemned? How shall he cast thee off returning, who came from heaven seeking thee?"[1] But greater still is the encouragement given us by this same Saviour of ours, when, speaking by Isaias, he says, *Behold, I have graven thee upon My hands; thy walls are always before My eyes.*[2] Be not distrustful, my sheep; see how much thou didst cost me. I keep thee engraven upon my hands, in these wounds which I have suffered for thee; these are ever reminding me to help thee, and to defend thee from thine enemies: love me and have confidence.

Yes, my Jesus, I love Thee, and feel confidence in Thee. To rescue me, yea, this has cost Thee dear; to save me will cost Thee nothing. It is Thy will that all should be saved, and that none should perish. If my sins cause me to dread, Thy goodness reassures me, more desirous as Thou art to do me good than I am to receive it. Ah, my beloved Redeemer, I will say to Thee with Job: *Even though Thou shouldst kill me, yet I will hope in Thee, and Thou wilt be my Saviour.*[3] Wert Thou

[1] "Quid times, peccator? quomodo te damnabit pœnitentem, qui moritur, ne damneris? quomodo te abjiciet redeuntem, qui de cœlo venit quærere te?"—*Tr. de Adv. D.*

[2] "Ecce in manibus meis descripsi te; muri tui coram oculis meis semper."—*Isa.* xlix. 16.

[3] "Etiam si occiderit me, in ipso sperabo. . . . Et ipse erit Salvator meus."—*Job,* xlii. 15.

even to drive me away from Thy presence, O my love, yet would not I leave off from hoping in Thee, who art my Saviour. Too much do these wounds of Thine and this blood encourage me to hope for every good from Thy mercy. I love Thee, O dear Jesus; I love Thee, and I hope.

V.

The glorious St. Bernard one day, in sickness, saw himself before the judgment-seat of God, where the devil was accusing him of his sins, and telling him that he did not deserve paradise: "It is true that I deserve not paradise," the saint replied; "but Jesus has a two-fold title to this kingdom,—in the first place, as being by nature Son of God; in the next place, as having purchased it by his death. He contents himself with the first of these, and the second he makes over to me; and therefore it is that I ask and hope for paradise." We, too, can say the same ; for St. Paul tells us that the will of Jesus Christ to die, consumed by sufferings, had for its end the obtaining of paradise for all sinners that are penitent, and resolved to amend: *And, being perfected, He was made the cause of eternal salvation to all that obey Him.*[1] And hence the Apostle subjoins: *Let us run to the fight proposed unto us, looking on Jesus, the Author and Finisher of faith, who, having joy proposed unto Him, underwent the cross, despising the shame.*[2] Let us go forth with courage to fight against our enemies, fixing our eyes on Jesus Christ, who, together with the merits of his Passion, offers us the victory and the crown.

He has told us that he is gone to heaven to prepare a

[1] "Et consummatus, factus est omnibus obtemperantibus sibi causa salutis æternæ."—*Heb.* v. 9.

[2] "Curramus ad propositum nobis certamen, aspicientes in Auctorem fidei et Consummatorem Jesum, qui, proposito sibi gaudio, sustinuit crucem, confusione contempta."—*Heb.* xii. 1.

place for us: *Let not your heart be troubled . . . ; for I go to prepare a place for you.*[1]   He has told, and is continually telling, his Father that, since he has consigned us to him, he wishes us to be with him in paradise : *Father, those whom Thou hast given Me, I will that where I am they also may be with Me.*[2]   "And what greater mercy could we have hoped for from the Lord, says St. Anselm, than for the Eternal Father to have said to a sinner, already for crimes condemned to hell, and with no means of delivering himself from its punishments, Take thou my Son, and offer him in thy stead?" And for the same Son to have said, Take me, and deliver thyself from hell? "What greater mercy can we imagine than that to one who, being a sinner, cannot redeem himself, God the Father should say, Accept of my only-begotten Son, and deliver him over to be punished in thy stead; and that the Son should say, Take me and redeem thyself?"[3]

Ah, my loving Father, I thank Thee for having given me this Thy Son for my Saviour; I offer to Thee his death; and, for the sake of his merits, I pray Thee for mercy.   And ever do I return thanks to Thee, O my Redeemer, for having given Thy blood and Thy life to deliver me from eternal death.   "We pray Thee, therefore, help Thy servants, whom Thou hast redeemed with Thy precious blood."[4]   Help, then, us, Thy rebellious servants, since Thou hast redeemed us at so great a cost. O Jesus, my one and only hope ! Thou dost love me.

---

[1] "Non turbetur cor vestrum . . . , quia vado parare vobis locum."—*John,* xiv. 1-2.

[2] "Pater, quos dedisti mihi, volo ut, ubi sum ego, et illi sint mecum."—*John,* xvii. 24.

[3] "Quid misericordius intelligi valet, quam cum peccatori, unde se redimat non habenti, Deus Pater dicit : Accipe Unigenitum meum. et da pro te ;—et ipse Filius : Tolle me, et redime te ?"—*Cur D. H.* l. 2, c. 20.

[4] "Te ergo quæsumus, tuis famulis subveni, quos pretioso sanguine redemisti."

Thou hast power to do all things : make me a saint. If I am weak, do Thou give me strength; if I am sick, in consequence of the sins I have committed, do Thou apply to my soul one drop of Thy blood, and heal me. Give me the love of Thee, and final perseverance, making me die in Thy grace. Give me paradise; through Thy merits do I ask it of Thee, and hope to obtain it. I love Thee, O my most lovely God, with all my soul; and I hope to love Thee always. Oh, help a miserable sinner, who is wishing to love Thee.

VI.

Having, therefore, a great High-Priest, who hath penetrated the heavens, Jesus the Son of God, let us hold fast our confession. For we have not a high-priest who cannot have compassion on our infirmities, but one tempted in all things like as we are, yet without sin.[1] Since, says the Apostle, we have this Saviour, who has opened to us paradise, which was at one time closed to us by sin, let us always have confidence in his merits; because, from having of his goodness willed to suffer in himself also our miseries, he well knows how to compassionate us: *Let us, therefore, go with confidence to the throne of grace, that we may obtain mercy, and find grace in seasonable aid.*[2] Let us, then, go with confidence to the throne of the divine mercy, to which we have access by means of Jesus Christ, that so we may there find all the graces that we need. And how can we doubt, subjoins St. Paul, but that God, having given us his Son, has given us together with that

---

[1] " Habentes ergo Pontificem magnum, qui penetravit cœlos, Jesum Filium Dei, teneamus confessionem. Non enim habemus Pontificem qui non possit compati infirmitatibus nostris ; tentatum autem per omnia pro similitudine, absque peccato."—*Heb.* iv. 14.

[2] " Adeamus ergo cum fiducia ad thronum gratiæ, ut misericordiam consequamur, et gratiam inveniamus in auxilio opportuno."—*Ibid.* 14-16.

Son all his goods: *He delivered Him up for us all ; how hath He not, with Him, given us all things ?*[1] Cardinal Hugo comments on this: "He will give the lesser, that is to say eternal life, who hath given the greater, that is to say his own Son."[2] That Lord will not deny us the lesser, which is eternal life, who has gone so far as to give us the greater, which is his own Son himself.

O my chief and only good ! what shall I render Thee, miserable as I am, in return for so great a gift as that which Thou hast given me of Thy Son? To Thee will I, with David, say, *The Lord shall repay for me.*[3] Lord, I have not where with to recompense Thee. That same Son of Thine can alone render Thee worthy thanks; let him thank Thee in my stead. O my most merciful Father! by the wounds of Jesus, I pray Thee to save me. I love Thee, O infinite goodness; and because I love Thee, I repent of having offended Thee. My God, my God, I wish to be all Thine own; accept of me for the sake of the love of Jesus Christ. Ah, my sweet Creator, is it possible that Thou, after having given me Thy Son, shouldst deny me the good things that belong to Thee,— Thy grace, Thy love, Thy paradise ?

VII.

St. Leo declares that Jesus Christ, by his death, has brought us more good than the devil brought us evil in the sin of Adam: "We have gained greater things through the grace of Christ than we had lost through the envy of the devil."[4] And this the Apostle distinctly

[1] " Pro nobis omnibus tradidit illum ; quomodo non etiam cum illo omnia nobis donavit ?"— *Rom*. viii. 32.

[2] "Dabit minus, id est, vitam æternam, qui dedit majus, id est, Filium suum."

[3] " Dominus retribuet pro me."—*Ps*. cxxxvii. 8.

[4] " Ampliora adepti sumus per Christi gratiam, quam per diaboli amiseramus invidiam."—*De Asc. D., s.* 1.

says, when writing to the Romans: *Not as the offence so also is the gift. Where the offence abounded, grace did super-abound.*' Cardinal Hugo explains it: '' The grace of Christ is of greater efficacy than is the offence.''' There is no comparison, says the Apostle, between the sins of man and the gift which God has made us in giving us Jesus Christ; great as was the sin of Adam, much greater by far was the grace which Jesus Christ, by his Passion, merited for us: *I have come that they may have life, and that they may have it more abundantly.*' I am come into the world, the Saviour protests, to the end that mankind, who were dead through sin, may receive through me not only the life of grace, but a life yet more abundant than that which they had lost by sin. Wherefore it is that Holy Church calls the sin happy which has merited to have such a Redeemer: "O happy fault, which de-served such and so great a Redeemer."'

Behold, God is my Saviour, I will deal confidently, and will not fear.' If, then, O my Jesus, Thou, who art an om-nipotent God, art also my Saviour, what fear shall I have of being damned? If, in time past, I have offended Thee, I repent of it with all my heart. From this time forth I wish to serve Thee, to obey Thee, and to love Thee. I firmly hope that Thou, my Redeemer, who hast done and suffered so much for my salvation, wilt not deny me any grace that I shall need in order to be saved: " I will act with confidence, firmly hoping that

---

' '' Non sicut delictum. ita et donum.—Ubi autem abundavit de-lictum, superabundavit gratia.''—*Rom.* v. 15-20.

' '' Christi gratia majoris est efficaciæ, quam delictum.''

' '' Ego veni ut vitam habeant, et abundantius habeant.''—*John*, x, 10.

' "O felix culpa, quæ talem ac tantum meruit habere Redemp-tcrem !''

' '' Ecce Deus Salvator meus ; fiducialiter agam, et non timebo.''—*Isa.* xii. 2.

nothing necessary to salvation will be denied me by Him who has done and suffered so much for my salvation."[1]

VIII.

You shall draw water from the fountains of the Saviour, and you shall say in that day, Praise ye the Lord, and call upon His name.[2] The wounds of Jesus Christ are now the blessed fountains from which we can draw forth all graces, if we pray unto him with faith: *And a fountain shall come forth from the house of the Lord, and shall water the torrent of thorns.*[3] The death of Jesus, says Isaias, is precisely this promised fountain, which has bathed our souls in the water of grace, and, from being thorns of sins, has, by his merits, transformed them into flowers and fruits of life eternal. He, the loving Redeemer, made himself, as St. Paul tells us, poor in this world, in order that we, through the merit of his poverty, might become rich: *For your sakes He became poor, that, through His poverty, you might be rich.*[4] By reason of sin we were ignorant, unjust, wicked, slaves of hell; but Jesus Christ, says the Apostle, by dying and making satisfaction for us, *is by God made for us Wisdom, Justice, Sanctification, and Redemption.*[5] That is to say, as St. Bernard explains it, "Wisdom, in his preaching, justice in his absolving, sanctification in his conduct, redemption in his Pas-

---

[1] "Fiducialiter agam, immobiliter, sperans nihil ad salutem neces-sarium ab eo negandum, qui tanta pro mea salute fecit et pertulit."

[2] "Haurietis aquas in gaudio de fontibus Salvatoris ; et dicetis in illa die : Confitemini Domino, et invocate nomen ejus."—*Isa.* xii. 3.

[3] "Et fons de domo Domini egredietur, et irrigabit torrentem spi-narum."—*Joel,* iii. 8.

[4] "Propter vos egenus factus est, cum esset dives, ut illius inopia vos divites essetis."—2 *Cor.* viii. 9.

[5] "Factus est nobis sapientia a Deo, et justitia, et sanctificatio, et redemptio."—1 *Cor.* i. 30.

sion."[1] He has made himself our wisdom by instructing us, our justice by pardoning us, our sanctity by his example, and our redemption by his Passion, delivering us from the hands of Lucifer. In short, as St. Paul says, the merits of Jesus Christ have enriched us with all good things, so that we no more want for anything in order to be able to receive all graces: *In all things you are made rich; so that nothing is wanting to you in any grace.*[2]

O my Jesus, my Jesus, what beautiful hopes does Thy Passion give me! O my beloved Saviour, how much do I owe Thee! Oh, would that I had never offended Thee! Oh, pardon me all the wrongs that I have done Thee; inflame me fully with Thy love, and save me in eternity. And how can I be afraid of not receiving forgiveness, salvation, and every grace, from an omnipotent God who has given me all his blood? Ah, my Jesus, my hope, Thou, in order not to lose me, hast been willing to lose Thy life; I will not lose Thee, O infinite good. If, in time past, I have lost Thee, I repent of it; I wish, for the future, never to lose Thee more. It is for Thee to aid me, that I may not lose Thee again. O Lord, I love Thee, and I will love Thee always. Mary, thou, next after Jesus, art my hope; tell thy Son that thou dost protect me, and I shall be safe. Amen. So may it be.

[1] "Sapientia in prædicatione, justitia in absolutione, sanctificatio in conversatione, redemptio in passione."—*In Cant.* s. 22.

[2] "In omnibus divites facti estis in illo . . . , ita ut nihil vobis desit in ulla gratia."—I *Cor.* i. 5.

CHAPTER XV.

THE LOVE OF THE ETERNAL FATHER IN HAVING GIVEN US HIS SON.

I.

God so loved the world, that He gave His only-begotten Son.[1] God, says Jesus Christ, has loved the world to that degree that he has given it his own and only Son. In this gift there are three things demanding our consideration: Who is the giver, what is the thing given, and the greatness of the love wherewith he gives it? We are already aware that the more exalted the donor is, the more to be prized is the gift. One who receives a flower from a monarch will set a higher value on that flower than on a large amount of money. How much ought we not, then, to prize this gift, coming to us, as it does, from the hands of one who is God! And what is it that he has given us? His own Son. The love of this God did not content itself with having given us so many good things on this earth, until it had reached the point of giving us its whole self in the person of the Incarnate Word : "He gave us not a servant, not an Angel, but his own Son,"[2] says St. John Chrysostom. Wherefore Holy Church exultingly exclaims, "O wondrous condecension of Thy mercy in our regard! O unappreciable love of charity! that Thou mightest redeem a slave, Thou deliveredst up Thy Son."[3]

---

[1] "Sic Deus dilexit mundum, ut Filium suum unigenitum daret."—*John*, iii. 16.

[2] "Non servum, non Angelum, sed Filium suum donavit."—*In Jo. hom.* 26.

[3] "O mira circa nos tuæ pietatis dignatio ! o inæstimabilis dilectio charitatis ! ut servum redimeres, Filium tradidisti."

O infinite God, how couldst Thou condescend to exercise towards us so wondrous a compassion! Who shall ever be able to understand an excess so great as that, in order to ransom the slave, Thou wert willing to give us Thine only Son? Ah, my kindest Lord, since Thou hast given me the best that Thou hast, it is but just that I should give Thee the most that I can. Thou desirest of me my love : of Thee I desire nothing else, but only Thy love. Behold this miserable heart of mine; I consecrate it wholly to Thy love. Depart from my heart, all ye creatures; give room to my God, who deserves and desires to possess it wholly, and without companions. I love Thee, O God of love; I love Thee above everything: and I desire to love Thee alone, my Creator, my treasure, my all.

II.

God hath given us his Son; and why? For love alone. Pilate, for fear of men, gave Jesus up to the Jews : *He delivered Him up to their will.*[1] But the Eternal Father gave his Son to us for the love which he bore us: *He delivered Him up for us all.*[2] St. Thomas says that "love has the nature of a first gift."[3] When a present is made us, the first gift that we receive is that of the love which the donor offers us in the thing that he gives: because, observes the Angelic Doctor, the one and only reason of every voluntary gift is love ; otherwise, when a gift is made for some other end than that of simple affection, the gift can no longer rightly be called a true gift. The gift which the Eternal Father made us of his Son was a true gift, perfectly voluntary, and without any merit of ours; and therefore it is said that the Incarnation of the Word was effected through the operation of the Holy

[1] "Tradidit voluntati eorum."—*Luke.* xxiii. 25.
[2] "Pro nobis omnibus tradidit illum."—*Rom.* viii. 32.
[3] "Amor habet rationem primi doni."—P. 1, q. 38, a. 2.

Spirit: that is, through love alone; as the same holy
Doctor says : " Through God's supreme love it was
brought to pass, that the Son of God assumed to himself
flesh." [1]

But not only was it out of pure love that God gave
unto this his Son, he also gave him to us with an immensity of love. This is precisely what Jesus wished to
signify when he said: *God so loved the world.*[2] The word
"so" (says St. John Chrysostom) signifies the magni-
tude of the love wherewith God made us this great gift:
" The word 'so' signifies the vehemence of the love."[3]
And what greater love could one who was God have been
able to give us than was shown by his condemning to
death his innocent Son in order to save us miserable
sinners? *Who spared not His own Son, but delivered
Him up for us all.*[4] Had the Eternal Father been capable of suffering pain, what pain would he not, have then
experienced, when he saw himself compelled by his justice to condemn that Son, whom he loved with the same
love wherewith he loved himself, to die by so cruel a
death in the midst of so many ignominies? *And the Lord
willed to bruise Him in infirmity.*[5] He willed to make him
die consumed by torments and sufferings.

Imagine thyself, then, to behold the Eternal Father,
with Jesus dead in his arms, and saying to us: This, O
men, is my beloved Son, in whom I have found all my
delights: *This is My beloved Son in whom I am well
pleased.*[6] Behold how I have willed to see him ill-treated

---

[1] " Ex maximo Dei amore provenit, ut Filius Dei carnem sibi as-
sumeret."—P. 3, q. 32, a. 1.

[2] " Sic Deus dilexit mundum."—*John*, iii. 16.

[3] " Verbum ' Sic ' significat amoris vehementiam."—*In Jo. hom.* 26.

[4] " Qui etiam proprio Filio suo non pepercit, sed pro nobis omnibus
tradidit illum."—*Rom.* viii. 32.

[5] " Et Dominus voluit conterere eum in infirmitate."—*Isa.* liii. 10.

[6] " Hic est Filius meus dilectus, in quo mihi complacui."—*Matt.* iii.
17.

on account of your iniquities: *For the wickedness of My people have I smitten Him.*[1] Behold how I have condemned him to die upon this cross, afflicted, and abandoned even by myself, who love him so much. This have I done in order that you may love me.

O infinite goodness! O infinite mercy! O infinite love! O God of my soul! since Thou didst will that the object most dear to Thy heart should die for me, I offer to Thee in my own behalf that great sacrifice of himself which this Thy Son made Thee; and for the sake of his merits I pray Thee to give me the pardon of my sins, Thy love, and Thy paradise. Great as are these graces which I ask of Thee, the offering which I present unto Thee is greater still. For the love of Jesus Christ, O my Father, pardon me and save me. If I have offended Thee in time past, I repent of it above every evil. I now prize Thee, and love Thee, above every good.

III.

Ah, who but a God of infinite love could ever have loved us to such a degree? St. Paul writes: *But God, who is rich in mercy, on account of the too great love wherewith He loved us when we were dead in sins, quickened us together in Christ.*[2] The Apostle calls too great this love which God showed us in giving to men, by means of the death of his Son, the life of grace which they had lost by their sins. But to God, who is love itself, this love was not too great: *God is love.*[3] St. John says that herein he wished to make us see the extent to which the greatness of the love of a God towards us reached, in sending his own Son into the world to obtain for us, by

[1] " Propter scelus populi mei percussi eum."—*Isa.* liii. 8.
[2] "Deus autem, qui dives est in misericordia, propter nimiam charitatem suam qua dilexit nos, et cum essemus mortui peccatis, convivificavit nos in Christo."—*Ephes.* ii. 4.
[3] " Deus charitas est."—I *John,* iv. 16.

his death, forgiveness and life eternal: *By this hath appeared the charity of God in us, because God hath sent His
own only-begotten Son into the world, that we might have life
through Him.*[1]

By sin, we were dead to the life of grace ; and Jesus,
by his death, has brought us back to life. We were
miserable, deformed objects of abomination ; but God,
by means of Jesus Christ, has rendered us pleasing and
precious in his divine sight. *He hath made us* (wrote
the apostle) *acceptable through His beloved Son.*[2] He hath
made us acceptable, i.e., " He hath made us pleasing,"
says the Greek text. And therefore St. John Chrysostom adds that were there to be a poor leper all covered
with wounds and disfigurements, and any one were to
heal his body of the leprosy, and make him beautiful
and rich besides, how great would be the sense of obligation that he would retain towards this his benefactor!
How much more, then, are we now beholden to God,
since, when our souls were disfigured and hateful on
account of our sins, he hath, by means of Jesus Christ,
not only delivered us from our sins, but has made them
beautiful and lovely besides: *He hath blessed us with all
spiritual blessings in heavenly places in Christ.*[3] Cornelius à
Lapide comments upon this: " He hath bestowed upon
us every spiritual gift."[4] God's blessing involves bene-
faction. The Eternal Father, then, in giving us Jesus
Christ, hath loaded us with all gifts, not indeed earthly
ones in the body, but spiritual ones in the soul: *In
heavenly places;*[5] giving us, together with his Son, a

---

[1] " In hoc apparuit charitas Dei in nobis, quoniam Filium suum unigenitum misit Deus in mundum, ut vivamus per eum."—1 *John*, iv. 9.

[2] " Gratificavit nos in dilecto Filio suo."—*Ephes.* i. 6.

[3] " Benedixit nos in omni benedictione spirituali in cœlestibus in
Christo."—*Ibid.* 3.

[4] " Benefecit nobis omni dono spirituali."

[5] " In cœlestibus in Christo."

heavenly life in this world, and a heavenly glory in the other.

Give me, then, Thy blessings and Thy benefactions, O my most loving God, and may the benediction draw me wholly to Thy love : " Draw me by the chains of Thy love,"[1] Let the love which Thou hast borne me make me enamoured of Thy goodness. Thou dost deserve an infinite love ; I love Thee with all the love I can command ; I love Thee above everything ; I love Thee more than myself. I give Thee my whole will; and this is the grace that I ask of Thee: make me from this day forth to live and do everything according to Thy divine will, wherewith Thou desirest nothing but my good, and my eternal salvation.

IV.

The King hath brought me into the cellar of wine ; He hath set in order charity in me.[2] My Lord, said the holy spouse, hath taken me into the cellar of wine; that is to say, hath placed before mine eyes all the benefits that he hath done me in order that I may be induced to love him: *He hath set in order charity in me.* A certain writer says that God, in order to gain our love, has, so to say, despatched against us an army of the graces of love. " He drew up charity against me like an armed host."[3] But, says Cardinal Hugo, the gift of Jesus Christ to us was the reserved arrow of which Isaias prophesied: *He hath made me as a chosen arrow : in his quiver He hath hidden me.*[4] As the hunter, says Hugo, keeps the best arrow in

---

[1] " Trahe me vinculis amoris tui."

[2] "Introduxit me in cellam vinariam, ordinavit in me charitatem."—*Cant.* ii. 4.

[3] "Instruxit contra me charitatem tamquam exercitum."—*G. Sanch. ap. Corn. a Lap.*

[4] " Posuit me sicut sagittam electam, in pharetra sua abscondit me."—*Isa.* xlix. 2.

reserve to give the finishing stroke to his game, so did
God, amongst all his other benefits, keep Jesus in reserve, until the time of grace had arrived, and then he
sent him forth, as if to give the finishing stroke of love
to the hearts of men: " The chosen arrow is kept in reserve: so was Christ kept in reserve in the bosom of the
Father, until the fulness of time should come; and
then he was sent forth to wound the hearts of the faithful." [1] St. Peter, wounded by this arrow, says St John
Chrysostom,[2] said to his Master: Lord, Thou knowest
well that I love Thee: *Lord, Thou knowest that I love
Thee.*[3]

Ah, my God, I behold myself surrounded on all sides
with the artifices of Thy love. I do, likewise, love Thee;
and if I love Thee, I know that Thou too dost love me.
And what power shall ever deprive me of Thy love? Sin
only.   But from this infernal monster it is for Thee,
through Thy mercy, to deliver me. I am content to suffer every evil, the most cruel death, or even to be torn
to pieces, sooner than offend Thee by mortal sin. But
Thou already knowest my past falls; Thou knowest my
weakness; help me, O my God, for love of Jesus Christ:
Despise not Thou the work of Thine hands,[4] I am the workmanship of Thy hands; Thou hast created me; despise
me not. If I merit to be left to myself by reason of
my sins, I merit nevertheless that Thou be merciful towards me for love of Jesus Christ, who hath sacrificed
his life to Thee for my salvation. I offer up to Thee his
merits, which all are mine; and, through them, I ask of
Thee, and hope for, from Thee, the gift of holy persever-

---

[1] "Sagitta electa reservatur; ita Christus quasi reservatus est in
sinu Patris, donec venit plenitudo temporis, et tunc missus est ad
vulnerandum corda fidelium."

[2] *Hom. de Turt.*

[3] "Domine ! tu scis quia amo te."—*John,* xxi. 15.

[4] "Opera manuum tuarum ne despicias."—*Ps.* cxxxvii. 8.

ance, together with a good death; and meanwhile to live the remainder of my life entirely to Thy glory. Long enough have I offended Thee! I now repent of it with all my heart, and I wish to love Thee to the uttermost of my power. I desire no longer to offer resistance to Thy love: I surrender myself wholly unto Thee. Give me Thy grace, and Thy love, and then do with me what Thou wilt. I love Thee, O my God, and I wish, and I ask of Thee, to love Thee always. Oh, for the merits of Jesus Christ, hearken unto my prayer. Mary, my Mother, pray to God for me. Amen. So may it be.

CHAPTER XVI.

THE LOVE OF THE SON OF GOD IN HAVING WILLED TO DIE FOR US.

I.

And behold Thy time was the time of lovers. . . . And Thou wast made exceeding beautiful.[1] How deeply are we Christians indebted to the Lord, in that he has caused us to be born after the coming of Jesus Christ! Our time is no longer a time of fear, as was that of the Jews, but a time of love; having seen a God dead for our salvation, and in order to gain our love. It is of faith that Jesus has loved us, and for love of us has given himself over unto death: *Christ hath loved us, and hath delivered Himself up for us.*[2] And where would ever have been the power to make an omnipotent God die,

[1] " Et ecce tempus tuum, tempus amantium. . . . Et decora facta es vehementer nimis."—*Ezech.* xvi. 8, 13.
[2] " Christus dilexit nos et tradidit semetipsum pro nobis."—*Ephes.* v. 2.

had not he of himself voluntarily willed to give his life for us ? *I give My life . . . no one taketh it from Me; but I lay it down of Myself.*¹ Wherefore St. John observes that Jesus, by his death, gave us the uttermost proof that he could have given us of his love: *Having loved His own, He loved them to the end.*² Jesus, by his death, says a devout writer, gave us the greatest possible sign of his love, beyond which there remained for him nothing that he could do in order to show how much he loved us: "The highest proof of love was that which he showed forth at the end of his life upon the cross."³

O my beloved Redeemer, Thou hast for love given Thyself wholly unto me; for love I give myself wholly unto Thee. Thou for my salvation hast given Thy life; I for Thy glory wish to die, when and as Thou dost please. There was nothing more that Thou couldst do in order to gain my love; but I have ungratefully exchanged Thee away for nothing. I repent of it, O my Jesus, with all my heart. Pardon me through Thy Passion; and in token of pardon, help me to love Thee. Through Thy grace I feel within myself a great desire of loving Thee, and I resolve to be all Thine own; but I see my languidness and the betrayals of which I have been guilty. Thou alone canst help me and render me happy. Help me, then, O my love. Make me love Thee: I ask Thee for nothing more.

II.

The Blessed Denis, the Carthusian, says that the Passion of Jesus Christ was called an excess—*And they spake*

---

¹ "Ego pono animam meam . . .; nemo tollit eam a me, sed ego pono eam a meipso."—*John*, x. 17.

² "Cum dilexisset suos, qui erant in mundo, in finem dilexit eos."—*John*, xiii. 1.

³ "Summum dilectionis testimonium circa finem vitæ suæ in ipsa ara crucis monstravit."—*Contens.* l. 10, d. 4, c. 1, *sp.* 1.

of His excess, which he would accomplish in Jerusalem'—
because it was an excess of mercy and of love: " The Passion of Jesus Christ is said to be an excess, because in it
was shown forth an excess of love and of compassion." '
O my God, and where is the believer that could live
without loving Jesus Christ, if he were frequently to
meditate upon his Passion? The wounds of Jesus, says
St. Bonaventure, are all of them wounds of love. They
are darts and flames which wound the hardest hearts,
and kindle into a flame the most frozen souls: "O
wounds that wound stony hearts, and set frozen minds
on fire !" ' In order the more strongly to impress upon
his heart a love towards Jesus in his Passion, the Blessed
Henry Suso one day took a knife, and cut out in letters
upon his breast the name of his beloved Lord. And
when thus bathed in blood, he went into the church, and,
prostrating himself before the crucifix, he said, Behold,
O Lord, Thou only Love of my soul, behold my desire.
I would gladly have written Thee deeper within my
heart; but this I cannot do. Do Thou, who canst do all
things, supply what is wanting in my powers, and imprint Thy adorable name in the lowest depths of my
heart, that so it may no more be possible to cancel in it
either Thy name or Thy love.

My Beloved is white and ruddy, chosen out of thousands.'
O my Jesus, Thou art all white through Thy spotless
innocence: but upon this cross Thou art also all ruddy
with wounds suffered for me. I choose Thee for the one
and only object of my love. And whom shall I love, if

' " Et dicebant excessum ejus, quem completurus erat in Jerusa-
lem."—*Luke*, ix. 31.
' " Dicitur passio Christi excessus, quia in ea ostensus est excessus
dilectionis et pietatis."
' "O vulnera, corda saxea vulnerantia, et mentes congelatas in-
flammantia !"—*Stim. div. am.* p. 1, c. 1.
' " Dilectus meus candidus et rubicundus, electus ex millibus."—
Cant. v. 10.

I love not Thee? What is there that I can find amongst all other objects more lovely than Thee, my Redeemer, my God, my all? I love Thee, O most lovely Lord. I love Thee above everything. Do Thou make me love Thee with all my affection, and without reserve.

III.

" Oh, if thou didst know the mystery of the cross," [1] said St. Andrew to the tyrant. O tyrant (it was his wish to say), wert thou to understand the love which Jesus Christ has borne thee, in willing to die upon a cross to save thee, thou wouldst abandon all thy possessions and earthly hopes, in order to give thyself wholly to the love of this thy Saviour. The same ought to be said to those Catholics who, believing as they do, the Passion of Jesus, yet do not think of it. Ah, were all men to think upon the love which Jesus Christ has shown forth for us in his death, who would ever be able not to love him? It was for this end, says the Apostle, that he, our beloved Redeemer, died for us, that, by the love he displayed towards us in his death, he might become the possessor of our hearts: *To this end Christ died, and rose again, that he might be Lord both of the dead and of the living; therefore, whether we live, or whether we die, we are the Lord's.* [2] Whether, then, we die or live, it is but just that we belong wholly to Jesus, who has saved us at so great a cost. Oh, who is there that could say, as did the loving martyr St. Ignatius, whose lot it was to give his life for Jesus Christ, " Let fire, cross, beasts, and torments of every kind come upon me ; let me only have fruition of Thee, O Christ." [3] Let flames, crosses, wild beasts, and every

---

[1] " O ! si scires mysterium crucis !"

[2] " In hoc enim Christus mortuus est et resurrexit, ut et mortuorum et vivorum dominetur. Sive ergo morimur, sive vivimus, Domini sumus."—*Rom.* xiv. 9.

[3] " Ignis, crux, bestiæ, et tota tormenta in me veniant ; tantum te, Christe, fruar."—*Epist. ad Rom.* c. 5.

kind of torture come upon me, provided only that I obtain and enjoy my Jesus Christ.

O my dear Lord! Thou didst die in order to gain my soul; but what have I done in order to gain Thee, O infinite good? Ah, my Jesus, how often have I lost Thee for nothing! Miserable that I was, I knew at the time that I was losing Thy grace by my sin; I knew that I was giving Thee great displeasure; and yet I committed it. My consolation is, that I have to deal with an infinite goodness, who remembers his offences no more when a sinner repents and loves him. Yes, my God, I do repent and love Thee. Oh, pardon me; and do Thou from this day forth bear rule in this rebellious heart of mine. To Thee do I consign it; to Thee do I wholly give myself. Tell me what Thou dost desire; wishing, as I do, to perform it all. Yes, my Lord, I wish to love Thee; I wish to please Thee in everything. Do Thou give me strength, and I hope to do so.

IV.

Jesus has not, by dying, ceased to love us. He loves us, and seeks us with the self-same love wherewith he first of all came down from heaven to seek us and to die for us. That artifice of love, too, which was manifested by our Redeemer to St. Francis Xavier, while on his travels, is celebrated far and wide. In a storm at sea there came a wave which carried away from him his crucifix. As the saint, after landing, was standing upon the shore, sorrowing, and earnestly longing to recover, if he might, the image of his beloved Lord, behold he saw a crab coming towards him, holding up the crucifix between its claws. Then, going forward to meet it with tears of tenderness and love, he received it, and clasped it to his bosom.

Oh, with what love does Jesus go to that soul that seeks him—*The Lord is good . . . to the soul that seeketh*

Him [1]—to the soul that seeketh him, however, with true love! But can they think that they possess this true love who refuse the crosses which the Lord sends them? *Christ pleased not Himself.* [2] " Christ," (as Cornelius à Lap- ide explains this passage) " served not his own will and convenience ; but all this and his life itself did he ex- pose for our salvation." [3] Jesus, for love of us, sought not earthly pleasures ; but he sought sufferings and death, all innocent though he was ; yet what is there that we are seeking for love of Jesus Christ? St. Peter the Martyr was one day standing in his prison, complain- ing of an unjust acccusation which had been preferred against him, saying, " But, Lord, what have I done that I should have had to suffer this persecution?" When the crucifix made him this reply, " And I, what evil have I done that I should have had to be upon this cross ?"

O my dear Saviour, Thou didst say, what evil hast Thou done? Too much hast Thou loved us ; since for love of us Thou hast been willing to suffer so much. And shall we, who deserved hell for our sins, refuse to suffer that which Thou dost will for our good? Thou, my Jesus, art all love with whomsoever seeketh Thee. It is not Thy sweetnesses and consolations that I seek ; I seek only Thyself and Thy will. Give me Thy love, and then do with me whatsoever Thou dost please. I embrace all the crosses which Thou wilt send me—pov- erty, persecutions, sickness, and pain. Deliver me only from the evil of sin, and then lay upon me every other evil. All will be but little in comparison with the evils which Thou hast suffered for love of me.

---

[1] " Bonus est Dominus . . . animæ quærenti illum."—*Lam.* iii. 25.

[2] " Christus non sibi placuit."—*Rom.* xv. 3.

[3] " Christus suæ voluntati et commodis non servivit, sed ea omnia et vitam suam pro nostra salute exposuit."

V.

"That he might redeem a slave, the Father neither spared the Son, nor did the Son spare himself."[1] To liberate the slave, then, the Father hath not pardoned the Son, neither hath the Son pardoned himself. And after so great a love to men, will it be possible for there to be one who loves not this God, so loving as he is? The Apostle says that Jesus died for us all, to the end that we might live only to him and to his love : *Christ died for all, that they who live may no longer live unto themselves, but unto Him who died for them.*[2] But, alas ! the greater portion of mankind, although one who is God has died for them, live unto sin, unto the devil, and not unto Jesus Christ. It was said by Plato that "love is the magnet of love."[3] And Seneca replied, Do thou love, if thou wouldst be beloved: "If you would be loved, love."[4] And how does it happen that Jesus, who, by dying for men, would seem to have gone foolish, as it were, out of love for us—"It seemed foolish that the author of life should die for all,"[5] says St. Gregory— how does it happen that he, after so many tokens of love on his part, has not been able to draw to himself our hearts ? How is it that, loving us so much, he has not yet been able to make himself beloved by us ?

Oh that all men loved Thee, my most lovely Jesus ! Thou art a God worthy of infinite love. But, my poor Lord,—give me leave so to call Thee,—Thou art so love-

---

[1] " Ut servum redimeret, nec Pater Filio, nec sibi Filius ipse pepercit."—*S. de Pass. D.*

[2] " Pro omnibus mortuus est Christus, ut et qui vivunt, jam non sibi vivant, sed ei qui pro ipsis mortuus est."—*2 Cor.* v. 15.

[3] " Magnes amoris, amor."

[4] " Si vis amari, ama."—*Epist.* ix.

[5] "Stultum visum est ut pro hominibus Auctor vitæ moreretur."— *In Evang. hom.* 6.

ly, Thou hast done and suffered so much in order to be loved by men : and, after all, how many are they that do love Thee ? I see almost all men applying themselves to the love—some of their parents, some of their friends, some of wealth, honors, or pleasures, and some even of dumb animals ; but how many are they that love Thee, O infinite loveliness? O God, too few, indeed, they are; yet amongst these few I wish to be—I, miserable sinner as I am, who at one time also offended Thee by loving that which is but mire, going astray from Thee. But now I love Thee, and I prize Thee above every good : and Thee only do I wish to love. Do Thou pardon me, O my Jesus, and come to my assistance.

VI.

God, then, O Christian, says St. Cyprian, rests content with thee, even to dying in order to gain thy love ; and wilt not thou rest content with God, so that thou wilt love objects other than thy Lord ? " God is content with thee, and wilt thou not be content with thy God ?'[1] Ah, no ; my beloved Jesus, I will not have any love in me which is not for Thee. I am content with Thee ; I renounce all other loves : Thy love alone is enough for me. I hear Thee saying to me, *Put Me as a seal upon thy heart.*[2] Yes, my crucified Jesus, I do set Thee, and do Thou, too, set Thyself, as a seal upon my heart, that it may remain closed against every other love which tends not to Thee. In time past I have given Thee displeasure by means of other loves ; but, at the present moment, there is no pain that afflicts me excepting the remembrance of having, by my sins, lost my love of Thee. For the future, *Who shall separate me from*

---

[1] " Contentus est te Deus, et tu non eris contentus Deo tuo ?"—*Contens.* l. 10, d. 4, c. 1, *sp.* 1.

[2] " Pone me ut signaculum super cor tuum."—*Cant.* viii. 6.

the love of Christ ? [1] Who shall ever again separate me
from my love for Thee ?

No, my most lovely Saviour, since Thou hast made
me know the love which Thou hast borne me, I have not
the heart to live any more without loving Thee. I love
Thee, my crucified Love ; I love Thee with all my heart ;
and I give unto Thee this soul of mine, which Thou hast
so much sought and loved. Oh, by the merits of Thy
death, which so painfully separated Thy blessed soul
from Thy body, do Thou detach me from every love
which can hinder me from being all Thine own, and
from loving Thee with all my heart. Mary, my hope,
do thou help me to love thy sweetest Son alone, that so
I may be able with truth, throughout my whole life,
ever to repeat, " My Love is crucified ; my Love is crucified." [2] Amen.

Prayer of St. Bonaventure.

O Jesus ! who, for my sake, hast not pardoned Thyself, do
Thou so impress upon me Thy Passion that, wheresoever I
turn, I may behold Thy wounds, and find no repose but in
Thee and in the contemplation of Thy sufferings. Amen.

[1] " Quis ergo nos separabit a charitate Christi ?'—*Rom.* viii. 33.
[2] " Amor meus crucifixus est.

Simple Exposition of the Circumstances of the Passion of Jesus Christ,

ACCORDING TO THE NARRATION OF THE HOLY EVANGEL-
ISTS, WITH SOME REFLECTIONS AND AFFECTIONS.*

INTRODUCTION.

St. Augustine says that there is nothing more con-
ducive to the attainment of eternal salvation than to
think every day on the pains which Jesus Christ has suffered for the love of us. "Nothing is more salutary
than to think daily on what the Man-God has endured
for us."[1] And before him, Origen said that sin cannot
reign in the soul that frequently meditates on the death
of the Saviour. "It is certain that, when the death of
Christ is carried about in the soul, sin cannot reign in it.[2]
Besides, our Lord revealed to a holy solitary that there
is no exercise better calculated to kindle in the heart the
fire of divine love than the meditation on his Passion.
Hence, Father Balthazar Alvarez used to say that ignorance of the treasures that we have in the Passion of
Jesus Christ is the ruin of Christians. Hence, he would
tell his penitents that they should not consider themselves to have done anything until they had succeeded in
always keeping in the heart Jesus crucified. According
to St. Bonaventure, the wounds of Jesus are wounds

[1] "Nihil tam salutiferum, quam quotidie cogitare quanta pro nobis
pertulit Deus-Homo."—*Ad Fr. in er.* s. 32.
[2] "Certum est quia, ubi Christi mors animo circumfertur, non
potest regnare peccatum."—*Lib. 6 in Rom.* 6.

---

* This little work was published about two years after the preceding
one, that is, in the year 1761 (*Tannoia*, b. 2, ch. 48).—ED.

which soften the hardest hearts, and inflame the most frozen souls.'

Hence, a learned author, Father Croiset,' writes that there is nothing which unfolds to us the treasures contained in the sufferings of Jesus Christ better than the simple history of his Passion. To inflame a faithful soul with divine love, it is enough to reflect on the narration which the holy Evangelists have given of the sorrows of the Redeemer, and to view with the eyes of a Christian all that the Saviour has suffered in the three principal theatres of his Passion; that is, in the garden of Olives, in the city of Jerusalem, and on Mount Calvary. The contemplations which devout authors have made and written on the Passion are useful and beautiful; but certainly a single word from the Sacred Scriptures makes a greater impression on a Christian than a hundred and a thousand contemplations and revelations ascribed to certain holy souls; for the Scripture assures us that whatever they attest is certain with the certainty of divine faith.

Hence I have resolved, for the benefit and consolation of souls enamoured of Jesus Christ, to arrange in order, and to relate in simple language (adding a few brief reflections and affections) what the holy Evangelists say of the Passion of Jesus Christ. They supply abundant matter for the meditations of a hundred and a thousand years, and at the same time the most powerful motives to inflame us with holy charity towards our most loving Redeemer.

O God, how is it possible for a soul that has faith, and reflects on the sorrows and ignominies which Jesus Christ has suffered for us, not to burn with love for him, and not to conceive strong resolutions to become a saint, in

¹ "O vulnera, corda saxea vulnerantia, et mentes congelatas inflammantia!"—*Stim. div. am.* p. 1, c. 1.
² *Exerc. de p. Mardi S.*

order not to be ungrateful to so loving a God? Faith is necessary; for had not faith assured us of it, who could ever believe what a God has actually done for the love of us? *He emptied Himself, taking the form of a servant.*[1] Who, had he not the infallible assurance of faith, could, at the sight of Jesus, born in a stable, believe that he is the God who is adored by the angels in heaven? How, without the aid of faith, can he who beholds the Saviour flying into Egypt, in order to escape from the hands of Herod, believe that he is omnipotent? How could we, without the assurance of faith, believe that he whom we see sorrowful unto death in the Garden, is infinitely happy? or that he who was bound to a pillar, and suspended on a gibbet, is the Lord of the universe?

How great should be our astonishment if we saw a king become a worm, crawling along the earth, living in a filthy hole, and thence making laws, appointing ministers, and governing his kingdom? O holy faith, unfold to us who Jesus Christ is, who this man is, who appears as insignificant as the rest of men. *The Word was made flesh.*[2] St. John assures us that he is the eternal Word, the only-begotten of God. And what sort of life has this Man-God led on earth? Behold it described by the prophet Isaias: *And we have seen him . . . despised and most abject of men, a man of sorrows.*[3] He wished to be a man of sorrows; that is, he wished to be afflicted with all sorrows, and not to be for a moment free from pain. He was a man of sorrows and loaded with insults: *Despised and the most abject of men.* Yes, for Jesus was the most insulted and maltreated of all mortals, as if he had been the last and most contemptible of men. A God bound as a malefactor by the officers of justice! A God

[1] "Semetipsum exinanivit, formam servi accipiens."—*Phil.* ii. 7.
[2] "Verbum caro factum est."—*John*, i. 14.
[3] "Vidimus eum . . . despectum, et novissimum virorum, virum dolorum."—*Isa.* liii. 2–3.

11

scourged as a slave! A God treated as a mock king!
A God dying on an infamous gibbet!

How great the impression which these prodigies should
ₘake on him who believes them? How great the desire
which they should infuse of suffering for Jesus Christ? St.
Francis de Sales has said, "All the wounds of the Redeemer are, as it were, so many mouths which teach us
how we ought to suffer for him. The science of the
the saints consists in constantly suffering for Jesus; by
constantly suffering for him we shall soon become
saints. How ardent the love with which we shall be inflamed at the sight of the flames which are found in the
bosom of the Redeemer? Oh, what a happiness to burn
with the same fire with which our God burns? How
delightful to be united to God with the chains of love!"

But why do so many Christians behold with indifference Jesus on the cross? During the holy week they
are present at the celebration of his death, but without
sentiments of tenderness or gratitude, and as if they
commemorated an event which never happened, or
which does not concern them. Perhaps they neither
know nor believe what the Gospels relate of the Passion
of Jesus Christ? I answer and say, that they know it
and believe it, but they do not reflect on it. Ah! for
those who believe and reflect on the Passion of the Redeemer, it is impossible not to burn with love for a God
who suffers such torments, and dies for the love of them.
The charity of Christ presseth us.[1] The Apostle meant to
say that, in thinking on the Passion of our Lord, we
should consider not so much the sorrows and insults which
he suffered as the love with which he bore them; for Jesus
Christ wished to submit to such torments, not only to
save us (since for our salvation a single petition offered
by him to his Father would be sufficient), but also to

---

[1] " Charitas enim Christi urget nos."—2 *Cor.* v. 14.

make us understand the affection which he entertained for us, and thus gain our hearts. Ah! a soul that thinks of this love of Jesus Christ cannot but love him. *The charity of Christ presseth us.* It will feel itself bound and constrained, as it were by force, to consecrate all its affections to him. Hence Jesus Christ has died for us all, that we may live no longer to ourselves, but to this most loving Redeemer, who has sacrificed his divine life for our salvation.

O happy you, O loving souls, who frequently meditate on the Passion of Jesus! *You shall,* says Isaias, *draw waters with joy out of the Saviour's fountains.*[1] From the blessed fountains of the wounds of the Saviour you shall continually draw waters of love and confidence. And how can even the greatest sinner (if he repent of his sins) ever despair of the divine mercy at the sight of Jesus crucified, when he knows that the Eternal Father has placed on his beloved Son all our sins, that he might atone for them? *And the Lord hath laid on him the iniquities of us all.*[2] How, says St. Paul, can we be afraid that God will refuse us any grace after having given us his own Son? *He that spareth not even His own Son, but delivereth Him up for us all, how hath He not also with Him given us all things?*[3]

[1] "Haurietis aquas in gaudio de fontibus Salvatoris."—*Isa.* xii. 3.

[2] "Posuit Dominus in eo iniquitatem omnium nostrum."—*Isa.* liii. 6.

[3] "Qui etiam proprio Filio suo non pepercit, sed pro nobis omnibus tradidit illum, quomodo non etiam cum illo omnia nobis donavit?"—*Rom.* viii. 32.

CHAPTER I.

JESUS ENTERS JERUSALEM.

I.

*Behold thy king cometh to thee, meek and sitting on an ass,
and a colt the foal of her that is used to the yoke.*[1] Our Redeemer, at the approach of the time of his Passion, sets
out from Bethania for Jerusalem. Let us here consider
the humility of Jesus Christ, who is the king of heaven,
in condescending to enter that city sitting on an ass. O
Jerusalem, behold thy king comes to thee in humility
and meekness. Be not afraid that he comes to rule over
thee and to take possession of thy riches; for he comes all
love and mercy to save thee, and to purchase life for
thee by his own death. The people, who for some time
entertained a veneration for him on account of his miracles, and particularly of the last which he wrought, in
raising Lazarus from the dead, go out to meet him.
Some strewed their garments on the way before him,
others spread out branches of trees to do him honor.
Oh ! who would have ever imagined that that Lord, who
was received with so many honors, should have to appear
in a few days with a cross on his shoulders, as a criminal
condemned to death ?

Didst Thou then, my dear Jesus, wish to make this
glorious entry, that the greater the honor with which
Thou wast received, the more ignominious might be Thy
Passion and death ? The praises which this ungrateful
city now gives Thee will be changed into insults and

---

[1] "Ecce Rex tuus venit tibi mansuetus, sedens super asinam et
pullum filium subjugalis."—*Matt.* xxi. 5.

maledictions. They now say, *Hosanna to the Son of David; blessed is he that cometh in the name of the Lord.*[1] Glory to Thee, O Son of David: be forever blessed, since Thou comest for our welfare in the name of the Lord. And afterwards they will raise their voice and exclaim, *Away with Him, away with Him, crucify Him, crucify Him.*[2] Pilate (they will say), take away this miscreant from before our eyes; crucify him, and do not leave him any longer in our sight. Now they spread their garments before Thee, and they will afterwards strip Thee of Thy clothes in order to scourge and crucify Thee. They now take branches of palm to spread them under Thy feet, and afterwards they will take branches of thorns to pierce Thy head. Now they pour so many benedictions upon Thee, and afterwards they will load Thee with contumely and blasphemies. Go then, my soul, and say to him with love and gratitude : *Blessed is he that cometh in the name of the Lord.*[3] My beloved Redeemer, be forever blessed, since Thou art come to save us ; if Thou hadst not come, we should be all lost.

II.

And when he drew near the city, he wept over it.[4] When Jesus approached the unhappy city of Jerusalem, he looked at it, and wept over its ingratitude and destruction.

Ah, my Lord, in weeping over the ingratitude of Jerusalem, Thou didst also weep over my ingratitude and the destruction of my soul. My beloved Redeemer,

[1] " Hosanna Filio David! benedictus, qui venit in nomine Domini !" —*Matt.* xxi. 9.

[2] " Tolle, tolle, crucifige eum !—*John*, xix. 15.

[3] " Benedictus, qui venit in nomine Domini !"

[4] " Et ut appropinquavit, videns civitatem, flevit super illam."— *Luke*, xix. 41.

Thou didst weep at the sight of the injury that I have done myself in banishing Thee from my soul, and in constraining Thee to condemn me to hell after Thou hadst died for my salvation. Ah, leave weeping to me, for I alone should weep at the thought of the injury that I have offered to Thee, in offending Thee and separating myself from Thee after Thou hadst loved me so tenderly. Eternal Father, for the sake of the tears which Thy Son then shed over me, give me sorrow for my sins. And Thou, O loving and tender heart of my Jesus, have mercy on me, for I detest above all things the offences that I have given Thee, and I resolve to love nothing but Thee.

III.

After his entry into Jerusalem, Jesus labored the entire day in preaching and curing the sick; but in the evening there was no one to invite him to sleep in his house; and therefore he was obliged to return to Bethania.

My sweet Lord, if others banish Thee, I will not banish Thee. There was once an unhappy time when I ungratefully banished Thee from my soul; but now I set a greater value on being united with Thee than on the possession of all the kingdoms of the earth. Ah, my God, who shall be able ever again to separate me from Thy love?

CHAPTER II.

THE COUNCIL OF THE JEWS, AND THE TREACHERY OF JUDAS.

I.

The chief priests, therefore, and the Pharisees gathered a council and said: What do we, for this man doeth many miracles?[1] Behold, at the very time that Jesus Christ was employed in working miracles for the benefit of all, the first personages of the city assembled to plan the death of the author of life.   Behold what the impious Caiphas said :   *It is expedient for you that one man should die for the people, and that the whole perish not.*[2]   From that day, says St. John, they sought a means of putting Jesus to death.

Ah, Jews, fear not; this your Redeemer does not fly away ; no, he has come on earth to die, and by his death to deliver you and all men from eternal death !

II.

But behold, Judas presents himself to the high priests and says : *What will you give me, and I will deliver him unto you?*[3]   Oh, how great was the joy with which the Jews exulted through the hatred that they bore to Jesus Christ, when they saw that one of his own disciples offered to betray him, and to deliver him into their hands!

---

[1] " Collegerunt ergo Pontifices et Pharisæi concilium, et dicebant : Quid facimus, quia hic homo multa signa facit ?"—*John*, xi. 47.

[2] " Expedit vobis ut unus moriatur homo pro populo, et non tota gens pereat."—*Ibid.* 50.

[3] " Quid vultis mihi dare, et ego vobis eum tradam ?"—*Matt.* xxvi. 15.

Let us here consider the exultation of hell when a soul that has served Jesus Christ for several years betrays him for a miserable good or a vile pleasure. But, O Judas, since you wish to sell your God, at least demand the price which he is worth. He is an infinite good, and is therefore worth an infinite price. But, O God! you conclude the sale for thirty pieces of silver: *But they appointed him thirty pieces of silver.*[1] Ah, my unhappy soul, leave Judas, and turn thy thoughts on thyself. Tell me for what price hast thou so often sold the grace of God to the devil?

Ah, my Jesus, I am ashamed to appear before Thee when I think of the injuries I have done Thee. How often have I turned my back upon Thee, and preferred to Thee some temporal interest, the indulgence of caprice, or a momentary and vile pleasure? I knew that by such a sin I should lose Thy friendship, and I have voluntarily exchanged it for nothing. Oh that I had been dead rather than have offered Thee so great an outrage! My Jesus, I repent with my whole heart ; I would wish to die of sorrow for it.

III.

Let us here consider the benignity of Jesus Christ, who, though he knew the appointment which Jesus had made, did not banish him from his presence when he saw him, nor look at him with an unfriendly eye, but admitted him into his society, and even to his table, and reminded him of his treachery, for the sole purpose of making him enter into himself. When he saw him obstinate, he even prostrated himself before him, and washed his feet in order to soften his heart.

Ah, my Jesus, I see that Thou dost treat me in the same manner. I have despised and betrayed Thee, and Thou dost not cast me off. Thou dost regard me with love,

[1] " At illi constituerunt ei triginta argenteos."—*Matt.* xxvi. 15.

Thou dost admit me even to Thy table of the Holy Communion. My dear Saviour, oh that I had always loved Thee! And how shall I be ever again able to depart from Thy feet and renounce Thy love?

CHAPTER III.

THE LAST SUPPER OF JESUS WITH HIS DISCIPLES.—THE WASHING OF THE FEET.

Jesus knowing that his hour was come to pass out of this world to the Father; having loved his own who were in the world, he loved them unto the end.[1] Knowing that the time of his death and departure from this world was come, and having hitherto loved men even to excess, he wished to give them the last and the greatest proof of his love. Behold him seated at table, all on fire with charity, turning to his disciples and saying, *With desire I have desired to eat this Pasch with you.*[2] My disciples (and he then said the same to us all), know that I have desired nothing during my whole life but to eat this last supper with you; for after it I shall go to sacrifice my life for your salvation.

Then, O my Jesus, dost Thou desire so ardently to give Thy life for us, Thy miserable creatures? Ah! this Thy desire inflames our hearts with a desire to suffer and die for the love of Thee, since Thou dost condescend to suffer and die for the love of us. O beloved Redeemer, make known to us what Thou willest from us: we are willing to please Thee in all things. We sigh

---

[1] "Sciens Jesus quia venit hora ejus, ut transeat ex hoc mundo ad Patrem, cum dilexisset suos, . . . in finem dilexit eos."—*John*, xiii. 1.

[2] "Desiderio desideravi hoc pascha manducare vobiscum, antequam patiar."—*Luke*, xxii. 15.

to give Thee pleasure, to correspond at least in part to Thy great love for us. Increase always more and more this blessed flame within us : may it make us forget the world and ourselves, that from this day forward we may think only of pleasing Thy enamoured heart.

II.

Behold at table the Paschal lamb, the figure of our Saviour ; as the former was consumed at supper, so on the following day the world was to behold on the altar of the cross Jesus Christ, the Lamb of God, consumed by torments. *He therefore leaning on the breast of Jesus.*[1] Happy thou, O beloved John, who, leaning thy head on the bosom of Jesus, didst then understand the tenderness of the love of this loving Redeemer for the souls that love him ! Ah my sweet Lord, Thou hast frequently favored me with a similar grace. Yes, I too have felt the tenderness of Thy affection for me, when Thou didst console me with celestial lights and spiritual sweetness ; but, after all Thy favors, I have not been faithful to Thee. Ah, do not permit me to live any longer ungrateful to Thy goodness. I wish to be all Thine : accept me and assist me.

III.

He riseth from supper, and layeth aside His garments, and having taken a towel girded Himself. After that He putteth water into a basin, and began to wash the feet of the disciples, and to wipe them with the towel wherewith He was girded.[2] My soul, behold thy Jesus, rising from the table, laying aside his garments, taking a white cloth and girding himself with it : he afterwards puts water into a basin,

---

[1] "Cum recubuisset ille supra pectus Jesu."—*John*, xiii. 25.

[2] "Surgit a coena, et ponit vestimenta sua; et cum accepisset linteum præcinxit se. Deinde mittit aquam in pelvim, et cœpit lavare pedes discipulorum, et extergere linteo quo erat præcinctus."—*John*, xiii. 4-5.

kneels down before his disciples, and begins to wash their feet. Then the sovereign of the universe, the only-begotten of God, humbles himself so as to wash the feet of his creatures. O angels, what do you say? It would have been a great favor if Jesus Christ had permitted them, as he did Magdalene, to wash his divine feet with their tears. But no; he wished to place himself at the feet of his servants in order to leave us at the end of his life this great example of humility, and this proof of the great love that he bears to men.

And, O Lord, shall we be always so proud as not to be able to bear a word of contempt, or the smallest inattention, without instantly feeling resentment, and thinking of seeking revenge, after we had by our sins deserved to be trampled on by the devils in hell? Ah, my Jesus, Thy example has rendered humiliations and insults amiable to us. I purpose henceforth to bear every injury and affront for the love of Thee.

CHAPTER IV.

THE INSTITUTION OF THE MOST HOLY SACRAMENT.

I.

And whilst they were at supper, Jesus took bread and blessed and broke it, and gave to His disciples and said, Take ye and eat, this is My body.[1] After the washing of the feet, an act of humility the practice of which Jesus recommended to his disciples, he took his garments, and, sitting down again to table, wished to give men the last proof of the tender love that he had for them, and that was

[1] "Cœnantibus autem eis, accepit Jesus panem, et benedixit, ac fregit, deditque discipulis suis, et ait : Accipite et comedite ; hoc est corpus meum."—*Matt.* xxvi. 26.

the institution of the Most Holy Sacrament of the altar. He took for that purpose bread, consecrated it, broke it, and gave it to his disciples, saying, Take and eat, this is my body. He then recommended them as often as they should communicate to remember the death which he suffered for their sake. *As often as you shall eat this bread . . . you shall show the death of the Lord.*[1] Jesus Christ did then, what a dying prince who tenderly loved his spouse would do : he selects among all his gems and jewels the most beautiful and costly; he then calls his spouse and says to her, O my dear spouse, I am going to die ; and, that thou mayest not forget me, I leave thee this gem as a memorial of me :[2] when thou dost look at it, remember me and the love I have borne thee. " No tongue," says St. Peter of Alcantara, in his meditations, " is able to express the greatness of the love which Jesus bears to every soul. Hence, that his absence might not be an occasion of forgetting him, he left, before his departure from this world, to his spouse this Most Holy Sacrament, in which he himself remained, wishing that between them there should be no other pledge than himself to keep alive the remembrance of him." We may then imagine how pleasing it is to Jesus Christ that we remember his Passion, since he has instituted the sacrament of the altar, that we may preserve a continual remembrance of the immense love which he has shown us in his death.

O my Jesus, O God enamoured of souls ! has Thy affection for men enraptured Thee to such a degree as to make Thyself their food ? Tell me what more remains for Thee to do in order to oblige us to love Thee ? In the Holy Communion Thou givest Thyself to us entirely and without reserve : it is then but just that we give our

---

[1] " Quotiescumque manducabitis panem hunc et calicem bibetis, mortem Domini annuntiabitis."—1 *Cor.* xi. 26.

[2] *De l'Or. et de la Med.* p. 1, ch. 4

whole being unreservedly to Thee. I wish to be all Thine, I wish to love nothing but Thee, my God. Thou hast said that he who eats Thy flesh lives only for Thee. *He that eateth Me, the same also shall live by Me.*[1] Since then Thou hast so often permitted me to eat Thy flesh, make me die to myself that I may live only for Thee, only to serve Thee, and give Thee pleasure. My Jesus, I wish to fix all my affections in Thee : assist me to be faithful to Thee.

II.

St. Paul remarks the time in which Jesus Christ instituted this great sacrament, and says, *The Lord Jesus, the same night in which He was betrayed, took bread, and giving thanks, broke, and said, Take ye and eat : this is My body.*[2] O God, on the very night in which men were preparing to put him to death, the loving Redeemer prepared for us this bread of life and of love to unite us entirely to himself, as he declared when he said, *He that eateth My flesh abideth in Me, and I in him.*[3]

O love of my soul, worthy of infinite love! Thou canst not give greater proofs of Thy affection and tender love for me. Ah, draw me entirely to Thyself : if I know not how to give Thee my whole heart, take it Thou to Thyself. Ah, my Jesus, when shall I be all Thine, as Thou dost make Thyself all mine when I receive Thee in this sacrament of love? Ah, enlighten me, and unfold to me always more and more Thy amiable qualities, which render Thee so worthy of love, that I may be always more and more enamoured of Thee, and may be

---

[1] "Qui manducat me, et ipse vivet propter me."—*John*, vi. 58.

[2] "Dominus Jesus, in qua nocte tradebatur, accepit panem, et gratias agens fregit, et dixit: Accipite, et manducate ; hoc est corpus meum."—1 *Cor.* xi. 23, 24.

[3] "Qui manducat meam carnem et bibit meum sanguinem, in me manet, et ego in illo."—*John*, vi. 57.

wholly employed in pleasing Thee. I love Thee, O my sovereign good, my joy, my love, my all.

CHAPTER V.

AGONY OF JESUS IN THE GARDEN OF OLIVES.

I.

And a hymn being said, they went out to Mount Olivet. . . . *Then Jesus came with them into a country place, which is called Gethsemani.*[1] As soon as they had said grace, Jesus leaves the supper room with his disciples, goes into the garden of Gethsemani, and begins to pray. But, alas, at the commencement of his prayer, he is assailed with a great fear, an oppressive tediousness, and an overwhelming sadness. *He began to fear and be heavy,*[2] says St. Mark. St. Matthew adds, *He began to grow sorrowful and to be sad.*[2] Hence our Redeemer, overwhelmed with sadness, said that his blessed soul was sorrowful even unto death. Then was presented before him the melancholy scene of all the torments and ignominies which were prepared for him. In his Passion these afflicted him one by one; but in the garden, the buffets, the spittle, the scourges, the thorns, the nails, and the reproaches which he was to suffer, came all together to torment him. He there embraced them all, but in embracing them, he trembled, he agonized, and prayed: *And being in an agony, He prayed the longer.*[4] But, my Jesus, who compels Thee to submit to such torments? The

---

[1] " Hymno dicto, exierunt in montem Olivetl."—*Matt.* xxvi. 30.
[2] "Cœpit pavere et tædere,—contristari et mœstus esse."—*Mark,* xiv. 33.—*Matt.* xxvi. 37.
[3] "Tristis est anima mea usque ad mortem."—*Mark,* xiv. 34.
[4] "Factus in agonia, prolixius orabat."—*Luke,* xxii. 43.

love, he answers, which I bear to men constrains me to endure them. Ah, how great must have been the astonishment of heaven at the sight of omnipotence become weak, of the joy of paradise oppressed with sadness! A God afflicted! And why? To save men, his own creatures. In the garden he offered the first sacrifice : Jésus was the victim, love was the priest, and the ardor of his affection for men was the blessed fire with which the sacrifice was consummated.

II.

My Father, if it be possible, let this chalice pass from Me.[1] Thus Jesus prayed. My Father, he says, if it be possible, save me from drinking this bitter chalice. But he prayed thus not so much to be delivered from the torments that he was to endure, as to make us understand the pain which he suffered and embraced for the love of us. He prayed thus, also, to teach us that in tribulations we may ask God to deliver us from them, but that we should at the same time conform entirely to his divine will, and say with him, *Nevertheless, not as I will, but as Thou wilt.*[2] And during the whole time of his prayer he repeated the same petition. *Thy will be done. . . . And He prayed the third time, saying the self-same word.*[3]

Yes, my Lord, for Thy sake, I embrace all the crosses which Thou wilt send me. Thou, an innocent, hast suffered for my sake, and shall I, a sinner, after having so often deserved hell, refuse to suffer in order to please Thee, and to obtain from Thee the pardon of my sins, and Thy grace? *Not as I will, but as Thou wilt : let not my will, but Thine, be always done.*

---

[1] "Pater mi ! si possibile est, transeat a me calix iste."—*Matt.* xxvi. 39.

[2] "Verumtamen, non sicut ego volo, sed sicut tu."—*Ibid.*

[3] "Fiat voluntas tua . . . . ; et oravit tertio, eundem sermonem dicens."—*Ibid.* 44.

III.

He fell flat on the ground.[1] In his prayer in the garden, Jesus fell prostrate on the ground, because, seeing himself clothed with the sordid garment of all our sins, he felt, as it were, ashamed to raise his eyes to heaven.

My dear Redeemer, I would not dare to ask pardon for so many insults which I have committed against Thee, if Thy sufferings did not give me confidence. *Eternal Father, look on the face of Thy Christ:*[2] look not on my iniquities, behold this, Thy beloved Son, trembling, agonizing, and sweating blood in order to obtain Thy pardon for me. *And his sweat became as drops of blood, trickling down upon the ground.*[3] Behold me, and have pity on me. But, my Jesus, in this garden there are not executioners to scourge Thee, nor thorns, nor nails to torture Thee; what, then, extracts so much blood from Thee? Ah! I understand Thee: it was not the foresight of Thy approaching sufferings that then afflicted Thee so grievously; for to these pains Thou didst spontaneously offer Thyself: *He was offered because it was His own will.*[4] It was the sight of my sins; these were the cruel press which forced so much blood from Thy sacred veins. Hence, it was not the executioners, nor the nails, nor the thorns, that were cruel and barbarous in Thy regard: no, my sins, which made Thee so sorrowful in the garden, have been barbarous and cruel to Thee, my sweet Redeemer. Then, in Thy great affliction, I too have added to Thy sorrows, and have grievously afflicted Thee by the weight of my sins. Had I been guilty of fewer sins, Thou shouldst have suffered less. Behold, then,

---

[1] " Procidit super terram."—*Mark,* xiv. 35.
[2] " Respice in faciem Christi tui."—*Ps.* lxxxiii. 10.
[3] " Et factus est sudor ejus sicut guttæ sanguinis decurrentis in terram."—*Luke,* xxii. 44.
[4] "Oblatus est, quia ipse voluit."—*Isa.* liii. 7.

the return I have made for Thy love in dying for me.   I
have added to Thy great sufferings !   My beloved Lord,
I repent of having offended Thee, I am sorry for my sins,
but my sorrow is not great ; I would wish for sorrow
that would take away my life.   Ah ! through the bitter
agony which Thou didst suffer in the garden, give me
a portion of that abhorrence which Thou didst then feel
for my sins.   And if my ingratitude was then a cause of
affliction to Thee, grant that I may now please Thee by
my love.   Yes, my Jesus, I love Thee with my whole
heart.   I love Thee more than myself, and for Thy love
I renounce all the pleasures and goods of this earth.
Thou alone art, and shalt always be, my only good and
my only love.

CHAPTER VI.

JESUS IS TAKEN AND BOUND.—FLIGHT OF THE DISCIPLES.

I.

Rise up, let us go.   Behold he that will betray Me is at hand.[1]
Knowing that Judas, along with the Jews and soldiers
who came to capture him, was at hand, the Redeemer,
still bathed in the sweat of death, rises with a pallid
countenance, but with a heart all on fire with love, and
goes to meet his enemies, in order to deliver himself into
their hands.   On seeing them he said, *Whom do you
seek ?*[2]   Imagine, O my soul, that Jesus then said to
thee, Tell me whom dost thou seek ?

Ah ! my Lord, and whom will I seek but Thee, who
art come from heaven on earth to seek after me, and
save me from perdition ?

[1] "Surgite eamus; ecce, qui me tradet, prope est."—*Mark.* xiv. 42.
[2] "Quem quæritis?"—*John,* xviii. 4.

II.

They took Jesus and bound Him.[1] Alas, a God bound! What should we say if we saw a king taken and bound in chains by his own servants? And what do we say now that we see a God in the hands of the rabble? O blessed cords that bound my Redeemer, bind me also to him; but bind me so that I can nevermore withdraw myself from his love ; bind my heart to his most holy will, so that henceforth I may wish only what he wishes.

Behold, O my soul, how one seizes his hands, another binds him, and others insult and strike him : the innocent Lamb permits them to bind and strike him as they please. He makes no effort to escape from their hands, he does not call for aid, he does not complain of so many injuries, nor does he ask why he is so maltreated. Behold the prediction of Isaias verified : *He was offered because it was his own will, and he opened not his mouth : he shall be led as a sheep to the slaughter.*[2] He neither speaks nor complains ; for he offered himself to the divine justice in order to make satisfaction and to die for us ; and therefore he permits himself to be led as a sheep to the slaughter, without opening his mouth.

III.

Behold him in chains, dragged from the garden, in the midst of a tumultuous crowd, and brought in haste before the high priest! And where are his disciples? What do they do? If they are unable to liberate him from the hands of enemies, they surely accompany him in order to defend his innocence before the judges, or at least to console him by their presence. But no, the

---

[1] "Comprehenderunt Jesum, et ligaverunt eum."—*John*, xviii. 12.
[2] "Oblatus est quia ipse voluit, et non aperuit os suum ; sicut ovis ad occisionem ducetur."—*Isa.* liii. 7.

Gospel says, *Then his disciples leaving him, all fled away.*[1] How great was the pain which Jesus Christ felt at seeing himself forsaken and abandoned by his beloved disciples. Alas! Jesus then saw all those who, after having been specially favored by him, would afterwards abandon him, and ungratefully turn their back upon him. Ah, my Lord, I have been one of these unhappy souls, who having received so many graces, lights and calls, have ungratefully forgotten and forsaken Thee. Accept me for the sake of Thy mercy, now that I return to Thee with a penitent and sorrowful heart, never again to leave Thee. O treasure of life, O love of my soul!

CHAPTER VII.

JESUS IS PRESENTED TO THE HIGH-PRIESTS, AND IS CONDEMNED BY THEM TO DEATH.

I.

But they holding Jesus, led him to Caiphas the high-priest, where the scribes and the ancients were assembled.[2] Bound as a malefactor, our Saviour enters Jerusalem, where he was received a few days before with so much honor and applause. He passes, during the night, through the streets, amid torches and lanterns ; and such were the noise and tumult that all the citizens were given to understand that some notorious malefactor was conducted in chains by the officers of justice. The people run to the windows, and ask, Who is the prisoner? They are told that he is Jesus of Nazareth, who has been proved

[1] "Tunc discipuli ejus, relínquentes eum, omnes fugerunt."— *Mark*, xiv. 50.

[2] "At illi, tenentes Jesum, duxerunt ad Caipham, principem sacerdotum, ubi Scribæ et Seniores convenerant."—*Matt.* xxvi. 57.

to be a seducer, an impostor, and worthy of death. But what must have been the sentiments of contempt and indignation which all felt when they saw Jesus Christ, who was hailed before as the Messiah, now imprisoned as an impostor, by order of the judges? Oh! how each person changed his veneration into hatred, and through shame of having saluted a malefactor as the Messiah, repented of having treated him with honor. Behold the Redeemer presented, as if in triumph, before Caiphas, who waited for his arrival, and who was filled with joy when he saw him alone and abandoned by his disciples. Behold, O my soul, thy sweet Lord, bound as a criminal, standing with downcast countenance, all meekness and humility, before the haughty pontiff. Behold that beautiful countenance, which, in the midst of so much contempt and so many injuries, has not lost its natural serenity and sweetness.

Ah, my Jesus, what shall I do, now that I see Thee surrounded, not by angels praising Thee, but by a vile rabble that hates and despises Thee? Will I continue to despise Thee as I have hitherto done? Ah, no; during the remainder of my life I wish to esteem and love Thee as Thou dost deserve, and I promise to love nothing but Thee. Thou shalt be my only love, my good, my all : *My God and my all.*[1]

II.

The impious high-priest interrogates Jesus regarding his disciples and doctrine, in order to find some grounds of condemnation against him. Jesus humbly answers : *I have spoken to the world. . . . Behold, they know what things I have said.*[2] I have not spoken in secret, I have spoken in public ; they who are present can bear wit-

---

[1] "Deus meus, et omnia !"

[2] "Ego palam locutus sum mundo; . . . ecce hi sciunt quæ dixerim ego."—*John,* xviii. 20.

ness to what I have said. He appeals to the testimony of his very enemies. But after an answer so just and meek, an insolent servant rushes forward through the crowd, and, as if to chastise him for his insolence to Caiphas, gives him a severe blow on the cheek, saying : *Is it thus thou answerest the high-priest ?*[1] And when he had said these things, one of the servants standing by gave Jesus a blow, saying, *Answerest thou the high-priest so ?* O God, how could an answer so humble and modest merit so gross an insult? The unworthy pontiff sees it, and instead of rebuking the guilty servant, remains silent, and by his silence approves of his conduct. On receiving the blow, Jesus, in order to show that he was not wanting in respect to the high-priest, said : *If I have spoken evil, give testimony of the evil : but if well, why strikest thou Me ?*[2]

Ah, my amiable Redeemer, Thou dost submit to all these affronts in order to atone for the insults that I have offered to the divine majesty by my sins. Ah, pardon me through the merit of the insults Thou hast suffered for my sake.

III.

They sought false witnesses against Jesus, that they might put him to death, and they found not.[3] They seek for false witnesses in order to condemn the Saviour, but find none; hence the high-priest endeavors again to discover in the words of Jesus grounds for declaring him guilty, and therefore says : *I adjure thee by the living God, that Thou tell us if Thou be the Christ the Son of God.*[4] When

---

[1] " Hæc autem cum dixisset, unus assistens ministrorum dedit alapam Jesu, dicens : Sic respondes Pontifici ?"—*John.* xviii. 22.

[2] " Si male locutus sum, testimonium perhibe de malo ; si autem bene, quid me cædis ?"—*Ibid.* 23.

[3] " Quærebant falsum testimonium contra Jesum, ut eum morti traderent ; et non invenerunt."—*Matt.* xxvi. 59.

[4] "Adjuro te per Deum vivum, ut dicas nobis si tu es Christus Filius Dei."—*Matt.* xxvi. 63.

asked in the name of God, he confessed the truth, saying, *I am. And you shall see the Son of Man sitting on the
right hand of the power of God, and coming with the clouds
of heaven.*[1] I am ; and you shall one day see me, not in
the lowliness in which I now appear, but seated as on a
throne of majesty, on the clouds of heaven, with power
to judge all men. At these words the high-priest, instead
of falling prostrate on his face to adore his God and his
judge, rends his garments and exclaims, What further
testimony do we require? Have you heard the blasphemy which he has spoken? *Then the high-priest rent
his garment, saying, He hath blasphemed, what further need
have we of witnesses? Behold now you have heard the blasphemy. What think you?*[2] All the other priests immediately answered that he certainly deserved death : *But
they answering said, He is guilty of death.*[3]

Ah, my Jesus, Thy eternal Father pronounced the
same sentence when Thou didst offer Thyself to atone
for our sins. He then said : My Son, since Thou dost
wish to make satisfaction for men, Thou art guilty of
death, and shalt die.

VI.

*Then did they spit in his face and buffet him, and others
struck his face with the palms of their hands, saying,
Prophesy unto us, O Christ, who is he that struck Thee.*[4] Then
they all begin to maltreat him, as a criminal already
condemned to death, and deserving of all kinds of re-

[1] "Ego sum : et videbitis Filium hominis sedentem a dextris virtutis Dei et venientem cum nubibus cœli."—*Mark.* xiv. 62.

[2] "Tunc Princeps sacerdotum scidit vestimenta sua, dicens : Blas-
phemavit ; quid adhuc egemus testibus? Ecce nunc audistis blasphemiam ; quid vobis videtur ?"—*Matt.* xxvi. 65.

[3] "At illi respondentes dixerunt : Reus est mortis."—*Ibid.* 66.

[4] "Tunc exspuerunt in faciem ejus, et colaphis eum ceciderunt ; alii
autem palmas in faciem ejus dederunt, dicentes : Prophetiza nobis,
Christe, quis est qui te percussit ?"—*Ibid.* 67.

proaches. Some spit in his face, others buffet him, and others strike him with their hands, and blindfolding him, *they*, says St. Mark, *began to spit on him, and cover his face.*[1] They mock him as a false prophet, saying, Since Thou art a prophet, guess who it is that has struck Thee. St. Jerome has written that the ignominies and cruelties which our Lord suffered on that night were so manifold that they shall not be all known till the day of judgment.

Then, my Jesus, on that night Thou didst not repose; no, Thou wast the object of the derision and cruelty of that ferocious rabble. O men, how can you behold a God so humbled, and continue to indulge in pride? How can you behold your Redeemer suffering such torments for your sake, and not love him? O God! how can they who believe, and reflect on the pains and ignominies which, according to the narration of the Evangelists, Jesus has suffered for our sake, live without burning with love for a God so benignant and so enamoured of us?

V.

The fall of Peter, who denied him, and even swore that he never knew him, added to the sufferings of Jesus. Go, my soul, go to that prison where my Lord is sorrowful, mocked, and abandoned; thank him, and console him by thy repentance, for thou also hast despised and derided him. Tell him that thou wouldst wish to die of sorrow, at the thought of having hitherto caused so much bitterness to the sweet heart of a God who has loved thee so tenderly. Tell him that now thou dost love him, and dost desire nothing else than to suffer and die for the love of him.

Ah, my Jesus, forget all the displeasure that I have given Thee, and look on me with that love with which

[1] " Et cœperunt . . . velare faciem ejus."—*Mark*, xiv. 65.

Thou didst look on Peter after he denied Thee ; after the look which Thou didst then cast upon him, he did not cease to bewail his sin until he ceased to live. O great Son of God, O infinite love, who dost suffer for the very men who hate and maltreat Thee, Thou art the glory of paradise; Thou wouldst have done great honor to men by merely permitting them to kiss Thy feet. But, O God ! what has reduced Thee to such a degree of ignominy as to become the sport of the vilest rabble ? Tell me, O my Jesus, what I can do in order to compensate the honor which Thy enemies take from Thee by their insults and reproaches. I hear Thee answer: Bear insults for my sake, as I have borne them for the love of thee. Yes, my Redeemer, I wish to obey Thee. My Jesus, despised for the love of me, I am willing, and desire to be despised for Thee as much as Thou pleasest.

CHAPTER VIII.

JESUS IS BROUGHT BEFORE PILATE, AFTERWARDS BEFORE HEROD; BARABBAS IS PREFERRED TO HIM.

I.

And when the morning was come, the chief priests and the ancients of the people took counsel against Jesus, that they might put Him to death. And they brought Him bound, and delivered Him to Pontius Pilate, the governor.[1] In the morning the chief priests again declared him deserving of death, and then brought him before Pilate, in order to have him condemned to the death of the cross. After

[1] " Mane autem facto, consilium inierunt . . . adversus Jesum, ut eum morti traderent; et vinctum adduxerunt eum et tradiderunt Pontio Pilato præsidi."—*Matt.* xxvii. 1.

having asked many questions as well of the Jews as of our Redeemer, Pilate felt convinced that Jesus was innocent, and that the accusations were all calumnies. Hence he went out and told the Jews that he found no grounds for condemnation against him. *He went out again to the Jews, and said to them, I find no fault in Him.*[1] But afterwards, seeing that the Jews were so intent on the death of Jesus, and hearing that he was from Galilee, Pilate, in order to get rid of his embarrassment, *sent Him away to Herod.*[2]

II.

Herod was delighted to see Jesus Christ in his court; he hoped that our Lord would perform some miracles in his presence. Hence he proposed many questions to him, but Jesus remained silent, and gave no answer, thus reproving the vain curiosity of the haughty ruler. *And he questioned Him in many words. But He answered him nothing.*[3] Miserable the soul to whom the Lord speaks no longer !

My Jesus, this I have deserved, because I have been deaf to Thy merciful inspirations, by which Thou hast so often called me to Thy love. I have deserved that Thou shouldst speak to me no longer, and that Thou shouldst abandon me ; but no, my dear Redeemer, have pity on me and speak to me. *Speak, Lord, for Thy servant heareth.*[4] Tell me what Thou willest from me; I wish to obey Thee, and to please Thee in all things.

[1] " Exivit ad Judæos, et dicit eis: Ego nullam invenio in eo causam."—*John*, xviii. 38.
[2] " Remisit eum ad Herodem, qui et ipse Jerosolymis erat illis diebus."—*Luke*, xxiii. 7.
[3] "Interrogabat autem eum multis sermonibus; at ipse nihil illi respondebat."—*Ibid.* 9.
[4] " Loquere, Domine, quia audit servus tuus."—1 *Reg.* iii. 10.

III.

But Herod felt indignant at the silence of Jesus; regarding him as a fool, he ordered him to be clothed, through derision, with a white garment, and despised him with all his court ; after having thus treated him with contempt and mockery, he sent him back to Pilate. *And Herod with his army, set Him at nought; and mocked Him, putting on Him a white garment, and sent Him back to Pilate.*[1]   Behold how Jesus, clothed with that mock garment, is led through the streets of Jerusalem.

O my despised Saviour, Thou wouldst submit even to the ignominy of being treated as a fool ! O Christians, behold how the world treats the Eternal Wisdom ! Happy the man who delights in being treated by the world as a fool, and wishes to know nothing but Jesus crucified, loving suffering and insults, and saying, with St. Paul, *For I judge not myself to know anything among you but Jesus Christ, and Him crucified.*[1]

IV.

The Jews had a right to demand of the Roman governor the liberation of a criminal at the Paschal solemnity. Hence Pilate proposed to them Jesus and Barabbas, saying, *Whom will you that I release to you, Barabbas or Jesus?*[1]   He felt certain that the people would prefer Jesus to Barabbas, who was a wicked man, a homicide, a public robber, and an object of universal abhorrence. But the people, instigated by the heads of the synagogue, instantly and without deliberation demanded Barabbas:

---

[1] "Sprevit autem illum Herodes cum exercitu suo; et illusit indutum veste alba, et remisit ad Pilatum."—*Luke,* xxiii. 11.

[1] "Non enim judicavi me scire aliquid inter vos, nisi Jesum Christum, et hunc crucifixum."—*1 Cor.* ii. 2.

[1] "Quem vultis dimittam vobis, Barabbam an Jesum?"—*Matt.* xxvii. 17.

But they said Barabbas.[1] Being astonished and at the same time indignant at seeing so great a miscreant preferred to an innocent mán, Pilate said, *What shall I then do with Jesus? They say all, Let Him be crucified.*[2] Pilate then said, *What evil hath he done? But they cried out the more, saying, Let Him be crucified.*[3]

My Lord, this I have done when I have committed sin. I had then the choice of loving Thee or a vile pleasure; and I have answered, I wish for the pleasure, and care not to lose God. This I then said, O my Lord, but I now say that I prefer Thy grace before all the pleasures and riches of the world. O infinite good, O my Jesus! I love Thee above every other good; I wish for Thee and for nothing else.

V.

As Jesus and Barabbas were proposed to the people, so it was proposed to the Eternal Father to save his Son or sinful man. The Eternal Father answered, Let my Son die, and let sinful man be saved. This the Apostle has declared: *He that spared not even His own Son, but delivered Him up for us all.*[4] The Father would not spare his own Son, but consigned him to death for us all. Yes, said our Saviour, God has so loved the world that for its salvation he delivered up his only-begotten Son to torments and death. *God so loved the world as to give His only-begotten Son.*[5] Hence, the Holy Church exclaims, "O wonderful condescension of Thy mercy in

---

[1] "At illi dixerunt: Barabbam."—*Matt.* xxvii. 21.

[2] "Quid igitur faciam de Jesu? Dicunt omnes: Crucifigatur!"—*Ibid.* 22.

[3] "Quid enim mali fecit? At illi magis clamabant, dicentes: Crucifigatur!"—*Ibid.* 23.

[4] "Qui etiam proprio Filio suo non pepercit, sed pro nobis omnibus tradidit illum."—*Rom.* viii. 32.

[5] "Sic Deus dilexit mundum, ut Filium suum unigenitum daret."—*John,* iii. 16.

our regard! O inestimable love of charity! To redeem a slave Thou hast delivered up Thy Son!"[1] O admirable condescension of Thy mercy, O my God! O inconceivable tenderness of love! To ransom a slave, Thou hast condemned Thy Son! O holy faith! How is it possible for him who believes this not to be all fire in loving a God who loves men so tenderly? Oh that we had always before our eyes this infinite charity of God!

CHAPTER IX.

JESUS IS SCOURGED AT THE PILLAR.

I.

Then, therefore, Pilate took Jesus and scourged Him.[2] Seeing that the two means that he had taken of saving the innocent Jesus from the Jews—namely, sending him to Herod, and proposing him along with Barabbas—had failed, he tried another; he ordered the Saviour to be scourged, intending afterwards to dismiss him. *You have*, he said, *presented unto me this man . . . and behold, I, having examined Him before you, find no cause in this man. . . . No, nor Herod, neither. . . . I will chastise Him, therefore, and release Him.*[3] You have accused this man as a criminal before me; but I find no guilt in him, neither has Herod found any. However, to satisfy you, I will chastise him and will afterwards release him. O God!

---

[1] " O mira circa nos tuæ pietatis dignatio ! o inæstimabilis dilectio charitatis ! ut servum redimeres, Filium tradidisti."—*In Sabb. S.*

[2] " Tunc ergo apprehendit Pilatus Jesum, et flagellavit."—*John*, xix. 1.

[3] "Obtulistis mihi hunc hominem. . . ; et ecce ego, coram vobis interrogans, nullam causam inveni. . . ; sed neque Herodes. . . ; emendatum ergo illum dimittam."—*Luke*, xxiii. 14, 15.

what an injustice! He declares Jesus Christ perfectly innocent: I find no cause in this man; and afterwards condemns him to be chastised.

O my Jesus, Thou art innocent, but I am guilty ; and since Thou dost wish to make satisfaction to the divine justice for my sins, it is not unjust; no, it is just that Thou be punished.

II.

What, O Pilate, is the chastisement to which thou dost condemn this innocent ? Dost thou condemn him to be scourged ? Dost thou sentence an innocent man to a punishment so cruel and so shameful ? Yes, he commanded him to be scourged. *Then therefore Pilate took Jesus and scourged Him.*[1] Behold, O my soul, how, after this most iniquitous order, the officers of justice seize with fury the meek Lamb, conduct him amid shouts and yells of triumph to the hall, and bind him to the pillar. And what does Jesus do? With humble submission he accepts this painful and ignominious punishment in satisfaction for our sins. Behold how they take the lash in their hands, and when the signal is given, raise their arms, and begin to scourge every part of his sacred body. O executioners, you have erred ; this man is not guilty, it is I that have deserved these scourges.

III.

The virginal body of Jesus first appears all livid, and then begins to send forth blood from every member. Alas ! the executioners, after having lacerated the whole body, continue without mercy to lash the wounds already inflicted, and to add pain to pain. *They have added to the*

---

[1] " Tunc ergo apprehendit Pilatus Jesum, et flagellavit."—*John,* xix. 1.

grief of My wounds.' O my soul, wilt thou be one of those who look with indifference on thy God torn with scourges? Reflect on his sufferings, but still more on the love with which thy sweet Lord submits to so excruciating a torture for thy sake. In his scourging, Jesus certainly thought of thee. O God! had he borne but a single stripe for thy sake, thou shouldst burn with love for him, and say, A God has suffered to be struck for my sake. But for the atonement of thy sins he has, as Isaias foretold, permitted all his flesh to be mangled. *He was wounded for our iniquities, He was bruised for our sins.*' Alas! says the same Prophet, the most beautiful of men no longer appears beautiful. *There is no beauty in Him, nor comeliness; and we have seen him, and there was no sightliness.*' The scourges have so deformed him that he can be no longer recognized : *His look was, as it were, hidden and despised, whereupon we esteemed Him not.*' He is reduced to such a degree of misery that he appears to be a leper covered with wounds from head to foot ; such the manner in which God wished to see him maltreated and humbled : *And we have thought Him, as it were, a leper, and as one struck by God and afflicted.*' And why? Because this loving Redeemer wished to suffer the pains that were due to us. *Surely He hath borne our infirmities, and carried our sorrows.*'

[1] " Et super dolorem vulnerum meorum addiderunt."—*Ps.* lxviii. 27.

[2] " Ipse autem vulneratus est propter iniquitates nostras, attritus est propter scelera nostra."—*Isa.* liii. 5.

[3] " Non est ei species neque decor ; et vidimus eum, et non erat aspectus."—*Isa.* liii. 2.

[4] " Et quasi absconditus vultus ejus et despectus : unde nec reputavimus eum."—*Ibid.* 3.

[5] " Et nos putavimus eum quasi leprosum, et percussum a Deo, et humiliatum."—*Ibid.* 4.

[6] " Vere languores nostros ipse tulit, et dolores nostros ipse portavit."—*Ibid.* 4.

Blessed forever be Thy mercy, O my Jesus, who didst voluntarily submit to torments in order to deliver me from eternal torments. Oh! miserable and unhappy the soul that loves not Thee, O God of love!

IV.

But what does our amiable Saviour do while the executioners scourge him so cruelly? He neither speaks, nor complains, nor sighs; but patiently offers all to God to appease his anger against us. *Like a lamb without voice before his shearer, so openeth He not His mouth.*[1]

Ah, my Jesus, innocent Lamb, these barbarians shear Thee not of wool, but of Thy skin and flesh. But behold the baptism of blood which Thou didst so ardently desire when Thou didst say, *I have a baptism wherewith I am to be baptized; and how am I straightened until it be accomplished?*[2] Go, my soul, and wash thyself in the precious blood with which that fortunate floor is bathed. And, O my sweet Saviour, how can I any longer doubt of Thy love, when I see Thee wounded and mangled for my sake? I know that every wound in Thy body is a most certain testimony of the affection Thou hast for me. I hear every wound demanding my love. A single drop of Thy blood was sufficient to save me; but Thou dost wish to give me the entire of it without reserve, that I might give myself to Thee entirely and without reserve. Yes, my Jesus, I give my whole being to Thee without any reserve; assist me and help me to be faithful to Thee.

---

[1] "Sicut agnus coram tondente se sine voce, sic non aperuit os suum."—*Acts*, viii. 32.

[2] "Baptismo autem habeo baptizari; et quomodo coarctor usque-dum perficiatur!"—*Luke*, xii. 50.

CHAPTER X.

JESUS IS CROWNED WITH THORNS AND TREATED AS A MOCK KING.

I.

Then the soldiers of the governor taking Jesus into the hall, gathered together unto Him the whole band, and stripping Him, they put a scarlet cloak about Him : and platting a crown of thorns, they put it on His head, and a reed in His right hand.[1] Let us now consider the other torments which the soldiers inflicted on our tortured Lord. The entire band is assembled, they put on his shoulders a scarlet cloak (which was an old mantle worn by soldiers over their armor), in imitation of the purple, as the emblem of royalty : they then placed in his hand a reed for a sceptre, and for a crown they put on a wreath of thorns which surrounded the entire head. And because by the pressure of the hands the thorns did not enter sufficiently into his sacred head, which was already wounded by the scourges, they took a reed, and spitting in his face, beat with all their might the cruel crown into the head of Jesus. *And spitting on Him, they took the reed and struck His head.*[2]

O thorns! O ungrateful creatures! what is it you do ? Do you thus torment your Creator? But why reprove

---

[1] "Tunc milites Præsidis, suscipientes Jesum in prætorium, congregaverunt ad eum universum cohortem: et exuentes eum chlamydem coccineam circumdederunt ei ; et plectentes coronam de spinis, posuerunt super caput ejus, et arundinem in dextera ejus."—*Matt.* xxvii. 27.

[2] "Et exspuentes in eum, acceperunt arundinem, et percutiebant caput ejus."—*Matt.* xxvii. 30.

the thorns? O sinful thoughts of men! it was you that
pierced the head of the Redeemer. Yes, my Jesus, by
our criminal consent to sin we have formed Thy crown
of thorns. I now detest this compliance with sin, and
abhor it more than death or any other evil. To you, O
thorns, consecrated with the blood of the Son of God, I
again turn with an humble heart ; ah, pierce this soul of
mine, make it always sorrowful for having offended so
good a God. And since Thou, O Jesus my love, hast
suffered so much for me, detach me from creatures and
from myself, so that I may be able to say with truth
that I am no longer mine, that I belong to Thee alone,
and am all Thine.

II.

O my afflicted Saviour! O King of the world! to what
do I see Thee reduced? I behold Thee a king of mockery and sorrow! In a word, I see Thee the laughing-
stock of all Jerusalem! From the wounded head of our
Lord, streams of blood flow down his face and breast.
I am filled with astonishment, O my Jesus! at the
cruelty of Thy enemies, who are not content with having,
as it were, excoriated Thy flesh from head to foot, but
still continue to torment Thee with fresh cruelties and
insults : but I admire still more Thy meekness and Thy
love in suffering and accepting all with so much patience
for the love of us: *Who when He was reviled, did not revile:
when He suffered, He threatened not ; but delivered Himself to
him that judged Him unjustly.*[1] The prediction of Jeremias,
that our Saviour would be satiated with sorrows and
ignominies, is verified. *He shall give His cheek to him that
striketh Him, He shall be filled with reproaches.*[2]

[1] "Qui, cum malediceretur, non maledicebat ; cum pateretur, non
comminabatur ; tradebat autem judicanti se injuste."—1 *Pet.* ii. 23.
[2] "Dabit percutienti se maxillam, saturabitur opprobriis."—*Lam.*
iii. 30.

13

III.

But, O soldiers, are you not satisfied? *And bowing the knee before Him, they mocked Him, saying, Hail, king of the Jews.*[1] St. John writes: *And they came to Him, and said, Hail king of the Jews ; and they gave Him blows.*[2] After having thus tormented him, and clothed him as a mock king, they kneel before him in derision, and say, We salute thee, O king of the Jews. Then, rising up, they laugh at him, mock him, and buffet him. O God! the sacred head of Jesus is all wounded by the punctures of the thorns, so that every motion produced the pangs of death. Thus every buffet and blow was to him a most cruel torment. Go, my soul, and do thou at least confess the Saviour to be what he really is, the Lord of the universe ; and thank and love him as the King of sorrow and of love, since he suffers in order to be loved by Thee.

CHAPTER XI.

PILATE SHOWS JESUS TO THE PEOPLE, SAYING, "BEHOLD THE MAN."

I.

Pilate therefore went forth again, and saith to them, . . . Behold the man.[3] When Jesus was brought before Pilate after the scourging and crowning with thorns, Pilate looked at him, and seeing him so mangled and deformed, felt persuaded that he would move the people to com-

[1] "Et genu flexo ante eum, illudebant ei, dicentes: Ave. Rex Judæorum!"—*Matt.* xxvii. 29.
[2] "Et dabant ei alapas."—*John.* xix. 3.
[3] "Exivit iterum Pilatus foras . . ., et dicit eis : Ecce Homo."—*John.* xix. 4, 5.

passion by merely exposing him to their view. Hence
he went forth to the balcony, bringing with him our
afflicted Saviour, and said to the people, *Behold the man;*
as if he said, O Jews, be content with what this innocent man has already suffered. *Behold the man ;* behold
the man whom you suspected of wishing to become your
king: behold him, see the miserable condition to which
he is reduced. What fear can you now have of him,
when it is impossible for him to recover from his
wounds ? Let him go and die in his own house; he has
but a short time to live.

II.

*Jesus therefore came forth, bearing the crown of thorns,
and the purple garment.*[1] Behold, O my soul, on that balcony, Thy Lord bound and dragged by a soldier; behold him half naked, covered with wounds and blood,
his flesh all torn; behold him clothed with a rag of
purple which only excites derision, and carrying that
barbarous crown which continues to torment him. Behold the state to which thy pastor is reduced, in order
to find thee, his lost sheep.

Ah, my Jesus, in how many characters do men exhibit
Thee, but all in order to add to Thy pain and ignominy !
Ah, my sweet Redeemer, Thou dost excite the compassion of the beasts of the forest, and still Thou dost not
find mercy. Behold the answer of the people : *When
the chief priests therefore and the servants had seen Him,
they cried out, saying, Crucify Him; crucify Him.*[1] But
what shall they say on the day of judgment, when they
shall see him gloriously seated as a judge on a throne
of light ? But, alas, my Jesus, I too once said: *Crucify*

---

[1] " Exivit ergo Jesus portans coronam spineam et purpureum vestimentum."—*John*, xix. 5.

[1] "Cum ergo vidissent eum Pontifices et ministri, clamabant
dicentes: Crucifige, crucifige eum."—*Ibid.* 6.

him, crucify him, when I offended Thee by my sins. But, O God of my soul, I now am sorry for them above all things, and I love Thee above every good. Pardon me through the merits of Thy Passion, and grant that on the last day I may see Thee appeased, and not enraged against me. `

III.

Pilate showed Jesus to the Jews, saying, *Behold the man,* and, at the same time, the Eternal Father from heaven invited us to look at Jesus Christ in the miserable state to which he was reduced, and said, *Behold the man.* O men, this man whom you see tormented and despised is my beloved Son, who, for the love of you, and to atone for your sins, submits to such torments; look at him, thank him, and love him.

My God and my Father, Thou dost tell me to look at this Thy Son; but I pray Thee to look at him for me; look at him, and for the love of this Son have mercy on me.

IV.

Seeing that Pilate, in spite of all their clamor, sought to save Jesus,[1] the Jews, by exclaiming that, were he to release him, he would declare himself the enemy of Cæsar, endeavored to force him to condemn the Saviour. *The Jews cried out, saying, If thou release that man, thou art not Cæsar's friend; for whosoever maketh himself a king speaketh against Cæsar.*[2] Unfortunately for them, their efforts were successful. Pilate is afraid of losing the friendship of Cæsar, and therefore he brings Jesus Christ into the hall, and sits in judgment in order to pass sentence of condemnation upon him. *When Pilate had heard these words, he brought Jesus forth, and sat*

---

[1] "Quærebat Pilatus dimittere eum."—*John,* xix. 12.

[2] "Judæi autem clamabant dicentes: Si hunc dimittis non es amicus Cæsaris; omnis enim qui se regem facit, contradicit Cæsari."—*Ibid.*

down in the judgment-seat.[1]   But stung with remorse of conscience at the thought of condemning an innocent man, he again turns to the Jews, and says to them: *Behold your king.*[2]   Shall I condemn your king ?   *But they cried out, Away with Him, away with Him, crucify Him.*[3]   The Jews exclaim with greater fury than before, What king ?   What king ?   Ah, Pilate, you always keep him before our eyes.   Away with him, away with him; take him out of sight, and condemn him to die on a cross.

Ah, my Lord, incarnate Word, Thou art come from heaven on earth to converse with men, and to save them; but they cannot bear to see Thee any longer among them; they labor with all their might to put Thee to death, and to take Thee out of sight.

V.

Pilate still resists, and says: *Shall I crucify your king ?*[4]   *The chief priests answered, We have no king but Cæsar.*[5]   Ah, my adorable Jesus, they are unwilling to acknowledge Thee for their Lord, and say that they have no other king than Cæsar.   I acknowledge Thee for my king and my God, and I protest that I wish for no other king in my heart than Thee, my Redeemer.   Unhappy me !   I have once submitted to the domination of my passions, and have banished Thee, my divine king, from my soul.   I now wish that Thou alone reign in my heart ; that Thou command, and that it obey.   I will say to Thee, with St. Teresa: O lover, who lovest me more than I am able to conceive, grant that my soul may serve

---

[1] " Pilatus autem, cum audisset hos sermones, adduxit foras Jesum, et sedit pro tribunali."—*John,* xix. 13.

[2] " Dicit Judæis : Ecce Rex vester."—*Ibid.* 14.

[3] " Illi autem clamabant: Tolle, tolle, crucifige eum."—*Ibid.* 15.

[4] " Regem vestrum crucifigam ?"—*Ibid.* 15.

[5] " Responderunt Pontifices : Non habemus regem, nisi Cæsarem!" *Ibid.* xix. 15.

Thee more in conformity with Thy pleasure than its own. May this self die, and may another live in me. May he live and give me life. May he reign, and may I be his slave. May my soul wish for no other liberty; My Jesus, Thou art my only king, my only good, my only love.

CHAPTER XII.

JESUS IS CONDEMNED BY PILATE.

I.

Then, therefore, he delivered Him to them to be crucified.[1] Behold how Pilate, after having so often declared the innocence of Jesus, declares it again by washing his hands, and protesting that he is innocent of the blood of that just man, and that, should he die, the Jews must render an account of his death. *Pilate . . . taking water, washed his hands before the people, saying, I am innocent of the blood of this just man : look you to it.*[2] He then pronounces the sentence, and condemns Jesus to death. O injustice no longer known in the world ! A judge condemns the accused, and at the same time declares him innocent ! St. Luke says that Pilate delivered Jesus into the hands of the Jews, that they might treat him as they pleased. *Jesus was delivered up to their will.*[3] This is what really happens when an innocent man is condemned. He is given over to the hands of his enemies, that they may take away his life by the death which is most pleasing to them. Unhappy Jews ! you then said, *His blood be upon*

[1] "Tunc ergo tradidit eis illum, ut crucifigeretur."—*John*, xix. 16.
[2] "Accepta aqua, lavit manus coram populo, dicens: Innocens ego sum a sanguine justi hujus; vos videritis."—*Matt.* xxvii. 24.
[3] "Jesum vero tradidit voluntati eorum."—*Luke*, xxiii. 25.

us and upon our children.[1] You have prayed for the chastisement; it has already come. Your nation bears, and shall bear to the end of the world, the punishment due to the shedding of that innocent blood.

II.

Behold the unjust sentence of death is read in the presence of our condemned Lord. He listens to it, and, with entire resignation to the just decree of his Eternal Father, who condemns him to the cross, he humbly accepts it, not for the crimes falsely imputed to him by the Jews, but in atonement for our real sins, for which he offered to make satisfaction by his death. Pilate says on earth, Let Jesus die. And the Eternal Father from heaven confirms the sentence, saying, Let my Son die. The Son himself answers, Here I am; I obey; I accept death, and the death of the cross. *He humbled Himself, becoming obedient unto death, even the death of the cross.*[2]

My beloved Redeemer, Thou dost accept the death due to me, and by Thy death dost obtain life for me. I thank Thee for it, O my love, and I hope to go one day to praise Thy mercies forever in heaven : *The mercies of the Lord I will sing forever.*[3] But since Thou, an innocent, dost accept the death of the cross, I, a sinner, cheerfully accept the death Thou dost appoint for me, and I accept it with all the pains that shall accompany it; and from this moment I offer it to Thy Eternal Father, in union with Thy holy death. Thou hast died for the love of me; I wish to die for the love of Thee. Ah, through the merits of Thy bitter death, grant me, O my Jesus, the happy lot of dying in Thy grace, and burning with Thy holy love.

[1] " Sanguis ejus super nos, et super filios nostros."—*Matt.* xxvii. 25.

[2] " Humiliavit semetipsum, factus obediens usque ad mortem, mortem autem crucis."—*Phil.* ii. 8.

[3] " Misericordias Domini in æternum cantabo."—*Ps.* lxxxviii. 2.

CHAPTER XIII.

JESUS CARRIES THE CROSS TO CALVARY.

I.

As soon as the sentence is proclaimed, the unhappy people raise a shout of exultation, and say: Rejoice, rejoice; Jesus is already condemned. Make haste, lose no time; prepare the cross, and put him to death before to-morrow. which will be the Paschal solemnity. They instantly seize him; tear off the scarlet cloak, and put on his own clothes, that (says St. Ambrose) he might be recognized by the people as the impostor (as they called him), whom they had a few days before hailed as the Messiah. *They took off the cloak from Him, and put on His own garments, and led Him away to crucify Him.*[1] They then take two large beams, make a cross, and insolently command him to carry it on his shoulders to the place of his execution. O God! what barbarity! to put so heavy a burden on a man who has been so tortured and exhausted of strength.

II.

Jesus lovingly embraces the cross. *And bearing His own cross, He went forth to that place which is called Calvary.*[2] Behold the officers of justice set out along with the criminals, and among these goes the Saviour loaded with the very altar on which he is to sacrifice his life. A devout author justly remarks that the Passion of Jesus Christ was, in all its circumstances, an object of aston-

[1] "Exuerunt eum chlamyde, et induerunt eum vestimentis ejus, et duxerunt eum ut crucifigerent."—*Matt.* xxvii. 31.

[2] "Et bajulans sibi crucem, exivit in eum. qui dicitur Calvariæ, locum."—*John*, xix. 17.

ishment and an excess, as it was called by Moses and
Elias on Mount Thabor.[1] Who would have ever imagined that the sight of Jesus covered with wounds
should only serve to increase the rage of the Jews and
their desire to see him crucified? What tyrant has ever
made a criminal carry his own gibbet on his shoulders
after he had been consumed by torments? It fills one
with horror to think on the accumulation of cruelties,
insults, and derisions which his enemies made Jesus
suffer in less than half a day, from his capture till his
death. The fetters, the buffets, the spittle, the mockery, the scourges, the thorns, the nails, the agony and
death, succeed one after another without interruption.
In a word, the Jews and Gentiles, the priests and the
people, all united to make Jesus Christ (as Isaias had
foretold) a man overwhelmed with insults and sorrows.
The judge defends the innocence of Jesus, but the defence served only to add to the pain and ignominies of
the Redeemer ; for had Pilate at once condemned him
to death, Jesus would not see Barabbas preferred before
him, he would not have been treated as a fool, he would
not have been so cruelly scourged and crowned with
thorns.

III.

But let us return to the consideration of the astonishing
spectacle of the Son of God going to die for the very
men who conduct him to death. Behold the prediction
of Jeremias verified : *And I was as a meek lamb that is
carried to be a victim.*[2] Behold how they lead the innocent Saviour as a lamb to the slaughter. O ungrateful
city, dost thou thus banish from thee thy Redeemer with

---

[1] " Et dicebant excessum ejus, quem completurus erat in Jerusalem."
—*Luke*, ix. 31.

[2] " Ego quasi agnus mansuetus qui portatur ad victimam."—*Jer.*
xi. 19.

so much contempt, after he had conferred so many favors upon thee? O God, such too is the ingratitude of the Christian, who, after being favored with many divine gifts, banishes Jesus from his soul by sin.

IV.

The appearance of Jesus in the journey to Calvary was so pitiable that the women followed him weeping and lamenting over his sufferings. *And there followed Him a great multitude of people and of women who bewailed and lamented Him.*[1] But the Redeemer turning to them, said, Weep not over me, but over your children: *For if in the green wood they do these things, what shall be done in the dry?*[2] By these words he wished to give us to understand the great punishment which our sins deserve: for if he who was innocent and the Son of God, merely because he had offered to make satisfaction for our transgressions, was treated in this manner, how shall men be treated for their own sins?

V.

Look at him, O my soul: see him moving along with his flesh all torn, carrying a crown of thorns on his head and a heavy cross on his shoulders, surrounded by enemies who load him with insults and maledictions. O God! his sacred body is all mangled, so that at every step the pain of his wounds is renewed. The cross torments him before he is fastened to it, for it presses on his wounded shoulders, and cruelly beats into his head the thorns of that barbarous crown. Alas, how great and manifold his pain at every step! But Jesus leaves not the cross; no, he does not leave it, because through

---

[1] " Sequebatur autem illum multa turba populi et mulierum, quæ plangebant et lamentabantur eum."—*Luke,* xxiii. 27.

[2] " Si in viridi ligno hæc faciunt, in arido quid fiet ?"—*Ibid.* 31.

it he wishes, as Isaias foretold, to reign in the hearts of men: *And the government is on His shoulders.*[1]

Ah, my Jesus, with what sentiments of love for me didst Thou then go to Calvary, where Thou wast to consummate the great sacrifice of Thy life! My soul, do thou also embrace thy cross for the love of Jesus, who suffers so much for thy sake. See how he goes before with his cross, and invites thee to follow him with thine. *If any man will come after Me, let him take up his cross and follow Me.*[2] My Jesus, I do not wish to leave Thee; I wish to follow Thee till death; but, through the merits of this painful journey, give me strength to carry with patience the crosses which Thou dost send me. Ah, Thou hast rendered sorrows and insults amiable by embracing them with so much love for our sake.

VI.

They found a man of Cyrene, named Simon, him they forced to take up his cross.[3] *And they laid the cross on him to carry after Jesus.*[4] Was it through compassion that they unburdened Jesus of the cross, and placed it on the Cyrenian? No, it was through wickedness and hatred. Seeing that our Lord almost breathed forth his soul at every step, they began to fear that he would not reach Calvary alive; they wished not only that he should die, but also that he should die on the cross, that his memory might be forever infamous: for to die on a cross was the same as to be the object of universal malediction : *For he is accursed that hangeth on a tree.*[5] Hence, in seeking the

---

[1] " Et factus est principatus super humerum ejus."—*Isa.* ix. 6.

[2] "Si quis vult post me venire, . . . tollat crucem suam, et sequatur me."—*Matt.* xvi. 24.

[3] "Invenerunt hominem Cyrenæum, nomine Simonem; hunc angariaverunt ut tolleret crucem ejus."—*Matt.* xxvii. 32.

[4] " Et imposuerunt illi crucem portare post Jesum."—*Luke,* xxiii. 26.

[5] "Maledictus omnis qui pendet in ligno."—*Gal.* iii. 13.

death of Jesus, they not only called on Pilate to put him to death, but always demanded his crucifixion: "Let him be crucified, crucify him, crucify him," that his name might be so infamous on earth, that it would be no longer mentioned : *Let us cut him off from the land of the living, and let his name be remembered no more.*[1] Hence they took the cross off his shoulders that he might reach Calvary alive ; thus they gained their object, and saw him dying the shameful death of the cross. Ah, my despised Jesus, Thou art my hope and all my love.

CHAPTER XIV.

JESUS IS CRUCIFIED.

I.

As soon as Jesus arrived on Calvary, oppressed with pain and fatigue, they gave him to drink wine mixed with gall, which was ordinarily given to persons con-demned to the death of the cross, in order to diminish their sensibility to pain. But because Jesus wished to die without comfort, he tasted, but would not drink it. *And they gave him wine to drink mingled with gall. And when he had tasted, he would not drink.*[2] The people there-fore formed a circle round Jesus; the soldiers took off his garments, which, because they were fastened to his wounded and mangled body, took with them pieces of flesh. They then threw him on the cross. Jesus stretched out his sacred hands, offered to the Eternal Father the

[1] " Eradamus eum de terra viventium, et nomen ejus non memore-tur amplius."—*Jer.* xi. 19.
[2] " Et dederunt ei vinum bibere cum felle mixtum ; et cum gustasset, noluit bibere."—*Matt.* xxvii. 34.

great sacrifice of himself, and prayed him to accept it for our salvation.

II.

Behold they took the nails and hammers, and piercing the hands and feet of the Saviour, they fastened him to the cross. The noise of the hammers resounded through the mountains, and was heard by Mary, who followed her Son, and had already arrived at the place of execution. O sacred hands, which by your touch have healed so many invalids, why are you now pierced on this cross? O sacred feet, so often wearied in seeking after lost sheep, why are you now transfixed with nails? Why do you suffer so intense a pain? When a nerve is punctured, the pain is so acute that it causes the swoons and spasms of death. How great, then, must have been the pain which Jesus suffered when his hands and feet— parts of the body which are full of bones and nerves— were pierced with the nails?

O my sweet Saviour, how dearly has my salvation, and Thy desire of gaining the love of me, a miserable worm, cost Thee! And I have so often ungratefully refused Thee my love, and have turned my back upon Thee.

III.

Behold the cross is raised along with Jesus Christ who is fastened to it, and is let fall with violence into the hole prepared for it. It is then made fast in its place, and Jesus nailed, to it, hangs between two thieves, there to leave his life. *They crucified him, and with him two others, one on each side, and Jesus in the midst.*[1] This Isaias had foretold: *He was reputed with the wicked.*[2] To the cross was affixed a paper, on which was written: *Jesus of*

[1] "Crucifixerunt eum, et cum eo alios duos, hinc et hinc, medium autem Jesum."— *John*, xix. 18.

[2] "Et cum sceleratis reputatus est."—*Isa.* liii. 12.

Nazareth, King of the Jews. The priests wanted Pilate to change the title, but he refused. God wished that all should know that the Jews put to death their true King and Messiah, whom they themselves had so long expected and sighed for.

IV.

Jesus on the cross! Behold the proof of the love of a God. Behold the last appearance of the incarnate Word on earth. The first was in a stable : the last is on a cross : both display his love and infinite charity for men. Contemplating one day the love of Jesus in dying for us, St. Francis of Paul, wrapt in ecstasy and raised in the air, exclaimed three times, in a loud voice : "O God, charity ! O God, charity ! O God, charity !" By these exclamations the Lord wished, through the saint, to teach us that we shall never be able to comprehend the infinite love which this God has shown us in condescending to suffer such torments, and to die for our salvation. My soul, approach with an humbled and penitent heart that cross; kiss the altar on which thy loving Lord dies. Place thyself under his feet, that his divine blood may flow upon thee, and say to the Eternal Father (but in a sense different from that which the Jews intended), *His blood be upon us.*[1] O Lord, may this blood descend on us, and wash us from our sins : this blood does not demand vengeance from Thee, as did the blood of Abel, but implores of Thee for us mercy and pardon. This Thy Apostle encourages us to hope for, saying, *You are come to Jesus, the Mediator of the New Testament, and to the sprinkling of blood, which speaketh better than that of Abel.*[2]

---

[1] "Sanguis ejus super nos."—*Matt.* xxvii. 25.

[2] "Accessistis ad . . . Mediatorem Jesum, et sanguinis aspersionem, melius loquentem, quam Abel."—*Heb.* xii. 24.

V.

O God, how great the torture of our dying Saviour on the cross ! Every member suffers pains ; one member cannot assist another, for the hands and feet are fastened with nails. Alas ! in every moment he suffers the pangs of death, so that it may be said that during the three hours of his agony, Jesus suffered as many deaths as he was moments on the cross. On that bed of pain, our afflicted Lord had not a moment of comfort or repose, He had at one time to rest on his hands, and at another on his feet ; but wheresoever he rested, his sufferings were increased. In a word, that sacred body was suspended on his very wounds, so that the pierced hands and feet had to sustain the weight of the entire body.

O my dear Redeemer, if I look at Thy body I see nothing but wounds and blood, if I look at Thy heart ; I behold it overwhelmed with affliction and desolation. I read on this cross that Thou art king ; but what badges of royalty dost Thou wear ? I see no other throne than a gibbet of infamy ; I see no other purple than Thy flesh covered with blood and wounds ; no other crown than this wreath of thorns which continues to torture Thee. Ah, all exhibit Thee as a king, not of majesty, but of love : the cross, the blood, the nails, the crown, are all so many proofs of love.

VI.

Hence from the cross Jesus seeks not so much our compassion as our love. And if he seeks pity, he asks it only that it may induce us to love him. He merits our love on account of his own goodness ; but, on the cross he appears to ask us to love him at least through compassion.

Ah, my Jesus, Thou hadst just reason to say, before the time of Thy Passion, that, when Thou shouldst be exalted on the cross, Thou wouldst draw all our hearts to Thee. *And I, if I be lifted up from the earth, will draw all things to myself.*[1] Oh, what darts of fire didst Thou cast at our hearts from this throne of love! Oh, how many happy souls hast Thou drawn to Thee from this cross, and rescued from the jaws of hell? Permit me, then, to say to Thee: Justly, O my Lord, have they caused Thee to die between two thieves, since by Thy love Thou hast snatched from Lucifer so many Christians who justly belonged to him on account of their sins One of these I hope to be. O wounds of my Jesus, O blessed furnaces of love! receive me, that I may burn not in the fire of hell, as I have deserved, but with the holy flames of love for that God who has condescended to die consumed by torments for my salvation.

VII.

After the crucifixion of Jesus, the executioners cast lots for his garments, thus verifying the prediction of David: *They parted my garments amongst them, and upon my venture they cast lots.*[2] They then sat down waiting for his death. My soul, do thou also sit at the foot of the cross, and under its saving shadow repose during thy whole life, that with the sacred spouse thou mayest be able to say, *I sat down under his shadow whom I desired.*[3] Oh! how delightful the repose which the souls that love God enjoy amid the tumults of the world, the temptations of hell, and the terrors of the divine judgments at the sight of Jesus crucified!

VIII.

In the midst of his bodily pains, and the desolation

---

[1] " Et ego, si exaltatus fuero a terra, omnia traham ad meipsum."—*John*, xii. 32.

[2] " Diviserunt sibi vestimenta mea, et super vestem meam miserunt sortem."—*Ps.* xxi. 19.

[3] "Sub umbra illius, quem desideraveram, sedi."—*Cant.* ii. 3.

and sadness of his soul, our dying Jesus looked for some one who would console him. But, my Redeemer, there is no one to comfort Thee. Perhaps there are at least some to pity Thee, and weep at the sight of Thy bitter agony. But, alas! I hear some insult Thee, others mock Thee, and others blaspheme Thee. One says, *If Thou be the Son of God, come down from the cross.*[1] Another, *Vah! Thou that destroyest the temple of God . . . save thyself.*[2] Others say, *He saved others ; himself he cannot save.*[3] O God, what criminal has been ever loaded with so many insults and reproaches while he was dying on a gibbet?

CHAPTER XV.

WORDS THAT JESUS SPOKE ON THE CROSS.

I.

But what does Jesus do? What does he say at the sight of all the outrages which he received? He prays for them that maltreat him: *Father*, he says, *forgive them, for they know not what they do.*[4] Jesus also prayed from the cross for us sinners. Let us then turn to the Eternal Father, and say to him with confidence:

O Father, hear the voice of this beloved Son, who implores Thee to pardon us. To grant us pardon is an act of mercy in our regard, because we do not deserve mercy ; but it is an act of justice to Jesus Christ, who

---

[1] " Si Filius Dei es, descende de cruce."—*Matt.* xxvii. 40.

[2] " Vah! qui destruis templum Dei, et in triduo illud reædificas, salva temetipsum."—*Ibid.*

[3] " Alios salvos fecit, seipsum non potest salvum facere."—*Ibid.* 42.

[4] " Pater! dimitte illis ; non enim sciunt quid faciunt."—*Luke,* xxiii. 34.

14

has superabundantly atoned for our sins. Thou hast obliged Thyself to pardon us through his merits, and to receive into favor all who repent of the offences that they have offered Thee. My Father, I repent with my whole heart of having offended Thee; and in the name of this Son, I ask Thy pardon. Pardon me, and receive me into Thy favor.

II.

Lord, remember me when Thou shalt come into Thy kingdom.[1] Thus the good thief prayed to Jesus dying on the cross, and Jesus answered: *Amen, I say to thee, This day thou shalt be with me in paradise.*[2] Here was verified what the Lord said long before by the prophet Ezechiel, that when sinners repent of their transgressions, God pardons them, and forgets the insults that they have offered to him : *But if the wicked do penance . . . I will not remember all his iniquities.*[3]

O immense mercy, O infinite goodness of my God! who will not love Thee? O my Jesus! forget the injuries I have done Thee, and remember the painful death Thou hast suffered for my salvation, and for the sake of that death bring me to Thy kingdom in the life to come, and grant that during this life Thy holy love may reign in me. May Thy love rule in my heart, and may it be my only lord, my only desire, my only love. Happy thief, who didst merit by thy patience to partake of the fruits of the death of Jesus. And happy me, O my Jesus! if I shall have the happiness to die loving Thee, and uniting my death to Thy holy death.

[1] " Domine ! memento mei, cum veneris in regnum tuum."—*Luke*, xxiii. 42.

[2] " Amen dico tibi: Hodie mecum eris in paradiso."—*Ibid.* 43.

[3] " Si autem impius egerit pœnitentiam . . . , omnium iniquitatum ejus . . . non recordabor." *Ezek.* xviii. 21.

III.

There stood by the cross of Jesus his mother.[1] Behold, O my soul, Mary at the foot of the cross, transfixed with sorrow, and with her eyes fixed on her beloved and innocent Son, contemplating the external and internal pains in the midst of which he dies. She is perfectly resigned, and in peace offers to the Eternal Father the death of her Son for our salvation; but her compassion and love are to her a source of great affliction. O God! who would not pity a mother standing beside the gibbet on which a son dies before her eyes? But here we should consider who this mother and this Son are. Mary's love for her Son immensely surpassed the love of all mothers for their children. She loved Jesus, who was at the same time her Son and her God: a Son infinitely amiable, all beauty and sanctity; a Son who had been always respectful and obedient to her; a Son who had loved her so tenderly, and had, from eternity, chosen her for his mother. This was the mother who had to behold such a Son dying before her eyes on an infamous gibbet, without being able to afford him any comfort; who saw that even the agony which she suffered at the foot of the cross, through love to him, added to his sorrows.

O Mary, through the pain which thou didst suffer at the death of Jesus, have pity on me, and recommend me to thy Son. Listen to him on the cross, recommending me to thee, in the person of St. John: *Woman, behold thy Son.*[2]

IV.

And about the ninth hour, Jesus cried out with a loud voice, saying, Eli, Eli, lamma sabacthani? that is, My God, my God,

[1] "Stabant autem juxta crucem Jesu Mater ejus. . . ."—*John*, xix. 25.

[2] "Mulier, ecce filius tuus!"—*John*, xix. 26.

why hast Thou forsaken me?[1] Jesus, agonizing on the cross, afflicted with pain of body and sadness of soul (for the sadness which assailed him in the garden, when he said, *My soul is sorrowful unto death,*[2] did not leave him until his last breath), seeks for some one to console him, but finds none. *I looked for one who would grieve together with Me, but there was none; and for one that would comfort Me, and I found none.*[3] He looks at his mother, and, as has been said, her presence gives him no consolation; the sight of her sorrows adds to his affliction. He looks about, and sees enemies on every side; hence, finding himself bereft of every comfort, he turns to his Eternal Father, to seek consolation. But the Father, seeing him charged with the sins of all men, for which he was then atoning to the divine justice on the cross, abandons him to a death of pure unmixed pain. Then it was that Jesus cried out with a loud voice, to show the intensity of his sufferings, and said, *My God, why hast Thou also forsaken me?* Hence the death of Jesus Christ was more painful than the death of all the martyrs, because it was full of desolation and bereft of all comfort.

But, my Jesus, why dost Thou complain after having voluntarily offered Thyself to so cruel a death? Ah! I understand Thee; Thou dost complain in order make us comprehend the intense pain with which Thou dost expire, and at the same time to encourage us to have confidence, and to practise resignation when we find ourselves in desolation and deprived of the sensible aid of the divine grace. My sweet Redeemer, Thy abandonment makes me hope that God, although I have betrayed him, will not abandon me. O my Jesus, how have I been

---

[1] " Circa horam nonam, clamavit Jesus voce magna, dicens . . . Deus meus ! Deus meus ! ut quid dereliquisti me ?"—*Matt.* xxvii. 46.

[2] " Tristis est anima mea usque ad mortem."—*Matt.* xxvi. 38.

[3] " Et sustinui qui simul contristaretur, et non fuit ; et qui consolaretur, et non inveni."—*Ps.* lxviii. 21.

able to live so long forgetful of Thee? I thank Thee for not having forgotten me. Ah! I entreat Thee to remind me always of the desolation to which Thou hast submitted for my sake, that I may never more forget Thee and the love Thou hast borne me.

V.

Knowing that his sacrifice was consummated, the Saviour said that he was thirsty, and the soldiers applied to his mouth a sponge full of vinegar. *Afterwards, Jesus knowing that all things were now accomplished, that the Scripture might be fulfilled, said, I thirst. . . . And they putting a sponge full of vinegar about hyssop, put it to his mouth.*[1] The Scripture, which was to be fulfilled, is the text of David: *And in my thirst they gave me vinegar to drink.*[2] But, O Lord, Thou art silent about the intense pains which hasten Thy death, and dost Thou complain of thirst? Ah! the thirst of Jesus was very different from that which we imagine it to be. His thirst is the desire of being loved by the souls for whom he dies. Thus, my Jesus, Thou dost thirst after me, a miserable worm, and shall I not thirst after Thee, who art an infinite good? Ah, I long for Thee, I love Thee, I desire to please Thee in all things. Assist me, O Lord, to banish from my heart all earthly desires, and grant that nothing may reign in me but the desire to please Thee and to do Thy will. O holy will of God, blessed fountain that dost fill enamoured souls! fill me also, and be the object of all my thoughts and affections.

[1] " Postea, sciens Jesus quia omnia consummata sunt, ut consummaretur Scriptura, dixit : Sitio! . . . Illi autem spongiam plenam aceto . . . obtulerunt ori ejus."—*John*, xix. 28, 29.

[2] " Et in siti mea potaverunt me aceto."—*Ps.* lxviii. 22.

CHAPTER XVI.

DEATH OF JESUS.

I.

The amiable Redeemer approaches the end of life. My soul, behold those eyes grow dim; that beautiful countenance becomes pale; that heart palpitates feebly; that sacred body is abandoned to death. *Jesus, therefore, when he had taken the vinegar, said, It is consummated.*[1] When on the point of expiring, Jesus placed before his eyes all the sufferings of his life,—the poverty, fatigues, pains, and injuries which he had suffered,—and, again offering them all to his Eternal Father, he said. All is now accomplished—all is consummated. All that the prophets foretold of me is consummated; in a word, the sacrifice which God expected in order to be appeased with the world is perfectly consummated, and full satisfaction is made to the divine justice. *It is consummated,* said Jesus, turning to his Eternal Father : *It is consummated,* he said, at the same time turning to us. As if he had said, O men, I have done all that I can do, in order to save your souls and to gain your love. I have done my part; do you now do yours. Love me, and be not unwilling to love a God who has gone so far as to die for you.

Ah, my Jesus, that I also, at the hour of my death. could say, at least for the part of my life which yet remains, *It is consummated.* Lord, I have accomplished Thy will; I have obeyed all Thy wishes! Give me strength, O my Jesus, for with Thy aid I purpose and hope to do Thy will in all things.

[1] "Cum ergo accepisset Jesus acetum, dixit : Consummatum est."—*John*, xix. 30.

And Jesus, crying with a loud voice, said, Father, into Thy hands I commend my spirit.[1] These were the last words which Jesus spoke on the cross. Seeing that his blessed soul was about to be separated from his mangled body, he said, with perfect resignation to the divine will, and with filial confidence, Father, to Thee I recommend my spirit. As if he had said, My Father, I have no will; I do not wish either to live or die. If it is pleasing to Thee that I continue to suffer on this cross, behold, I am ready; into Thy hands I consign my spirit; do with it what Thou wilt. Oh that we also would say the same when we meet any cross, leaving ourselves to be guided by the Lord in all things, according to his good pleasure! This, says St. Francis de Sales, is that holy abandonment in God which constitutes all perfection. We ought to act in this manner particularly at the hour of death; but, in order to do it well then, we should practise it frequently during life.

Yes, my Jesus, in Thy hands I place my life and my death; in Thee I abandon myself entirely, and I recommend my soul to Thee now for the last moments of my life. Receive it into Thy wounds, as Thy Father received Thy spirit, when Thou didst expire on the cross.

III.

But behold, Jesus dies. O angels of heaven, come, come to be present at the death of your God; and thou, O sorrowful mother of God, approach nearer to the cross, raise thy eyes to behold thy Son ; look at him more steadfastly, for he is about to expire. Behold, the Redeemer already calls on death, and gives it permission to come and take away his life. O death, he says, perform thy office; take away my life and save my sheep. Behold, the earth trembles, the graves are opened, the

---

[1] "Et clamans voce magna, Jesus ait : Pater ! in manus tuas commendo spiritum meum."—*Luke.* xxiii. 46. .

veil of the Temple is rent in two ; behold, in fine, how the violence of his pains deprives the dying Lord of strength, of the natural heat, of respiration ; his body is abandoned to death ; he bows down his head on his breast, he opens his mouth, and expires: *And bowing down His head, He gave up the ghost.*[1] Go forth, O beautiful soul of my Saviour, go forth; go to open paradise, which has been hitherto shut against us; go to present thyself to the divine Majesty, and to obtain for us pardon and salvation. The crowd, turning to Jesus, on account of the loud voice in which he spoke these words, look at him with attention and in silence; they see him expire, and, observing that he is motionless, they exclaim, He is dead—he is dead. Mary hears this from all the by-standers, and she also says, Ah, my Son, Thou art dead.

IV.

He is dead. O God, who is dead ? The author of life, the only-begotten of God, the Lord of the world. O death which was the astonishment of heaven and of nature ! A God to die for his creatures ! O infinite charity ! A God to sacrifice himself entirely ! To sacrifice his delights, his honor, his blood, his life ; and for whom ? For ungrateful creatures. And to die in a sea of sorrows and insults, and in order to atone for our sins. My soul, raise thy eyes, and behold that crucified Man-God. Behold that divine Lamb sacrificed on that altar of pain; consider that he is the beloved Son of the Eternal Father, and consider he has died through the love he has borne thee. See how his arms are stretched out to embrace thee; his head bowed down to give thee the kiss of peace; his side opened to receive thee. What dost thou say ? Does a God so good and so loving deserve to be loved ? Listen to what the Lord says to thee

[1] " Et inclinato capite, tradidit spiritum."—*John*, xix. 30.

from the cross: My Son, see if there is any one in this world who has loved thee more than I, thy God, have loved thee.

Ah, my God and my Redeemer, Thou, then, hast died, and died a death the most infamous and painful. And why? To gain my love. But what love of a creature can ever compensate the love of his Creator, who has died for him? O my adored Jesus, O love of my soul! how shall I be ever able to forget Thee? How shall I be able to love anything but Thee, after having seen Thee dying through pain on this cross in order to atone for my sins and to save my soul? How can I behold Thee dead, hanging on this tree, and not love Thee with all my strength? Can I think that my sins have reduced Thee to this condition, and not weep always with intense sorrow for the offences that I have committed against Thee?

V.

O God, had the vilest of all men suffered for me what Jesus Christ has suffered; had I beheld a man torn with scourges, fastened to a cross, and made the laughing-stock of the people in order to save my life, could I remember his sufferings without feeling for him the tenderest affection? And were the likeness of my expiring lover brought before me, could I behold it with indifference, and say, Oh! the miserable man has died thus in torture for the love of me? Had he not loved me he would not have died for me. Alas, how many Christians keep a beautiful crucifix in their room, but only as a fine piece of furniture! They praise the workmanship and the expression of grief, but it makes as little impression on their hearts as if it were not the image of the incarnate Word, but of a man who was a stranger and unknown to them.

Ah, my Jesus, do not permit me to be one of them.

Remember that Thou didst promise that when Thou wouldst be elevated on the cross, Thou wouldst draw all hearts to Thee. Behold, my heart, softened into tenderness by Thy death, will no longer resist Thy calls. Ah, draw all its affections to Thy love. Thou hast died for me, and I wish to live only for Thee. O sorrows of Jesus, O ignominies of Jesus, O death of Jesus, O love of Jesus ! may you be fixed in my heart, and may the sweet remembrance of you remain there forever, to wound me continually, and to inflame me with love. O Eternal Father, behold Jesus dead for my sake, and, through the merits of this Son, show me mercy. My soul, be not diffident on account of the sins thou hast committed against God. It is the Father himself that has given the Son to the world for our salvation, and it is the Son that has voluntarily offered himself to atone for our sins. Ah, my Jesus, since to pardon me Thou hast not spared Thyself, behold me with the same affection with which Thou didst one day behold me, agonizing for me on the cross. Behold me and enlighten me; and pardon particularly my past ingratitude to Thee, in thinking so little of Thy Passion, and on the love Thou hast shown me in Thy sufferings. I thank Thee for the light which Thou givest me, in making me see in these wounds and lacerated members, as through so many lattices, Thy great and tender affection for me. Unhappy me, if, after this light, I should neglect to love Thee, or if I loved anything out of Thee. May I die (I will say with the enamoured St. Francis of Assisi) for the love of Thee, O my Jesus, who hast condescended to die for the love of me. O pierced heart of my Redeemer, O blessed dwelling of loving souls ! do not disdain to receive also my miserable soul. O Mary, O mother of sorrows ! recommend me to thy Son, whom thou dost hold lifeless in thy arms. Behold his lacerated flesh, behold his divine blood shed for me, and see in them how pleasing it is to

him that thou shouldst recommend my salvation to him.
My salvation consists in loving him; this love thou
hast to obtain for me, but let it be a great and eternal
love.

Commenting on the words of St. Paul, *The charity of
Christ presseth us*,' St. Francis de Sales says: "Since we
know that Jesus, the true God, has loved us so as to suffer death, and the death of the cross, for our salvation,
must not our hearts be under a press which squeezes
and forces love from them by a violence which is strong
in proportion as it is amiable?"' The saint afterwards
says that " the hill of Calvary is the mountain of lovers."'
He then adds: " Ah, why, then, do we not cast ourselves
on Jesus crucified, in order to die on the cross with him
who has voluntarily died upon it for the love of us? I
will hold him, we ought to say, and will never forsake
him; I will die with him, and will burn in the flames of
his love. One and the same fire shall consume this
divine Creator and his miserable creature. My Jesus
gives himself to me, and I give myself entirely to him.
I will live and die on his bosom; neither life nor death
shall separate me from him. O eternal love! my soul
seeks Thee, and chooses Thee for eternity. Ah! come,
O Holy Ghost, and inflame our hearts with the love of
Thee. Either to love or to die. To die to every other
love, in order to live to that of Jesus. O Saviour of our
souls! grant that we may sing for eternity: "Live Jesus;
I love Jesus. Live Jesus, whom I love; I love Jesus, who
lives forever and ever."'

Let us, in conclusion, say: O Lamb of God, who hast
sacrificed Thyself for our salvation! O victim of love,
who hast been consumed by sorrows on the cross! Oh

---

¹ "Charitas Christi urget nos."—2 *Cor.* v. 14.
² *Love of God.*—B. 7, ch. 8.
³ Ibid. bk. 12, ch. 13.
⁴ Ibid. bk. 7, ch. 8; bk. 12, ch. 13.

that I knew how to love Thee as Thou dost deserve to be loved! Oh that I could die for Thee, who hast died for me! By my sins I have been a cause of pain to Thee during Thy entire life; grant that I may please Thee during the remainder of my life, living only in Thee, my love, my all. O Mary, my mother, thou art my hope after Jesus; obtain for me the grace to love Jesus.

Considerations on the Passion of Jesus Christ.*

INTRODUCTION.

How pleasing is it to Jesus Christ that we should often remember his Passion, and the shameful death which he suffered for us, can be well understood from his having instituted the most holy Sacrament of the Altar for this very end, that there might ever dwell in us the lively memory of the love which he bore to us in sacrificing himself on the cross for our salvation. Let us, then, recollect that on the night preceding his death he instituted this sacrament of love, and, when he had distributed his body to the disciples, he said to them, and through them to all of us, that in receiving the Holy Communion we should bear in mind what great things he has suffered for us: *As often as ye shall eat this bread and drink this cup, ye shall show forth the Lord's death.*[1] Therefore, in the Mass the Holy Church ordains that after the consecration the celebrant shall say, in the

---

[1] "Quotiescumque enim manducabitis panem hunc, et calicem bibetis, mortem Domini annuntiabitis."—1 *Cor.* xi. 26.

---

* In this introduction, the saintly author informs us that when he wrote this treatise he was seventy-seven years of age. This was thirteen years after he had written the *Simple Exposition of the Passion.* The considerations he wrote less for the use of others than for his own spiritual advantage, being desirous of preparing himself well for death. He sent the little work to a pious person, with a letter dated September 8, 1773, in which he says: " You may use this little book in your prayers when you meditate on the Passion. I am using it myself every day. I desire that you should not allow a day to pass without recalling to your mind, with the aid of this or another book, something of the Passion. The Passion was for the saints a continual subject of meditation."—ED.

name of Jesus Christ, *As often as ye do this, ye shall do it
in memory of Me.*[1]   And the angelic St. Thomas writes,
"That the memory of the great things that he has done
for us might ever remain with us, he left us his own
body to be received as our food."[2]   The saint then goes
on to say that through this sacrament is preserved the
memory of the boundless love which Jesus Christ has
shown us in his Passion.[3]

If we were to endure injuries and stripes for the sake
of a friend, and were then to learn that our friend, when
he heard any one speak of what we had done, would
not pay any heed to it, but turned the conversation,
and said, "Let us talk of something else," what pain
we should suffer at the sight of the neglect of the ungrateful man!   And, on the other hand, how glad we
should be to find that our friend admitted that he was
under an eternal obligation to us, that he constantly bore
it in mind, and spoke of it with affection and with tears.
Therefore the saints, knowing how much it pleases Jesus
Christ that we should often call to mind his Passion,
have been almost perpetually occupied in meditating on
the pains and insults which our loving Redeemer suffered during his whole life, and still more in his death.
St. Augustine writes that there is no more profitable
occupation for the soul than to meditate daily on the
Passion of the Lord.[4]   It was revealed by God to a holy
anchorite, that there is no exercise more adapted to inflame the heart with divine love than the thought of
the death of Jesus Christ.   And to St. Gertrude, as

---

[1] " Hæc quotiescumque feceritis, in mei memoriam facietis."

[2] " Ut autem tanti beneficii jugis in nobis maneret memoria, corpus
suum in cibum sumendum dereliquit."—*Opusc.* 57.

[3] " Per quod recolitur memoria illius, quam in sua passione Christus
monstravit, excellentissimæ charitatis."

[4] " Nihil tam salutiferum, quam quotidie cogitare quanta pro nobis
pertulit Deus Homo."—*Ad Fr. in er.* s. 32.

Blosius' records, it was revealed that as often as we look with devotion upon the crucifix, so often does Jesus look upon us with love. Blosius² adds, that to consider or read of any portion of the Passion brings greater profit than any other devout exercise. Therefore St. Bonaventure writes, "O Passion worthy of love, which renders divine him who meditates upon it."³ And, speaking of the wounds of the Crucified, he calls them wounds which pierce the hardest hearts, and inflame the coldest souls with divine love.⁴

It is related in the life of the Blessed Bernard of Corlione, a Capuchin, that when his brother religious desired to teach him to read, he went to take advice from Him who was crucified, and that the Lord replied to him, "What is reading? what are books? I who was crucified will be thy book, in which thou mayest read the love I bore thee." Jesus crucified was also the beloved book of St. Philip Benitius; and when the saint was dying, he desired to have his book given him. Those who stood by, however, did not know what book he wanted ; but Brother Ubaldo, his confidential friend, offered to him the image of the Crucified, on which the saint said, "This is my book;" and, kissing the sacred wounds, breathed out his blessed soul.

For myself, in my spiritual works, I have often written of the Passion of Jesus Christ, but yet I think that it will not be unprofitable to devout souls if I here add many other points and reflections which I have read in various books, or which have occurred to myself ; and I have determined to commit them to writing, both for the use of others, and especially for my own profit;

---

¹ *Concl. an.* p. 2, c. 2.
² *Sac. an.* p. 3, c. 21.
³ "O passio mirabilis. quæ suum meditatorem reddit divinum!"
⁴ "Vulnera. corda saxea vulnerantia. et mentes congelatas inflam-mantia."—*Stim. div. am.* p. 1, c. 1.

for finding myself, now that I am putting together this little treatise, near to death, at the age of seventy-seven years, I have been desirous to prolong these considerations, by way of preparing myself for the great day of account. And, in fact, I make my own poor meditations on these very points; often and often reading some portion, in order that, whenever my last hour shall come, I may find myself occupied in keeping before my eyes Jesus crucified, who is my only hope, and thus I hope to breathe out my soul into his hands. Let us, then, begin the proposed reflections.

CHAPTER I.

THE PASSION OF JESUS CHRIST IN GENERAL.

I.

Necessity of a Redeemer and His Qualities—The Incarnation of the Word—Errors of the Jews—Prophecies.

Adam sinned and rebelled against God, and, being the first man, and the progenitor of all men, he fell into a state of perdition, together with the whole human race. The injury was done to God; so that neither Adam nor all the rest of mankind, by all the sacrifices that they could have offered, even of their own life, could furnish a worthy satisfaction to the divine majesty which was offended. To appease this there was need that a divine person should satisfy the divine justice. Behold, then, the Son of God, who, moved to compassion for men, and excited by the bowels of his mercy, offered himself to take human flesh, and to die for men, that he might thus give to God a complete satisfaction for all their sins, and obtain for them the divine grace which they had lost.

Our loving Redeemer thus came into this life, and became man, in order that he might find a remedy for all the miseries which sin had brought upon men. At the same time, he chose to lead men to an observance of the divine precepts, and thus to the acquisition of eternal life, not only by his instructions, but also by the example of his own holy life. For this end Jesus Christ renounced all honors, delights, and riches, which he might have enjoyed upon this earth, and which belonged to him as Lord of the world; and he chose for

15

himself a life of humility, poverty, and tribulation, until he died in anguish upon a cross.

The Jews were possessed with a delusion that the Messiah would come upon earth to triumph over all his enemies by force of arms, and that, having conquered them, and acquired the rule of all the earth, he would make his followers rich and glorious. But if the Messiah had been what the Jews imagined him to be, a prince triumphant and honored by all men as the sovereign of all the earth, he would not have been the Redeemer promised by God, and predicted by the prophets. This he himself declared, when he replied to Pilate, *My king-dom is not of this world.*[1] On this St. Fulgentius writes : " Why, Herod, art thou thus troubled? This king who is born is not come to conquer kings in battle, but won-derfully to subdue them by his death."[2]

The Jews had two false notions respecting the Re-deemer whom they expected; the first was, the idea that the spiritual and eternal blessings with which the proph-ets foretold that the Messiah would enrich his people, were earthly and temporal blessings: *There shall be faith in thy days ; the riches of salvation, wisdom, and knowledge; the fear of the Lord, that shall be thy treasure.*[3] These were the blessings promised by the Redeemer : faith, the knowledge of virtue, and holy fear. These were the riches of the salvation which he had promised. Besides this, he promised that he would bring medicine for the peni-tent, pardon for sinners, and liberty to the captives of the devil: *He hath sent Me to bring tidings to those who are meek, that I should heal those who are contrite of heart, and*

---

[1] " Regnum meum non est de hoc mundo."—*John*, xviii. 36.

[2] " Quid est quod sic turbaris, Herodes ? Rex iste, qui natus est, non venit reges pugnando superare, sed moriendo mirabiliter subju-gare."—*S. de Epiph. et Inn. nece.*

[3] " Et erit fides in temporibus tuis ; divitiæ salutis, sapientia et scientia; timor Domini ipse est thesaurus ejus."

preach pardon to the captives, and liberty to those who are in bondage.[1] The other delusion of the Jews was, that what was predicted by the prophets respecting the second coming of the Saviour when he should come to judge the world at the end of ages, was to be understood of his first coming. David wrote of the future Messiah, that he would conquer the princes of the earth, and beat down the pride of many, and with the force of his sword would subdue the whole earth : *The Lord, upon Thy right hand, shall beat down kings in the day of His wrath ; He shall judge among the nations; He shall shatter the heads of many upon the earth.*[2] And the prophet Jeremias wrote: *The sword of the Lord shall devour from the one end of the earth to the other.*[3] But all this is to be understood of the second advent, when he shall come as a judge to condemn the wicked.

When the prophets spoke of the first advent, in which he would accomplish the work of redemption, they most clearly foretold that the Redeemer would live upon this earth a life of poverty and contempt. This was what was written by the prophet Zacharias, when speaking of the life of Jesus Christ: *Behold thy king cometh to thee as a just one, and the Saviour; He is poor, and sitteth upon an ass, and upon a colt the foal of an ass.*[4] All this was specially fulfilled when he entered into Jerusalem sitting upon a young ass, and was honorably received as the desired Messiah, as St. John writes, *And Jesus found an*

[1] "Ad annuntiandum mansuetis misit me, ut mederer contritis corde, et prædicarem captivis indulgentiam, et clausis apertionem." —*Isa.* xxxiiî. 6; lxi. 1.

[2] "Dominus a dextris tuis, confregit in die iræ suæ reges; judicabit in nationibus, implebit ruinas ; conquassabit capita in terra multorum."—*Ps.* cix. 5.

[3] "Gladius Domini devorabit ab extremo terræ usque ad extremum ejus."—*Jer.* xii. 12.

[4] "Ecce Rex tuus veniet tibi justus et Salvator; ipse pauper et ascendens super asinam et super pullum filium asinæ."—*Zach.* ix. 9.

ass and sat upon it, as it is written, Fear not, daughter of Sion, behold thy king cometh to thee, sitting upon an ass's colt.[1] We know, also, that he was poor from the time of his birth, being born in Bethlehem, a place of no celebrity, and in a cave: *And thou, Bethlehem Ephrata, art little among the thousands of Judah; from thee cometh forth to Me He who is the ruler of Israel; and His going forth is from the beginning, and from the days of eternity.*[2] This prophecy, also, is referred to by St. Matthew and St. John.[3] Further, also, the prophet Osee writes: *From Egypt I have called My Son;*[4] which was fulfilled when Jesus Christ was carried as an infant into Egypt, where he remained about seven years, as a stranger in the midst of a barbarous race, far from his kindred and friends, which was sufficient to make his life one of poverty. And so, also, he continued to live the life of the poor when he had returned to Judea. He himself had foretold, by the mouth of David, that throughout all his life he would remain poor and afflicted with toils: *I am poor, and in the midst of labors from my youth.*[5]

Almighty God could not consider his justice sufficiently satisfied by all the sacrifices that men could offer, even of their own lives; and therefore he ordained that his own Son should take a human body, and become a victim worthy to reconcile him with men, and obtain salvation for them. *Sacrifice and oblation Thou wouldst not, but a body hast Thou prepared for Me.*[6] The

[1] "Et invenit Jesus asellum et sedit super eum, sicut scriptum est: Noli timere, filia Sion; ecce Rex tuus venit sedens super pullum asinæ."—*John*, xii. 14.

[2] "Et tu, Bethlehem Ephrata, parvulus es in millibus Juda : ex te mihi egredietur, qui sit dominator in Israel; et egressus ejus ab initio, a diebus æternitatis."—*Mich.* v. 2.

[3] *Matt.* ii. 6; *John*, vii. 42.

[4] "Ex Ægypto vocavi Filium meum."—*Os.* xi. 1.

[5] "Pauper sum ego et in laboribus a juventute mea."—*Ps.* lxxxvii. 16.

[6] "Hostiam et oblationem noluisti, corpus autem aptasti mihi."—*Heb.* x. 5.

only-begotten Son offered himself willingly to be a sacrifice for us, and came down on earth in order that he might accomplish the sacrifice with his death, and thus complete the redemption of man. *Then He said, Behold, I come ; in the volume of the book it is written of Me, that I should do Thy will, O God!* [1]

The Lord said, speaking to sinners, *Why should I strike you any more?* [2] This God said in order that we should understand, that, however much he might punish those who offended him, their punishments would never be sufficient to make reparation to his offended honor; and therefore he committed it to his own Son to make satisfaction for the sins of men, because his Son alone could give worthy compensation to the divine justice. Therefore he declared, by Isaias, speaking of Jesus being made a victim for our sins, *For the wickedness of My people I have stricken him.* [3] Nor was he satisfied with a light satisfaction, but chose to see him consumed with torments: *The Lord willed to exhaust Him with weakness.* [4]

O my Jesus, O victim of love, consumed by pangs upon the cross to atone for my sins, I am ready to die with grief when I think that I have so often despised Thee, after Thou hast so much loved me. Oh, suffer it not that I should continue longer ungrateful for Thy goodness. Draw me wholly to Thee; grant it through the merits of that blood which Thou hast poured forth for me.

II.

Figures of the Old Testament—Other Prophecies—Thanks Due to the Father and to the Son.

When the divine Word offered himself to redeem mankind, there were before him two ways of redemp-

[1] "Tunc dixi : Ecce venio; in capite libri scriptum est de me, ut faciam, Deus, voluntatem tuam."—*Heb.* x. 5-7.

[2] "Super quo percutiam vos ultra?"—*Isa.* i. 5.

[3] "Propter scelus populi mei percussi eum."—*Isa.* liii. 8.

[4] "Et Dominus voluit conterere eum in infirmitate."—*Ibid.* 10.

tion, the one of joy and glory, the other of pains and insults. At the same time, it was his will, not only by his coming to deliver man from eternal death, but also to call forth the love of all the hearts of men, and therefore he rejected the way of joy and glory, and chose that of pains and insults: *The joy being set before Him, He endured the cross.*[1] In order that he might satisfy the divine justice for us, and, at the same time, inflame us with his holy love, he was willing to endure this burden of all our sins; that, dying upon a cross, he might obtain for us grace and the life of the blessed. This is what Isaias intended to express when he said: *He Himself hath borne our pains, and carried our sorrows.*[2]

Of this there were two express figures in the Old Testament; the first was the annual ceremony of the scape-goat,[3] which the high-priest represented as bearing all the sins of the people, and therefore all, loading it with curses, drove it into the desert, to be the object of the wrath of God.[4] This goat was a figure of our Redeemer, who was willing to load himself with all the curses deserved by us for our sins; being made a curse for us, in order that he might obtain for us the divine blessing. Therefore the Apostle wrote in another place, *He made Him to be sin for us, who knew not sin, that we might be made the justice of God in Him.*[5] That is, as St. Ambrose and St. Anselm explain it, he made him to be sin who was innocence itself; that is, he presented himself to God as if he had been sin itself. In a word, he took upon himself the character of a sinner, and en-

---

[1] " Proposito sibi gaudio, sustinuit crucem."—*Heb.* xii. 2.

[2] "Vere languores nostros ipse tulit, et dolores nostros ipse portavit."—*Isa.* liii. 4.

[3] *Lev.* xvi. 5.

[4] " Factus pro nobis maledictum."—*Gal.* iii. 13.

[5] " Eum, qui non noverat peccatum, pro nobis peccatum fecit, ut nos efficeremur justitia Dei in ipso."—*2 Cor.* v. 21.

dured the pains due to us sinners, in order to render us just before God. The second type of the sacrifice that Jesus Christ offered to the Eternal Father for us upon the cross was, that brazen serpent[1] fixed to a tree, by looking upon which the Jews who were bitten by fiery serpents were healed. Accordingly, St. John writes: *As Moses lifted up the serpent in the wilderness, so must the Son of Man be lifted up, that every one who believeth in Him should not perish, but have eternal life.*[2]

We must here notice that in the Book of Wisdom, the shameful death of Jesus Christ is clearly foretold. Although the words of the passage referred to may apply to the death of every just man, yet, say Tertullian, St. Cyprian, St. Jerome, and many other holy Fathers, that they principally refer to the death of Christ. It is said: *If He is the true Son of God, He will accept Him, and deliver Him.*[3] These words exactly correspond with what the Jews said when Jesus was upon the cross: *He trusted in God; let Him deliver Him, if He will have Him; for He said, I am the Son of God.*[4] The Wise Man goes on to say, *Let us try Him with insults and torments* (that is, those of the cross), *and let us prove His patience; let us condemn Him to the most shameful death.*[5] The Jews chose the death of the cross for Jesus Christ, because it is shameful, in order that his name might be forever infamous, and no more held in remembrance, according to

---

[1] *Num.* xxi. 8.
[2] "Sicut Moyses exaltavit serpentem in deserto, ita exaltari oportet Filium hominis, ut omnis qui credit in ipsum, non pereat, sed habeat vitam æternam."—*John,* iii. 14.
[3] "Si enim est verus Filius Dei, suscipiet illum et liberabit eum."—*Wisd.* ii. 18.
[4] "Confidit in Deo; liberet nunc, si vult eum; dixit enim: Quia Filius Dei sum."—*Matt.* xxvii. 43.
[5] "Contumelia et tormento interrogemus eum . . . , et probemus patientiam illius; morte turpissima condemnemus eum."—*Wisd.* ii. 19.

the other text of Jeremias: *Let us cast wood into His bread, and wipe Him out from the land of the living, and His name shall be remembered no more.*' How, then, can the Jews of the present day say that it is false that Christ was the promised Messiah, because his life was ended by a most shameful death, when the prophets themselves foretold that he should die with a most dishonorable death?

And Jesus accepted such a death. He died to pay the price of our sins; and therefore, as a sinner, he desired to be circumcised; to be redeemed with a price when he was presented in the temple ; to receive the baptism of repentance from the Baptist; and lastly, in his Passion, to be nailed upon the cross to atone for our guilty wanderings: to atone for our avarice, by being stripped of his garments; for our pride, by the insults he endured: for our desires of power, by submitting himself to the executioner; for our evil thoughts, by his crown of thorns; for our intemperance, by the gall he tasted; and by the pangs of his body, for our sensual delights. Therefore, we ought continually, with tears of tenderness, to thank the Eternal Father for having given his innocent Son to death, to deliver us from eternal death: *He spared not His own Son, but delivered him up for us all ; and how shall He not also with Him give us all things?*' Thus said St. Paul; and thus Jesus himself said, in the Gospel of St. John: *God so loved the world, that He gave His only-begotten Son.*' On this account, the holy Church exclaims on Holy Saturday, "Oh, wonderful is it which Thy love has done for us! O inestimable gift of love,

---

' "Mittamus lignum in panem ejus, et eradamus eum de terra viventium; et nomen ejus non memoretur amplius."—*Jer.* xi. 19.

' "Qui etiam proprio Filio suo non pepercit, sed pro nobis omnibus tradidit illum; quomodo non etiam cum illo omnia nobis donavit ?"—*Rom.* viii. 32.

³ "Sic enim Deus dilexit mundum, ut Filium suum unigenitum daret."— *John,* iii. 16.

that to redeem a servant, Thou shouldst give Thy Son." [1]
O infinite mercy, O infinite love of our God! O holy
faith! How can he who believes and confesses this, live
without burning with holy love for a God who is so loving, and so worthy of love?

O eternal God, look not upon me thus overwhelmed
with sins; look upon Thy innocent Son hanging upon
a cross, who offers Thee the many pangs and insults
which he has suffered, that Thou mayst have mercy
upon me. O God, most worthy of love, and my true
lover, for the love of this Thy Son, so beloved by Thee,
have mercy upon me. The mercy I ask is, that Thou
shouldst give me Thy holy love. Oh, draw me wholly
to Thyself, from the mire of my corruption. Burn up,
O Thou consuming fire, all that Thou seest impure in
my soul, and that hinders me from being wholly Thine.

Let us give thanks to the Father, and let us give equal
thanks to the Son, that he has been willing to take upon
him our flesh, and, together with it, our sins, to offer to
God, by his Passion, a worthy satisfaction. It is on this
account that the Apostle says that Jesus Christ has become our mediator; that is, that he has bound himself to
pay our debts: *Jesus is made the mediator of a better testament.*[2] As the mediator between God and man, he has
established a covenant with God, by which he has bound
himself to satisfy the divine justice for us; and, on the
other hand, has promised to us eternal life on the part of
God. Therefore, in anticipation of this, the Preacher
warns us not to forget the grace of this' divine surety,
who, to obtain salvation for us, has been willing to sacrifice his life. *Forget not the grace of the Surety, for He
hath given His soul for thee.*[3] It is to give us the better

[1] "O mira circa nos tuæ pietatis dignatio! o inæstimabilis dilectio
charitatis! ut servum redimeres, Filium tradidisti."

[2] "Melioris Testamenti sponsor factus est Jesus."—*Heb.* vii. 22.

[3] "Gratiam fidejussoris ne obliviscaris; dedit enim pro te animam
suam."—*Ecclus.* xxix. 20.

assurance of pardon, says St. Paul, that Jesus Christ with his blood has blotted out the decree of our condemnation, in which the sentence of eternal death stands written against us, and has nailed it to the cross on which he died to satisfy the divine justice for us.[1]

O my Jesus! by that love which caused Thee to give Thy blood and Thy life upon Calvary for me, make me die to all the affections of this world; make me forget everything, that I may not think of anything but to love Thee and give Thee pleasure! O my God, worthy of infinite love, Thou hast loved me without reserve, I desire to love Thee also without reserve. I love Thee, my greatest good; I love Thee, O my love, my all.

III.

The Death of Jesus Christ is our Salvation. It is an Instruction and an Example; it is a Motive of Confidence and of Love.

In a word, whatever blessing, whatever salvation, whatever hope we have, we have it all in Jesus Christ, and in his merits; as St. Peter says, *There is salvation in none other; for there is no other name under heaven given among men in which we must be saved.*[2] Thus, there is no hope of salvation for us except through the merits of Jesus Christ; from which St. Thomas and all theologians[3] conclude, that, since the promulgation of the Gospel, we are bound to believe explicitly, of necessity, not only by precept, but by the necessity of the truth,

---

[1] " Delens quod adversus nos erat chirographum decreti, quod erat contrarium nobis, et ipsum tulit de medio, affigens illud cruci."—*Col.* ii. 14.

[2] " Et non est in alio aliquo salus; nec enim aliud nomen est sub coelo datum hominibus, in quo oporteat nos salvos fieri."—*Acts.* iv. 12.

[3] *Theol. mor.* l. 2, tr. 1.

that it is only through the means of our Redeemer that we can be saved.

All the foundation, then, of our salvation consists in the redemption of man wrought out by the divine Word upon earth. We must, therefore, reflect that although the actions of Jesus Christ upon earth, being the acts of a divine person, were of an infinite merit, so that the least of them was enough to satisfy the divine justice for all the sins of men, yet nevertheless the death of Jesus Christ is the great sacrifice by which our redemption was completed; so that, in the holy Scriptures, the redemption of man is attributed chiefly to the death suffered by him upon the cross: *He humbled Himself, and was made obedient to death, even the death of the cross.*[1] Wherefore the Apostle writes, that in receiving the Holy Eucharist, we ought to remember the Lord's death: *As often as ye shall eat this bread and drink this cup, ye shall show forth the Lord's death till He come.*[2] But why does he mention the death of the Lord, and not his incarnation, birth, or resurrection? He speaks of his death because this was the suffering of greatest pain and greatest shame that Jesus Christ endured, and that completed our redemption.

Hence St. Paul says, *I have determined that I would know nothing among you, except Jesus Christ, and Him crucified.*[3] The Apostle well knew that Jesus Christ was born in a cave; that, for thirty years, he inhabited a carpenter's shop; that he had risen from the dead, and had ascended into heaven. Why, then, did he say that he would know nothing but Jesus crucified? Because the death suffered

---

[1] "Humiliavit semetipsum, factus obediens usque ad mortem, mortem autem crucis."—*Phil.* ii. 8.

[2] "Quotiescumque enim manducabitis panem hunc, et calicem bibetis, mortem Domini annuntiabitis."—1 *Cor.* xi. 26.

[3] "Non enim judicavi me scire aliquid inter vos, nisi Jesum Christum, et hunc crucifixum."—*Ibid.* ii. 2.

by Jesus Christ on the cross was that which most moved
him to love him, and induced him to exercise obedience
towards God and love towards his neighbor, which were
the virtues most specially inculcated by Jesus Christ
from the chair of his cross. St. Thomas, the angelic
Doctor, writes: "In whatever temptation we fall, in the
cross is our protection; there is obedience to God, love
to our neighbor, patience in adversity; whence St. Augustine says, "The cross was not only the instrument
of death to the sufferer, but his chair of teaching."[1]

O devout souls, let us labor to imitate the Spouse of
the Canticles, who said, *I have sat under the shadow of
Him whom I desired.*[2]   Let us place often before our
eyes, especially on Fridays, Jesus dying on the cross;
and let us rest there for a while, and contemplate with
tender affection his sufferings, and the love which he
bore to us, while he continued in agony upon that bed
of pain.   Let us also say, *I have sat under the shadow of
Him whom I desired.*   Oh, how sweet is the repose that is
found by souls who love God in the midst of the tumult
of this world, and in the temptations of hell, and even in
fears of the divine justice. when they contemplate in
solitude and silence our loving Redeemer, as he hangs in
agony upon the cross, while his divine blood flows forth
in drops from all his limbs, stricken and laid open with
stripes, and thorns, and nails !   Oh, how the desires of
worldly honors, of earthly riches, of sensual pleasures,
depart from our minds at the sight of Jesus crucified !
Then does there breathe from that cross a heavenly gale,
which sweetly detaches us from earthly things, and
lights up in us a holy desire to suffer and die for love of

[1] "In quacumque tribulatione invenitur ejus remedium in cruce;
ibi est obedientia ad Deum, ibi charitas ad proximum, ibi patientia in
adversis. Unde Augustinus : Crux non solum fuit patibulum patientis,
sed etiam cathedra docentis."—*In Heb.* xii. *lect.* 1.

[2] "Sub umbra illius, quem desideraveram, sedi."—*Cant.* ii. 3.

him who has been willing to suffer and die for love of
us.

O God, if Jesus Christ had not been what he really is,
the Son of God, and true God, our Creator and supreme
Lord, but a mere man, who would not be moved to compassion at the sight of a youth of noble blood, innocent
and holy, dying through the strength of his torments
upon a shameful tree, to atone for sins not his own, but
those of his enemies themselves, and thus to deliver them
from the death which was their due? How, then, is it
that the affections of all hearts are not drawn to a God
who died in a sea of insults and pains for love of his
creatures? How can these creatures love anything but
God? How can they think of anything but being grateful to him who is their so loving benefactor?

"Oh, if thou knewest the mystery of the cross!" [1] said
St. Andrew to the tyrant who sought to induce him to
deny Jesus Christ because Jesus had been crucified as a
malefactor. "Oh, if thou couldst understand, O tyrant,
the love which Jesus Christ hath borne thee, in being
willing to die upon the cross to make satisfaction for
thy sins, and to obtain for thee eternal happiness, certainly thou wouldst not labor to persuade me to deny
him; but thou thyself wouldst abandon everything that
thou hast and hopest for upon this earth, in order to
please and satisfy a God who has so loved thee." What
have not so many saints and holy martyrs done, who
have left all for Jesus Christ! Oh, shame unto us! how
many young virgins have renounced the marriage of
the great, royal riches, and all earthly delights, and
have willingly sacrificed their life to return some recompense of love for that love which was shown to them by
this crucified God! How is it, then, that the Passion of
Jesus Christ makes so little impression upon so many

[1] "Oh! si scires mysterium crucis!"

Christians? It results from this, that they apply themselves so little to consider what Jesus Christ has suffered for love of us.

O my Redeemer, I have been of the number of these ungrateful ones! Thou hast sacrificed Thy life upon a cross that Thou mightest not see me perish, and have I repeatedly been willing to lose Thee, an infinite good, by losing Thy grace? At this time the devil would have me believe that it is impossible that I should be saved, by bringing my sins to my remembrance; but the sight of Thee crucified, O my Jesus, assures me that Thou wilt not drive me from Thy face, if I repent of having offended Thee, and desire to love Thee. Yea, I repent, and desire to love Thee with all my heart. I detest these accursed pleasures, which have caused me to lose Thy grace. I love Thee, O Thou who art infinitely worthy of love, and I desire ever to love Thee; and the memory of my sins will serve to inflame me the more in the love of Thee, who hast come to seek me when I fled from Thee. No ; I desire to be separated from Thee no more, and not to cease to love Thee, O my Jesus.

O Mary, refuge of sinners, thou who hast so much shared in the sufferings of thy Son in his death, pray to him to pardon me, and to give me grace to love him.

CHAPTER II.

THE SEPARATE SUFFERINGS THAT JESUS CHRIST ENDURED AT HIS DEATH.

I.

Prophecy of Isaias—Abasement of the Promised Redeemer.

We now come to consider the separate sufferings which Jesus Christ endured in his Passion, and which had been foretold for many ages by the prophets, and especially by Isaias, in the fifty-third chapter of his prophecy. This prophet, as St. Irenæus, St. Justin, St. Cyprian, and others say, spoke so distinctly of the sufferings of our Redeemer that he seems to be another Evangelist. Hence St. Augustine says that the words of Isaias, which refer to the Passion of Jesus Christ, call rather for meditations and tears than for the explanations of sacred writers; and Hugo Grotius records that even the old Hebrews themselves could not deny that Isaias (especially in his fifty-third chapter) spoke of the Messiah promised by God. Some have wished to apply the passages of Isaias to persons named in Scripture and not to Jesus Christ; but Grotius ' answers that no one can be found to whom these texts may be referred.

Isaias writes: *Who hath believed our report ; and to whom is the arm of the Lord revealed?* [2] This was fulfilled, as St. John writes, when the Jews, notwithstand-

---

[1] "Quis potest nominari aut Regum aut Prophetarum, in quem hæc congruant? Nemo sane !"—*De ver. rel. chr.* l. 5, n. 10.

[2] "Quis credidit auditui nostro? et brachium Domini cui revelatum est ?"—*Isa.* liii. 1.

ing all the miracles which they had seen wrought by Jesus Christ, which proved him to be truly the Messiah sent by God, would not believe in him: *When He did so many miracles before them, they did not believe in Him, that the word of Isaias the prophet might be fulfilled, when he said, Lord, who hath believed our report; and to whom is the arm of the Lord revealed?*[1] Who will believe, says Isaias, what has been heard by us; and who has recognized the arm, that is, the power of the Lord? In these words he foretold the obstinacy of the Jews in not choosing to believe in Jesus Christ as their Redeemer. They fancied that this Messiah would exhibit upon earth great pomp, and the splendor of his greatness and power; and that, triumphing over all his enemies, he would thus load the people of the Jews with riches and honors; but no, the prophet adds these words to those above named: *He shall grow up as a slender plant before Him, and as a root out of a thirsty ground.*[2] The Jews thought that the Saviour would appear like a cedar of Libanus; but Isaias foretold that he would show himself like an humble shrub, or a root which grows in an arid soil, stripped of all beauty and splendor: *There is no beauty in Him, nor comeliness.*[3]

He then goes on to describe the Passion of the Lord: *We have seen Him and there was no sightliness, that we should be desirous of Him.*[4] We desired to recognize him, but we could not, for we have seen nothing but a man despised and vile upon the earth, and a man of sorrows:

[1] "Cum autem tanta signa fecisset coram eis, non credebant in eum; ut sermo Isaiæ Prophetæ impleretur, quem dixit: Domine, quis credidit auditui nostro? et brachium Domini cui revelatum est?"—*John*, xii. 37.

[2] "Et ascendet sicut virgultum coram eo, et sicut radix de terra sitienti."—*Isa.* liii. 2.

[3] "Non est species ei neque decor."—*Ibid.*

[4] "Et vidimus eum, et non erat aspectus, et desideravimus eum."—*Ibid.*

Despised, and the most abject of men,—a man of sorrows; whereupon we esteemed Him not.[1]

Adam, through his pride in not obeying the divine commands, brought ruin upon all men ; therefore the Redeemer, by his humility, chose to bring a remedy to this great evil, and was content to be treated as the lowest and most abject of men : that is, by being reduced to the lowest depths of humiliation. Therefore St. Bernard cried out, " O Thou who art lowest and highest ; O Thou humble and lofty ; O shame of men and glory of angels ! None is loftier than he; none more humble."[2] If, then, adds the saint, the Lord, who is higher than all things, has made himself the lowest of all things, every one of us ought to desire that all others should be preferred to him, and fear to be preferred to any.[3] But I, O my Jesus, fear that any should be preferred to me, and desire to be preferred above all. O Lord, give me humility. Thou, O My Jesus, with such love, hast embraced contempt, to teach me to be humble, and to love a hidden and an abject life ; and shall I desire to be esteemed by all, and to display myself in everything ? O my Jesus! grant me Thy love ; it will make me like to Thee. Let me no more live ungrateful to the love which Thou hast borne to me. Thou art almighty ; make me humble, make me holy, make me all Thine own.

[1] " Despectum, et novissimum virorum, virum dolorum, . . . unde nec reputavimus eum."—*Isa.* liii. 3.

[2] " O novissimum et altissimum ! o humilem et sublimem ! o opprobrium hominum et gloriam angelorum ! nemo illo sublimior, neque humilior."—*S. de Pass. D.*

[3] " Desiderabis subjici omnibus, et reformidabis præferri etiam minimo."—*Ibid.*

16

II.

Humiliations and Sufferings of Jesus Christ.

Isaias also called Jesus Christ the man of sorrows. It is to Jesus crucified that the words of Jeremias are especially applicable : *Thy grief is great as the sea.*[1] As all the waters of the rivers meet in the ocean, so in Jesus Christ are united all the pains of the sick, the penitential sufferings of anchorites, and all the pangs and contempts endured by martyrs. He was laden with sorrows both of soul and body. *Thou hast brought all Thy waves over me.*[2] "O my Father!" said our Redeemer by the mouth of David, "Thou hast sent upon me all the waves of Thy wrath;" and therefore, in the hour of death, he said, that he died sunk in a sea of sorrow and shame : *I have come unto the depths of the sea, and the storm hath sunk me.*[3] The Apostle writes that Almighty God, in commanding his Son to pay for our sins with his blood, desired thus to show how great was his justice: *Whom God hath proposed to be a propitiation, through faith in His blood, to the showing forth of His justice.*[4]

To form a conception of what Jesus Christ suffered in his life, and still more in his death, we must consider what the same Apostle says in his letter to the Romans : *God sending His own Son, in the likeness of sinful flesh, and by sin condemned sin in the flesh.*[5] Jesus Christ being sent by the Father to redeem man, clothed himself with that

[1] "Magna est velut mare contritio tua."—*Lam.* ii. 13.
[2] "Et omnes fluctus tuos induxisti super me."—*Ps.* lxxxvii. 8.
[3] "Veni in altitudinem maris, et tempestas demersit me."—*Ps.* lxviii. 3.
[4] "Quem proposuit Deus propitiationem per fidem in sanguine ipsius, ad ostensionem justitiæ suæ."—*Rom.* iii. 25.
[5] "Deus Filium suum mittens in similitudinem carnis peccati, et de peccato damnavit peccatum in carne."—*Ibid.* viii. 3.

flesh which was infected with sin ; and though he had
not contracted the pollution of sin, nevertheless he took
upon him the miseries contracted by human nature, as
the punishment of sin ; and he offered himself to the
Eternal Father, to satisfy the divine justice for all the
sins of men by his sufferings ; he was offered because he
himself willed it;[1] and the Eternal Father, as Isaias
writes, *laid upon Him the iniquity of us all.*[2] Behold Jesus,
therefore, laden with all the blasphemies, all the sacrileges, trespasses, thefts, cruelties, and abominable deeds
which men have committed and will commit. Behold
him, in a word, the object of all the divine curses which
men have deserved through their sins : *Christ hath redeemed us from the curse of the law, being made a curse for
us.*[3]

Therefore St. Thomas writes that both the internal
and outward pains of Jesus Christ exceeded all the pains
which can be endured in this life.[4] As for the external
pains of the body, it is enough to know that Jesus Christ
received from the Father a body prepared on purpose
for suffering; and on this account he himself said, *A body
hast Thou prepared for Me.*[5] St. Thomas remarks that
our Lord suffered pains and torments in all his senses:
he suffered in his sense of touch, because all his flesh
was torn; he suffered in his taste, with gall and vinegar;
he suffered in his hearing, through the blasphemies and
mockeries that were offered to him; he suffered in his
sight, at beholding his mother, who was present at his
death. He suffered also in all his members: his head

---

[1] "Oblatus est, quia ipse voluit."—*Isa.* liii. 7.

[2] "Et posuit Dominus in eo iniquitatem omnium nostrum."—
Ibid. 6.

[3] "Factus pro nobis maledictum."—*Gal.* iii. 13.

[4] "Uterque autem dolor in Christo fuit maximus inter dolores
præsentis vitæ."—P. 3, q. 46, a. 6.

[5] "Corpus autem aptasti mihi."—*Heb.* x. 5.

was tortured with thorns, his hands and feet with nails, his face with buffeting and spitting, and all his body with scourging, in the way that was foretold by Isaias, who said that the Redeemer would appear in his Passion like a leper, who has no sound portion in his body, and strikes horror into every one who sees him, as a man who is all wounds from head to foot. It is enough to say, that by such a sight of Jesus scourged, Pilate hoped to be allowed by the Jews to exempt him from death, when he showed him to the people from the balcony, saying, *Behold the Man.*[1]

St. Isidore says that other men, when their pains are great and last long, through the very severity of the pain, lose all power of feeling it.[2] But in Jesus Christ it was not so; his last sufferings were as bitter as his first, and the first stripes in his scourging were as torturing as the last; for the Passion of our Redeemer was not the work of man, but of the justice of God, who thought fit to chastise his Son with all the severity which the sins of all mankind deserved.

Thou, O my Jesus, Thou hast desired by Thy sufferings to take upon Thee the punishment due to my sins. Thus, if I had less offended Thee, Thou wouldst have suffered less in Thy death. And knowing this, can I live henceforward without loving Thee, and without mourning continually for the offences that I have committed against Thee? O my Jesus, I grieve that I have despised Thee, and I love Thee above everything. Oh, despise me not; receive me, that I may love Thee, since now I love Thee, and desire to love nothing but Thee. Too ungrateful should I be, if, after all the mercies Thou hast shown me, I should henceforth love anything but Thee.

[1] " Ecce homo !"—*John*, xix. 5.
[2] " Præ doloris magnitudine sensum doloris amittunt."

III.

Jesus Christ suffered voluntarily for Us.

Observe how it was foretold by Isaias: *We have thought Him as it were a leper, and as one stricken by God and afflicted. But He was wounded for our iniquities, He was bruised for our sins; the chastisement of our peace was upon Him, and by His stripes we are healed. All we like sheep have gone astray, every one hath turned aside into his own way; and the Lord hath laid on Him the iniquity of us all.*[1] Jesus, full of love, of his own will, offered himself, without a reply, to accomplish his Father's will, whose will it was to behold him outraged by executioners at their own pleasure. *He was offered because it was His own will, and He opened not His mouth: He shall be led as a sheep to the slaughter, and shall be dumb as a lamb before his shearer.*[2] As a lamb offers itself to be shorn without complaint, so our loving Redeemer in his Passion caused himself to be shorn, not of his wool, but of his very skin, without opening his mouth.

What obligation did he lie under to offer satisfaction for our sins? Yet he chose to take it upon him, that he might deliver us from eternal damnation; and therefore every one of us ought to give him thanks, and say, *Thou hast brought forth my soul, that it should not perish; Thou hast cast all my sins behind Thy back.*[3]

[1] "Et nos putavimus eum quasi leprosum, et percussum a Deo, et humiliatum. Ipse autem vulneratus est propter iniquitates nostras, attritus est propter scelera nostra. Disciplina pacis nostræ super eum, et livore ejus sanati sumus. Omnes nos quasi oves erravimus, unusquisque in viam suam declinavit; et posuit Dominus in eo iniquitatem omnium nostrum."—*Isa.* liii. 4-6.

[2] "Oblatus est, quia ipse voluit; et non aperuit os suum. Et quasi agnus coram tondente se, obmutescet."—*Isa.* liii. 7.

[3] "Tu autem eruisti animam meam ut non periret, projecisti post tergum tuum omnia peccata mea."—*Isa.* xxxviii. 17.

And thus Jesus voluntarily, through his own goodness, making himself the debtor for our debts, chose to sacrifice himself altogether, even to death in the pains of the cross, as he himself says in the Gospel of St. John: *I lay down My life; no one taketh it away from Me, but I lay it down of Myself.*[1]

IV.

The Sufferings of Jesus were Extreme.

St. Ambrose, writing of the Passion of our Lord, says that Jesus Christ has followers, but no equals.[2] The saints have endeavored to imitate Jesus Christ in suffering, to render themselves like him; but who ever attained to equalling him in his sufferings? He truly suffered for us, more than all the penitents, all the anchorites, all the martyrs have suffered, because God laid upon him the weight of a rigorous satisfaction to the divine justice for all the sins of men: *The Lord laid on Him the iniquity of us all.*[3] And, as St. Peter writes, Jesus bore all our sins upon the cross, to pay our punishment with his most holy body: *He Himself bore our sins in His own body on the tree.*[4] St. Thomas writes that Jesus Christ, in redeeming us, not only accomplished the virtue and infinite merit which belonged to his sufferings, but chose to suffer a depth of pain which might be sufficient to satisfy abundantly and rigorously for all the sins of the human race.[5] And St. Bonaventure writes: "He chose to suffer

---

[1] "Ego pono animam meam. . . . Nemo tollit eam a me, sed ego pono eam a meipso."—*John,* x. 17.

[2] "Æmulos habebat, pares non habet."—*In Luc.* xxii.

[3] "Et posuit Dominus in eo iniquitatem omnium nostrum."—*Isa.* liii. 6.

[4] "Peccata nostra ipse pertulit in corpore suo super lignum."—I *Pet.* ii. 24.

[5] "Non solum attendit quantam virtutem dolor ejus haberet, sed etiam quantum dolor ejus sufficeret secundum humanam naturam ad tantam satisfactionem."—P. 3, q. 46, a. 6.

as much pain as if he himself had committed all our
sins."¹ God himself thought right to aggravate the
pains of Jesus Christ, until they were equal to the entire
payment of all our debts; and thus the prophecy of
of Isaias was fulfilled: *The Lord was pleased to bruise Him
in infirmity.*

When we read the lives of the martyrs, it seems at
first as if some of them had suffered pains more bitter
tha. those of Jesus Christ; but St. Bonaventure says
that the pains of no martyr could ever equal in acuteness
the pains of our Saviour, which were more acute than
all other pains.' In like manner, St. Thomas writes
that the sufferings of Christ were the most severe pains
that can be felt in this present life.' Upon which St.
Laurence Justinian writes that in each of the torments
which our Lord endured, on account of the agony and
intensity of the suffering, he suffered as much as all the
tortures of martyrs.' And all this was predicted by King
David in a few words, when, speaking in the person of
Christ, he said, *Thy wrath is strong over Me; Thy terrors
have troubled Me.* Thus all the wrath of God, which he
had conceived against our sins, poured itself out upon
the person of Jesus Christ; and thus we must interpret
what the Apostle said, *He was made a curse for us;*' that
is, the object of all the curses deserved by our sins.

¹ "Tantum voluit doloris sufferre, quantum si ipse omnia peccata
fecisset."

' " Et Dominus voluit conterere eum in infirmitate."—*Isa.* liii. 10.

' " Nullus potuit ei æquari vivacitate sensus; dolor illius omnium
dolorum fuit acutissimus."—*In Sent.* l. 3, d. 16, a. 1, q. 2.

⁴ " Dolor in Christo fuit maximus inter dolores præsentis vitæ."—
P. 3, q. 46, a. 6.

⁵ "In singulis singula Martyrum sustinebat tormenta."—*De Tr.
Chr. Ag.* c. 19.

⁸ " Super me confirmatus est furor tuus . . . ; in me transierunt
iræ tuæ."—*Ps.* lxxxvii. 8, 17.

¹ " Factus pro nobis maledictum."—*Gal.* iii. 13.

V.

Interior Sufferings of Our Saviour.

Hitherto, also, we have spoken only of the outward bodily pains of Jesus Christ. And who can ever explain and comprehend the inward pains of his soul, which a thousand times exceeded his outward pains? This inward torment was such that in the Garden of Gethsemani it caused a sweat of blood to pour forth from all his body, and compelled him to say that this was enough to slay Him: *My soul is sorrowful even unto death.*[1] And since this anguish was enough to cause death, why did he not die? St. Thomas answers that he did not die because he himself prevented his own death, being ready to preserve his life, in order to give it in a while upon the tree of the cross. This sorrow also, which most deeply afflicted Jesus Christ in the garden, afflicted him also throughout his whole life; since, from the first moment when he began to live, he had ever before his eyes the causes of his inward grief; among which the most afflicting was, the sight of the ingratitude of men towards the love which he showed them in his Passion. ·

Nevertheless, an angel came to comfort him in the garden, as St. Luke relates.[2] Yet Venerable Bede says that this comfort, instead of lightening his pains, increased them.[3] The angel, indeed, strengthened him to endure with greater constancy for the salvation of men; upon which Bede remarks that Jesus was then strengthened for suffering, by a representation of the greatness of the fruits of his Passion, without the least diminution

---

[1] " Tristis est anima mea usque ad mortem."—*Matt.* xxvi. 38.

[2] " Apparuit autem illi Angelus de cœlo, confortans eum."—*Luke*, xxii. 43.

[3] " Confortatio dolorem non minuit, sed auxit."

of the greatness of his sufferings.[1] Therefore the Evangelist relates that immediately after the appearance of the angel, Jesus Christ was in an agony, and sweated blood in such abundance that it fell to the ground.[2]

St. Bonaventure further relates that the agony of Jesus then reached its height;[3] so that our afflicted Lord, at the sight of the anguish that he must suffer at the termination of his life now come, was so terrified that he prayed his divine Father that he might be delivered from it: *Father, if it be possible, let this cup pass from Me.*[4] Yet he said this, not that he might be delivered from the pains, for he had already offered himself to suffer them,—*He was offered, because He Himself willed,*[5]—but to teach us to understand the agony which he experienced in enduring this death so bitter to the senses; while in his will, in order to accomplish the will of his Father, in order to obtain for us the salvation he so ardently desired, he immediately added: *Nevertheless, not as I will, but as Thou wilt.*[6] And he continued thus to pray and to resign himself for the space of three hours: *He prayed the third time, saying the same words.*[7]

VI.

Patience of Jesus Christ—Fruits of His Death.

But let us follow the prophecy of Isaias. He foretold the blows, the buffetings, the spitting, and the other in-

[1] " Confortatus est ex fructus magnitudine, non subtracta doloris magnitudine."

[2] " Et factus in agonia, prolixius orabat. Et factus est sudor ejus sicut guttæ sanguinis decurrentis in terram."—*Luke,* xxii. 43, 44.

[3] " Dolor fuit in summo."

[4] " Pater mi ! si possibile est, transeat a me calix iste."—*Matt.* xxvi. 39.

[5] " Oblatus est, quia ipse voiuit."

[6] ' Verumtamen, non sicut ego volo, sed sicut tu."—*Matt.* xxvi. 44.

[7] " Et oravit tertio, eundem sermonem dicens."—*Mark,* xiv. 39.

sults which Jesus 'Christ endured the night before his death from the hands of the executioners, who kept him in bondage in the palace of Caiphas, in order to take him the next morning to Pilate, and to make him condemn him to death. *I have given My body to the strikers, and My cheeks to them that plucked them; I have not turned away My face from them that rebuked Me and spit upon Me.*[1] These insults are described by St. Mark, who adds that these soldiers, treating Jesus as a false prophet, in order to mock him, covered his face with a cloth, and then striking him with blows and buffetings, bade him prophesy who it was that smote him.[2]

Isaias goes on to speak of the death of Jesus Christ: *He shall be led as a sheep to the slaughter.*[3] The eunuch of Queen Candace, as we read in the Acts of the Apostles, reading this passage, asked of St. Philip, who, by a divine inspiration, had come to join himself with him, of whom these words were to be understood? and the saint then explained to him the whole mystery of the redemption accomplished by Jesus Christ; upon which the eunuch, then enlightened by God, desired at once to be baptized.

Isaias then continues, and foretells the great fruits which the world would derive from the death of the Saviour, and says that from it great numbers of saints would be spiritually born: *Because His soul hath labored, He shall see and be filled; by His knowledge shall this my just servant justify many, and He shall bear their iniquities.*[4]

---

[1] "Corpus meum dedi percutientibus, et genas meas vellentibus: faciem meam non averti ab increpantibus et conspuentibus in me."—*Isa.* l. 6.

[2] "Et cœperunt quidam conspuere eum, et velare faciem ejus, et colaphis eum cædere, et dicere ei : Prophetiza !—Et ministri alapis eum cædebant."—*Mark,* xiv. 65.

[3] "Sicut ovis ad occisionem ducetur."—*Isa.* liii. 7.

[4] "Si posuerit pro peccato animam suam, videbit semen longævum . . . ; in scientia sua justificabit ipse justus servus meus multos."—*Isa.* liii. 10, 11.

VII.

Prophecies of David—Various Circumstances.

David also predicted other circumstances more in detail respecting the Passion of Jesus Christ. Especially in the twenty-first Psalm he foretold that he should be pierced with nails in his hands and in his feet, so that they should be able to count all his bones.[1] He foretold that before he should be crucified, his garments should be stripped off from him, and divided among the executioners ;[2] speaking of his outer garments alone, because the inner vestment, which was made without seam, was to be given by lot: *They parted My garments amongst them, and upon My vesture they cast lots.* This prophecy is recalled both by St. Matthew and St. John.

David also foretold what St. Matthew thus relates respecting the blasphemies and mockeries of the Jews against Jesus Christ while he hung upon the cross: *They that passed by blasphemed Him, wagging their heads and saying, Vah, Thou that destroyest the temple of God, and in three days dost rebuild it, save Thy own self; if Thou be the Son of God, come down from the cross.[3] In like manner also, the chief priests, with the scribes and ancients, mocking, said, He saved others, Himself He cannot save ; if He be the king of*

[1] "Foderunt manus meas et pedes meos; dinumeraverunt omnia ossa mea."

[2] "Diviserunt sibi vestimenta mea, et super vestem meam miserunt sortem."—*Ps.* xxi. 19 ; *Matt.* xxvii. 35 ; *John*, xix. 23.

[3] "Prætereuntes autem blasphemabant eum, moventes capita sua et dicentes: Vah, qui destruis templum Dei, et in triduo illud reædificas, salva temetipsum; si Filius Dei es, descende de cruce. Similiter et Principes sacerdotum illudentes cum Scribis et Senioribus dicebant : Alios salvos fecit, seipsum non potest salvum facere ; si Rex Israel est, descendat nunc de cruce, et credimus ei. Confidit in Deo; liberet nunc, si vult eum; dixit enim: Quia Filius Dei sum."—*Matt.* xxvii. 40–43.

*Israel, let Him now come down from the cross, and we will
believe Him. He trusted in God, let Him now deliver Him if
He will have Him ; for He said, I am the Son of God.* All
this was in accordance with what David had foretold in
the following words: *All they that saw Me have laughed Me
to scorn ; they have spoken with the lips and wagged the head.
He hoped in the Lord, let Him deliver Him, let Him save
Him, seeing He delighteth in Him.*[1]

David further foretold the great pains which Jesus
should suffer on the cross in seeing himself abandoned
by all, and even by his own disciples, except St. John
and the Blessed Virgin; while his beloved Mother, by
her presence, did not lessen the sufferings of her Son,
but rather increased them through the compassion that
he felt for her, in seeing her thus afflicted by his death.
Thus our suffering Lord, in the agonies of his bitter
death, had none to comfort him. This also was foretold
by David: *I looked for one that would grieve together with
Me, but there was none ; and for one that would comfort Me,
and I found none.*[2] The greatest suffering, however, of
our afflicted Redeemer consisted in his beholding himself abandoned by his Eternal Father, upon which he
cried out, according to the prophecy of David, *O God, my
God, look upon me ; why hast Thou forsaken me ? Far
from My salvation are the words of My sins;*[3] as though he
had said, " O my Father, the sins of men, which I call my
own, because I have taken them upon me, forbid me to
be delivered from these sufferings which are ending my
life; and why hast Thou, O my God, abandoned me in this

---

[1] " Omnes videntes me deriserunt me; locuti sunt labiis et moverunt caput: Speravit in Domino, eripiat eum; salvum faciat eum,
quoniam vult eum."—*Ps.* xxi. 8, 9.

[2] " Et sustinui qui simul contristaretur, et non fuit; et qui consolaretur, et non inveni."—*Ps.* lxviii. 21.

[3] " Deus meus, respice in me; quare me dereliquisti ? longe a salute
mea verba delictorum meorum."—*Ps.* xxi. 2.

my great agony?" To these words of David correspond the words which St. Matthew records as uttered by Jesus upon the cross a little while before his death: *Eli, Eli, lamma sabachthani? that is, My God, My God, why hast Thou forsaken Me?* [1]

VIII.

Jesus Christ is the True Messias—Superabundance of His Merits.

From all this it clearly appears how unjustly the Jews refuse to recognize Jesus Christ as their Messiah and Saviour, because he died so shameful a death. They do not perceive that if, instead of dying as a malefactor upon the cross, Jesus Christ had died a death accounted honorable and glorious by men, he would not have been that Messiah who was promised by God and predicted by the prophets, who, so many ages before, had foretold that our Redeemer should die a death loaded with insults: *He shall give His cheek to the smiter, He shall be overwhelmed with insults.* [2] All these humiliations, and all the sufferings of Jesus Christ, already foretold by the prophets, were not understood even by his disciples until after his resurrection and ascension into heaven: *These things His disciples did not understand at first; but when Jesus was glorified, then they remembered that these things were written of Him.* [3]

In a word, by the Passion of Jesus Christ, which was accompanied by so great sufferings and so great igno-

---

[1] "Eli! Eli! lamma sabacthani?—Hoc est: Deus meus! Deus meus! ut quid delerequisti me?"—*Matt.* xxvii. 46.

[2] "Dabit percutienti se maxillam, saturabitur opprobriis."—*Lam.* iii. 30.

[3] "Hæc non cognoverunt discipuli ejus primum; sed, quando glorificatus est Jesus, tunc recordati sunt quia hæc erant scripta de eo, et hæc fecerunt ei."—*John,* xii. 16.

miny, that which David wrote was fulfilled: *Justice and peace have kissed each other.*[1] They kissed each other, because, by the merits of Jesus Christ, men obtained peace with God, while, at the same time, the divine justice was more than abundantly satisfied by the death of the Redeemer. We say, *more than abundantly*, because to save us, it was not actually necessary that Jesus Christ should endure so many sufferings and insults. One single drop of blood, one single prayer, would have been sufficient (so to say) to save the whole world; while, in order to strengthen our hopes, and to inflame our love, he thought fit that our redemption should not only be sufficient, but more than abundant, as David foretold: *Let Israel hope in the Lord; for with the Lord there is mercy, and with Him is plentiful redemption.*[2]

This had also been clearly announced by Job, when, speaking in the person of Christ, he said, *Oh that my sins were weighed, and my calamities which I suffer in a balance! As the sand of the sea, it would appear very heavy.*[3] Here Jesus, by the mouth of Job, calls our sins his sins, because he had bound himself to make satisfaction for us, in order to make his justice ours, as St. Augustine expresses it.[4] On this account the gloss upon the text quoted from Job contains this remark: "In the balance of the divine justice the Passion of Christ outweighs the sins of human nature."[5] All the lives of men would not have been sufficient to make satisfaction for a single sin;

---

[1] " Justitia et Pax osculatæ sunt."—*Ps.* lxxxiv. 11.

[2] " Speret Israel in Domino, quia apud Dominum misericordia, et copiosa apud eum redemptio."—*Ps.* cxxix. 6.

[3] " Utinam appenderentur peccata mea . . . . , et calamitas quam patior, in statera ! quasi arena maris hæc gravior appareret."—*Job*, vi. 2.

[4] " Delicta nostra sua delicta fecit, ut justitiam suam nostram justitiam faceret."—*In Ps.* xxi. *en.* 2.

[5] " In statera divinæ Justitiæ, passio Christi præponderat peccatis humanæ naturæ."

but the pains of Jesus Christ have paid for all our sins : *He is the propitiation of our sins.*[1] Therefore, St. Laurence Justinian encourages every sinner who truly repents to hope confidently for pardon through the merits of Jesus Christ, saying to them, " Measure thy sins by the afflictions of Christ the sufferer ;"[2] meaning thereby to say, " O sinner, measure not thy guilt by thy contrition, for all thy works cannot obtain thee pardon ; measure it by the pains of Jesus Christ, and from them hope for pardon, for thy Redeemer hath abundantly paid thy debt."

O Saviour of the world ! in Thy flesh, torn with scourgings, with thorns, and with nails, I comprehend the love Thou hast borne me, and my ingratitude in having so injured Thee after such love ; but Thy blood is my hope, for, with the price of that blood, Thou hast redeemed me from hell as often as I have deserved it. O God ! what would become of me through all eternity, if Thou hadst not determined to save me by Thy death ! Miserable man that I am, I have well known that, by losing Thy grace, I condemned myself to live forever in despair, and far from Thee in hell ; and yet I have repeatedly dared to turn my back upon Thee. But yet I turn to say, Thy blood is my hope. Oh that I had died, and not offended Thee ! O infinite goodness ! I deserved to continue blind, and Thou hast enlightened me with new light; I deserved to continue still more hardened, and Thou hast given me tenderness and compunction ; wherefore I now abhor the offences I have committed against Thee more than death, and I feel a great desire to love Thee. These graces, which I have received from Thee, assure me that Thou hast now pardoned me,

[1] " Ipse est propitiatio fro peccatis nostris, . . . etiam pro totius mundi."—1 *John*, ii. 2.

[2] " Tua in ejus afflictionibus metire delicta."—*De Tr. Chr. Ag.* c. 20.

and desirest to save me. O my Jesus! who could cease to love Thee henceforth, or could love anything apart from Thee? I love Thee, O my Jesus, and I trust in Thee; increase in me this confidence and this love, that henceforth I may forget everything, and think of nothing but loving Thee and giving Thee pleasure.

O Mary, Mother of God, obtain for me the grace of being faithful to thy Son and my Redeemer.

CHAPTER III.

THE SCOURGING, THE CROWNING WITH THORNS, AND THE CRUCIFIXION OF JESUS CHRIST.

. I.

The Scourging.

St. Paul writes respecting Jesus Christ: *He emptied Himself, taking the form of a servant.*[1] On this text St. Bernard remarks, " He took not only the form of a servant, that he might obey, but that of a slave, that he might be beaten."[2] Our Redeemer, who is the Lord of all, was willing not only to take upon him the condition of a servant, but even that of a bad servant, that he might be punished as a malefactor, and thus make satisfaction for our sins.

It is certain that the scourging was the most cruel of the tortures that shortened the life of our Redeemer; for the great effusion of blood (already foretold by him, when he said, *This is My blood of the New Testament, which shall*

[1] " Semetipsum exinanivit, formam servi accipiens."—*Phil.* ii. 7.
[2] " Non solum formam servi accepit, ut subesset, sed etiam mali servi, ut vapularet."—*S. de Pass. D.*

be shed for many') was the principal cause of his death. It is true that this blood was first poured forth in the garden, and was also poured forth in the crowning with thorns, and by the driving-in of the nails ; but the largest portion was shed in the scourging, which was also a cause of great shame and insult to Jesus Christ, because this was a punishment inflicted only on slaves. On this account, also, the tyrants who condemned the holy martyrs to death scourged them after their condemnation, and then slew them ; while our Lord was scourged before he was condemned to death. He had himself particularly predicted the scourging to his disciples during his life : *He shall be given up to the Gentiles, and mocked and scourged.* Thus he signified to them the great anguish which this torture would inflict upon him.

It was revealed to St. Bridget that one of the executioners first commanded Jesus Christ to strip himself of his garments. He obeyed, and then embraced the pillar to which he was bound, and was then so cruelly scourged that his whole body was lacerated. The revelation stated that the stripes not only struck him, but ploughed into his most holy flesh. He was so torn open that, as the same revelation declares, his ribs appeared laid bare. With this agrees what was written by St. Jerome: "The stripes cut the most holy body of God ;" and also what St. Peter Damian wrote, that the executioners exhausted themselves with fatigue in scourging our Lord. All

---

1 " Hic est enim sanguis meus novi testamenti, qui pro multis effundetur."—*Matt.* xxvi. 28.
3 " Tradetur enim Gentibus, et illudetur, et flagellabitur."—*Luke*, xviii. 32.
3 " Jubente lictore, seipsum vestibus exuit, columnam sponte amplectens ligatur, et flagellis, non evellendo, sed sulcando, totum corpus laceratur."—*Rev.* l. 4, c. 70.
4 " Ita ut costæ viderentur."—*Ibid.* l. 1, c. 10.
5 " Sacratissimum corpus Dei flagella secuerunt."—*In Matt.* xxvii.
6 " Usque ad defatigationem."

17

this was already foretold by Isaias in the words, *He was bruised for our iniquities ;*[1] the word bruised signifying the same as being broken to pieces, or as being pounded in a mortar.

Behold me, O my Jesus! I am one of Thy most cruel executioners, who have scourged Thee with my sins; have pity upon me. O my loving Saviour! a heart is too little with which to love Thee. I desire no longer to live for myself, I desire to live only for Thee, my love, my all. Wherefore I say to Thee, with St. Catharine of Genoa, "O love! O love! let there be no more sins. It is enough that I have already offended Thee so much! now I hope to be wholly Thine, and with Thy grace I desire to be ever Thine through all eternity."

II.

The Crowning with Thorns.

The divine Mother revealed to the same St. Bridget that the crown of thorns surrounded the whole sacred head of her Son, as low down as the middle of his forehead; and that the thorns were driven in with such violence that the blood gushed out in streams over all his countenance, so that the whole face of Jesus Christ appeared covered with blood.[2]

Origen writes that this crown of thorns was not taken from the head of the Lord until he had expired upon the cross.[3] In the mean time, as the inner garment of Christ was not sewed together, but woven all in one

---

[1] " Attritus est propter scelera nostra."—*Isa.* liii. 5.

[2] " Quæ (corona) tam vehementer caput Filii mei pupugit, ut ex sanguine affluente replerentur oculi ejus.—Ad medium frontis descendebat, plurimis rivis sanguinis decurrentibus per faciem ejus, ut quasi nihil nisi sanguis totum videretur."—*Rev.* l. 1, c. 10; l. 4, c. 70.

[3] " Corona spinea, semel imposita, et nunquam detracta."—*In Matt.* tr. 35.

piece, on this account it was not divided among the soldiers, like his outer garments, but it was given by lot, as St. John writes: *The soldiers, therefore, when they had crucified Him, took His garments, and made four parts, to every soldier a part, and also His coat. Now the coat was without seam, woven from the top throughout. They said then one to another: Let us not cut it ; but let us cast lots for it, whose it shall be.*[1] As this garment, then, must have been drawn off over the head, many authors write, with great probability, that when Jesus was stripped of it, the crown of thorns was taken from his head, and was replaced before he was nailed to the cross.

In the book of Genesis it is written: *Cursed is the earth in thy work; thorns and thistles shall it bring forth to thee.*[2] This curse was inflicted by God upon Adam and upon all his posterity ; and by the earth here spoken of we must understand, not only the material earth, but the flesh of man, which, being infected by the sin of Adam, brings forth only the thorns of sin. In order to remedy this infection, says Tertullian, it was necessary that Jesus Christ should offer to God in sacrifice this great torment of the crowning with thorns.[3]

This torture also, besides being in itself most acute, was accompanied by blows and spitting, and by the mockings of the soldiers, as St. Matthew and St. John relate: *And plaiting a crown of thorns, they put it upon His head, and a reed in His right hand. And bowing the knee before Him, they mocked Him, saying, Hail, King of the*

[1] "Milites ergo, cum crucifixissent eum, acceperunt vestimenta ejus (et fecerunt quatuor partes, unicuique militi partem), et tunicam; erat autem tunica inconsutilis, desuper contexta per totum; dixerunt ergo ad invicem: Non scindamus eam, sed sortiamur de illa cujus sit."—*John*, xix. 23, 24.

[2] "Maledicta terra in opere tuo . . .; spinas et tribulos germinabit tibi."—*Gen.* iii. 17.

[3] "Hunc (Christum) enim oportebat pro omnibus gentibus fieri sacrificium."—*Adv. Judæos.*

Jews! And spitting upon Him, they took the reed, and struck His head.[1] *And the soldiers plaiting a crown of thorns, put it upon His head; and they put on Him a purple garment. And they came to Him and said, Hail, King of the Jews! and they gave Him blows.*[2]

O my Jesus! what thorns have I added to this crown with my sinful thoughts to which I have consented! I would I could die with grief! Pardon me, through the merit of this grief, which Thou didst then accept in order to pardon me. O my Lord, thus bruised and thus despised! Thou hast laden Thyself with all these pains and mockeries in order to move me to have compassion upon Thee, that, at least through compassion, I may love Thee, and no more displease Thee. It is enough, O my Jesus; cease to suffer more : I am convinced of the love that Thou bearest to me, and I love Thee with all my heart. But now I see that it is not enough for Thee; Thou art not satisfied with thorns, until Thou findest Thyself dead with anguish upon the cross. O goodness! O infinite love! Miserable is the heart that loves Thee not.

III.

Jesus Carries His Cross.

The cross began to torture Jesus Christ before be was nailed upon it ; for after he was condemned by Pilate, the cross on which he was to die was given to him to carry to Calvary, and, without refusing, he took it upon his shoulders.[3] Speaking of this, St. Augustine

[1] " Et exeuntes eum, chlamydem coccineam circumdederunt ei; et plectentes coronam de spinis, posuerunt super caput ejus, et arundinem in dextera ejus; et genu flexo ante eum, illudebant ei, dicentes: Ave, Rex Judæorum. Et expuentes in eum, acceperunt arundinem, et percutiebant caput ejus.— *Matt.* xxvii. 28-30.

[2] " Et dabant ei alapas."— *John,* xix. 3.

[3] " Et bajulans sibi crucem, exivit in eum, qui dicitur Calvariæ, locum "— *John,* xix. 17.

writes: "If we regard the wickedness of his tormentors, the insult was great ; if we regard the love of Jesus, the mystery is great ; ¹ for in carrying the cross, our Captain then lifted up the standard under which his followers upon this earth must be enrolled and must fight, in order to be made his companions in the kingdom of heaven."

St. Basil, speaking of the passage in Isaias, *A child is born to us, and a son is given to us, and the government is upon His shoulder,*² says "that earthly tyrants load their subjects with unjust burdens, in order to increase their own power; but Jesus Christ chose to take upon himself the burden of the cross, and to carry it, in order to leave life to us therein, that he might obtain salvation for us." He further remarks that the kings of the earth found their sovereignties in the force of arms and in the heaping-up of riches; but Jesus Christ founded his sovereignty in the insults of the cross,—that is, in humbling himself and in suffering,—and on this account he willingly accepted it, and carried it on that painful journey, in order, by his example, to give us courage to embrace with resignation every cross, and thus to follow him. Wherefore, also, he said to his disciples, *If any man will come after Me, let him deny himself, and take up his cross and follow Me.*³

It is useful here to note the beautiful expressions applied to the cross by St. John Chrysostom:

He calls it *the hope of the despairing;*⁴ for what hope of salvation would sinners have were it not for the cross on which Jesus Christ died to save them?

---

¹ "Si pectet impietas, grande ludibrium; si pietas, grande mysterium."—*In Jo. tr.* 117.

² "Factus est principatus super humerum ejus."—*Isa.* ix. 6.

³ "Si quis vult post me venire, abneget semetipsum, et tollat crucem suam, et sequatur me."—*Matt.* xvi. 24.

⁴ "Spes Christianorum, desperatorum Via."

The guide of the voyager;[1] for the humiliation of the cross (that is, of tribulation) is the cause which, in this life that is like a sea of dangers, gives us grace to keep the divine law, and to amend ourselves after our trangressions; as the prophet says, *It is good for me that Thou hast humbled me, that I might learn Thy justifications.*[2]

The counsellor of the just;[3] because in adversities the just learn wisdom, and gain motives for uniting themselves more closely to God.

The rest of the troubled;[4] for where can the troubled find relief but in beholding that cross on which their Redeemer and God died of pain for love of them?

The glorying of the martyrs;[5] because in this consists the glory of the holy martyrs, that they were able to unite their deaths to the pains and death which Jesus Christ suffered on the cross; as St. Paul says, *God forbid that I should glory, save in the cross of our Lord Jesus Christ.*[6]

The physician of the sick;[7] and great indeed is the remedy of the cross to those who are sick in spirit; tribulations make them repent, and detach them from the world.

The fount for the thirsty;[8] the cross, that is, suffering for Jesus Christ, being the desire of the saints, as St. Teresa was wont to say, "Oh that I might suffer! oh that I might die!" and as St. Mary Magdalen of Pazzi said, "May I suffer, and not die;" meaning that she would

[1] "Navigantium Gubernator."
[2] "Bonum mihi quia humiliasti me, ut discam justificationes tuas."—*Ps.* cxviii. 71.
[3] "Justorum Consiliarius."
[4] "Tribulatorum Requies."
[5] "Martyrum Gloriatio."
[6] "Mihi absit gloriari, nisi in cruce Domini nostri Jesu Christi."—*Gal.* vi. 14.
[7] "Ægrotantium Medicus."
[8] "Sitientium Fons."

refuse to die and to go to rejoice in heaven, in order that she might continue to suffer upon this earth.

Finally, to speak of all alike, both the just and sinners, every one has his own cross. The just, though they enjoy peace of conscience, yet all have their vicissitudes; at one time they are comforted by visits of divine mercy, at another they are afflicted by bodily vexations and infirmities, and especially by desolation of spirit, by darkness and weariness, by scruples and temptations, and by fears for their own salvation. Much heavier are the crosses of sinners, through remorse of conscience, through the terrors of eternal punishment, which from time to time affright them, and through the pains they suffer when things go wrong with them. The saints, when adversities befall them, unite themselves with the divine will, and suffer them with patience; but how can the sinner calm himself by recollecting the divine will, when he is living at enmity with God? The pains of the enemies of God are unmixed pains, pains without relief. Wherefore St. Teresa was wont to say "that he who loves God embraces the cross, and thus does not feel it ; while he who does not love him drags the cross along by force and thus cannot but feel it."

IV.

The Crucifixion.

It was revealed to St. Bridget that when the Saviour saw himself laid upon the cross, he stretched out his right hand to the place where it was to be nailed.[1] They then immediately nailed the other hand, and then his sacred feet; and Jesus Christ was left to die upon this bed of anguish. St. Augustine says that the punishment of the cross was a most bitter torment, because, upon

[1] "Voluntarie extendit brachium, et, aperta sua dextera manu, posuit eam in cruce; quam tortores crucifixerunt."—*Rev.* l. 7, c. 15.

the cross, death itself was prolonged, lest the pain should be speedily ended.[1]

O God ! what horror must then have smitten heaven, at the sight of the Son of the Eternal Father crucified between two thieves ! Such, in truth, was the prophecy of Isaias: *He was reputed with the wicked.*[2] Therefore St. John Chrysostom, contemplating Jesus upon the cross, cried out, full of amazement and love, "I see him in the midst, in the holy Trinity ; I see him in the midst, between Moses and Elias ; I see him in the midst, be-tween two thieves."[3] As though he had said, "I see my Saviour first in heaven between the Father and the Holy Ghost; I see him upon the Mount Tabor, between two saints, Moses and Elias; how, then, can I see him crucified upon Calvary between two thieves?" How could this come to pass, but through the divine decree, that thus he must die, to satisfy by his death for the sins of men, and to save from death, as Isaias had fore-told: *He was reputed with the wicked, and He hath borne the sins of many.*[4]

The same prophet also asks, *Who is this that cometh from Edom, with dyed garments from Bosra; this beautiful one in His robe, walking in the greatness of His strength ?*[5] (Edom signifying a red color, though somewhat dark, as is explained in Gen. xxv. 30); and he gives the

---

[1] "Mors ipsa protendebatur, ne dolor citius finiretur."—*In Jo. tr.* 36.

[2] "Et cum sceleratis reputatus est."—*Isa.* liii. 12.

[3] "Medium in Sancta Triade, medium inter Moysen et Eliam, medium inter Latrones!"

[4] "Et cum sceleratis reputatus est, et ipse peccata multorum tulit."—*Isa.* liii. 12.

[5] "Quis est iste qui venit de Edom, tinctis vestibus de Bosra ? iste formosus in stola sua, gradiens in multitudine fortitudinis suæ."—*Isa.* lxiii. 1.

answer, *I that speak justice, and am a defender to save.*[1] The person who thus replies is, according to the interpreters, Jesus Christ, who says, I am the promised Messiah, who am come to save men, by triumphing over their enemies.

Then, further, he is again asked, *Why is Thy apparel red, and Thy garments like theirs that that tread in the wine-press?*[2] And he answers, *I have trodden the wine-press alone, and of the Gentiles there is not a man with Me.*[3] Tertullian, St. Cyprian, and St. Augustine explain the wine-press to mean the Passion of Jesus Christ, in which his garments—that is, his most holy flesh—was covered with blood and wounds, according to what St. John wrote : *He was clothed with a garment sprinkled with blood; and His name is called the Word of God.*[4] St. Gregory, explaining the expression *I have trodden the wine-press alone,* says, " He trod the wine-press, and was himself trodden."[5] He trod it, because Jesus Christ, by his Passion, overcame the devil ; he was trodden, because, in his Passion, his body was bruised and broken, as the grapes are broken in the wine-press, and, as Isaias expresses it in another text, *The Lord was pleased to bruise Him in infirmity.*[6]

And now behold this Lord, who was fairest among men,[7] appears on Calvary with his form so disfigured by torments, that it struck horror into all who saw it. Yet this deformity makes him seem more beautiful in the eyes

[1] " Ego, qui loquor justitiam, et propugnator sum ad salvandum."—*Isa.* lxiii. 1.

[2] " Quare ergo rubrum est vestimentum tuum, et vestimenta tua sicut calcantium in torculari ?"—*Ibid.* 2.

[3] " Torcular calcavi solus, et de gentibus non est vir mecum."—*Ibid.* 3.

[4] " Et vestitus erat veste aspersa sanguine, et vocatur nomen ejus Verbum Dei."—*Apoc.* xix. 13.

[5] " Torcular in quo calcatus calcavit."—*In Es. hom.* 13.

[6] " Et voluit Dominus conterere eum in infirmitate."—*Isa.* liii. 10.

[7] " Speciosus forma præ filiis hominum."—*Ps.* xliv. 3.

of souls that love him, because these wounds, these marks
of the scourging, this lacerated flesh, are all tokens and
proofs of the love he bears them ; upon which the poet
Petrucci beautifully sings, " O Lord, if Thon sufferest
scourgings for us, to the souls that are bound to Thee,
the more deformed Thou art, the more fair dost Thou
appear."

St. Augustine adds, " He hung in deformity upon the
cross, but his deformity is our beauty." [1]   And truly so,
because this deformity of Jesus crucified was the cause
of the beauty of our souls, which, when they were deformed, were washed with his divine blood, and became
fair and lovely, according to what St. John wrote, *Who
are these that are clothed in white garments ?   These are
they who have come out of great tribulation, and have washed
their garments, and made them white in the blood of the Lamb.*[2]
All the saints, as being children of Adam (with the ex-
ception of the Blessed Virgin), were at one time covered
with a foul garment, and soiled with Adam's sin and
with their own; but being washed with the blood of the
Lamb, they became white and agreeable in the sight of
God.

Well, then, didst Thou say, O my Jesus, that, when
Thou shouldst be lifted up upon the cross, Thou wouldst
draw everything unto Thee;[3] "and this he said, signifying by what death he should die."   Truly Thou hast left
undone nothing to draw all hearts unto Thee.   Many
are the happy souls who, in seeing Thee crucified and
dying for love of them, have abandoned everything—

---

[1] " Pendebat in cruce deformis, sed deformitas illius pulchritudo
nostra erat."—*Serm.* 27, *E. B.*

[2] " Hi qui amicti sunt stolis albis, qui sunt ? . . . Hi sunt qui
venerunt de tribulatione magna, et laverunt stolas suas et dealbaver·
unt eas in sanguine Agni."—*Apoc.* vii. 13.

[3] " Et ego, si exaltatus fuero a terra, omnia traham ad meipsum."
—*John.* xii. 32.

possessions, dignities, country, and kindred, even to the embracing of torments and death—in order to give themselves wholly to Thee. Unhappy they who resist Thy graces, which Thou hast gained for them with Thy great labors and sorrows. O my God, this will be their great torment in hell, to think that they have lost a God who, to draw them to love him, gave his life upon a cross, that of their own choice they have perished, and that there will be no remedy for their ruin through all eternity. O my Redeemer, I have already deserved to fall into this ruin, through the sins I have committed against Thee. Alas, how often have I resisted Thy grace, which sought to draw me unto Thee, and, in order to cleave to my own inclinations, have despised Thy love, and turned my back upon Thee! Oh that I had died before I had offended Thee! Oh that I had ever loved Thee! I thank Thee, O my love, that Thou hast borne with me with so much patience, and that, instead of abandoning me, as I deserved, Thou hast repeated Thy calls, and increased Thy lights and Thy loving impulses upon me. *I will sing the mercies of God forever.*[1] Oh, cease not, my Saviour and my hope, to continue to draw me, and to multiply Thy graces upon me, that I may love Thee in heaven with more fervor, remembering the many mercies that Thou hast shown me, after all the offences that I have committed against Thee. I hope for all, through that precious blood which Thou hast shed for me, and that bitter death which Thou hast endured for me.

O holy Virgin Mary, protect me ; pray to Jesus for me.

V.

Jesus upon the Cross.

Jesus upon the cross was a spectacle which filled heaven and earth with amazement, at the sight of an Almighty

---

[1] " Misericordias Domini in æternum cantabo."—*Ps.* lxxxviii. 2.

God, the Lord of all, dying upon an infamous gibbet,
condemned as a malefactor between two other malefactors. It was a spectacle of justice, in displaying the
Eternal Father, in order that his justice might be satisfied ; punishing the sins of men in the person of his only-
begotten Son, loved by him as himself. It was a
spectacle of mercy, displaying his innocent Son dying a
death so shameful and so bitter, in order to save his
creatures from the punishment that was due to them.
Especially was it a sight of love, in displaying a God who
offered and gave his life to redeem from death his slaves
and enemies.

It is this spectacle which ever was and ever will be the
dearest object of the contemplations of the saints, through
which they have counted it little to strip themselves of
all earthly pleasures and goods, and to embrace with
desire and joy both pain and death, in order to make
some return of gratitude to a God who died for love of
them.

Comforted by the sight of Jesus derided upon the
cross, the saints have loved contempt more than worldly
people have loved all the honors of the world. At the
sight of Jesus naked and dying upon the cross, they
have sought to abandon all the good things of this earth.
At the sight of him all wounded upon the cross, while
the blood flowed forth from all his limbs, they have
learnt to abhor sensual pleasures, and have sought to
afflict their flesh as much as they could, in order to accompany with their own sufferings the sufferings of the
Crucified. At the sight of the obedience and conformity of will retained by Jesus Christ to the will of his
Father, they have labored to conquer all those appetites
which were not conformed to the divine pleasure; while
many, though occupied in works of piety, yet, knowing
that to be deprived of their own will was the sacrifice the
most welcome to the heart of God which they could of-

fer, have entered into some religious Order, to lead a life of obedience, and subject their own will to that of others. At the sight of the patience of Jesus Christ, in being willing to suffer so many pains and insults for the love of us, they have received with satisfaction and joy injuries, infirmities, persecutions, and the torments of tyrants. At the sight of the love which Jesus Christ has shown to us in sacrificing to God his life upon the cross for us, they have sacrificed to Jesus Christ all they possessed, —their property, their pleasures, their honors, and their life.

How is it, then, that so many Christians, although they know by faith that Jesus Christ died for love of them, instead of devoting themselves wholly to love and serve him, devote themselves to offend and despise him for the sake of brief and miserable pleasures? Whence comes this ingratitude? It comes from their forgetfulness of the Passion and death of Jesus Christ. And, O my God, what will be their remorse and shame at the day of judgment, when the Lord shall reproach them with all that he has done and suffered for them?

Let us not, then, cease, O devout souls, ever to keep before our eyes Jesus crucified, and dying in the midst of torments and insults through love of us. From the Passion of Jesus Christ all the saints have drawn those flames of love which made them forget all the good things of this world, and even their own selves, to give themselves up wholly to love and please this divine Saviour, who has so loved men that it seems as if he could not have done more in order to be loved by them. In a word, the cross, that is, the Passion of Jesus Christ, is that which will gain for us the victory over all our passions and all the temptations that hell will hold out to us, in order to separate us from God. The cross is the road and ladder by which we mount to heaven. Happy he who embraces it during his life, and does not put it off till the hour of death. He that dies embracing the cross has a sure pledge of eternal life, which is promised to all those who follow Jesus Christ with their cross.

O my crucified Jesus! to make Thyself loved by men Thou has spared nothing; Thou hast even given Thy life with a most painful death; how, then, can men who love their kindred, their friends, and even animals from whom they receive any token of affection, be so ungrateful to Thee as to despise Thy grace and Thy love, for the sake of miserable and vain delights! Oh, miserable that I am, I am one of those ungrateful beings who, for things of no worth, have renounced Thy friendship, and have turned my back upon Thee. I have deserved that Thou shouldst drive me from Thy face, as I have often banished Thee from my heart. But I know that Thou dost not cease to ask my heart of me: *Thou shalt love the Lord thy God.*[1] Yea, O my Jesus, as Thou desirest that I should love Thee and offerest me pardon, I renounce all creatures, and henceforth I desire to love Thee alone, my Creator and my Redeemer. Thou dost deserve to be the only object of my soul's love.

O Mary, Mother of God, and refuge of sinners, pray for me; obtain for me the grace of loving God, and I ask for nothing more.

---

[1] " Diliges Dominum Deum tuum."—*Deut.* vi. 5.

CHAPTER IV.

THE INSULTS OFFERED TO JESUS CHRIST WHILE HE WAS HANGING UPON THE CROSS.

I.

Agony of Jesus on the Cross.

Pride, as we have said, was the cause of the sin of Adam, and, consequently, of the ruin of the human race. On this account Jesus Christ came to repair this ruin by his own humiliation; not refusing to embrace the shame of all the insults that his enemies offered him, as he had himself predicted by David : *Since for thy sake I have endured reproach, confusion hath covered My face.*[1] The whole life of our Redeemer was filled with shame and insults which he received from men; and he did not refuse to accept them, even to the extent of death itself, in order to deliver us from eternal shame : *Who, having joy set before Him, endured the cross, despising the shame.*[2]

O God, who would not mourn with pity, and love Jesus Christ, if he would consider that he suffered for the three hours during which his crucifixion lasted, and he was in agonies upon the cross? Every one of his limbs was stricken and tormented, and one could not relieve the other. The afflicted Lord on that bed of pain could not move, being fastened with nails in his hands and feet ; all his most sacred flesh was full of wounds, while those of his hands and feet were most painful, and were

---

[1] "Quoniam propter te sustinui opprobrium, operuit confusio faciem meam."—*Ps.* lxviii. 8.

[2] "Qui, proposito sibi gaudio, sustinuit crucem, confusione contempta."—*Heb.* xii. 2.

compelled to sustain his whole body ; so that wheresoever he rested upon that cross, whether on his hands or
his feet, there his pains increased.   It may be truly said,
that in those three hours of agony Jesus suffered as
many deaths as he passed moments upon the cross.   O
innocent Lamb, who hast suffered such things for me,
have mercy upon me !   Lamb of God, that takest away
the sins of the world, have mercy upon me ! [1]
Yet these outward pains of the body were the least
bitter; the inward pains of the soul were far geater.   His
blessed soul was all desolate, and deprived of every drop
of consolation and sensible relief ; all was weariness,
sorrow, and afflictions.   This he uttered in the words,
My God, my God, why hast Thou forsaken Me ? [2]   Drowned
in this sea of inward and outward griefs, our Saviour, so
worthy of our love, thought fit to end his life, as he had
foretold by the mouth of David : *I have come into the
depths of the sea, and the storm hath sunk Me.* [3]

II.

"If Thou be the Son of God, come down from the Cross."

Behold also, that, at the very time when he was thus
in agonies upon the cross, and was drawing near to
death, all they who stood near him, priests, scribes,
elders, and soldiers, wearied themselves in adding to his
pangs with insults and mockeries.   St. Matthew writes,
They that passed by blasphemed Him, wagging their heads. [4]
This was already prophesied by David, when he wrote,

[1] "Agnus Dei, qui tollis peccata mundi ! miserere mei."
[2] "Deus meus! Deus meus! ut quid dereliquisti me ?"—*Matt.*
xxvii. 46.
[3] "Veni in altitudinem maris, et tempestas demersit me."—*Ps.*
lxviii. 3.
[4] "Prætereuntes autem blasphemabant eum, moventes capita sua."
—*Matt.* xxvii. 39.

in the person of Christ, *All they that saw Me reviled Me, they spoke with their lips, and wagged their head.*[1]

They who passed before him said, *Vah, Thou that destroyest the temple of God, and in three days dost rebuild it, save Thy own self; if Thou be the Son of God, come down from the cross.*[2] Thou hast boasted, they said, that Thou wouldst destroy the temple, and rebuild it in three days. Yet Jesus had not said that he could destroy the material temple, and raise it again in three days ; but he had said: *Destroy this temple and in three days I will raise it up again.*[3] With these words he indeed intended to express his own power ; but he really (as Euthymius and others explain it) spoke allegorically, foretelling that, through the act of the Jews, his soul would be one day separated from his body, but that in three days it would rise again.

They said, *Save Thyself.*[4] O ungrateful men ! If this great Son of God, when he was made man, had chosen to save himself, he would not voluntarily have chosen death.

If Thou art the Son of God, come down from the cross;[5] yet, if Jesus had come down, he would not have accomplished our redemption by his death; we could not have been delivered from eternal death. " He would not come down," says St. Ambrose, "lest when he came down, I should die."[6] Theophylact writes, that they who said this spoke by the instigation of the devil, who

---

[1] " Omnes videntes me deriserunt me, locuti sunt labiis et moverunt caput."—*Ps.* xxi. 8.

[2] " Vah, qui destruis templum Dei, et in triduo illud reædificas!"—*Matt.* xxvii. 40.

[3] " Solvite templum hoc, et in tribus diebus excitabo illud."—*John,* ii. 19.

[4] " Salva temetipsum !"

[5] " Si Filius Dei es, descende de cruce."—*Matt.* xxvii. 40.

[6] " Noluit descendere, ne descenderet sibi, sed ut moreretur mihi."

sought to hinder the salvation which was about to be accomplished by Jesus by means of the cross.[1] And then
he adds that the Lord would not have mounted the
cross, if he had been willing to come down from it without accomplishing our redemption.[2] Also St. John
Chrysostom says that the Jews uttered this insult in
order that Jesus might die insulted as an impostor in
the sight of all men, and be proved unable to deliver
himself from the cross, after he had boasted that he was
the Son of God.[3]

St. John Chrysostom also remarks that the Jews
ignorantly said, *If Thou be the Son of God, come down from
the cross;* for if Jesus had come down from the cross before he had died, he would not have been that Son of God
who was promised, and who was to save us by his death.
On this account, says the saint, he did not come down
from the cross until he was dead, because he had come
for the very purpose of giving his life for our salvation.[4]
St. Athanasius makes the same remark, saying that our
Redeemer chose to be known as the true Son of God,
not by coming down from the cross, but by continuing
upon it till he was dead.[5] And thus it was foretold by
the prophets that our Redeemer must be crncified and
die, as St. Paul wrote, *Christ hath redeemed us from the
curse of the law, being made a curse for us, for it is written,
that cursed is every one who hangeth on a tree.*[6]

---

[1] " Diabolus incitabat illos ut dicerent : Descendat nunc de cruce,—
quia cognoscebat quod salus per crucem fieret."—*In Marc.* xv.

[2] " Si voluisset descendere, neque a principio ascendisset."

[3] " Volebant enim ut tamquam seductor in conspectu omnium vitu-
peratus decederet."—*In Matt. hom.* 88.

[4] " Qui Filius Del est, ideo non descendit de cruce; nam ideo venit,
ut crucifigeretur pro nobis."—*De Cruce et Latr. hom.* 2.

[5] " Neque descendendo de cruce voluit Filius Dei agnosci, sed ex eo
quod in cruce permaneret."—*Serm. de Pass. et Cr.*

[6] " Christus nos redemit de maledicto legis, factus pro nobis maledictum; quia scriptum est: Maledictus omnis qui pendet in ligno."—
Gal. iii. 13.

III.

"He saved Others, Himself He cannot save."

St. Matthew goes on to relate the other insults which the Jews offered to Jesus Christ : *He saved others, Himself He cannot save.*[1]

Thus they treated him as an impostor, by referring to the miracles which had been wrought by him in the restoration of the dead to life, and by treating him as one who was unable to save his own life.

St. Leo replies to them, that this was not the proper hour for Jesus to display his divine power; and that he would not hinder the redemption of man in order to confound their blasphemies.[2]

St. Gregory suggests another motive why Jesus would not descend from the cross: "If he had then come down, he would not have shown to us the virtue of patience."[3] Truly could Jesus Christ deliver himself from the cross and from these insults ; yet this was not the time for making a display of his power, but to teach us patience in our toils, in order that we may fulfil the divine pleasure ; and therefore Jesus would not deliver himself from death before he had fulfilled his Father's will, and in order that he might not deprive us of this great example of patience. "Because he taught patience, he laid aside his power,"[4] says St. Augustine.

The patience which Jesus Christ exercised in enduring

[1] "Alios salvos fecit, seipsum non potest salvum facere."—*Matt.* xxvii. 42.

[2] "Non vestræ cæcitatis arbitrio, o stulti Scribæ, ostendenda erat potentia Salvatoris; nec secundum preces blasphemantium linguarum, humani generis redemptio debebat omitti."—*De Pass.* s. 17.

[3] "Si de cruce tunc descenderet, virtutem nobis patientiæ non demonstraret."—*In Evang. hom.* 21.

[4] "Quia patientiam docebat, ideo potentiam differebat."—*In Jo. tr.* 37.

the shame of all the insults which were offered him by the Jews obtained for us grace to endure with patience and peace of mind all the humiliations and persecutions of the world. Therefore St. Paul, speaking of the journey of Jesus Christ to Calvary when he carried the cross, thus exhorts us to accompany him, *Let us, therefore, go forth to meet him without the camp. bearing his reproach.*[1] The saints, when they received injuries, did not think of revenging themselves, nor were they disturbed; they were even comforted at seeing themselves despised, as Jesus Christ was despised. Therefore let us not fear to embrace, for the love of Jesus Christ, all the insults that were offered to him, since Jesus Christ has suffered so many insults for love of us.

O my Redeemer, for the time past I have not done this. For the future I desire to suffer everything for love of Thee: give me strength to put my desires into execution.

IV.

"If God loves him, let him deliver him now."

The Jews, not satisfied with the injuries and blasphemies which they had offered to Jesus Christ, reproached him with the name of his Father, saying, *He trusted in God, let Him now deliver Him, if He will have Him; for He said, I am the Son of God.*[2] This sacrilegious expression of the Jews was already foretold by David, when he said in the name of Christ, *All they that saw Me derided Me; they spoke with their lips, and shook their head, saying, He trusted in God, let Him deliver Him, let Him save Him; for He desireth Him.*[3] These very men who thus

---

[1] " Exeamus igitur ad eum extra castra, improperium ejus portantes."—*Heb.* xiii. 13.

[2] "Confidit in Deo; liberet nunc si vult eum; dixit enim: Quia Filius Dei sum."—*Matt.* xxvii. 43.

[3] " Speravit in Domino, eripiat eum; salvum faciat eum, quoniam vult eum."—*Ps.* xxi. 9.

spoke were called bulls, dogs, and lions, by David in the same Psalm: *Fat bulls encompassed me. Many dogs surrounded me. Save me from the mouth of the lion.*[1] Thus, when the Jews said, *Let Him now deliver Him, if He will have Him,*[2] they truly showed that they were these bulls, dogs, and lions which had been foretold by David.

These very same blasphemies, which were one day to be spoken against the Saviour and against God, were already foretold by the Wise Man with even more exactness: *He declares that He has the knowledge of God, and calls Himself the Son of God, and He glories that He has God for His Father. If he is the true Son of God, let Him accept Him, and deliver Him from the hands of His adversaries. Let us try Him with insults and torments, that we may know His reverence, and prove His patience; let us condemn Him to a most shameful death.*[3]

The chief priests were stirred up by envy and hatred against Jesus Christ thus to insult him; but, at the same time, they were not exempt from the fear of some great punishment, as they could not deny the miracles wrought by the Lord. Wherefore all the priests and chiefs of the synagogue continued disturbed and in terror, and therefore desired to be present at his death, in order to be freed from this fear which tormented them. Seeing him then fastened upon the cross, and that he was not delivered from it by his Father, they proceeded with increased audacity to taunt him with his impotence and his persuasion that he was the Son of God. They said,

---

[1] " Tauri pingues obsederunt me. . . . Circumdederunt me canes multi. . . . Salva me ex ore leonis."—*Ps.* xxi. 13, 17, 22.

[2] " Liberet nunc, si vult eum."—*Matt.* xxvii. 43.

[3] " Promittit se scientiam Dei habere, et Filium Dei se nominat . . ., et gloriatur Patrem se habere Deum. Si enim est verus Filius Dei, suscipiet illum, et liberabit eum de manibus contrariorum. Contumelia et tormento interrogemus eum, ut sciamus reverentiam ejus, et probemus patientiam illius; morte turpissima condemnemus eum." —*Wisd.* ii. 13, 16, 18-20.

" He trusted in God, that he was his Father; why, then, does not God deliver him if he loves him as his Son ?" But grievously were these malicious men in error, for God did truly love Jesus Christ, and loved him as his Son; and he loved him on this very account, that Jesus was sacrificing his life upon the cross for the salvation of men, in order to obey his Father. This Jesus himself had said, *I lay down My life for My sheep . . . therefore hath the Father loved Me, because I lay down My life.*[1] The Father had already destined him to be the victim of this great sacrifice, which would bring to him an infinite glory, as the God-man would be sacrificed, and which would ensure the salvation of all men; but if the Father had delivered him from death, the sacrifice would have been imperfect, and then the Father would have been deprived of that glory, while men would have been deprived of their salvation.

Tertullian writes that all the insults that were offered to Jesus Christ were a secret remedy for our pride; for these injuries, which were unjust, and unworthy of him, were nevertheless necessary to our salvation,[2] and worthy of a God who chose to suffer so much in order to save man. And then, speaking of the reproaches laid against Jesus, he adds: " Of him they were unworthy, but to us they were necessary, and therefore they were worthy of God, because nothing is so worthy of God as the salvation of man." [3]

Let us, therefore, who boast that we are disciples of Jesus Christ, be ashamed of angrily resenting the in-

---

[1] " Animam meam pono pro ovibus meis. . . . Propterea me diligit Pater, quia ego pono animam meam."—*John*, x. 15, 17.

[2] " Totum denique Dei mei penes vos dedecus, sacramentum est humanæ salutis."

[3] " Sibi quidem indigna. homini autem necessaria: et ita jam Deo digna, quia nihil tam dignum Deo, quam salus hominis."—*Adv. Marr.* l. 2.

juries which we receive from men, because a God made man suffered the same for our salvation with so much patience. And let us not be ashamed of imitating Jesus Christ in pardoning those who offend us, as he himself declares that in the day of judgment he will be ashamed of those who in this life have been ashamed of him.[1]

O my Jesus! how can I grieve for any insults that I may receive, who have so often deserved to be trodden under foot by the devils in hell! Oh, by the merits of all the insults which Thou didst suffer in Thy Passion, give me grace to suffer with patience all the insults which may be offered to me, through love of Thee, who hast embraced so many for love of me. I love Thee above everything, and desire to suffer for Thee, who hast suffered so much for me. I hope for everything from Thee, who hast bought me with Thy blood. And I also hope in thy intercession, O my mother Mary.

CHAPTER V.

THE SEVEN WORDS SPOKEN BY JESUS CHRIST ON THE CROSS.

I.

Pater! dimitte illis ; non enim sciunt quid faciunt.[2]

" Father, forgive them, for they know not what they do."

O loving tenderness of Jesus towards men! St. Augustine says that when the Saviour was injured by his enemies, he besought pardon for them; for he thought not so much of the injuries he received from them, and the

---

[1] " Qui me erubuerit et meos sermones, hunc Filius hominis erubescet, cum venerit in majestate sua."—*Luke,* ix. 26.

[2] *Luke,* xxiii. 34.

death they inflicted upon him, as upon the love which brought him to die for them.'

But some may say, Why did Jesus pray to the Father to pardon them, when he himself could have forgiven their injuries? St. Bernard replies that he prayed to the Father, not because he could not himself forgive them, but that he might teach us to pray for them that persecute us.' The holy abbot says also in another place: "O wonderful thing! He cries, Forgive; they cry, Crucify."' Arnold of Chartres remarks that while Jesus was laboring to save the Jews, they were laboring to destroy themselves; but the love of the Son had more power with God than the blindness of this ungrateful people.' St. Cyprian writes, "Even he who sheds the blood of Christ is made to live by the blood of Christ."' Jesus Christ, in dying, had so great a desire to save all men, that he made even those enemies who shed his blood with torments partakers of that blood.' Look, says St. Augustine, at thy God upon his cross; see how he prays for them that crucify him; and then deny pardon to thy brother who has offended thee!

St. Leo writes' that it was through this prayer of Christ that so many thousands of Jews were converted

---

[1] "Illis petebat veniam a quibus adhuc accipiebat injuriam; non enim attendebat, quod ab ipsis moriebatur, sed quia pro ipsis moriebatur."—*In Jo. tr.* 31.

[2] "Non quia non posset ipse relaxare, sed ut nos pro persequentibus orare doceret."

[3] "Mira res! ille clamabat: Ignosce !—Judæi : Crucifige!"—*S. de Pass. D.*

[4] "Cum ipse ad hoc nitatur ut salventur, Judæi ad hoc ut damnentur. Plus debet apud Deum posse Filii charitas, quam populi cæcitas."—*De 7 Verbis.*

[5] "Vivificatur Christi sanguine, etiam qui fudit sanguinem Christi." —*De Bono pat.*

[6] *Serm.* 49, *E. B.*

[7] "Impetravit quod petierat Christus, multaque statim de Judæis millia crediderunt."—*Ad Hedib.* q. 8.

at the preaching of St. Paul, as we read in the Acts of the Apostles; whilst (says St. Jerome) God did not will that the prayer of Jesus Christ should continue without effect, and therefore at the very time he caused many of the Jews to embrace the faith. But why were they not all converted? I reply that the prayer of Jesus Christ was conditional, and that they who were converted were not of the number of those of whom it was said, *Ye have resisted the Holy Ghost.*[1]

In this prayer Jesus Christ further included all sinners; so that we all may say to God:

O Eternal Father, hear the prayer of Thy beloved Son, who prayed to Thee to pardon us. We deserve not this pardon, but Jesus Christ has merited it, who by his death has more than abundantly satisfied for our sins: No, my God, I would not be obstinate like the Jews; I repent, O my Father, with all my heart, for having offended Thee, and through the merits of Jesus Christ I ask for pardon. And Thou, O my Jesus, Thou dost know that I am poor and sick, and lost through my sins; but Thou hast come from heaven on purpose to heal the sick, and to save the lost, when they repent of having offended Thee. Of Thee Isaias said, *He came to save that which had perished.*[2] And of Thee St. Matthew writes, *The Son of Man is come to save that which was lost.*[3]

II.

Amen dico tibi: Hodie mecum eris in paradiso.[4]

"Amen I say to thee, this day thou shalt be with Me in paradise."

St. Luke writes that of the two thieves who were cru-

---

[1] "Vos semper Spiritui Sancto resistitis."—*Acts*, vii. 51.

[2] "Misit me, ut mederer contritis corde."—*Isa.* lxi. 1.

[3] "Venit enim Filius hominis salvare quod perierat."—*Matt.* xviii. 11.

[4] *Luke*, xxiii. 43.

cified with Jesus Christ, one continued obstinate, the other was converted; and seeing his miserable companion blaspheming Jesus Christ, and saying, *If Thou art the Christ, save Thyself and us,* he turned and reproved him, saying that they were deservedly punished, but that Jesus was innocent. Then he turned to Jesus himself and said, *Lord, remember me when Thou comest into Thy kingdom;* by which words he recognized Jesus Christ as his true Lord and the king of heaven. Jesus then promised him paradise on that very day; *Amen I say to thee, this day thou shalt be with me in paradise.*[1] A learned author writes that, in conformity with this promise, the Lord, on that very day, immediately after his death, showed himself openly, and rendered the repentant thief blessed, though he did not confer on him all the delight of heaven before he entered there.

Arnold of Chartres, in his treatise on the seven words, remarks upon all the virtues which the good thief exercised at the time of his death: "He believed, he repented, he confessed, he preached, he loved, he trusted, he prayed."[2]

He exercised faith when he said, *When Thou comest into Thy kingdom;* believing that Jesus Christ, after his death, would enter into his glorious kingdom. He believed, says St. Gregory, that he whom he saw dying was about to reign.[3]

He exercised penitence together with the confession of his sins, saying, *We indeed justly; for we received the due reward of our deeds.* St. Augustine observes that before

---

[1] "Si tu es Christus, salvum fac temetipsum et nos. Et nos quidem juste, nam digna factis recipimus; hic vero nihil mali gessit. Domine, memento mei, cum veneris in regnum tuum. Amen dico tibi: Hodie mecum eris in paradiso "—*Luke,* xxiii. 39-43.

[2] "Ibi credit, timet, compungitur et pœnitet, confitetur et prædicat, amat, confidit, orat."—*De 7 Verbis.*

[3] "Regnaturum credidit, quem morientem vidit."—*Mor.* l. 18, c. 25.

his confession he had not boldness to hope for pardon; he did not dare to say *Remember me*, until, by the confession of his guilt, he had thrown off the burden of his sins.[1] On this St. Athanasius exclaims, O blessed thief, thou hast stolen a kingdom by that confession![2]

This holy penitent also exercised other noble virtues; he preached, declaring the innocence of Jesus Christ, *This man hath done no evil.* He exercised love to God, receiving death with resignation, as the punishment due to his sins, saying, *We receive the due reward of our deeds.* Hence St. Cyprian, St. Jerome, and St. Augustine do not scruple to call him a martyr; and Silveira says[3] that this happy thief was a true martyr, as the executioners broke his legs with increased fury, because he had declared the innocence of Jesus; and that the saint willingly accepted this torment for the love of his Lord.

Let us also in this circumstance remark the goodness of God, who always gives us more than we ask for, as St. Ambrose says, " The Lord always grants more than we ask; the thief prayed that Jesus would remember him, and Jesus said, *To-day thou shalt be with Me in paradise.*[4] St. John Chrysostom further remarks that no one merited the possession of paradise before this thief.[5] Thus is confirmed what God said by Ezechiel, that, when the sinner heartily repents of his sins, God pardons him in the same way as if he had forgotten all the sins

[1] " Non est ausus ante dicere, ' Memento mei;' quam, post confessionem iniquitatis, sarcinam peccatorum deponeret."—*Serm.* 155, *E. B. app.*

[2] "O beatum latronem! rapuisti regnum ista confessione."—*S. contra omn. hær.*

[3] *Lib.* 8, c. 16, q. 12.

[4] "Semper plus Dominus tribuit, quam rogatur. Ille rogabat ut memor sui esset: Dominus autem ait, ' Hodie mecum eris in paradiso.' "—*In Luc.* xxiii.

[5] " Nullum ante Latronem invenies repromissionem paradisi meruisse."

he had committed.[1]   And Isaias gives us to understand
that God is so urgent for our good, that when we pray
he instantly hears us.[2]   St. Augustine says that God is
ever prepared to embrace penitent sinners.[3]

And thus it was that th. cross of the wicked thief,
being endured with impatience, became to him a precipice leading to hell; while the cross endured with patience by the good thief became to him a ladder to paradise.   Happy wert thou, O holy thief, who hadst the
fortune to unite thy death to the death of thy Saviour.

O my Jesus! henceforth I sacrifice to Thee my life, and
I seek for grace to enable me, at the hour of my death,
to unite the sacrifice of my life to that which Thou didst
offer to God upon the cross, and through which I hope
to die in Thy grace, and, loving Thee with pure love
stripped of every earthly affection, to attain to love Thee
with all my powers through all eternity.

III.

Mulier, ecce filius tuus. . . . Ecce Mater tua.[4]

"Woman, behold thy son. . . . Behold thy mother."

We read in St. Mark that on Calvary there were present many women, who watched Jesus on the cross, but
from afar off, among whom was Mary Magdalen.[5]   We
believe, also, that among these holy women was the divine mother also; while St. John says that the Blessed
Virgin stood, not afar off, but close to the cross, together

---

[1] "Si autem impius egerit pœnitentiam . . . , omnium iniquitatum
ejus . . . non recordabor."—*Esech.* xviii. 21, 22.

[2] "Ad vocem clamoris tui, statim ut audierit, respondebit tibi."—
Isa. xxx. 19.

[3] "Paratus in amplexus peccatorum."—*Man.* c. 23.

[4] *John,* xix. 26, 27.

[5] "Erant autem et mulieres de longe aspicientes, inter quas erat
Maria Magdalene."—*Mark,* xv. 40.

with Mary of Cleophas and Mary Magdalen.[1] Euthymius attempts to reconcile this discrepancy, and says that the Holy Virgin, seeing her son drawing nearer to death, came from among the rest of the women close up to the cross, overcoming her fear of the soldiers who surrounded it, and enduring with patience all the insults and repulses which she had to suffer from these soldiers who watched the condemned, in order that she might draw near her beloved Son.[2] Thus also a learned author, who wrote the life of Jesus Christ, says, "There were his friends, who watched him from afar; but the Holy Virgin, the Magdalen, and another Mary stood close to the cross, with John; wherefore Jesus, seeing his mother and John, spoke to them the words above mentioned. Truly it was the mother who not even in the terror of death deserted her Son.[3] Some other mothers fly when they see their children dying; their love does not suffer them to be present at their death without the power of relieving them; but the holy mother, the nearer her Son approached to death, the nearer she drew to his cross."

The afflicted mother thus was standing close to the cross; and as the Son sacrificed his life, so she offered her pangs for the salvation of men, sharing with perfect resignation all the pains and insults which her Son suffered in his death. A writer says that they who would describe her fainting at the foot of the cross dishonor the constancy of Mary. She was the strong woman, who neither fainted nor wept, as St. Ambrose writes: "I read of her standing, but not of her weeping."[4]

---

[1] "Stabant autem juxta crucem Jesu Mater ejus, et soror Matris ejus, Maria Cleophæ, et Maria Magdalene."—*John,* xix. 25.

[2] "Tunc Dei Mater propinquius cruci astitit, quam cæteræ mulieres, Judæorum vincens timorem."—*In Matt.* c. 67.

[3] "Plane Mater, quæ nec in terrore mortis Filium deserebat."—*In Ass. B. M.* s. 4.

[4] "Stantem lego, flentem non lego."—*Or. de ob. Val.*

The pain which the Holy Virgin endured in the Passion of her Son exceeded all the pains which a human heart can endure; but the grief of Mary was not a barren grief, like that of other mothers who behold the sufferings of their children; it was a fruitful grief, since through the merits of her so great grief, and through her love (according to the opinion of St. Augustine), as she was the natural mother of our head Jesus Christ,[1] so she then became the spiritual mother of us who are his faithful members, in co-operating with him by her love in causing us to be born, and to be the children of the Church.

St. Bernard writes that upon Mount Calvary both of these two great martyrs, Jesus and Mary, were silent, because the great pain that they endured took from them the power of speaking.[2] The mother looked upon her Son in agony upon the cross, and the Son looked upon the mother in agony at the foot of the cross, and torn with compassion for the pains he suffered.

Mary and John then stood nearer to the cross than the other women, so that they could more easily hear the words and mark the looks of Jesus Christ in so great a tumult. St. John writes: *When Jesus then saw His mother and the disciple standing, whom He loved, he saith to His mother: Woman, behold thy son.*[3] But if Mary and John were accompanied by other women, why is it said that Jesus beheld his mother and the disciple, as if the other women had not been perceived by him? St. John Chrysostom writes that love always makes us look more

---

[1] " Plane mater membrorum ejus, quod nos sumus; quia cooperata est charitate ut fideles in Ecclesia nascerentur, qui illius Capitis membra sunt."—*De S. Virg.* c. 6.

[2] " Tacebant ambo illi Martyres, et, præ nimio dolore, loqui non poterant."—*De Lam. V. M.*

[3] " Cum vidisset ergo Jesus Matrem et Discipulum quem diligebat . . . "—*John,* xix. 26.

closely at the object of our love.[1] And St. Ambrose in a
similar way writes, It is natural that we should see those
we love before any others.[2] The Blessed Virgin revealed
to St. Bridget that in order that Jesus might look upon
Mary, who stood by the side of the cross, he was obliged
first to compress his eyebrows in order to remove the
blood from his eyes, which prevented him from seeing.[3]

Jesus said to her, Woman, behold thy son ! with his
eyes pointing out St. John, who stood by his side. But
why did he call her *woman*, and not *mother ?* He called
her " woman," we may say, because, drawing now near to
death, he spoke as if departing from her, as if he had
said, Woman, in a little while I shall be dead, and thou
wilt have no Son upon earth; I leave thee, therefore, John,
who will serve and love thee as a son. And from this we
may understand that St. Joseph was already dead, since
if he had been still alive he would not have been separated from his wife.

All antiquity asserts that St. John was ever a virgin, and
specially on this account he was given as a son to Mary,
and honored in being made to occupy the place of Jesus
Christ; on which account the holy Church sings, " To
him a virgin He commended his Virgin Mother." [4] And
from the moment of the Lord's death, as it is written,
St. John received Mary into his own house, and assisted
and obeyed her throughout her life, as if she had been
his own mother.[5] Jesus Christ willed that this beloved
disciple should be an eye-witness of his death, in order
that he might more confidently bear witness to it in his

---

[1] " Semper amoris oculus acutius intuetur."—*Serm.* 78.

[2] "Morale est ut, quos diligimus, videamus præ cæteris."—*De Jos.*
patr. c. 10.

[3] " Nec ipse me adstantem cruci videre potuit, nisi sanguine ex-
presso per ciliorum compressionem."—*Rev.* l. 4, c. 70.

[4] "Cui Matrem Virginem virgini commendavit."—*Off. de S. Jo.*

[5] " Et ex illa hora accepit eam Discipulus in sua."—*John*, xix. 27.

Gospel, and might say, *He that saw it has borne witness;*[1] and in his Epistle, *What we have seen with our eyes, that we both testify and make known to you.*[2]   And on this account the Lord, at the time when the other disciples abandoned him, gave to St. John strength to be present until his death in the midst of so many enemies.

But let us return to the holy Virgin, and examine more deeply the reason why Jesus called Mary *woman*, and not *mother*.   By this expression he desired to show that she was the great woman foretold in the Book of Genesis, who would crush the serpent's head: *I will put enmities between thee and the woman, and thy seed and her seed : she shall crush thy head, and thou shalt lie in wait for her heel.*[3] It is doubted by none that this woman was the Blessed Virgin Mary, who, by means of her Son, would crush the head of Satan,—if it be not more correct to say that her Son, by means of her who would bear him, would do this. Naturally was Mary the enemy of the serpent, because Lucifer was haughty, ungrateful, and disobedient, while she was humble, grateful, and obedient.   It is said, *She shall crush thy head*, because Mary, by means of her Son, beat down the pride of Lucifer, who lay in wait for the heel of Jesus Christ, which means his holy humanity, which was the part of him which was nearest to the earth ; while the Saviour by his death had the glory of conquering him, and of depriving him of that empire which, through sin, he had obtained over the human race.

God said to the serpent, *I will put enmities between thy seed and the woman.*   This shows that after the fall of man, through sin, notwithstanding all that would be done

---

[1] "Qui vidit, testimonium perhibuit."—*John*, xix. 35.

[2] "Quod vidimus oculis nostris . . . , testamur et annuntiamus."—1 *John*, i. 1.

[3] "Inimicitias ponam inter te et Mulierem, et semen tuum et semen illius : ipsa conteret caput tuum, et tu insidiaberis calcaneo ejus."—*Gen*. iii. 15.

by the redemption of Jesus Christ, there would be
two families and two posterities in the world, the
seed of Satan signifying the family of sinners, his
children corrupted by him, and the seed of Mary signifying the holy family, which includes all the just, with
their head Jesus Christ. Hence Mary was destined to
be the mother both of the head and of the members,
namely, the faithful. The Apostle writes: *Ye are all one
in Christ Jesus; and if ye are Christ's, then ye are the seed of
Abraham.*[1] Thus, Jesus Christ and the faithful are one
single body, because the head cannot be divided from
the members, and these members are all spiritual children of Mary, as they have the same spirit of her Son according to nature, who was Jesus Christ. Therefore, St.
John was not called *John,* but the disciple beloved by the
Lord, that we might understand that Mary is the mother
of every good Christian who is beloved by Jesus Christ,
and in whom Jesus Christ lives by his Spirit. This was
expressed by Origen, when he said, " Jesus said to Mary,
Behold thy son, as if he had said, This is Jesus, whom
thou hast borne, for he who is perfected lives no more
himself, but Christ lives in him."[2]

Denis the Carthusian writes that in the Passion of
Jesus Christ the breast of Mary was filled with the blood
which flowed from his wounds, in order that with it she
might nourish her children. And he adds that this
divine mother by her prayers and merits, which she especially acquired by sharing in the death of Jesus Christ,
obtained for us a participation in the merits of the Passion of the Redeemer.[3]

---

[1] "Omnes enim vos unum estis in Christo Jesu; si autem vos
Christi, ergò semen Abrahæ estis."—*Gal.* iii. 28.

[2] " Dixitque Jesus Matri : 'Ecce filius tuus;' perinde ac si dixisset :
Ecce hic Jesus quem genuisti.—Etenim, qui perfectus est, non amplius vivit ipse, sed in ipso vivit Christus."

[3] " Promeruit ut, per preces ejus ac merita, meritum passionis
Christi communicetur hominibus."—*De Laud. V. M.* l. 2, a. 23.

O suffering Mother! Thou knowest that I have deserved hell; I have no hope of being saved, except by sharing the merits of the death of Jesus Christ ; Thou must pray for me, that I may obtain this grace ; and I pray thee to obtain it for me by the love of that Son whom thou sawest bow his head and expire on Calvary before thy eyes. O queen of martyrs, O advocate of sinners, help me always, and especially in the hour of my death ! Even now I seem to see the devils, who, in my last agony, will strive to make me despair at the sight of my sins; oh ! abandon me not then, when thou seest me thus assaulted ; help me with thy prayers, and obtain for me confidence and holy perseverance. And because then, when my speech is gone, and perhaps my senses, I cannot invoke thy name, and that of thy Son, I now call upon thee ; Jesus and Mary, I recommend my soul unto you.

IV.

Dens mens ! Dens mens ! ut quid dereliquisti me ?[1]

" Eli, Eli, lamma sabacthani ? that is, My God, my God, why hast Thou forsaken Me ?"

St. Matthew writes that Jesus uttered these words with a loud voice. Why did he thus utter them ? Euthymius says that he thus cried out in order to show us his divine power, inasmuch as, though he was on the point of expiring, he was able thus to cry aloud, a thing which is impossible to dying men, through their extreme exhaustion. Also, he thus cried out in order to show us the anguish in which he died. It might, perhaps, have been said that as Jesus was both God and man, by the power of his divinity he had diminished the pains of his torments ; and in order to prevent this idea, he thought fit in these words to declare that his death was more

[1] *Matt.* xxvii. 46.

bitter than that which any man had endured, and that while the martyrs in their torments were comforted with divine sweetness, he, the king of martyrs, chose to die deprived of every consolation, satisfying the utmost rigor of the divine justice for all the sins of men. And therefore Silveira remarks that Jesus called his Father God, and not Father, because he was then regarding him as a Judge, and not as a son regards his father.[1]

St. Leo writes that this cry of the Lord was not a lamentation, but a doctrine,[2] because he thus desired to teach us how great is the wickedness of sin, which, as it were, compelled God to abandon his beloved Son without a comfort, because he had taken upon him to make satisfaction for our sins. At the same time, Jesus was not abandoned by the divinity, nor deprived of the glory which had been communicated to his blessed soul from the first moment of his creation; but he was deprived of all that sensible relief by which God is wont to comfort his faithful servants in their sufferings ; and he was left in darkness, fear, and bitterness, pangs which were deserved by us. This deprivation of the sensible consciousness of the divine presence was also endured by Jesus in the Garden of Gethsemani ; but that which he suffered on the cross was greater and more bitter.

O Eternal Father, what offence had this Thy innocent and most obedient Son ever given Thee, that Thou shouldst punish him with a death so bitter? Look at him as he hangs upon this cross, with his head tortured with thorns, as he hangs upon the three iron nails, and is supported by his own wounds! All have abandoned him, even his own disciples, all deride him upon the cross, and blaspheme him; and why hast Thou abandoned him, who hast so greatly loved him? We must under-

---

[1] " Jesus, pendens in cruce, erat satisfaciens de toto rigore justitiæ suo Parenti, tamquam Judici, pro peccatis generis humani."—*Lib.* 8, c. 18, q. 3.

[2] " Vox ista doctrina est, non querela."—*De Pass.* s. 16.

stand that Jesus had taken upon himself the sins of the world, although he was himself the most holy of all men, and even sanctity itself; since he had taken upon himself to satisfy for all our sins, he seemed the greatest of all sinners ; and having thus made himself guilty for all, he offered himself to pay the price for all. Because we had deserved to be abandoned forever in hell to eternal despair, therefore he chose to be given up to a death deprived of every relief, that thus he might deliver us from eternal death.

Calvin, in his commentary on St. John, blasphemously asserts that Jesus Christ, in order to appease his Father, experienced all the wrath which God feels towards sinners, and felt all the pains of the damned, and particularly that of despair. O blasphemy and shocking thought! How could he satisfy for our sins by committing a sin so great as that of despair? And how could this despair, which Calvin imagines, be reconciled with the other words which Jesus uttered, *Father, into Thy hands I commend My spirit?*[1] The truth is, as St. Jerome and others explain it, that our Saviour uttered this lamentation to show not his own despair, but the bitterness which he endured in a death without consolation. And, further, despair could only have been produced in Jesus Christ by a knowledge that he was hated by God; but how could God hate that Son who, to obey his will, had offered himself to satisfy for the sins of men? It was this very obedience in return for which the Father looked upon him, and granted him the salvation of the human race, as the Apostle writes, *Who in the days of His flesh, offering with loud crying and tears, prayers and supplications to Him who could save Him from death, was heard because of His reverence.*[2]

[1] " Pater, in manus tuas commendo spiritum meum."—*Luke,* xxiii. 46.

[2] "Qui in diebus carnis suæ, preces supplicationesque ad eum, qui possit illum salvum facere a morte, cum clamore valido et lacrymis offerens, exauditus est pro sua reverentia."—*Heb.* v. 7.

Further, this abandonment of Jesus Christ was the most dreadful suffering in all his Passion; for we know that after suffering so many bitter pangs without complaining, he lamented over this; he cried with a loud voice, and with many tears and prayers, as St. Paul tells us. Yet all these prayers and tears were poured forth in order to teach us how much he suffered to obtain the divine mercy for us; and to enable us at the same time to comprehend how dreadful a punishment it would be to a guilty soul to be driven from God, and to be deprived forever of his love, according to the divine threat, *I will cast them forth form My house, I will not further love them.*[1]

St. Augustine also says that Jesus Christ was agitated at the sight of his death, but that he was so for the comfort of his servants; in order that if ever they should find themselves disturbed at their own death, they should not suppose themselves reprobates, or abandon themselves to despair, because even he was disturbed at the sight of death.[2]

Therefore, let us give thanks to the goodness of our Saviour for having been willing to take upon himself the pains which were due to us, and thus to deliver us from eternal death; and let us labor henceforth to be grateful to this our deliverer, banishing from our hearts every affection which is not for him. And when we find ourselves desolate in spirit, and deprived of the sense of the divine presence, let us unite our desolation to that which Jesus Christ suffered in his death. Sometimes he hides himself from the souls that he most loves, but he does not really leave their hearts; he aids them with his

[1] " De domo mea ejiciam eos; non addam ut diligam eos."—*Osee*, ix. 15.
[2] "Si imminente morte turbaris, non te existimes reprobum, nec desperationi te abjicias; ideo enim Christus turbatus est in conspectu mortis suæ."

inward grace. He is not offended, if in such an abandonment we say, as he himself said in the garden to his
divine Father, *O My Father, if it be possible, let this cup pass
from Me.*[1] But at the same time we must add, *Yet, not
as I will, but as Thou wilt.*[2] And if the desolation continues, we must continue the same acts of conformity to
the divine will, as he himself repeated them for the
three hours during which he prayed in the garden.[3] St.
Francis de Sales says that Jesus is as worthy of love
when he hides himself as when he makes himself seen.
Further, he who has deserved hell, and finds himself out
of it, should say only, *I will bless the Lord at all times.*[4]
O Lord, I do not deserve consolations; grant that
through Thy grace I may love Thee, and I am content
to live in desolation as long as it pleases Thee. If the
damned could thus in their pains unite themselves to
the divine will, hell would be no longer hell to them.

*But Thou, O Lord, remove not Thy help to a distance from
Me ; look towards my defence.*[5] O my Jesus, through the
merits of Thy desolate death, deprive me not of Thy
help in that great struggle which, in the hour of my
death, I must maintain with hell. At that hour all
things of earth will have deserted me and cannot help
me ; do not Thou abandon me, who hast died for me,
and canst alone help me in that extremity. Do this
through the merits of those pains which Thou didst
suffer in Thy abandonment, by which Thou hast merited
for us that we should not be abandoned by the divine
grace, as we have deserved through our sins.

---

[1] " Pater mi ! si possibile est, transeat a me calix iste."—*Matt.* xxvi.
39.

[2] "Verumtamen, non sicut ego volo, sed sicut tu."—*Ibid.*

[3] " Et oravit tertio, eundem sermonem dicens."—*Ibid.* 44.

[4] " Benedicam Dominum in omni tempore."—*Ps.* xxxiii. 2.

[5] " Tu autem, Domine, ne elongaveris auxilium tuum a me; ad de
fensionem meam conspice."—*Ps.* xxi. 20.

V.

Sitio.[1]

" I thirst."

St. John writes, *Jesus then, knowing that all things were accomplished, th.it the Scripture might be fulfilled, said: I thirst.*[2] Scripture here refers to the words of David, *They gave Me gall to eat, and in My thirst they gave Me vinegar to drink.*[3]

Severe was this bodily thirst, which Jesus Christ endured on the cross through his loss of blood, first in the garden, and afterwards in the hall of judgment, at his scourging and crowning with thorns; and, lastly, upon the cross, where four streams of blood gushed forth from the wounds of his pierced hands and feet as from four fountains. But far more terrible was his spiritual thirst, that is, his ardent desire to save all mankind, and to suffer still more for us, as Blosius says, in order to show us his love.[4] On this St. Laurence Justinian writes: "This thirst came from the fount of love."[5]

O my Jesus ! Thou hast thus desired to suffer for me; and I, when my sufferings at all increase, become so impatient that I am insupportable both to others and to myself. O my Jesus! through the merits of Thy patience, make me patient and resigned in the sicknesses and crosses which befall me; make me like Thyself before I die.

---

[1] *John*, xix. 28.

[2] " Postea, sciens Jesus quia omnia consummata sunt, ut consummaretur Scriptura, dixit : Sitio."— *John*, xix. 28.

[3] " Et dederunt in escam meam fel, et in siti mea potaverunt me aceto."— *Ps.* lxviii. 22.

[4] " Habuit et aliam sitim, puta, amplius patiendi atque evidentius suum nobis demcnstrandi amorem."— *Marg. sp.* p. 3, c. 18.

[5] " Sitis hæc de ardore nascitur charitatis."— *De Tr. Chr. Ag.* c. 10.

VI.

Consummatum est.[1]

"It is consummated."

St. John writes, *Jesus, therefore, when He had taken the vinegar said, It is consummated.*[2] At this moment Jesus, before breathing out his soul, placed before his eyes all the sacrifices of the old law (which were all figures of the sacrifice upon the cross), all the prayers of the patriarchs, and all the prophecies which had been uttered respecting his life and his death, all the injuries and insults which it was predicted that he would suffer; and, seeing that all was accomplished, he said, *It is consummated.*

St. Paul encourages us to run generously and encounter with patience the struggle which awaits us in this life with our enemies, in order to obtain salvation: *Let us run with patience to the contest which is set before us, looking to Jesus the author and the consummation of faith, who for the joy set before Him endured the cross.*[3] The Apostle thus exhorts us to resist temptations with patience unto the end, after the example of Jesus Christ, who would not come down from the cross while life remained. On this St. Augustine says, "What did he teach thee, who, when he hung upon the cross, would not come down, but that thou shouldst be strong in thy God?"[4] Jesus thought fit to complete his sacrifice even to death, in order to convince us that the reward of glory is not given by God except to those who persevere

[1] *John*, xix. 30.
[2] "Cum ergo accepisset Jesus acetum dixit : consummatum est."—*Ibid.*
[3] " Per patientiam curramus ad propositum nobis certamen, aspicientes in Auctorem fidei et Consummatorem Jesum, qui, proposito sibi gaudio, sustinuit crucem."—*Heb.* xii. 1.
[4] "Quid te docuit pendens, qui descendere noluit, nisi ut sis fortis in Deo tuo ?"—*In Ps.* lxx. s. 1.

to the end, as he teaches us in St. Matthew: *He that shall persevere unto the end, he shall be saved.*[1]

Therefore, when, through inward passions, or the temptations of the devil, or the persecutions of men, we feel ourselves disturbed and excited to lose our patience, and to abandon ourselves to displeasing God, let us cast our eyes on Jesus crucified, who poured forth all his blood for our salvation, and let us reflect that we have not yet poured forth one drop of blood for love of him : *Ye have not yet resisted unto blood, striving against sin.*[2] When, therefore, we are called to yield up any point of human esteem, to abstain from any resentful feeling, to deprive ourselves of any satisfaction, or of anything we are curious to see, or to do anything which is unpleasant to our tastes, let us be ashamed to deny this gift to Jesus Christ. He has treated us without holding anything back ; he has given his own life, and all his blood ; let us, then, be ashamed to treat him with any reserve.

Let us oppose to our enemies all the resistance that we are bound to make, and hope for victory from the merits of Jesus Christ alone, by means of which alone, the saints, and especially the holy martyrs, have overcome torments and death : *In all things we overcome, through Him who loved us.*[3] Therefore, when the devil paints to our thoughts any obstacles which, through our weakness, seem extremely difficult to overcome, let us turn our eyes to Jesus crucified, and, wholly trusting in his help and merits, let us say, with the Apostle, *I can do all things through Him that strengthens me.*[4] By myself

---

[1] "Qui autem perseveraverit usque in finem, hic salvus erit."— *Matt.* x. 22.

[2] "Recogitate enim eum. . . . Nondum enim usque ad sanguinem restitistis, adversus peccatum repugnantes."—*Heb.* xii. 3, 4.

[3] "In his omnibus superamus propter eum, qui dilexit nos."—*Rom.* viii. 37.

[4] "Omnia possum in eo qui me confortat."—*Phil.* iv. 13.

I can do nothing, but by the help of Jesus I can do everything.

Thus let us animate ourselves to endure the tribulations of the present life, by the sight of. the pains of Jesus on the cross. Behold, says the Lord from this cross—behold the multitude of the pains and the wrongs which I suffer for thee upon this tree. My body hangs by three nails, and rests alone upon my very wounds. The people who surround me blaspheme me and afflict me, and my spirit within me is more afflicted than my body. I suffer all for love of thee ; behold the affection I bear thee, and love me ; and be not wearied at suffering anything for me, who, for thee, have lived a life so afflicted, and now am dying so bitter a death.

O my Jesus ! Thou hast placed me in the world that I might serve Thee and love Thee ; Thou hast given me so many lights and graces that I might be faithful to Thee ; but, in my ingratitude, how often, in order that I might not deprive myself of my own satisfaction—how often have I been willing to lose Thy grace and turn my back upon Thee ! Oh, through Thy desolate death, which Thou didst accept for my sake, give me strength to be grateful to Thee for what remains to me of life, while from this day forth I intend to drive from my heart every affection which is not for Thee, my God, my love, and my all.

Mary, my mother, help me to be faithful to thy Son, who has so much loved me.

VII.

Pater ! in manus tuas commendo spiritum meum.[1]

" Jesus, crying with a loud voice, said, Father, into Thy hands I commend My spirit."

Eutychius writes that Jesus uttered these words with

---

[1] *Luke.* xxiii. 46.

a loud voice, to make all men understand that he was the true Son of God, calling God his Father.[1] But St. John Chrysostom writes that he cried with a loud voice to teach us that he did not die of necessity, but of his own free will,[2] uttering so strong a voice at the very moment when he was about to end his life. This was in comformity with what Jesus had said during his life, that he voluntarily sacrificed his life for his sheep, and not through the will and malice of his enemies : *I lay down my life for my sheep. . . . No man taketh it from me, but I lay it down of myself.* [3]

St. Athanasius adds that Jesus Christ, in thus recommending himself to the Father, recommended at the same time all the faithful, who through him would obtain salvation, since the head with the members form one single body.[4] On which the saint remarks that Jesus then intended to repeat the prayer that he had before offered : *O holy Father, keep them in Thy name, that they may be one, as We are one.* And then he added, *Father, I will that those whom Thou hast given me should be where I am, and that they should be with me.* [5]

This made St. Paul say, *I know in whom I have believed, and I am sure that he is able to keep that which I have committed to him until that day.* [6] Thus the Apostle wrote, while he

---

[1] "Clamavit voce magna, ut omnes scirent quod Patrem Deum appellaret."—*In Matt.* c. 67.

[2] "Ut ostenderet hæc sua potestate fieri."—*In Matt. hom.* 89.

[3] "Et animam meam pono pro ovibus meis. . . . Nemo tollit eam a me, sed ego pono eam a meipso."—*John,* x. 15.

[4] "In eo homines apud Patrem commendat per ipsum vivificandos ; membra enim sumus, et membra unum corpus sunt. . . . Omnes ergo in se Deo commendat."

[5] "Pater sancte ! serva eos in nomine tuo quos dedisti mihi, ut sint unum sicut et nos. Volo ut, ubi sum ego, et illi sint mecum."—*John,* xvii. 11, 24.

[6] "Scio enim cui credidi, et certus sum quia potens est depositum meum servare in illum diem."—2 *Tim.* I. 12.

was in prison, suffering for Jesus Christ, into whose
hands he committed the deposit of his sufferings and
of all his hopes, knowing how grateful and faithful he
is to those who suffer for his love.

David placed all his hope in the future Redeemer
when he said, *Into thy hands, O Lord, I commend my spirit,
for Thou hast redeemed me, O Lord God of truth.*[1] And
how much more ought not we to trust in Jesus Christ,
who has now completed our redemption? Let us say
with great courage, *Thou hast redeemed me, O Lord ; into
Thy hands I commend my spirit. Father, into Thy hands I
commend my spirit.* Great comfort do these words bring
to the dying at the moment of death, against the temptations of hell, and their fears on account of their sins.

But, O Jesus, my Redeemer ! I would not wait for
death to recommend my soul to Thee ; I commend it to
Thee now ; suffer me not to turn my back upon Thee
again. I see that my past life has only served to dishonor
Thee ; suffer me not to continue to displease Thee for my
days that yet remain. O Lamb of God, sacrificed upon
the cross, and dead for me as a victim of love, and consumed by all griefs, grant by the merits of Thy death
that I may love Thee with all my heart, and be wholly
Thine while life remains. And when I shall reach the
end of my days, grant me to die glowing with love for
Thee. Thou hast died through love of me : I would die
for love of Thee. Thou hast given Thyself wholly to
me ; I give myself wholly to Thee : *Into Thy hands, O
Lord, I commend my spirit ; Thou hast redeemed me, O Lord
God of truth.* Thou hast poured forth all Thy blood ;
Thou hast given Thy life to save me ; suffer not that
through my fault all should be lost unto me. O my
Jesus, I love Thee, and I hope through Thy merits that

---

[1] "In manus tuas commendo spiritum meum ; redemisti me,
Domine Deus veritatis."—*Ps.* xxx. 6.

I shall love Thee forever. *In Thee, O Lord, I have hoped; I shall not be confounded forever.*[1]

O Mary, mother of God, I trust in thy prayers ; pray that I may live and die faithful to thy Son. To thee I would say, with St. Bonaventure, " In thee, O Lady, I have hoped ; I shall not be confounded forever."

CHAPTER VI.

THE DEATH OF JESUS CHRIST.

I.

Jesus dies, and triumphs over Death.

St. John writes that our Redeemer, before he breathed his last, bowed his head.[2] He bowed his head as a sign that he accepted death with full submission from the hands of his Father, and thus accomplished his humble obedience : *He humbled himself, and was made obedient to death, even the death of the cross.*[3]

Jesus upon the cross, with his hands and feet nailed upon it, could move no part of his body except his head. St. Athanasius says that death did not dare to approach to take away life from the author of life ; wherefore it was needed that he himself, by bowing his head (which alone he then could move), should call death to approach and slay him.[4] On St. Matthew's words, *Jesus again crying with a loud voice, yielded up the ghost,*[5] St. Ambrose remarks that the Evangelist used

---

[1] " In te, Domine, speravi; non confundar in æternum."—*Ps.* xxx. 2.

[2] " Et inclinato capite, tradidit spiritum."—*John,* xix. 30.

[3] "Humiliavit semetipsum, factus obediens usque ad mortem, mortem autem crucis."—*Phil.* ii. 8.

[4] " Mors ad ipsum non audebat accedere ; ideo Christus, inclinato capite, eam vocavit."—*Interpr. par.* q. 41.

[5] " Jesus autem, iterum clamans voce magna, emisit spiritum."— *Matt.* xxvii. 50.

the expression *yielded up* to show that Jesus did not die of necessity, or through the violence of the executioners, but because he voluntarily chose to die.[1] He chose willingly to die, to save man from the eternal death to which he was condemned.

This was already foretold by the prophet Osee in the words, *I will deliver them from the hand of death, from death I will redeem them. O death, I will be thy death ; O hell, I will be thy bite.*[2] This is testified by the holy Fathers St. Jerome, St. Augustine, St. Gregory; and St. Paul, as we have seen, applies the prophecy literally to Jesus Christ, who, with his death delivered us from death, that is, from hell. In Hebrew also (as the interpreters explain) the word *sheol*, which is rendered *death*, properly signifies *hell*.

How, then, was Jesus Christ the death of death ? *O death, I will be thy death !* Because by his death our Saviour conquered death, and destroyed the death which had resulted from sin. Therefore the Apostle writes, *Death is swallowed up in victory. Where, O death, is thy victory? Where, O death, is thy sting? The sting of death is sin.*[3] Jesus, the divine Lamb, by his death destroyed sin, which was the cause of our death; and this was the victory of Jesus, since by dying he banished sin from the world, and consequently delivered it from eternal death, to which all the human race was subjected.

To this corresponds that other text of the Apostle, *That through death He might destroy him who had the power of death, that is, the devil.*[4] Jesus destroyed the devil, that

[1] " ' Emisit,' quia non invitus amisit : quod enim emittitur, voluntarium est ; quod amittitur, necessarium."—*In Luc.* xxiii.

[2] " De manu mortis liberabo eos, de morte redimam eos: ero mors tua, o mors ! morsus tuus ero, inferne."—*Osee*, xiii. 14.

[3] " Absorpta est mors in victoria. Ubi est, mors, victoria tua? ubi est, mors, stimulus tuus ? Stimulus autem mortis peccatum est."—I *Cor.* xv. 54.

[4] " Ut per mortem destrueret eum, qui habebat mortis imperium, id est, diabolum."—*Heb.* ii. 14.

is, the power of the devil, who, through sin, had the power of death; that is, who had power to inflict temporal and eternal death on all the sons of Adam who were corrupted with sin. This was the victory of the cross, on which Jesus, the author of life, dying, by his death acquired life for us. Whence the Church sings of the cross that by it " Life endured death, and by death brought forth life."[1]

And all this was the work of the divine love, which brought this Priest to sacrifice to the Eternal Father the life of his only-begotten Son for the salvation of men; for which reason the Church also sings, "The Priest, who is love, sacrifices the limbs of his tender body."[2]

And therefore St. Francis de Sales cries out, "Let us look upon this divine Saviour stretched upon the cross, as upon the altar of his love, where he dies for love of us. Ah, why do we not cast ourselves in spirit upon the same, that we may die upon the cross with him who has been willing to die for love of us?"[3]

Yes, O my sweet Redeemer, I embrace Thy cross; and holding it in my embrace, I would live and die ever lovingly kissing Thy feet, wounded and pierced for me.

II.

Jesus Dead on the Cross.

But before going farther, let us stay to contemplate our Redeemer now dead upon the cross. Let us first say to his divine Father:

"Eternal Father, look upon the face of Thy Christ,"[4]

[1] " Fulget Crucis mysterium,
    Qua Vita mortem pertulit,
    Et morte vitam protulit."—*Off. de Pass.*
[2] " Almique membra corporis
    Amor sacerdos immolat."
                                    —*Off. de Temp. Pasch.*
[3] *Love of God*, bk. 7, ch. 8.
[4] " Respice in faciem Christi tui."—*Ps.* lxxxiii. 10.

look upon this Thy only-begotten Son, who, in order to satisfy Thy will that lost man should be saved, came down upon earth, took human nature, and with that flesh took upon him all our miseries, save sin. In a word, he made himself man, and lived all his life among men, as the poorest, the most despised, the most troubled of all; in the end he was condemned to death, as Thou seest him, after these very men had torn his flesh with scourgings, wounded his head with thorns, and pierced his hands and feet with nails upon the cross. Thus he died on this tree of unmixed anguish, despised as the vilest of men, derided as a false prophet, blasphemed as a sacrilegious impostor for having said that he was Thy Son, and condemned to die as one of the most guilty of malefactors. Thou Thyself didst give him up to endure this terrible and desolate death, depriving him of all relief. Tell us, what fault did Thy beloved Son commit that he should deserve so horrible a punishment? Thou knowest his innocence and his sanctity; why hast Thou thus treated him? I hear Thee reply, "For the wickedness of my people have I stricken him."[1] No, he did not deserve, he could not deserve, any punishment, being innocence and holiness itself; the punishment was due to you for your sins by which you deserved eternal death; and that I might not see you, the beloved creatures of my hand lost eternally, to deliver you from so dreadful a destruction, I gave up this my Son to so mournful a life, and to so bitter a death. Think, O men, to what an excess I have loved you. *God so loved the world*, says St. John, *that He gave His only-begotten Son.*[2]

Let me now return to Thee, O Jesus, my Redeemer. I behold Thee upon this cross, pale and desolate; Thou speakest no more, nor breathest, for Thou art no longer

[1] "Propter scelus populi mei percussi eum."—*Isa.* liii. 8.
[2] "Sic enim Deus dilexit mundum, et Filium suum unigenitum daret."—*John,* iii. 16.

alive; Thou hast no more blood, for Thou hast poured it all forth, as Thou didst Thyself foretell: *This is My blood of the new covenant which is shed for many.*[1] Thou hast no longer life, for Thou hast given it in order to give life to my soul, which was dead through its sins. But why didst Thou destroy Thy life and pour forth Thy blood for us miserable sinners? Behold, St. Paul tells us: *He loved us and gave Himself for us."*[2]

III.

The Fruits of the Death of our Saviour.

Thus this divine Priest, who was both priest and victim, sacrificing his life for the salvation of the men he loved, completed the great sacrifice of the cross, and accomplished the work of human redemption.

Jesus Christ, by his death, stripped our death of its terrors; until this it was but the punishment of rebels; but by grace and the merits of our Saviour it became a sacrifice so dear to God that when we unite it to the death of Jesus, it makes us worthy to enjoy the same glory that God enjoys, and to hear him one day say to us, as we hope, *Enter thou into the joy of thy Lord.*[3]

Thus death, which was an object of pain and dread, was changed by the death of Jesus into a passage from a state of peril, of eternal misery, into one of security, of eternal blessedness, and from the miseries of this life to the boundless delights of paradise.

Therefore the saints have ever regarded death with joy and desire, and no longer with fear. St. Augustine says that they who love the crucified one "live with patience and die with joy."[4] And common experience shows

---

[1] "Hic est sanguis meus Novi Testamenti, qui pro multis effundetur."—*Mark*, xiv. 24.

[2] "Dilexit nos, et tradidit semetipsum pro nobis."—*Eph.* v. 2.

[3] "Intra in gaudium Domini tui."—*Matt.* xxv. 21.

[4] "Patienter vivunt, delectabiliter moriuntur."—*In* 1 *Jo. tr.* 9.

20

that they who in life have been most troubled with persecutions, temptations, scruples, or other painful events, in death are most comforted by the crucified one, conquering with great peace of mind all the terrors and pains of death. And if it has sometimes happened that some saints, as we read in their lives, have died in great fear of death, the Lord has permitted this in order to increase their merits; because the sacrifice that they made, the more painful it was to themselves, the more acceptable was it to God, and the more profitable to them for eternity.

Oh, how much harder was the death of the faithful of old before the death of Jesus Christ! Then, when the Saviour was not yet come, they sighed for his coming, they waited for his promise, but they knew not when it would be fulfilled; the devil had great power upon earth; heaven was closed to men. But after the death of the Redeemer, hell was conquered, divine grace was given to souls, God was reconciled to men, and the country of Paradise was opened to all those who die innocent, or who have expiated their sins by repentance. And if some who die in grace do not immediately enter heaven, this only results from the faults of which they are not yet cleansed; and death merely bursts their bonds, in order that they may go free to unite themselves perfectly to God, from whom they are far away in this land of banishment.

Let us, then, take heed, O Christian souls, while we are in this exile, not to look at death as a misfortune, but as the end of our pilgrimage, which is full of difficulties and dangers, and as the beginning of our eternal happiness, which we hope one day to attain through the merits of Jesus Christ. And with this thought of heaven, let us detach ourselves as much as possible from earthly things, which may cause us to lose heaven, and give us over to eternal pains. Let us offer ourselves to

God, declaring that we wish to die when it pleases him, and to accept death in the manner and at the time which he has appointed; ever praying him that, through the merits of Jesus Christ, he will cause us to depart from this life in his grace.

O my Jesus and my Saviour, who, to obtain for me a happy death, hast chosen for Thyself a death so painful and desolate, I abandon myself into the arms of Thy mercy. For many years passed I have deserved to be in hell, for the sins that I have committed against Thee, and to be separated from Thee forever. But Thou, instead of punishing me as I deserved, hast called me to repentance, and I hope that now Thou hast pardoned me; but if Thou hast not already pardoned me through my fault, pardon me now that in sorrow I ask for mercy at Thy feet. O my Jesus! I could die of grief when I think of the injuries that I have offered to Thee! " O blood of the innocent one, wash away the penitent's sins!" Pardon me, and give me help to love Thee with all my strength till death; and when I shall reach the end of my life, make me to die burning with love for Thee, that I may go on to love Thee forever. Jesus, henceforth I unite my death to Thy holy death, through which I hoped to be saved. *In Thee, O Lord, have I hoped; I shall not be confounded forever.*[1]

O thou great mother of God! next to Jesus thou art my hope. "In thee, O Lady, I have hoped; I shall not be confounded forever."

[1] "In te, Domine, speravi; non confundar in æternum."—*Ps.* xxx. 2.

CHAPTER VII.

THE PRODIGIES WHICH HAPPENED AT THE DEATH OF CHRIST.

I

Mourning of all Nature—Darkness.

It is reported (as Cornelius à Lapide relates) that St.
Dionysius the Areopagite, being at the time at Heliop-
olis in Egypt, at the time of the death of Jesus Christ
exclaimed, "Either the God of nature is suffering, or
the fabric of the world is being dissolved."[1]   Others,
such as Syncellus and Suidas, relate the story differently,
and state that he said, "God, unknown, is suffering in
the flesh, and therefore the universe is hidden in this
darkness."[2]

Eusebius[3] writes that Plutarch, being in the isle of
Praxos, heard a voice say, "The great Pan is dead;"[4]
and immediately afterwards heard a cry of many persons wailing. Eusebius considers that *Pan* means the
devil, who being, as it were, killed by the death of
Jesus, was stripped of the power he had possessed over
men; but Barrada[5] thinks that it means Jesus Christ
himself, because in Greek the word *Pan* means *All*, which
Jesus Christ, being the Son of God, and truly God,
really was; that is, all that is good.

[1] "Aut Deus, naturæ Auctor, patitur, aut mundi machina dissolvi-
tur."

[2] "Deus ignotûs in carne patitur ; ideoque universum hisce tenebris
obscuratur."—*Enc. B. Dion.*

[3] *Præp. ev.* l. 5, c. 17.

[4] "Magnus Pan mortuus est."

[5] T. iv. l. 7, c. 21.

What we have in the Gospels is, that on the day of the death of the Saviour, the whole earth was covered with darkness, from the sixth to the ninth hour. And when Jesus breathed his last, the veil of the temple was rent, and a great earthquake shook the mountains.[1]

Speaking of the darkness, St. Jerome says that this darkness was foretold by the prophet Amos in these words: *It shall come to pass in that day, saith the Lord, that the sun shall go down at mid-day; and I will make the earth dark in the day of light.*[2] On which St. Jerome remarks that the sun seemed to have withdrawn its light, in order that the enemies of Jesus Christ might not rejoice in it ;[3] and that the sun hid itself, because it dared not look upon the Lord hanging on the cross.[4] But St. Leo more justly says that then all creatures groaned, when the Creator hung upon the cross.[5] With this Tertullian agrees, saying that from the sixth hour the world was darkened, and celebrated the obsequies of the Lord.[6]

St. Athanasius, St. Chrysostom, and St. Thomas remark that this darkness was altogether miraculous, because it could not have happened as an eclipse of the sun, by the interposition of the moon between the earth and the sun, as this eclipse always takes place at the new moon, and not the full moon, as astronomers say.

[1] " A sexta autem hora, tenebræ factæ sunt super universam terram usque ad horam nonam. Et ecce velum Templi scissum est in duas partes a summo usque deorsum; et terra mota est, et petræ scissæ sunt."—*Matt.* xxvii. 45, 51.

[2] " Et erit in die illa, dicit Dominus Deus : occidet sol in meridie, et tenebrescere faciam terram in die luminis."—*Amos,* viii. 9.

[3] " Videtur luminare majus retraxisse radios suos, ne impii sua luce fruerentur."—*In Matt.* xxvii.

[4] " Retraxit radios suos, pendentem in cruce Dominum spectare non ausus."—*In Am.* viii.

[5] " Pendente in patibulo Creatore, universa creatura congemuit."— *De Pass.* s. 6.

[6] " A sexta hora contenebratus orbis defuncto Domino lugubre fecit officium."—*De Jejunio.*

And, further, as the sun is much larger than the moon, the moon could not hide the whole of its light; while the Gospel relates that darkness was spread over the whole earth. Further still, even if the moon could have darkened the whole light of the sun, we know that the course of the sun is so swift that such darkness could only have lasted a few minutes, while the Gospel relates that it lasted from the sixth to the ninth hour.

This miraculous darkness Tertullian especially pointed out, in his Apology to the heathen, reminding them that in their own archives this prodigy of the darkness of the sun was recorded.[1] Eusebius, confirming this statement, relates in his chronicle the words of Phlegon, the freedman of Augustus, an author of that period, who thus writes: " In the fourth year of the second Olympiad, the sun was completely darkened, more than at any other recorded time; and night came on at the sixth hour, so that the stars were visible." [2]

II.

The Rending of the Veil of the Temple.

In the Gospel of St. Matthew it is said, *The veil of the temple was rent in two parts, from the top to the bottom.*[3] The Apostle writes[4] that in the temple, as in the tabernacle, there was the Holy of Holies, where was the ark of the covenant, which contained the manna, the rod of Aaron, the tables of the law; and this ark was the Propitiatory.

---

[1] " Eodem momento diei, medium orbem signante sole, lux subducta est. Eum mundi casum relatum in archivis vestris habetis."— *Apolog.* c. 21.

[2] " Quarto anno Olympiadis 202, factum est deliquium solis omnibus cognitis majus, et nox facta est hora diei sexta, ita ut stellæ in cœlo conspicerentur."—*Chron.* l. 2.

[3] " Et velum Templi scissum est in duas partes a summo usque deorsum."—*Matt.* xxvii. 51.

[4] *Heb.* ix. 1.

Into the first tabernacle, which was outside the Holy of
Holies, and was covered with the first veil, the priests
went to offer sacrifices; and the priest who sacrificed,
dipping his finger into the blood of the victim that was
offered, sprinkled the veil seven times.[1] But into the
second tabernacle, the Holy of Holies, which was always
shut, and covered with the second veil, the high-priest
went solemnly once a year, carrying the blood of the
victim which was sacrificed by himself.[2]

The whole was a mystery: the sanctuary ever closed,
represented the separation of men from the divine grace,
which they would never have received but for the sacrifice
of himself which Jesus Christ was one day to offer, and
which was typified in all the old sacrifices; and therefore
he is called by St. Paul, a High-Priest of good things to
come, who by a more perfect tabernacle, that is, by his own
sacred body, would enter into the Holy of Holies of the
presence of God, as the mediator between God and men:
offering the blood, not of goats and calves, but his own
blood, with which he completed the work of human redemption, and thus opened to us the way of heaven.[3]

The Apostle says, he was a Priest of good things to
come, unlike the high-priest Aaron, who obtained present and earthly blessings; while Jesus Christ came to
obtain for us future blessings, which are heavenly and
eternal. He says, also, that he came by a greater and
more perfect tabernacle, which was the sacred humanity
of the Lord, which was the tabernacle of his divinity;
it was not made with hands, because the body of Jesus

---

[1] *Lev.* iv. 6-17.
[2] *Lev.* xvi. 12, 14; *Heb.* ix. 7.
[3] "Christus autem assistens Pontifex futurorum bonorum, per amplius et perfectius tabernaculum non manufactum, id est, non hujus
creationis: neque per sanguinem hircorum aut vitulorum, sed per
proprium sanguinem, introivit semel in Sancta, æterna Redemptione
inventa."—*Heb.* ix. 11.

was not formed by the work of man, but by the Holy Ghost. Nor did he come with the blood of goats and calves, but with his own blood ; for the blood of goats and calves effected merely a carnal purification, while the blood of Jesus effected the purification of the soul by the remission of sins. It is said, also, that he entered once into the Holies, having obtained eternal redemption ; which implies that this redemption could never have been obtained by ourselves, nor expected except from the divine promises: it was the work of the divine goodness ; and it is called eternal, because, while the high-priest of the Hebrews went into the Holy of Holies once every year, Jesus Christ, once only accomplishing the sacrifice of his death, merited for us an eternal redemption, which would be sufficient to atone for all our sins; as the same Apostle writes, *By one offering He perfected forever those who are sanctified.*[1]

The Apostle adds, *And therefore he is the Mediator of the New Testament.*[2] Moses was the mediator of the Old Testament, that is, the old covenant, which had no power to obtain for men reconciliation with God and salvation; for, as St. Paul explains in another place, the old law made nothing perfect.[3] But by the new covenant, Jesus Christ, fully satisfying the divine justice for the sins of men, by his merits obtained for men pardon and the divine grace. The Jews were offended at perceiving that the Messiah had wrought the redemption of man by so shameful a death; saying that they had read in the law that the Messiah would not die, but live forever.[4] But they were completely in error; for death was the means

---

[1] " Una enim oblatione consummavit in sempiternum sanctificatos."—*Heb.* x. 14.
[2] " Et ideo Novi Testamenti Mediator est."—*Ibid.* ix. 15.
[3] " Nihil enim ad perfectum adduxit Lex."—*Ibid.* vii. 19.
[4] " Nos audivimus ex Lege, quia Christus manet in æternum."—*John,* xii. 34.

by which Jesus Christ made himself the Mediator and Saviour of men, since by the death of Jesus Christ the promise of the eternal inheritance was made to those who are called.' Therefore St. Paul exhorts us to place all our hopes in the merits of the death of Jesus Christ: *Having a confidence in the entering into the Holies by the blood of Christ, a new and living way which He hath dedicated for us through the veil, that is to say, His flesh.*' We, he says, have a strong foundation for our hope of eternal life in the blood of Jesus Christ, who has opened to us the new way to paradise. He calls it a *new* way, because it was trodden by no one before; while Jesus, by treading it, has opened it to us through his flesh, which was sacrificed on the cross, of which the veil was a figure; because (as St. John Chrysostom writes), as when the veil was rent, the Holy of Holies continued open, so the body of Christ, when torn in his Passion, opened to us the heaven which was closed. The Apostle therefore exhorts us to go with confidence to the throne of grace to obtain the divine mercy.' This throne of grace is Jesus Christ, to whom, when we miserable sinners go in the midst of the dangers of destruction in which we stand, we find that mercy which we do not deserve.

Let us return to the text quoted from St. Matthew, *Jesus, crying with a loud voice, yielded up His spirit; and behold the veil of the temple was rent in two parts, from the top to the bottom.* This rending took place at the moment of

¹ "Et ideo Novi Testamenti Mediator est, ut morte intercedente in redemptionem earum prævaricationum quæ erant sub priori Testamento, repromissionem accipiant, qui vocati sunt, æternæ hereditatis."—*Heb.* ix. 15.

² "Habentes itaque, fratres, fiduciam in introïtu Sanctorum in sanguine Christi, quam initiavit nobis viam novam et viventem per velamen, id est, carnem suam."—*Heb.* x. 19.

³ "Adeamus ergo cum fiducia ad thronum gratiæ, ut misericordiam consequamur, et gratiam inveniamus in auxilio opportuno."—*Ibid.* iv. 16.

the death of Jesus Christ, which, as was remarked by all
the priests and the people, could not have taken place
except as a supernatural prodigy; for by the mere shak-
ing of the earthquake the veil would not thus have
been torn from the top to the bottom. It took place in
order to show that God no longer desired to keep this
sanctuary closed, as it had been commanded by the law,
but that he himself desired to be henceforth the sanctuary opened by means of Jesus Christ.

St. Leo writes [1] that the Lord, by this rending, showed
us plainly that the old priesthood was ended, and the
eternal priesthood of Jesus Christ was begun; and that
the old sacrifices were abolished, and a new law set up,
according to what the Apostle says: *A change being made
in the priesthood, it is necessary that there should be also a
change in the law.*[2] And by this we are assured that Jesus
Christ is the founder both of the first law and of the second; and that the old law, the tabernacle, the priesthood, and the old sacrifices had regard to the sacrifice
of the cross, which was to accomplish the redemption of
man. And thus everything which had been obscure or
mysterious in the old law, in the sacrifices, festivals, and
promises, became clear through the death of the Saviour.
Lastly, Euthymius says that the rent veil showed that
the wall which divided heaven and earth was taken
away, so that the way for man to reach heaven lay open
without any obstacle.[3]

---

[1] *De Pass.* s. 10.

[2] "Translato enim sacerdotio, necesse est ut et legis translatio
fiat."—*Heb.* vii. 12.

[3] "Scissum velum significavit divisum jam esse parietem inter
cœlum et terram, qui inter Deum erat et homines, et factum esse
hominibus cœlum pervium."—*In Matt.* c. 67.

III.

The Earthquake.

It is further said in the Gospel, *The earth was shaken, and the rocks cleft asunder.*[1] It is reported that at the death of Jesus Christ there happened a trembling so great and universal that it shook the whole globe of the earth, as Paul Orosius writes.[2] Didymus' also says that the earth was then shaken to its centre. Further, Phlegon, as quoted by Origen and by Eusebius,[4] says that in the year 33 after the birth of Christ, many buildings were thrown down by this earthquake at Nice in Bithynia. Pliny also, who lived in the time of Tiberius, under whom Christ was put to death, and Suetonius, attest that at this time twelve cities in Asia were prostrated by this earthquake; and thus the learned believe that the prophecy of Aggeus was fulfilled, *Yet a little while, and I will move the heaven and the earth.*[5] Upon this St. Paulinus writes that Jesus Christ, though fixed upon the cross, to show who he was, even from his cross struck terror into the world.[6]

Agricomius' relates that even to his day the signs of this earthquake were visible on the left side of Mount Calvary, where there was a fissure large enough to contain a man's body, and so deep that the bottom could not be reached. Baronius,[8] writing upon A.D. 34, says that in many other places the mountains were laid open

---

[1] " Et terra mota est, et petræ scissæ sunt."—*Matt.* xxvii. 51.

[2] *Hist.* l. 7, c. 4.

[3] *Fragm. in Job,* 9.

[4] *Chron.* l. 2.

[5] "Adhuc unum modicum est, et ego commovebo cœlum et terram."—*Agg.* ii. 7.

[6] " In cruce fixus homo est, Deus e cruce terruit orbem."—*De Ob. Celsi.*

[7] *Jerus. Descr.* n. 252.

[8] *Ann.* 34.

by the earthquake; especially at the present time there
is to be seen at Gaeta a hill of rock which, it is said,
was split open from the top to the bottom at the time of
our Lord's death; and it is clear that the aperture was
prodigiously large, for the sea flows through it, and
another portion of the hill is enlarged in an equal proportion. The same tradition is attached to Mount Co-
lombo, near Rieti; to Monserrat in Spain; and to several
mountains in Sardinia near Cagliari; while still more
remarkable is that which happened to Mount Alvernia
in Tuscany, where St. Francis received the gift of the
sacred *stigmata*, and where large masses of rock heaped
one upon another are to be seen, of which it is said
that it was revealed to St. Francis by an angel that
these rocks were thus thrown together at the death of
Jesus Christ, as Wading[1] relates.

St. Ambrose on this exclaims, " O Jewish hearts, harder
than rocks! the mountains are cleft, but the hearts of
these men are hardened."[2]

IV.

Resurrection of the Dead, and Conversions.

St. Matthew goes on to describe the prodigies which
happened at the death of Christ, and says, *The graves
were opened, and many bodies of the saints that had slept arose;
and coming out of the tombs after His resurrection, came into
the holy city, and appeared to many.*[3] Upon this, St. Ambrose says "What else is meant by this opening of the

---

[1] *Ann.* 1215, n. 15.

[2] " O duriora saxis pectora Judæorum ! finduntur petræ, sed horum
corda durantur."—*In Luc.* xxiii.

[3] " Et monumenta aperta sunt, et multa corpora Sanctorum, qui
dormierant, surrexerunt; et exeuntes de monumentis, post resurrectionem ejus, venerunt in Sanctam Civitatem et apparuerunt multis."
—*Matt.* xxvii. 52.

graves, but the resurrection of the dead?" [1] Thus the opening of the graves signified the discomfiture of death, and the restoration of life to man by the resurrection.

St. Jerome, Venerable Bede, and St. Thomas say that though the graves were opened at the death of Christ, yet the dead did not rise till after the resurrection of the Lord.[2] And this is conformable to what the Apostle says when he calls Christ the first begotten of the dead, and the first of them that rise.[3] For it was not fitting that any man should rise before Him who had triumphed over death.

It is said in St. Matthew that many saints then arose, and, leaving the graves, appeared to many. These were the just, who had believed and hoped in Jesus Christ; and God desired thus to honor them, as a reward for their faith and confidence in the future Messiah, according to the prediction of Zacharias, *Thou also, by the blood of Thy testament, hast sent forth Thy prisoners out of the pit, wherein is no water;*[4] that is, from what is called Limbo by the Fathers, in which there was none of the water of joy.

St. Matthew goes on to say that the centurion, and the other soldiers who were under him, who had put the Saviour to death, though the Jews continued obstinately to rejoice in his death, were themselves moved with the miracles of the darkness and earthquake, and recognized

[1] "Monumentorum reseratio quid aliud nisi, claustris mortis effractis, resurrectionem significat mortuorum?"—*In Luc.* xxiii.

[2] "Tamen, cum monumenta aperta sunt, non antea resurrexerunt quam Dominus resurgeret, ut esset primogenitus resurrectionis ex mortuis."

[3] "Principium, primogenitus ex mortuis, ut sit in omnibus ipse primatum tenens."—*Col.* i. 18.

[4] "Tu quoque, in sanguine Testamenti tui, emisisti vinctos tuos de lacu in quo non est aqua."—*Zach.* ix. 11.

him as the Son of God.' These soldiers were the first-fruits of the Gentiles, who embraced the faith of Jesus Christ after they had put him to death, though, through his merits, they had grace to understand their sin and to hope for pardon.

St. Luke adds that all the others who had either taken part in or applauded the death of Jesus Christ, when they saw the prodigies, smote their breasts in sign of repentance, and returned home.' And then, as we read in the Acts of the Apostles, many other Jews, being touched by the preaching of St. Peter, asked of him what they should do to be saved; and St. Peter bade them repent and be baptized; and they who received his words and were baptized were about three thousand.'

V.

The Heart of Jesus is pierced.

The soldiers then came, and broke the legs of the two thieves; but when they came to Jesus, they saw that he was already dead, and abstained from doing the same to him. One of them, however, with a spear pierced his side, from which immediately came forth blood and water.'

St. Cyprian says that the spear pierced straight into the heart of Jesus Christ; and the same thing was re-

---

[1] "Centurio autem et qui cum eo erant custodientes Jesum, viso terræ motu et his quæ fiebant, timuerunt valde, dicentes: Vere Filius Dei erat iste."—*Matt.* xxvii. 54.

[2] "Et omnis turba eorum qui simul aderant ad spectaculum istud, et videbant quæ fiebant, percutientes pectora sua revertebantur."—*Luke,* xxiii. 48.

[3] "Qui ergo receperunt sermonem ejus, baptizati sunt; et appositæ sunt in die illa animæ circiter tria millia."—*Acts,* ii. 41.

[4] "Sed unus militum lancea latus ejus aperuit, et continuo exivit sanguis et aqua."—*John,* xix. 34.

vealed to St. Bridget.' From which we understand
that, as both blood and water flowed forth, the spear,
in order to strike the heart, must first have pierced the
pericardium.

St. Augustine says that St. John used the words
opened the side, because in the heart of the Lord the way
of life was opened, whence came forth the sacraments,
by means of which we enter upon eternal life.' Further,
it is said that the blood and water which came from the
side of Jesus were figures of the sacraments; the water,
of baptism, which is the first of the sacraments; and the
blood, of the Eucharist, which is the greatest.

St. Bernard further says that, by receiving this visible
stroke, Jesus Christ wished to signify the invisible stroke
of love, by which his heart was pierced for us.'

St. Augustine also, speaking of the Eucharist, says
that the holy sacrifice of the Mass at this day is not less
efficacious before God than the blood and water which
flowed on that day from the side of Jesus Christ.'

VI.

Burial and resurrection of Jesus Christ.

We will conclude this chapter with some reflections
on the burial of Jesus Christ.

Jesus came into the world, not only to redeem us, but
by his own example to teach us all virtues, and especially

---

1 " Lancea attigit costam, et ambæ partes cordis fuerunt in lancea."
—*Rev.* l. 2, c. 21.

2 " Ut illic quodam modo vitæ ostium panderetur, unde sacramenta
Ecclesiæ manaverunt, sine quibus ad vitam non intratur."—*In Jo.
tr.* 120.

3 " Propterea vulneratum est, ut, per vulnus visibile, vulnus amoris
invisibile videamus ; carnale ergo vulnus vulnus spirituale ostendit."
—*Lib. de Pass.* c. 3.

4 " Non minus hodie in conspectu Patris oblatio illa est efficax,
quam die qua de saucio latere sanguis et aqua exivit."

humility and holy poverty, which is inseparably united
with humility. On this account he chose to be born in
a cave; to live, a poor man, in a workshop for thirty
years ; and finally to die, poor and naked, upon a cross,
seeing his garments divided among the soldiers before
he breathed his last; while after his death he was compelled to receive his winding-sheet for burial as an alms
from others. Let the poor be consoled, thus seeing
Jesus Christ, the King of heaven and earth, thus living
and dying in poverty in order to enrich us with his
merits and gifts; as the Apostle says, *For your sake He
became poor, when He was rich, that by His poverty you might
be rich.*[1] For this cause the saints, to become like Jesus in
his poverty, have despised all earthly riches and honors,
that they might go one day to enjoy with Jesus Christ
the riches and honors prepared by God in heaven for
them that love him; of which blessings the Apostle
says that eye hath not seen, nor ear heard, nor has it
entered into the mind of man to conceive what God has
prepared for them that love him.[2]

Jesus Christ, then, rose with the glory of possessing
all power in heaven and earth, not as God alone, but as
a man; wherefore all angels and men are subject to
him. Let us rejoice in thus seeing in glory our Saviour,
our Father, and the best friend that we possess. And
let us rejoice for ourselves, because the resurrection of
Jesus Christ is for us a sure pledge of our own resurrection, and of the glory that we hope one day to have in
heaven, both in soul and in body. This hope gave courage to the holy martyrs to suffer with gladness all the
evils of this life, and the most cruel torments of tyrants.
We must rest assured, however, that none will rejoice

---

[1] " Propter vos egenus factus est, cum esset dives, ut illius inopia
vos divites essetis."—2 *Cor.* viii. 9.

[2] " Oculus non vidit, nec auris audivit, nec in cor hominis ascendit,
quæ præparavit Deus iis qui diligunt illum."—1 *Cor.* ii. 9.

with Jesus Christ but they who are willing to suffer in this world with him; nor will he obtain the crown who does not fight as he ought to fight. *He that striveth in a wrestling is not crowned unless he has striven lawfully.*[1] At the same time let us be sure of what the same Apostle says, that all the sufferings of this life are short and light in comparison with the boundless and eternal joys which we hope to enjoy in Paradise.[2] Let us labor the more to continue in the grace of God, and continually to pray for perseverance in his favor; for without prayer, and that persevering, we shall not obtain this perseverance; and without perseverance we shall not obtain salvation.

O sweet Jesus, worthy of all love, how hast Thou so loved men that, in order to show Thy love, Thou hast not refused to die wounded and dishonored upon an infamous tree! O my God, how is it that there are so few among men who love Thee with their heart? O my dear Redeemer, of these few I would be one! Miserable that I am, for my past life I have forgotten Thy love, and given up Thy grace for miserable pleasures. I know the evil I have done; I grieve for it with all my heart; I would die for grief. Now, O my beloved Redeemer, I love Thee more than myself; and I am ready to die a thousand times rather than lose Thy friendship. I thank Thee for the light Thou hast given me. O my Jesus, my hope, leave me not in my own hands; help me until my death.

O Mary, Mother of God, pray to Jesus for me.

---

[1] " Nam et qui certat in agone, non coronatur, nisi legitime certaverit."—2 *Tim*. ii. 5.

[2] " Id enim quod in præsenti est momentaneum et leve tribulationis nostræ, supra modum in sublimitate æternum gloriæ pondus operatur in nobis."—2 *Cor*. iv. 17.

21

CHAPTER VIII.

THE LOVE SHOWN TO US BY JESUS CHRIST IN HIS PASSION.

I.

God so loved men, that He gave His own Son to redeem them.

St. Francis de Sales called Mount Calvary "the mountain of lovers," and says that the love which springs not
from the Passion is weak;' meaning, that the Passion
of Jesus Christ is the most powerful incentive to inflame
us to love our Saviour. To be able to comprehend a
part (for to comprehend the whole is impossible) of the
great love which God has shown us in the Passion of
Jesus Christ, it is sufficient to glance at what is said of
it in the divine Scriptures, of which I shall here set forth
some of the principal passages. Nor let any one complain that I thus repeat the texts which I have already
repeated several times in my other works when speaking
of the Passion. Many writers of mischievous books
constantly repeat their immodest jests, in order the more
to excite the passions of their thoughtless readers; and
shall it not be permitted to me to repeat those holy
texts which most inflame souls with divine love?

Speaking of this love, Jesus himself said, *God so loved
the world, that He gave His only-begotten Son.*' The word *so*
expresses much. It teaches us that when God gave his
only-begotten Son, he displayed to us a love which we
can never attain to comprehend. Through sin we were

' *Love of God*, b. 12, ch. 13.
' "Sic enim Deus dilexit mundum, ut Filium suum unigenitum
daret."—*John*, iii. 16.

all dead, having lost the life of grace; but the Eternal Father, in order to make known his goodness to the world, and to show us how much he loved us, chose to send on earth his Son, that by his death he might restore to us the life we had lost. *In this appeared the love of God to us, in that God sent His only-begotten Son into the world, that we might live by Him.*[1] Thus, in order to pardon us, God refused that pardon to his own Son, desiring that he should take upon him to satisfy the divine justice for all our faults ; *He spared not His own Son, but delivered Him up for us all.*[2] The words *delivered up* are used because God gave him into the hands of the executioners, that they might load him with insults and pains, until he died of agony on a shameful tree. Thus he first loaded him with all our sins. *The Lord laid on Him the iniquity of us all.* And then he chose to see him consumed with the most bitter inward and outward pangs and afflictions : *For the wickedness of My people I have stricken Him. The Lord bruised Him in infirmity.*[3]

St. Paul, considering this love of God, goes on to say: *On account of the too great love with which He loved us, when we were dead in sins, He raised us up in Christ.*[4] The Apostle calls it his *too great love.* Could there be anything indeed in excess in God? Yes; by this he means us to understand that God has done such things for us, that if faith had not assured us of them, none could have believed them. And therefore the Church cries out in

[1] "In hoc apparuit charitas Dei in nobis, quoniam Filium suum unigenitum misit Deus in mundum, ut vivamus per eum."—1 *John,* iv. 9.

[2] "Qui etiam proprio Filio suo non pepercit, sed pro nobis omnibus tradidit illum."—*Rom.* viii. 32.

[3] "Posuit Dominus in eo iniquitatem omnium nostrum.—Propter scelus populi mei percussi eum . . . et Dominus voluit conterere eum in infirmitate."—*Isa.* liii. 6–8.

[4] "Propter nimiam charitatem suam qua dilexit nos, et cum essemus mortui peccatis, convivificavit nos in Christo."—*Eph.* ii. 5.

astonishment, "Oh, wonderful is that which Thy love towards us has thought fit to do ! O inestimable Love of love ! that Thou mightest redeem Thy servant, Thou hast delivered up Thy Son."[1] Remark here the expression of the Church, *Love of love;* for the love of God to us is more than that he has shown to any other creatures. God, being love itself,[2] as St. John says, he loves all his creatures ; *Thou lovest all things that are, and hatest nothing that Thou hast made.*[3] But the love that he bears to man seems to be that which is the dearest and most beloved to him, for it appears as though, in love, he had preferred man to the angels, since he has been willing to die for men and not for the fallen angels.

II.

The Son of God offered Himself for the Love of us.

Speaking. then, of the love of the Son of God for man, let us remember that when he saw on one side man lost through sin, and on the other the divine justice requiring a perfect satisfaction for the offences committed by man, who was himself unable to offer such a satisfaction, he voluntarily offered himself to make satisfaction : *He was offered, because he willed it.*[4] And this humble lamb gave himself to the torturers, suffering them to lacerate his flesh, and to lead him to death, without lamenting or opening his mouth, as it was foretold: *He shall be brought as a lamb to the slaughter, and as a sheep is dumb before its shearer, and openeth not its mouth.*[5] St. Paul

[1] "O mira circa nos tuæ pietatis dignatio ! o inæstimabilis dilectio charitatis ! ut servum redimeres, Filium tradidisti."—*In Sabb. S.*

[2] "Deus charitas est."—1 *John,* iv. 8.

[3] "Diligis enim omnia, quæ sunt, et nihil odisti eorum, quæ fecisti."—*Wisd.* xi. 25.

[4] "Oblatus est, quia ipse voluit."—*Isa.* liii. 7.

[5] "Sicut ovis ad occisionem ducetur, et quasi agnus coram tondente se obmutescet, et non aperiet os suum."—*Ibid.*

writes that Jesus Christ accepted the death of the cross to obey his Father.[1] But let us not imagine that the Redeemer was crucified solely to obey his Father, and not with his own full will; he freely offered himself to this death, and of his own will chose to die for man, moved by the love he bore him, as he himself declares by St. John: *I lay down My life; no man will take it from Me, but I lay it down of Myself.*[2] And he said that it was the work of the Good Shepherd, to give his life for his sheep.[3] And why was this? what obligation was there on the shepherd to give his life for the sheep? *He loved us, and gave Himself for us.*[4]

This, indeed, our loving Redeemer himself declared, when he said, *If I be lifted up from the earth, I will draw all men unto Me;*[5] thereby showing the kind of death that he would die upon the cross, as the Evangelist himself explains it : *He said this, signifying by what death He would die.*[6] On these words St. John Chrysostom remarks, that he draws them as it were from the hands of a tyrant.[7] By his death he draws us from the hands of Lucifer, who, as a tyrant, keeps us enchained as his slaves, to torment us after our death forever in hell.

Miserable had we been if Jesus Christ had not died for us! We should all have been imprisoned in hell. For us who had deserved hell, it is a great motive to

---

[1] "Factus obediens usque ad mortem, mortem autem crucis."— *Phil.* ii. 8.

[2] "Ego pono animam meam. . . . Nemo tollit eam a me, sed ego pono eam a melpso."—*John.* x. 17.

[3] "Ego sum Pastor bonus. Bonus pastor animam suam dat pro ovibus suis."— *John.* x. 11.

[4] "Dilexit nos, et tradidit semetipsum pro nobis."—*Eph.* v. 2.

[5] "Et ego, si exaltatus fuero a terra, omnia traham ad meipsum." —*John.* xii. 32.

[6] "Hoc autem dicebat significans qua morte esset moriturus."— *Ibid.*

[7] " 'Omnia traham,' quasi a tyranno detenta."

us to love Jesus Christ, to think, that by his death, he has delivered us from this hell, by pouring forth his blood.

Let us, then, in passing, glance at the pains of hell, where at this hour are so many wretched souls. Oh, miserable beings! there they are sunk in a sea of fire, where they endure ceaseless agony, since in this fire they experience pains of all kinds. There they are given into the hands of devils, who, full of fury, are busied only in tormenting these miserable condemned ones. There, still more than by the fire and the other tortures, are they tormented by remorse of conscience in recollecting the sins of their life, which were the cause of their damnation. There they see the way of escape from this abyss of torments ever closed. There they find themselves forever excluded from the company of the saints, and from their country, heaven, for which they were created. But what most afflicts them, and constitutes their hell. is to see themselves abandoned by God, and condemned to be unable evermore to love him, and to look upon themselves with hatred and madness.

From this hell Jesus Christ has delivered us, redeeming us not with gold or any earthly good thing, but by giving his own life and blood upon the cross.[1] The kings of the earth send their subjects to die in war to preserve their own security; Jesus Christ chose himself to die, in order to give safety to his creatures.

III.

Jesus died not only for us all, but for each one of us.

Behold Jesus, then, presented by the scribes and priests to Pilate as a malefactor, that he might judge him and condemn him to the death of the cross; and see how

---

[1] "Non pro te dedit aurum, non prædia, sed proprium cruorem, in crucis moriendo patibulo."—*De Cont. m.* c. 7.

they follow him, in order to see him condemned and crucified. Oh, marvellous thing, cries St. Augustine, to see the judge judged ; to see justice condemned ; to see life dying ! [1] And for what cause were these marvels accomplished, except through the love which Jesus Christ bore to men ? *He loved us, and gave Himself for us.* [2] Oh that these words of St. Paul were ever before our eyes ! Truly then would every affection for earthly things depart from our heart. and we should think only of loving our Redeemer, reflecting that it was love which brought him to pour forth all his blood, to make for us a bath of salvation. *He hath loved us, and washed us from our sins in His own blood.* [3] St. Bernardine of Sienna says that Jesus Christ from the cross looked at every single sin of every one of us, and offered his blood for every one of them. [4] In a word, love brought the Lord of all to appear the most vile and low of all things upon earth.

" O power of love !" cries St. Bernard ; " the Supreme God of all is made the lowest of all ! Who hath done this ? Love, forgetting its dignity, powerful in its affections. Love triumphs over divinity." [5] Love hath done this, because, in order to make itself known to the beloved, it hath brought the loving one to lay aside his dignity, and to do that alone which aids and pleases the beloved. Therefore, St. Bernard says that God, who can be conquered by none, causes himself to be conquered by the love which he bore for men.

[1] " Ut judex judicaretur, Justitia damnaretur, Vita moreretur."— *Serm.* 191, *E. B.*

[2] " Dilexit nos, et tradidit semetipsum pro nobis."—*Eph.* v. 2.

[3] " Qui dilexit nos, et lavit nos a peccatis nostris in sanguine suo." —*Apoc.* i. 5.

[4] " Ad quamlibet culpam singularem habuit aspectum."—T. ii. s. 56, a. 1, c. 1.

[5] "O Amoris vim ! Summus omnium imus factus est omnium. Quis hoc fecit ? Amor, dignitatis nescius, affectu potens. Triumphat de Deo Amor."—*In Cant.* s. 64.

We must further reflect that whatever Jesus Christ suffered in his Passion, he suffered for each one of us individually ; on which account St. Paul says, *I live in the faith of the Son of God, who loved me, and delivered Himself for me.*[1] And what the Apostle said, every one of us may say; wherefore St. Augustine writes that man was redeemed at such a price that he seems to be of equal value with God.[2] The saint also goes on to say, " Thou hast loved me, not as Thyself, but more than Thyself, since, to deliver me from death, Thou hast been willing to die for me."[3]

But since Jesus could have saved us by a single drop of his blood, why did he pour it all forth in torments, even so as to die of mere agony upon the cross? "Yes," says St. Bernard, "what a drop might have done, he chose to do with a stream, in order to show us the excessive love he bore us."[4] He calls it *excessive*, as Moses and Elias on Mount Thabor called the Passion of the Redeemer an excess,—an excess of mercy and love ; *They spoke of His excess, which He was about to accomplish at Jerusalem.*[5] St. Augustine, speaking of the Passion of our Lord, says "that his mercy exceeded the debt of our sins."[6] Thus, the value of the death of Jesus Christ being infinite, infinitely exceeded the satisfaction due by us for our sins to the divine justice. Truly had the Apostle cause to say, *God forbid that I should glory, save*

[1] "In fide vivo Filii Dei, qui dilexit me, et tradidit semetipsum pro me."—*Gal.* ii. 20.
[2] "Tam copioso munere redemptio agitur, ut homo Deum valere videatur."—*De Dilig. D.* c. 6.
[3] "Dilexisti me plus quam te, quia voluisti mori pro me."—*Sol. an, ad D.* c. 13.
[4] "Quod potuit gutta, voluit unda."
[5] "Et dicebant excessum ejus, quem completurus erat in Jerusalem."—*Luke,* ix. 31.
[6] "Misericordiam magnam invenimus, pretium majus omni debito."—*Cur D. H.* l. 2, c. 21.

in the cross of our Lord Jesus Christ.[1]   And what St. Paul says, we may all say; what greater glory can we have, or hope for in the world, than to see a God dying for love of us?

O Eternal God, I have dishonored Thee by my sins; but Jesus, by making satisfaction for me by his death, has more than abundantly restored the honor due to Thee; for the love of Jesus, then, have mercy upon me. And Thou, my Redeemer, who hast died for me, in order to oblige me to love Thee, grant that I may love Thee. For, having despised Thy grace and Thy love, I have deserved to be condemned to be able to love Thee no more. But, O my Jesus, give me every punishment but this. And therefore, I pray Thee, consign me not to hell, for in hell I cannot love Thee. Cause me to love Thee, and then chastise me as Thou wilt. Deprive me of everything, but not of Thyself. I accept every infirmity, every ignominy, every pain that Thou willest me to suffer; it is enough that I love Thee. Now, I know, by the light Thou hast given me, that Thou art most worthy of love, and hast so much loved me: I trust to live no longer without loving Thee. For the time past I have loved creatures, and have turned my back upon Thee, the infinite good ; but now I say to Thee, that I would love Thee alone, and nothing else. O my beloved Saviour, if Thou seest that at any future time I should cease to love Thee, I pray Thee to cause me first to die ; and I shall be content to die before I am separated from Thee.

O holy Virgin Mary and Mother of God, help me with thy prayers; obtain for me, that I may never cease to love my Jesus, who died for me and thee, my queen, who hast already obtained for me so many mercies.

[1] "Mihi autem absit gloriari, nisi in cruce Domini nostri Jesu Christi."—*Gal.* vi. 14.

CHAPTER IX.

THE GRATITUDE THAT WE OWE TO JESUS CHRIST FOR HIS PASSION.

I.

Jesus died for us; we ought to live and die for Him.

St. Augustine says that Jesus Christ, having first given his life for us, has bound us to give our life for him; and, further, that when we go to the Eucharistic table to communicate, as we go to feed there upon the body and blood of Jesus Christ, we ought also, in gratitude, to prepare for him the offering of our blood and of our life, if there is need for us to give either of them for his glory.[1]

Full of tenderness are the words of St. Francis de Sales on this text of St. Paul: *The charity of Christ presseth us.*[2] To what does it press us? To love him. But let us hear what St. Francis de Sales says: "When we know that Jesus has loved us even to death, and that the death of the cross, is not this to feel our hearts constrained by a violence as great as it is full of delight?"[3] And then he adds, "My Jesus gives himself wholly to me, and I give myself wholly to him; I will live and die upon his breast, and neither death nor life shall ever separate me from him."

St. Peter, in order that we might remember to be ever

---

[1] "Debitores nos fecit, qui primus exhibuit. Mensa quæ sit, nostis; ibi est corpus et sanguis Christi; qui accedit ad talem mensam, præparet talia."—*In Jo.* tr. 47.

[2] "Charitas Christi urget nos."—2 *Cor.* v. 14.

[3] *Love of God,* B. 7, ch. 8.

grateful to our Saviour, reminds us that we were not redeemed from the slavery of hell with gold or silver, but
with the precious blood of Jesus Christ, which he sacrificed for us, as an innocent lamb, upon the altar of the
cross.[1] Great, therefore, will be the punishment of those
who are thankless for such a blessing, if they do not
correspond to it. It is true that Jesus came to save all
men who were lost;[2] but it is also true what was said
by the Venerable Simeon, when Mary presented the
child Jesus in the temple: *Behold, this child is placed for
the fall and the rising again of many in Israel, and as a sign
which shall be spoken against.*[3] By the words *for the rising
again* he expresses the salvation which all believers
should receive from Jesus Christ, who by faith should rise
from death to the life of grace. But first, by the words
he is set for the fall, he foretells that many shall fall into
a greater ruin by their ingratitude to the Son of God,
who came into the world to become a contradiction to
his enemies, as the following words imply : *He shall be a
sign which shall be spoken against;* for Jesus Christ was set
up as a sign, against which were hurled all the calumnies,
the injuries, and the insults which the Jews devised
against him. And this sign is spoken against not only
by the Jews of the present day, who deny him to be the
Messiah, but by those Christians who ungratefully
return his love with offences, and by neglecting his
commands.

Our Redeemer, says St. Paul, went so far as to give
his life for us, in order to make himself the Lord of all

---

[1] "Scientes quod non corruptibilibus auro vel argento redempti
estis . . . , sed pretioso sanguine, quasi agni immaculati, Christi."—
1 *Pet.* i. 18.

[2] "Venit enim Filius hominis quærere et salvum facere quod
perierat."—*Luke,* xix. 10.

[3] "Ecce positus est hic in ruinam et in resurrectionem multorum
in Israel, et in signum cui contradicetur."—*Ibid.* li. 34.

our hearts, by displaying to us his love in dying for us. *For this Christ both died and rose again, that He might be Lord of the dead and of the living.*[1] No, writes the Apostle, we are no longer our own, since we have been redeemed by the blood of Jesus Christ. *Whether we live, therefore, or die, we are the Lord's.*[1] Wherefore, if we do not love him and obey his precepts, of which the first is that we should love him, we are not only ungrateful, but unjust, and deserve a double punishment. The obligation of a slave rescued by Jesus Christ from the hands of the devil is, to devote himself wholly to love and serve him, whether he live or die.

St. John Chrysostom makes an excellent reflection upon the above-quoted text of St. Paul, saying that God has more care for us than we have for ourselves; and therefore regards our life as his own riches, and our death as his own loss; so that if we die, we die not to ourselves, but also to God.[1] Oh, how great is our glory while we live in this valley of tears, in the midst of so many dangers of perishing, that we should be able to say, "We are the Lord's," we are his possession; he will take care to preserve us in his grace in this life, and to keep us with himself throughout eternity in the life that is to come!

II.

What it is to live and die for Jesus.

Jesus Christ, then, died for every one of us, in order that every one of us might live only to his Redeemer, who died for love of him. *Christ died for us all, that both*

---

[1] " In hoc enim Christus mortuus est et resurrexit, ut et mortuorum et vivorum dominetur."—*Rom.* xiv. 9.

[1] " Sive ergo vivimus, sive morimur, Domini sumus."—*Ibid.* 8.

[1] " Majorem nostri habet curam Deus, quam nos ipsi; vitam nostram divitias suas, et mortem damnum, aestimat; non enim nobis ipsis tantum morimur, sed si morimur, Domino morimur."

they who live should live no longer to themselves, but to Him who died for them and rose again.[1] He that lives for himself directs all his desires, fears, and pains, and places all his happiness in himself. But he that lives to Jesus Christ places all his desires in loving and pleasing him; all his joys in gratifying him; all his fears are that he should displease him. He is only afflicted when he sees Jesus despised, and he only rejoices in seeing him loved by others. This it is to live to Jesus Christ, and this he justly claims from us all. To gain this he has bestowed all the pains which he suffered for love of us.

Does he ask too much in this? No, says St. Gregory, he cannot ask too much, when he has given such tokens of his love to us, that he seems to have become a fool for our sake.[2] Without reserve he has given himself wholly for us; he has, therefore, a right to require that we should give ourselves wholly to him, and should fix all our love upon him; and if we take from him any portion of it, by loving anything either apart from him or not for his sake, he has reason to complain of us; for then we do not love him as we should, says St. Augustine.[3]

And what but creatures can we love except Jesus Christ? And, in comparison with Jesus Christ, what are creatures but worms of the earth, dust, smoke, and vanity? To St. Clement, Pope, was offered a heap of silver, gold, and gems, if he would renounce Jesus Christ; the saint, however, gave only a sigh, and then exclaimed, "O my Jesus, Thou infinite good! how dost

---

[1] "Pro omnibus mortuus est Christus, ut, et qui vivunt, jam non sibi vivant, sed ei qui pro ipsis mortuus est et resurrexit."—*2 Cor.* v. 15.

[2] "Stultum visum est ut pro hominibus Auctor vitæ moreretur."— *In Evang. hom.* 6.

[3] "Minus te amat, qui tecum aliquid amat, quod non propter te amat."—*Conf.* l. 10, c. 20.

Thou endure to be esteemed by men as less than the rubbish of this earth?" "No," says St. Bernard, "it was not rashness which made the martyrs encounter hot irons, nails, and the most cruel deaths; it was love for Jesus Christ, when they saw him dead upon the cross." [1] For us all the example of St. Mark and St. Marcellian is of value, who, when they were fastened with nails through their hands and feet, were rebuked by the tyrants as fools for suffering so cruel a torment rather than renounce Jesus Christ; while they replied that they had never known greater delights than they now experienced when transfixed with these nails. [2] And all saints, in order to give pleasure to Jesus Christ, who was thus tormented and despised for our sake, gladly embrace poverty, persecutions, contempt, infirmities, pains, and death. Souls betrothed to Jesus Christ upon the cross know nothing more glorious to them than to bear the signs of the crucified, which are his sufferings.

Let us hear what St. Augustine says to us: "To you it is not lawful to love a little; let him who was wholly fixed upon the cross for you be wholly fixed in your hearts." [3] Let us, therefore, unite ourselves wholly to St. Paul, and say with him, *I am crucified with Christ. I live, and yet not I, for Christ liveth in me, who loved me, and gave Himself for me.* [4] On this St. Bernard remarks, "It is as if he had said, To all other things I am dead; I have no sensation, I pay no regard; but the things which are of Christ, these find me a living man, and prepared

---

[1] " Neque hoc facit stupor, sed amor."—*In Cant.* s. 61.

[2] " Nunquam tam jucunde epulati sumus, quam cum hic fixi esse cœpimus."

[3] " Parum vobis amare non licet ; toto vobis figatur in corde, qui pro vobis est fixus in cruce."—*De S. Virginit.* c. 55.

[4] " Christo confixus sum cruci ; vivo autem jam non ego, vivit vero in me Christus . . . , qui dilexit me, et tradidit semetipsum pro me."—*Gal.* ii. 19.

to act upon them.[1] Therefore St. Paul says, *To me to
live is Christ;*[2] meaning by these brief words, "Jesus
Christ is my life, for he is all my thoughts, all my inten-
tions, all my hope, all my desire, because he is all my
love." "It is a sure promise; if we are dead with him,
we shall also live with him; if we suffer with him, we
shall also reign with him; if we deny him, he will also
deny us." The kings of the earth, after a victory over
their enemies, confer a part of all they have gained upon
those who have fought on their side. Thus does Jesus
Christ on the day of judgment; he gives a share of the
blessings of heaven to all who have toiled and suffered
for his glory.

The Apostle says, *If we are dead with Him, we shall also
live with Him.*[3] To die with Christ means the denial of
ourselves, that is, of our own inclinations, which, if we
do not deny, we shall come to deny Jesus Christ, who
will justly deny us on the day of account. And here we
must remark, that we not only deny Jesus Christ when
we deny the faith, but also when we refuse to obey him
in anything he desires of us; as, for example, when, for
love of him, we will not forgive an injury we have received, when we give way to the love of vain honor,
when we will not break through a friendship which im-
perils the friendship of Jesus Christ, or yield to the fear
of being counted ungrateful, while our first gratitude is
due to Jesus Christ, who has given his blood and life for
us, which no creature whatever has done for us.

O divine love! how is it that thou art despised by

---

[1] "Vivo jam non ego, vivit vero in me Christus. Ac si diceret:
Ad alia omnia mortuus sum ; non sentio, non attendo ; si quæ vero
sunt Christi, hæc me vivum inveniunt et paratum."—*In Quadr.* s. 7.

[2] "Mihi enim vivere Christus est."—*Phil.* i. 21.

[3] "Fidelis sermo ; nam si commortui sumus. et convivemus; si
sustinebimus, et conregnabimus ; si negaverimus, et ille negabit
nos."—2 *Tim.* ii. 11.

men ? O man! look at this cross of the Son of God, who, as an innocent lamb, sacrifices himself to pay for thy sins, and thus to gain thy love! Look at him, look at him and love him!

O my Jesus, O infinitely lovely! grant that I may no longer live ungrateful to so great a good! For the past I have lived in forgetfulness of Thy love, and of all Thou hast suffered for me; but henceforth I would think of nothing but loving Thee. O wounds of Jesus, stricken with love! O blood of Jesus, inebriated with love! O death of Jesus! cause me to die to every love which is not love for him. O Jesus! I love Thee above everything. I love Thee with all my soul; I love Thee more than myself. I love Thee, and because I love Thee, I would die of grief because I have so often turned my back upon Thee, and have despised Thy grace. By Thy merits, O my crucified Saviour, give me Thy love, and make me all Thine own.

O Mary, my hope! make me love Jesus Christ, and I ask nothing more.

CHAPTER X.

WE MUST PLACE ALL OUR HOPES IN THE MERITS OF JESUS CHRIST.

I.

Jesus Crucified is our only Hope in all our Wants.

There is no salvation in any other.[1] St. Peter says that all our salvation is in Jesus Christ, who, by means of the cross, where he sacrificed his life for us, opened us a way for hoping for every blessing from God, if we would be faithful to his commands.

Let us hear what St. John Chrysostom says of the cross: "The cross is the hope of Christians, the staff of

---

[1] " Non est in alio aliquo salus."—*Acts*, iv. 12.

the lame, the comfort of the poor, the destruction of the proud, the victory over the devils, the guide of youth, the rudder of sailors, the refuge of those who are in danger, the counsellor of the just, the rest of the afflicted, the physician of the sick, the glory of martyrs." [1] The cross, that is, Jesus crucified, is—

The *hope* of the faithful, because if we had not Jesus Christ we should have no hope of salvation.

It is the *staff* of the lame, because we are all lame in our present state of corruption. We should have no strength to walk in the way of salvation except that which is communicated to us by the grace of Jesus Christ.

It is the *comfort* of the poor, which we all are, for all we have we have from Jesus Christ.

It is the *destruction* of the proud, for the followers of the Crucified cannot be proud, seeing him dead as a malefactor upon the cross.

It is *victory* over the devils, for the very sign of the cross is sufficient to drive them from us.

It is the *instructor* of the young, for admirable is the teaching which they who are beginning to walk in the ways of God learn from the cross.

It is the *rudder* of mariners, and guides us through the storms of this present life.

It is the *refuge* of those in danger, for they who are in peril of perishing, through temptations of strong passions, find a secure harbor by flying to the cross.

It is the *counsellor* of the just, for how many saints learn wisdom from the cross, that is, from the troubles of this life.

[1] " Crux, Spes Christianorum, claudorum Baculus, Consolatio pau-perum, Destructio superborum, contra dæmones Triumphus, adoles-centum Pædagogus, navigantium Gubernator, periclitantium Portus, justorum Consiliarius, tribulatorum Requies, ægrotantium Medicus, martyrum Gloriatio."—*Hom. de Cruce.*

It is the *rest* of the afflicted, for where can they find greater relief than in contemplating the cross, on which a God suffers for love of them?

It is the *physician* of the sick, for when they embrace it, they are healed of the wounds of the souL

It is the *glory* of martyrs, for to be made like Jesus Christ, the King of Martyrs, is the greatest glory they can possess.

In a word, all our hopes are placed in the merits of Jesus Christ. The Apostle says, *I know how to be humbled, and I know how to abound; how to be satisfied, and how to hunger; how to abound, and how to suffer poverty. I can do all things in Him who strengthens me.*[1] (In the Greek text, *In Christ who is strengthening me.*) Thus St. Paul, instructed by the Lord, says, I know how I ought to conduct myself: when God humbles me, I resign myself to his will; when he exalts me, to him I give all the honor; when he gives me abundance, I thank him; when he makes me endure poverty, still I bless him; and I do all this not by my own strength, but by the strength of the grace which God gives me. For he that trusts in Jesus Christ is strengthened with invincible power.

The Lord, says St. Bernard, makes those who hope in him all-powerful.[2] The saint also adds that a soul which does not presume upon its own strength, but is strengthened by the Word, can govern itself, so that no evil shall have power over it;[3] and that no force, no fraud, no snare can cast it down.[4]

[1] "Scio et humiliari, scio et abundare (ubique et in omnibus institutus sum); et satiari, et esurire; et abundare, et penuriam pati: omnia possum in eo qui me confortat."—*Phil.* iv. 12.

[2] "Omnia possum in corroborante me Christo."

[3] "Omnipotentes facit omnes qui in se sperant."

[4] "Ita animus, si non præsumat de se, sed confortetur a Verbo, poterit dominari sui, ut non dominetur ei omnis iniquitas."

[5] "Ita Verbo innixum nulla vis, nulla fraus, nulla illecebra, poterit stantem dejicere."—*In Cant.* s. 85

The Apostle prayed thrice to God that the impure temptations which troubled him might be driven away, and he was answered, *My grace is sufficient for thee, for My strength is accomplished in weakness.*[1] How is this that the virtue of perfection consists in weakness? St. Thomas, with St. Chrysostom, explains it, that the greater our weakness and inclination to evil, the greater is the strength given us by God. Therefore, St. Paul himself says, *I will gladly, therefore, glory in my infirmities, that the strength of Christ may dwell in me. Therefore, I take pleasure in my infirmities, in insults, in necessities, in persecutions, in straits for Christ's sake; for when I am weak, then I am strong.*[2]

For the word of the cross is to them that perish foolishness, but to those who are saved it is the power of God.[3] Thus St. Paul warns us not to follow after worldly men, who place their trust in riches, in their relatives and friends in the world, and account the saints fools for despising those earthly helps; yet men ought to place all their hopes in the love of the cross,—that is, of Jesus crucified, who gives every blessing to those who trust in him. We must further remark that the power and strength of the world is altogether different from that of God; it is exercised in worldly riches and honors, but the latter in humility and endurance. Wherefore St. Augustine says that our strength lies in knowing that we are weak, and in humbly confessing what we are.[4] And St. Jerome says, that this one thing constitutes the perfection of the pres-

[1] "Sufficit tibi gratia mea ; nam virtus in infirmitate perficitur."— 2 *Cor.* xii. 9.

[2] "Libenter igitur gloriabor in infirmitatibus meis, ut inhabitet in me virtus Christi. Propter quod placeo mihi in infirmitatibus meis, in contumeliis, in necessitatibus, in persecutionibus, in angustiis pro Christo ; cum enim infirmor, tunc potens sum."—*Ibid.* 9, 10.

[3] "Verbum enim crucis pereuntibus quidem stultitia est ; iis autem qui salvi fiunt, id est nobis, Dei virtus est."—1 *Cor.* i. 18.

[4] "Fortidudo nostra est infirmitatis in veritate cognitio et in humilitate confessio."

ent life, that we should know that we are imperfect.' For
then we distrust our own strength, and abandon ourselves to God, who protects and saves those who trust in
him. *He is the protector of all who hope in Him*, says
David. *Thou savest those who hope in Thee.'   He that trusts
in the Lord is like the Mount Sion, which is never removed.'*
Therefore St. Augustine reminds us that, when we are
tempted, we must hasten and abandon ourselves in Jesus
Christ, who will not suffer us to fall, but will embrace
and hold us up, and thus remedy our weakness.'

When Jesus Christ took upon himself the weaknesses
of humanity, he merited for us a strength which conquers
our weakness: *For in that He Himself hath suffered and
been tempted, He is powerful to help those who are tempted.'*
How is this, that the Saviour in being himself tempted,
became able to strengthen us in our temptations?   It is
meant that Jesus Christ, by being afflicted by temptations, became more ready to feel for us and help us when
we are tempted.   To this corresponds that other text of
the same Apostle, *We have not a High Priest who cannot
feel compassion for our infirmities; but was in all things
tempted like us, though without sin.   Therefore let us go with
confidence to the throne of grace, that we may obtain mercy,
and find grace in the help we need.'*

¹ "Hæc hominibus sola perfectio, si imperfectos esse se nove-
rint."—*Epist.* 43, *E. B.*
² "Protector est omnium sperantium in se.—Qui salvos facis
sperantes in te."—*Ps.* xvii. 31; xvi. 7.
³ "Qui confidunt in Domino, sicut mons Sion ; non commovebitur
in æternum, qui habitat in Jerusalem."—*Ps.* cxxiv. 1.
⁴ "Projice te in eum ; non se subtrahet, ut cadas ; excipiet et sana-
bit te."—*Conf.* l. 8, c. 11.
⁵ "In eo enim, in quo passus est ipse et tentatus, potens est et eis,
qui tentantur, auxiliari."—*Heb.* ii. 18.
⁶ "Non enim habemus Pontificem qui non possit compati infirmitatibus nostris ; tentatum autem peromni a pro similitudine absque
peccato.—*Heb.* iv. 15.   Adeamus ergo cum fiducia ad thronum gratiæ,
ut misericordiam consequamur, et gratiam inveniamus in auxilio
opportuno."—*Ibid.* 16.

Jesus himself, in enduring fears, weariness, and sorrows, as the Evangelists bear witness, speaking especially of the afflictions that he endured in the garden of Gethsemani the night before he suffered,[1] has merited for us a courage to resist the threats of those who would corrupt us, a strength to overcome the weariness we experience in prayer, in mortifications, and other devout exercises, and a power of enduring with peace of mind that sadness which afflicts us in adversity.

We must also know that he himself in the garden, at the sight of all the pains and the desolate death that he was about to endure, chose to suffer this human weakness. *The spirit indeed is ready, but the flesh is weak;*[2] and he prayed to his divine Father that, if it were possible, the cup might pass from him.[3]   But immediately he added, *Nevertheless, not as I will, but as Thou wilt.*[4]   And for the whole time that he continued praying in the garden, he repeated the same prayer, *Thy will be done;* and the third time he prayed, saying the same thing. With those words, *Thy will be done,*[5] Jesus Christ merited and obtained for us resignation in all adversity, and gained for his martyrs and confessors a strength to resist all the persecutions and torments of tyrants. "This world," says St. Leo, "inflamed all the confessors, it crowned all the martyrs."[6]

Thus also by the horror that he experienced through

---

[1] "Cœpit pavere, et tædere,—contristari et mœstus esse."—*Mark*, xiv. 33; *Matt.* xxvi. 37.

[2] "Spiritus quidem promptus est, caro autem infirma."—*Matt.* xxvi. 41.

[3] " Pater mi ! si possibile est, transeat a me calix iste."

[4] " Verumtamen, non sicut ego volo, sed sicut tu."—*Matt.* xxvi. 39.

[5] "Fiat voluntas tua ! . . . Et oravit tertio, eundem sermonem dicens."—*Ibid.* 44.

[6] "Hæc vox (Fiat) omnes Confessores accendit, omnes Martyres coronavit."—*De Pass.* s. 7.

our sins, which caused him to fall into a bitter agony in
the garden,[1] he merited for us contrition for our sins.
By the abandonment by the Father which he suffered
on the cross, he merited for us strength to retain our
courage in all desolations and darknesses of spirit.   By
bowing his head in death upon the cross, in obedience
to the will of the Father,[2] he merited for us all the victories which we gain over passions and temptations; and
patience in the pains of life, and especially in the bitternesses and straits which we endure in death.   In a word,
St. Leo writes that Jesus Christ came to take our infirmities and distresses, in order to communicate to us
his strength and constancy.[3]

St. Paul says, that though he was the Son of God, he
learned obedience in the things that he suffered ;[4] from
which we are to understand, not that Jesus in his Passion learned the virtue of obedience, and did not know
it beforehand, but, as St. Anselm says, he learned not
only by the knowledge which he had before, but by
actual experience, how grievous was the death he endured in order to obey his Father.   And at the same
time he experienced how great is the merit of obedience,
for by this he obtained for himself the utmost height
of glory, which is the seat at his Father's right hand,
and eternal salvation for us.   Therefore the Apostle
adds, *Being perfected, He became the cause of eternal life to
all them that obey Him.*[5]   He says, *being perfected*, because,
having completely fulfilled all obedience, by suffering
patiently what he endured in his Passion, Jesus Christ

[1] " Factus in agonia, prolixius orabat."—*Luke*, xxii. 43.
[2] " Factus obediens usque ad mortem, mortem autem crucis."—
Phil. ii. 8.
[3] " Venit nostra accipiens, et sua retribuens."—*De Pass.* s. 3.
[4] " Et quidem cum esset Filius Dei, didicit, ex iis quæ passus est,
obedientiam."—*Heb.* v. 8.
[5] " Et consummatus, factus est omnibus obtemperantibus sibi causa
salutis æternæ."—*Heb.* v. 9.

became the cause of eternal life to all those who obediently suffer with patience the troubles of this present life.

By this patience of Jesus Christ the holy martyrs were animated and strengthened to embrace with patience the most cruel torments that the cruelty of tyrants could devise ; and not only with patience, but with joy and desire to suffer for the love of Jesus Christ. In the celebrated letter which St. Ignatius the martyr wrote to the Romans after he had been condemned to be thrown to the wild beasts, and before he went to the place of his martyrdom, we read, "Suffer me, my children, to be ground down by the teeth of the wild beasts, that I may become corn for my Redeemer. I seek only him who died for me. He who is the only object of my love was crucified for me, and the love I bear to him makes me desire to be crucified for him." St. Leo[1] writes of St. Laurence the martyr, that when he lay upon the grid-iron, the flames which burned him without were less hot than the fire that burned within him. Eusebius'[2] and Palladius'[3] relate of St. Potamena, a virgin of Alexandria, that when she was condemned to be thrown in a caldron of boiling pitch, that she might suffer the more for the love of her crucified Spouse, she prayed the tyrant to have her thrust in little by little, that her death might become more torturing ; and she had her desire, for they began by thrusting her feet into the pitch, so that she was for three hours in this torment, and did not die till the pitch reached her neck. Such was the patience, such the fortitude which the martyrs gained from the Passion of Jesus Christ.

It was this courage which the Crucified infuses into those who love him, that made St. Paul say, *Who shall*

---

[1] *S. in fest. S. Laur.*
[2] *Hist. Eccl.* l. 6. c. 5.
[3] *Hist. Laus,* c. 3.

separate us from the love of Christ? Shall tribulation, or distress, or hunger, or nakedness, or perils, or persecution, or the sword?[1] And at the same time he says, *In all these things we are conquerors through Him who loved us.*[2] The love of the martyrs for Jesus Christ was unconquerable, because it gained its strength from him who is unconquerable, who strengthened them to suffer. And let us not imagine that the torments of the martyrs were miraculously deprived of their power of torturing, or that their heavenly consolations lulled the pains of the torments ; this perhaps may sometimes have happened, but ordinarily they truly felt all their pains, and many through weakness yielded to the pangs ; so that in the case of those who were constant in suffering, their patience was entirely the gift of God, who gave them their strength.

The first object of our hopes is eternal blessedness, that is, the blessedness of God,—the *fruition of God,* as St. Thomas teaches.[3] And all the means which are necessary for obtaining this salvation, which consists in the enjoyment of God,—such as the pardon of our sins, final perseverance in divine grace, and a good death,— we must hope for, not from our own strength, nor our good resolutions, but solely from the merits and grace of Jesus Christ. That our confidence, therefore, may be firm, let us believe with infallible certainty that we must look for the accomplishment of all these means of salvation only from the merits of Jesus Christ.

---

[1] " Quis ergo nos separabit a charitate Christi ? tribulatio ? an angustia ? an fames ? an nuditas ? an periculum ? an persecutio ? an gladius ?"—*Rom*. viii. 35.

[2] " Sed in his omnibus superamus propter eum qui dilexit nos."— *Ibid*. 37.

[3] " Fruitio Dei."—2. 2, q. 17, a. 2.

II.

The Hope that We have in Jesus Christ that He will pardon our Sins.

And first, in speaking of the pardon of sins, we must remember that for this very end our Redeemer came upon earth, that he might pardon sinners : *The Son of Man came to save that which was lost.*[1] Therefore the Baptist, when he showed to the Jews that their Messiah was already come, said, *Behold the Lamb of God, that taketh away the sin of the world.*[2] As it was foretold by Isaias, *As a sheep before her shearers, He shall be dumb;*[3] and also by Jeremias, *I am as a lamb that is carried to be a victim.*[4] And first, he was foreshadowed by Moses in the paschal lamb, and by the sacrifice of a lamb to God under the law every morning, and by other evening sacrifices. All these lambs, however, could not take away a single sin; they served only to represent the sacrifice of the divine Lamb Jesus Christ, who with his blood would wash our souls, and thus free them both from the stain of sin and from the eternal punishment of sin, for this is implied by the words *take away;* taking upon himself the duty of satisfying the divine justice for us by his death, according to what Isaias wrote, *The Lord hath laid upon Him the iniquity of us all.*[5] Wherefore St. Cyril writes, "One is slain for all, and the whole human race is restored to God the Father."[6] By dying,

[1] "Venit enim Filius hominis salvare quod perierat."—*Matt.* xviii. 11.

[2] "Ecce Agnus Dei, ecce qui tollit peccatum mundi."—*John*, i. 29.

[3] "Et quasi agnus coram tondente se, obmutescet." —*Isa.* liii. 7.

[4] "Et ego quasi agnus mansuetus, qui portatur ad victimam."— *Jer.* xi. 19.

[5] "Posuit Dominus in eo iniquitatem omnium nostrum."—*Isa.* liii. 6.

[6] "Unus pro omnibus occiditur, ut omne genus hominum Deo Patri lucrifaciat."

Jesus desired to regain for God all mankind who were lost.

Oh, how great is the debt we owe to Jesus Christ! If a criminal condemned to death were already standing at the gibbet with the rope around his neck, and a friend were to come and take the rope, and bind it round himself, and die in place of the guilty man, how great would be his obligation to love him! This is what Jesus Christ has done; He has been willing to die on the cross to deliver us from eternal death.

Jesus *bore our sins,* says St. Peter, *in His body on the tree, that, being dead to sin, we might live to justice; by whose stripes we were healed.*[1] "What can be more wonderful," cries St. Bonaventure, "than that wounds should heal, and death give life?"[2] St. Paul says that God *has graced us in His beloved Son, in whom we have redemption through His blood, the remission of sins, according to the riches of His grace, which have superabounded in us.*[3] And this resulted from the covenant made by Jesus Christ with his divine Father, that he would pardon us our offences, and receive us into his favor for the sake of the Passion and death of his Son.

And in this sense the Apostle called Jesus Christ the mediator of the New Testament. In the Holy Scriptures the word *Testament* has two senses; that of a *covenant,* or an agreement between two parties formerly disagreed; and that of a *promise,* or disposition by will, by which the testator leaves an inheritance to his heirs; and this testament is not valid until the testator's death. We have

[1] "Qui peccata nostra ipse pertulit in corpore suo super lignum, ut, peccatis mortui, justitiæ vivamus; cujus livore sanati sumus."—1 *Pet.* ii. 24.

[2] "Quid mirabilius quam quod mors vivificet, vulnera sanent?"— *Stim. div. am.* p. 1, c. I.

[3] "Gratificavit nos in dilecto Filio suo, in quo habemus redemptionem per sanguinem ejus, remissionem peccatorum, secundum divitias gratiæ ejus, quæ superabundavit in nobis."—*Eph.* i. 6.

formerly spoken of the Testament as a promise; we now
speak of it as a covenant, in the sense in which the
Apostle uses it when he calls Jesus Christ the Mediator
of the New Testament.[1]

Man, by reason of his sin, was a debtor to the divine
justice, and an enemy of God; the Son of God came on
earth and took man's flesh; and thus, being God and
man, he became a mediator between God and man, acting on behalf of both; and in order that he might bring
about peace between them, and obtain for man the divine grace, he offered himself to pay with his blood and
his death the debt due by man.   This was the reconciliation prefigured in the Old Testament by all the sacrifices and symbols ordained by God, such as the tabernacle, the altar, the veil, the candlestick, the censer, the
ark, wherein were contained the rod and the tables of
the law.   All these things were signs and figures of the
promised redemption; and because this redemption was
to be accomplished by the blood of Jesus Christ, therefore God appointed that all the sacrifices should be offered with the pouring-forth of the blood of the animals
(which was a figure of the blood of the Lamb of God),
while all the instruments above named were sprinkled
with the blood: *Wherefore, not even the Old Testament was
dedicated without blood.*[2]

St. Paul says that the first Testament—that is, the first
alliance, covenant, or mediation—which was accomplished
by the old law, and which prefigured the mediation of
Jesus Christ under the old law, was celebrated with the
blood of goats and calves; and that with this blood
were sprinkled the book, the people, the tabernacle, and
all the sacred vessels: *When the commandment of the law
of Moses was read to all the people, the priest taking the blood*

[1] "Et ideo Novi Testamenti Mediator est."—*Heb.* ix. 15.
[2] "Unde nec primum quide m (Testamentum) sine sanguine dedica-
tum est."—*Heb.* ix. 18.

of calves and goats with water and with scarlet wool [1] (the scarlet wool signified Jesus Christ, for as wool is by nature white, and becomes red by being dyed, thus Jesus, who was white by nature and innocence, appeared on the cross all red with blood, being condemned as a malefactor, and thus fulfilled in himself the words of the Spouse in the Canticles, *My beloved is white and is ruddy*)[2] *and with hyssop* (a lowly herb, which expressed the humility of Jesus Christ), *sprinkled both the book and all the people, saying, This is the blood of the covenant, which God has commanded; and in like manner he sprinkled the tabernacle and all the vessels of ministration with blood.*[3] *For all things are purged with blood according to the law, and without shedding of blood there is no remission.*[4] The Apostle repeats the word *blood* several times, in order to fix in the hearts of the Jews, and of all men, that without the blood of Jesus Christ we have no hope of pardon for our sins. As, then, in the old law, by the blood of the victims the outward defilement of sin was taken away, and the temporal punishment due to them was remitted; so, in the new law, the blood of Jesus Christ washes away the inward stain of sin, according to St. John's words, *He loved us, and washed us with His own blood.*[5]

St. Paul thus explains the whole truth in the same chapter of the Epistle to the Hebrews. *Christ being a High Priest of coming good things, by a greater and more perfect tabernacle, not made with hands, that is, not of this creation, neither by the blood of goats, but by His own blood,*

[1] " Lecto enim omni mandato Legis a Moyse universo populo, accipiens sanguinem vitulorum et hircorum cum aqua et lana coccinea et hyssopo. . . ."—*Heb.* ix. 19.
[2] " Dilectus meus candidus et rubicundus."—*Cant.* v. 10.
[3] " Ipsum quoque librum et omnem populum aspersit, dicens: Hic sanguis Testamenti quod mandavit ad vos Deus."—*Heb.* ix. 19, 20.
[4] " Et omnia pene in sanguine secundum Legem mundantur; et sine sanguinis effusione, non fit remissio."—*Ibid.* 22.
[5] " Lavit nos a peccatis nostris in sanguine suo."—*Apoc.* i. 5.

entered once into the Holies, having obtained eternal redemption.[1] The high-priest entered by the tabernacle into the Holy of Holies, and, by sprinkling the blood of animals, purged sinners from their outward defilement and from temporal punishment; for in order to the pardon of the sin, and for their liberation from eternal punishment, contrition, faith, and hope in the coming Messiah, who was about to die to obtain pardon for them, were absolutely necessary for the Jews. Jesus Christ, on the other hand, by means of his own body (which was the greater and more perfect tabernacle spoken of by the Apostle), which was sacrificed on the cross, entered into the Holy of Holies of heaven, which was closed to us, and opened it to us by means of this redemption.

Therefore St. Paul, in order to encourage us to hope for the pardon of all our sins, by trusting in the blood of Jesus Christ, goes on to say : *If the blood of goats and bulls, and the ashes of a heifer, sprinkled on the unclean, sanctifies to the purification of the flesh, how much more shall the blood of Christ, who, by the Holy Spirit, offered Himself without stain to God, purify our conscience from dead works to serve the living God!*[2] This he says because Jesus offered himself to God without shadow of sin, for otherwise he would not have been a worthy mediator, fit to reconcile God with sinful man, nor would his blood have had virtue to purge our consciences from dead works— that is, from sins, from the works without merit, and de-

---

[1] "Christus autem assistens Pontifex futurorum bonorum, per amplius et perfectius tabernaculum non manufactum, id est, non hujus creationis, neque per sanguinem hircorum aut vitulorum, sed per proprium sanguinem, introivit semel in Sancta, æterna redemptione inventa."—*Heb.* ix. 11, 12.

[2] "Si enim sanguis hircorum et taurorum, et cinis vitulæ aspersus, inquinatos sanctificat ad emundationem carnis ; quanto magis sanguis Christi, qui per Spiritum Sanctum semetipsum obtulit immaculatum Deo, emundabit conscientiam nostram ab operibus mortuis, ad serviendum Deo viventi !"—*Ibid.* 13, 14.

serving of eternal punishment, to serve the living God. God pardons us for no other end than that for the rest of our life we should devote it wholly to loving and serving him.

Finally, the Apostle concludes, *Therefore He is the mediator of the new covenant.* Because our Redeemer, through the boundless love he bore us, was willing by the price of his blood, to deliver us from eternal death, therefore he obtained for us from God pardon, grace, and eternal blessedness, if we are faithful to love him until death. This was the mediation or covenant accomplished between Jesus Christ and God, by the terms of which pardon and salvation are promised us.

This promise of pardon for our sins by the blood of Jesus Christ was confirmed to us by Jesus himself the day before his death, when, leaving to us the sacrament of the Eucharist, he said, *This is My blood of the new covenant, which shall be poured forth for many for the remission of sins.*[1] He says, *poured forth*, because in the sacrifice which was at hand he was about to shed not only a part, but the whole of his blood, to satisfy for our sins, and obtain pardon for us. Therefore he desired that the sacrifice should be renewed every day at every Mass that is celebrated, in order that his blood might continually plead in our favor. And therefore he is called a priest after the order of Melchisedech : *Thou art a priest forever after the order of Melchisedech.*[2] Aaron offered sacrifices of animals, but Melchisedech offered bread and wine, which was a figure of the sacrifice of the altar, in which our Saviour, under the species of bread and wine, offered at his last supper his body and blood to God, as he was about to sacrifice it on the following day in his Passion;

---

[1] " Hic est enim Sanguis meus Novi Testamenti, qui pro multis effundetur in remissionem peccatorum."—*Matt.* xxvi. 28.

[2] "Tu es Sacerdos in æternum secundum ordinem Melchisedech." —*Ps.* cix. 4.

and which he constantly offers by the hands of his priests, renewing by them the sacrifice of the cross. Therefore David called Jesus Christ an eternal priest, as St. Paul explains it, saying, *He that remaineth forever hath an eternal priesthood.*[1] The ancient priests came to an end by their death, but Jesus, being eternal, has an eternal priesthood. But how does he exercise his priesthood in heaven? The Apostle explains this, adding, *Wherefore he is able to save forever those who come to God by Him, ever living to intercede for us.*[2] The great sacrifice of the cross, represented still in that of the altar, has power forever to save those who, by means of Jesus Christ (being rightly prepared by faith and good works), approach to God; and this sacrifice, as St. Ambrose and St. Augustine write, Jesus, as man, continues to offer to the Father for our benefit, performing there, as he did on earth, the office of our advocate and mediator, and also of our priest, which is to intercede for us.

St. John Chrysostom says that the wounds of Jesus Christ are so many mouths,[3] which continually implore from God pardon for us sinners. Oh, how much better, says St. Paul, does the blood of Jesus Christ plead for us in calling down the divine mercy than the blood of Abel,[4] which called for vengeance against Cain! In the revelations of St. Mary Magdalene of Pazzi it is recorded that one day God spoke to her as follows: "My justice is changed into mercy through the vengeance that was taken upon the innocent flesh of Jesus Christ. The blood of my Son does not call for vengeance like

---

[1] "Hic autem, eo quod maneat in æternum, sempiternum habet sacerdotium."—*Heb.* vii. 24.

[2] "Unde et salvare in perpetuum potest accedentes per semetipsum ad Deum, semper vivens ad interpellandum pro nobis."—*Ibid.* 25.

[3] "Tot vulnera, tot ora."

[4] "Accessistis ad . . . Mediatorem Jesum, et sanguinis aspersionem melius loquentem. quam Abel."—*Heb.* xii. 22.

the blood of Abel, but for mercy only, and at this voice my justice is necessarily appeased. The blood binds my hands, so that they cannot move to take that revenge upon sins which they would otherwise have taken."

St. Augustine writes that God has promised us the remission of our sins and eternal life, but he has done more than he promised.[1] To give us pardon and paradise cost Jesus Christ nothing, but to redeem us cost him his blood and his life. The Apostle St. John exhorts us to flee from sin; and, in order that we may not despair of pardon for the sins we have committed, if we have a firm resolution not to commit them again, he gives us courage to hope for pardon, saying that we have to do with Jesus Christ, who not only died to pardon us, but, since his death, is become our advocate with the divine Father.[2] To our sins were due disgrace with God and eternal damnation ; but the Passion of our Saviour has acquired for us grace and eternal salvation ; and justice itself requires this, since, on account of his merits, the Eternal Father has promised to pardon and save us. if we are only disposed to receive his grace and to obey his commands, as St. Paul writes, *Being made perfect, He is the cause of eternal salvation to all that obey Him.*[3] Wherefore the Apostle exhorts us to run with patience the race that is before us, looking to Jesus, the author and finisher of faith; who, for the sake of the joy that was before him, endured the cross, and despised shame.[4]

---

[1] "Plus fecit, quam promisit."—*Enarr. in Ps.* cxlviii.

[2] "Filioli mei, hæc scribo vobis ut non peccetis; sed et si quis peccaverit, Advocatum habemus apud Patrem, Jesum Christum justum "—1 *John*, ii. 1.

[3] "Et consummatus, factus est omnibus obtemperantibus sibi causa salutis æternæ."—*Heb.* v. 9.

[4] "Per patientiam curramus ad propositum nobis certamen, aspicientes in Auctorem fidei et Consummatorem Jesum, qui, proposito sibi gaudio, sustinuit crucem, confusione contempta."—*Ibid.* xii. 1.

O precious blood! Thou art my hope. O blood of
the innocent one! wash the stains of the guilty.[1] O my
Jesus! my foes having betrayed me into offending
Thee, now tell me that I have no more hope of salva-
tion in Thee ; many say unto my soul, There is no salvation for him in his God.[2] But I trust in Thy blood that
Thou hast shed for me. I will say with David, Thou, O
Lord, wilt lift me up.[3] My foes terrify me, and say that
if I go to Thee, after so many sins, Thou wilt drive me
from Thee; but I read in St. John Thy promise, that
him who cometh to Thee, Thou wilt not cast out.[4] To
Thee, therefore, I come, full of confidence. We pray
Thee, help Thy servants, whom Thou hast redeemed with
Thy precious blood.[5] Thou, O my Saviour, who hast
poured forth all Thy blood in such agonies, and with
such love, that Thou mightest not see me perish, do
Thou have mercy on me, pardon me, and save me.

III.

**The Hope that we have in Jesus Christ that He will grant
us Final Perseverance.**

To obtain perseverance in good, we must not trust
in our resolutions and in the promises we have made to
God; if we trust in our own strength, we are lost. All
our hope of preserving the grace of God must be placed
in the merits of Jesus Christ, and thus, trusting in his
help, we shall persevere till death, though we were
attacked by all our enemies in earth and hell. Sometimes we find ourselves so cast down in mind, and so as-

---

[1] " O Sanguis Innocentis! lava sordes pœnitentis."

[2] " Multi dicunt animæ meæ : non est salus ipsi in Deo ejus."—*Ps.*
iii. 3.

[3] " Tu autem, Domine, susceptor meus es."—*Ibid.* 4.

[4] " Eum, qui venit ad me, non ejiciam foras."—*John*, vi. 37.

[5] " Te ergo quæsumus, tuis famulis subveni, quos pretioso sanguine
redemisti."

23

saulted by temptations, that we seem almost lost; let us not then lose courage, nor abandon ourselves to despair; let us go to the Crucified, and he will hold us up.

The Lord permits his saints sometimes to find themselves in tempests and fears. St. Paul says that the afflictions and terrors which he suffered in Asia were so overpowering that he became weary of life;[1] meaning that he was so, so far as he depended on his own strength, in order to teach us that God, from time to time, leaves us in desolations, in order that we may know our misery, and, distrusting ourselves, may humbly have recourse to his goodness, and gain from him strength not to fall.[2] More clearly he expresses the same in another place, *We are cast down, but we perish not.*[3] We find ourselves oppressed with sadness and passions, but do not abandon ourselves to despair; we are tossed about on the water, but do not sink, because the Lord, by his grace, gives us strength against our enemies. But the Apostle exhorts us ever to bear before our eyes that we are weak, and prone to lose the treasure of divine grace, and that all our strength for preserving it comes not from ourselves but from God: *We have this treasure in earthen vessels, that the loftiness of the power may be of God, and not of ourselves.*[4]

Let us, then, be firmly persuaded that in this life we must ever beware of placing any confidence in our own works. Our strongest armor with which we shall ever win the victory over the assaults of hell is prayer. This is the armor of God of which St. Paul speaks: *Put on*

---

[1] "Supra modum gravati sumus supra virtutem, ita ut tæderet nos etiam vivere."—2 *Cor.* i. 8.

[2] "Ut non simus fidentes in nobis, sed in Deo, qui suscitat mortuos."—*Ibid.* 9.

[3] "Aporiamur, sed non destituimur; . . . dejicimur, sed non perimus."—*Ibid.* iv. 8.

[4] "Habemus autem thesaurum istum in vasis fictilibus, ut sublimitas sit virtutis Dei, et non ex nobis."—2 *Cor.* iv. 7.

the armor of God, that ye may be able to stand against the deceits of the devil. For our wrestling is not against flesh and blood, but against principalities and powers, against the rulers of the world of this darkness, against the spirits of wickedness in high places. Therefore, take unto you the armor of God, that you may be able to resist in the evil day, and to stand in all things perfect. Stand, therefore, having your loins girt about with truth, and having on the breastplate of justice, and your feet shod with the preparation of the gospel of peace; in all things taking the shield of faith, wherewith you may be able to extinguish all the fiery darts of the most wicked one; and take unto you the helmet of salvation, and the sword of the Spirit (which is the word of God), *by all prayer and supplication, praying at all times in the Spirit.*[1]

Let us pause and weigh well these various expressions.

Stand, having your loins girt about with truth.[2] There the Apostle alludes to the military girdle with which soldiers gird themselves as a token of the fidelity which they have sworn to their sovereign. The girdle which the Christian must put on is the possession of the truth of the doctrine of Jesus Christ, in accordance with which we must repress all inordinate passions, especially those of impurity, which are the most dangerous of all.

Having on the breastplate of justice.[3] The Christian's breastplate is a good life, without which he will have little strength to resist the assaults of his foes.

And your feet shod with the preparation of the gospel of peace.[4] The military shoes which the Christian ought to wear, in order that he may go speedily where it is necessary, unlike those whose feet are bare, and who walk

---

[1] "Induite vos armaturam Dei, ut possitis stare adversus insidias diaboli. Quoniam non est nobis colluctatio adversus carnem et sanguinem, sed adversus principes et potestates."—*Eph.* vi. 11-15.

[2] "State ergo succincti lumbos vestros in veritate."—*Ibid.* 14.

[3] "Et induti loricam justitiæ."

[4] "Et calceati pedes in præparatione Evangelii pacis."

slowly, is the possession of a mind prepared to embrace in practice, and to teach by example, the holy maxims of the Gospel.

In all things taking the shield of faith.[1] The shield with which the soldier of Christ must defend himself against the fiery darts (that is, darts which pierce like fire) of the enemy is a steady faith, strengthened with holy hope, and especially with divine charity. *The helmet of salvation, and the sword of the spirit.*[2] The helmet, as St. Anselm teaches us, is the hope of eternal salvation; and, lastly, the sword of the Spirit, our spiritual sword, is the divine word, by which God repeatedly promises to hear those who pray to him. *Seek, and it shall be given you.*[3] *He that seeketh, receiveth.*[4] *Call to Me, and I will hear thee.*[5] *Call Me, and I will deliver thee.*[6]

Wherefore the Apostle continues, *By all prayer and supplication, praying at all times in the spirit; and in the same watching with all instance and supplication for all the saints.*[7] Thus, prayer is the most powerful of the arms with which the Lord gives us victory over our evil passions and the temptations of hell; but this prayer must be made *in the spirit;* that is, not with the mouth only, but with the heart. Moreover, it must last through our life,—"at all times;" for as the struggle endures, so must our prayers. It must be urgent and repeated; if the temptation does not yield at the first prayer, we must repeat it a second,

[1] "In omnibus sumentes scutum fidei, in quo possitis omnia tela nequissimi ignea extinguere."—*Eph.* vi. 16.
[2] "Et galeam salutis assumite, et gladium spiritus, quod est verbum Dei."—*Ibid.* 17.
[3] "Petite et dabitur vobis."—*Matt.* vii. 7.
[4] "Omnis enim qui petit, accipit."—*Luke,* xi. 10.
[5] "Clama ad me, et exaudiam te."—*Jer.* xxxiii. 3.
[6] "Invoca me . . ., eruam te."—*Ps.* xlix. 15.
[7] "Per omnem orationem et obsecrationem orantes omni tempore. In spiritu, et in ipso vigilantes in omni instantia et obsecratione pro omnibus sanctis."—*Eph.* vi. 18.

third, or fourth time; and if it still continues, we must
add sighs, tears, importunity, vehemence, as if we would
do violence to God, that he may give us the grace of
victory. This is what the Apostle's words, "with all instance and supplication," mean. The Apostle adds,
"for all saints," which means that we are not to pray
for ourselves alone; but for the perseverance of all the
faithful who are in the grace of God, and especially of
priests, that they may labor for the conversion of unbe-
lievers and all sinners, repeating in our prayers the words
of Zacharias, *To give light to them that sit in darkness, and
in the shadow of death.*[1]

It is of great use for resisting our enemies in spiritual
combats, to anticipate them in our meditations, by preparing ourselves to do violence to them to our utmost
power, on all occasions when they may suddenly come
upon us. Thus the saints have been able to preserve the
greatest mildness, or at least not to reply by a single
word, and not to be disturbed when they have received
a great injury, a violent persecution, a severe pang in
body or in mind, the loss of property of great value, the
death of a much-loved relative. Such victories are ordinarily not acquired without the aid of a life of long dis-
cipline, without frequenting sacraments, and a continual
exercise of meditation, spiritual reading, and prayer.
Therefore these victories are with difficulty obtained by
those who have not taken great heed to avoid dangerous
occasions, or who are attached to the vanities or pleasures of the world, and practise very little the mortification of the senses; by those, in a word, who live a soft
and easy life. St. Augustine says that in the spiritual
life, "first, pleasures are to be conquered, then pains;"[2]

---

[1] "Illuminare his qui in tenebris et in umbra mortis sedent."—
Luke, i. 79.

[2] "Primo vincendæ sunt delectationes, postea dolores."—*Serm.*
335, *E. B.*

meaning that a person who is given to seek the pleasures of the senses will scarcely resist a great passion or temptation which assails him; a man who loves too much the esteem of the world will scarcely endure a grave affront without losing the grace of God.

It is true that we must look for all our strength to live without sin, and to do good works, not from ourselves, but from the grace of Jesus Christ; but we must take great care not to make ourselves weaker than we are by nature through our own fault. The defects of which we take no account will cause the divine light to fail, and the devil will become stronger against us. For example, a desire to display to the world our learning, rank, or vanity in dress, or the seeking of any superfluous pleasure, or resentment at every inattentive word or action, or a wish to please every one, though at the loss of our spiritual profit, or neglect of works of piety through the fear of man, or little acts of disobedience towards our Superiors, little murmurings, trifling but cherished aversions, trivial falsehoods, slight attacks upon our neighbor, loss of time in gossip, or the indulgence of curiosity, —in a word, every attachment to earthly things, and every act of inordinate self-love, can serve as a help to our enemy to drag us over some precipice; or, at least, this defect deliberately consented to will deprive us of that abundance of divine help without which we may find ourselves fallen into ruin.

We grieve when we find ourselves so dry in spirit and desolate in prayer, in Communions, and in all our devout exercises; but how can God make us enjoy his presence and loving visits while we are thus niggardly and inattentive to him? *He that sows sparingly shall reap also sparingly.*[1] If we cause him so much displeasure, how can we expect to enjoy his heavenly consolations?

---

[1] "Qui parce seminat, parce et metet."—2 *Cor.* ix. 6.

If we do not detach ourselves in everything from earth, we shall never wholly belong to Jesus Christ, and where shall we go to protect ourselves? Jesus, by his humility, merited for us the grace of conquering pride; by his poverty he merited strength for us to despise earthly goods; and by his patience, constancy in overcoming slights and injuries. "What pride," writes St. Augustine, "could have been healed, if not healed by the humility of the Son of God? what avarice, except by the poverty of Christ? what anger, except by the Saviour's patience?"[1] But if we are cold in the love of Jesus Christ, and neglect to pray continually to him to help us, and nourish in our hearts any earthly affection, with difficulty shall we persevere in a good life. Let us pray, let us pray always. With prayer we shall obtain every thing.

O Saviour of the world! O my only hope! by the merits of Thy Passion, deliver me from every impure desire which may hinder me from loving Thee as I ought. May I be stripped of all desires that savor of the world; grant that the only object of my desires may be Thyself, who art the sovereign good, and the only good that is worthy of love. By Thy sacred wounds heal my infirmities, give me grace to keep far from my heart every love which is not for Thee, who deservest all my love. O Jesus, my love! Thou art my hope. O sweet words! sweet consolation! Jesus, my love, Thou art my hope!

IV.

The Hope that we have in Jesus Christ that He will grant us Eternal Happiness.

And therefore He is the mediator of the New Testament, that by means of His death . . . they that are called may receive

---

[1] "Quæ superbia sanari potest, si humilitate Filii Dei non sanatur? quæ avaritia, si paupertate Filii Dei non sanatur? quæ iracundia, si patientia Filii Dei non sanatur?"—*De Ag. Chr.* c. 11.

the promise of eternal inheritance.[1]   Here St. Paul speaks
of the New Testament not as a covenant, but as a promise, or testamentary disposition, by which Jesus Christ
left us heirs of the kingdom of heaven.   And because a
testament is not in force until the death of the testator,
therefore it was necessary that Jesus Christ should die,
that we might become his heirs, and enter into the possession of paradise.   Wherefore the Apostle adds, *For
where there is a testament, the death of the testator must of
necessity come in.   For a testament is of force after men are
dead; otherwise it is as yet of no strength whilst the testator
liveth.*[2]

Through the merits of Jesus Christ our mediator we
have received grace in baptism to become the sons of
God; unlike the Jews, who, under the old covenant,
though they were the elect, were yet all servants.
Whence the Apostle writes, *For there are two covenants, of
which one on Mount Sina engendereth to bondage.*[3]   The first
mediation was made with God by Moses on Mount Sina,
when God, through Moses, promised to the Jews the
abundance of temporal blessings, if they observed the
laws which he gave them; but this mediation, says St.
Paul, only produced servants, unlike the mediation of
Jesus Christ, which produces sons: *We, brethren, like
Isaac, are the children of promise.*[4]   If, then, being Christians, we are the sons of God, by consequence, says the

---

[1] " Et ideo Novi Testamenti Mediator est, ut, morte intercedente,
. . . repromissionem accipiant, qui vocati sunt, æternæ hereditatis."
—*Heb.* ix. 15.

[2] " Ubi enim Testamentum est, mors necesse est intercedat testa-
toris.   Testamentum enim in mortuis confirmatum est; alioquin,
nondum valet, dum vivit qui testatus est."—*Ibid.* 16, 17.

[3] " Hæc enim sunt duo Testamenta : unum quidem in monte Sina .
in servitutem generans."—*Gal.* iv. 24.

[4] " Nos autem, fratres, secundum Isaac, promissionis filii sumus."
—*Gal.* iv. 28.

Apostle, we are also heirs;[1] for a portion of the father's
inheritance is given to all sons, and this is the inheritance of eternal glory in paradise, which Jesus Christ
has merited for us by his death.

St. Paul nevertheless adds, in the same place, *If we
suffer with Him, we shall also be glorified with Him.*[2] It is
true that, by our sonship to God, which Jesus Christ has
obtained for us by his death, we have acquired a right
to paradise; but this is on the supposition that we are
faithful to correspond to the divine grace by our good
works, and especially by holy patience. Therefore the
Apostle says that in order to obtain eternal glory, as
Jesus Christ has obtained it, we must suffer upon earth
as Jesus Christ suffered. He goes before, as our captain,
with his cross; under this standard we must follow him,
each bearing his own cross, as the same Lord admon-
ishes us, *He that will come after Me, let him deny himself,
and take up his cross and follow Me.*[3]

St. Paul also exhorts us to suffer with courage, stength-
ened by the hope of paradise, reminding us that the
glory which will be given us in the next life will be infinitely greater than all our sufferings, if we suffer here
with good will, in order to fulfil the divine pleasure : *I
reckon that the sufferings of this present time are not worthy
to be compared with the glory to come that shall be revealed in
us.*[4] What beggar would be so foolish as not to give
gladly all his rags for a great kingdom? We do not as
yet enjoy this glory, because we are not yet saved, not
having finished our life in the grace of God; but hope

---

[1] "Si autem filii, et hæredes; hæredes quidem Dei, cohæredes
autem Christi."—*Rom.* viii. 17.

[2] "Si tamen compatimur, ut et conglorificemur."—*Ibid.*

[3] "Si quis vult post me venire, abneget semetipsum, et tollat crucem suam, et sequatur me."—*Matt.* xvi. 24.

[4] "Existimo enim quod non sunt condignæ passiones hujus temporis ad futuram gloriam, quæ revelabitur in nobis."—*Rom.* viii. 18.

in the merits of Jesus Christ, says St. Paul, will save us: *We are saved by hope.*[1] He will not fail to give us every help to save us, if we are faithful to him, and continue to pray; and the promise of Jesus Christ assures us that he hears every one who prays: *Every one that seeketh, receiveth.*[2] Some one will say, I fear, not that God will refuse to hear me, if I pray to him, but I fear for myself, that I should not know how to pray as I ought. No, says St. Paul, fear not this, for when we pray, God himself aids our weakness, and makes us pray so as to be heard. *The Spirit helpeth our infirmity, and asketh for us.*[3] He asks, explains St. Austin, that is, he helps us to ask.[4]

The Apostle would still further increase our confidence; he says, *We know that all things work together for good to those that love God.*[5] By this he teaches us that shame, sickness, poverty, persecutions, are not evils, as men of the world account them; for God turns them all into blessings and glory for those who suffer with patience. Finally, he says, *Those whom He foreknew, He also predestinated to be conformed to the image of His Son.*[6] With these words he would persuade us that, if we would be saved, we must resolve to suffer everything rather than lose the divine grace, for no one can be admitted to the glory of the blessed, unless at the day of judgment his life be found conformed to the life of Jesus Christ.

And that sinners may not, through these words, abandon themselves to despair on account of their guilt, St. Paul encourages them to hope for pardon, telling them

[1] "Spe enim salvi facti sumus."—*Rom.* viii. 24.
[2] "Omnis enim qui petit, accipit."—*Luke*, xi. 10.
[3] "Spiritus adjuvat infirmitatem nostram, . . . postulat pro nobis."—*Rom.* viii. 26.
[4] "'Postulat,' id est, postulare facit."—*Ep.* 194. c. 4. *E. B.*
[5] "Scimus autem quoniam, diligentibus Deum, omnia cooperantur in bonum."—*Rom.* viii. 28.
[6] "Nam quos præscivit, et prædestinavit conformes fieri imaginis Filii sui."—*Ibid.* 29.

that for this end the Eternal Father has not spared his own son, who was offered to satisfy for our sins, but gave him up to death,[1] that he might pardon us sinners; and still further to increase the hope of penitent sinners, he says, *Who is he that shall condemn? Is it Jesus Christ who died?*[2] as though he had said, Sinners, you who detest your sins, why do you fear to be condemned to hell? Tell me who is your judge,—who is to condemn you? Is it not Jesus Christ? How, then, can you fear that you will be condemned to death by this loving Redeemer, who, that he might not condemn you, has been willing to condemn himself to die as a malefactor upon the infamous gibbet of the cross? He speaks, indeed, of those sinners who, being contrite, have washed their souls in the blood of the Lamb, according to the words of St. John.[3]

O my Jesus! if I look at my sins, I am ashamed to seek for paradise, after the many times that I have openly renounced Thee, for the sake of short and miserable pleasures; but looking to Thee upon this cross, I cannot cease to hope for paradise, knowing that Thou hast been willing to die upon this tree to atone for my sins, and to obtain for me this paradise which I had despised. O my sweet Redeemer! I hope, through the merits of Thy death, that Thou hast already pardoned me the sins I have committed against Thee, for which I repent, and now I would rather die for grief of them; and yet, O my God, I see that, with all that Thou hast pardoned me, it will ever be true, that, in my ingratitude, I have had the heart to cause Thee so much displeasure, who hast

[1] "Qui etiam proprio Filio suo non pepercit, sed pro nobis omnibus tradidit illum."—*Rom.* viii. 32.

[2] "Quis est qui condemnet? Christus Jesus, qui mortuus est."—*Ibid.* 34.

[3] "Hi sunt qui . . . laverunt stolas suas et dealbaverunt eas in sanguine Agni."—*Apoc.* vii. 14.

so much loved me.   But what is past is past.   At least
for the rest of my life, O my Lord, I would love Thee
with all my powers; I would live only for Thee; I would
be wholly Thine; wholly, wholly, wholly Thine.   But
Thou must accomplish this.   Detach me from every
earthly thing, and give me light and strength to seek
Thee alone, my only good, my love, my all.

O Mary, hope of sinners! thou must help me with thy
prayers.   Pray, pray for me, and cease not to pray, until
thou seest me wholly given to God.

CHAPTER XI.

THE PATIENCE THAT WE MUST EXERCISE IN COMPANY WITH
JESUS CHRIST, IN ORDER TO OBTAIN ETERNAL SALVA-
TION.

I.

It is Necessary to suffer, and to suffer with Patience.

To speak of patience and suffering is a thing neither
practised nor understood by those who love the world.
It is understood and practised only by souls who love
God.   "O Lord," said St. John of the Cross to Jesus
Christ, "I ask nothing of Thee but to suffer and to be
despised for Thy sake."   St. Teresa frequently exclaimed, "O my Jesus, I would either suffer or die."   St.
Mary Magdalene of Pazzi was wont to say, "I would
suffer and not die."   Thus speak the saints who love
God, because a soul can give no surer mark to God of
love for him than voluntarily to suffer to please him.
This is the great proof which Jesus Christ has given of
his love to us.   As God he loved us in creating us, in
providing us so many blessings, in calling us to enjoy

the same glory that he himself enjoys; but in nothing
else has he more fully shown how much he loves us
than in becoming man, and embracing a painful life,
and a death full of pangs and ignominies, for love of
us. And how shall we show our love for Jesus Christ?
By leading a life full of pleasures and earthly delights?

Let us not think that God delights in our pains; the
Lord is not of so cruel a nature as to be delighted to
see us, his creatures, groan and suffer. He is a God of
infinite goodness, who desires to see us fully content and
happy, so that he is full of sweetness, affability, and
compassion to all who come to him.[1] But our unhappy
condition, as sinners, and the gratitude we owe to the
love of Jesus Christ, require that, for his love, we should
renounce the delights of this earth, and embrace with
affection the cross which he gives us to carry during this
life, after him who goes before, bearing a cross far
heavier than ours; and all this in order to bring us, after
our death, to a blessed life, which will never end. God,
then, has no desire to see us suffer, but, being himself infinite justice, he cannot leave our faults unpunished; so
that, in order that they may be punished, and yet we
may one day attain eternal happiness, he would have us
purge away our sins with patience, and thus deserve to
be eternally blessed. What can be more beautiful and
sweet than this rule of divine Providence, that we see at
once justice satisfied, and ourselves saved and happy?

All our hopes, then, we must derive from the merits of
Jesus Christ, and from him we must hope for all aid to
live holily, and save ourselves; and we cannot doubt that
it is his desire to see us holy: *This is the will of God, your
sanctification.*[2] But true as this is, we must not neglect to
do our part to satisfy God for the injuries we have done

---

[1] "Quoniam tu, Domine, suavis et mitis, et multæ misericordiæ
omnibus invocantibus te."—*Ps.* lxxxv. 5.

[2] "Hæc est enim voluntas Dei, sanctificatio vestra."—1 *Thess.* iv. 3.

to him, and to attain with our good works to eternal
life. This the Apostle expressed when he said, *I fill up
that which is wanting of the Passion of Christ in my flesh.*¹
Was the Passion of Christ, then, not complete, not
enough alone to save us? It was most complete in its
value, and most sufficient to save all men ; nevertheless,
in order that the merits of the Passion may be applied
to us, says St. Teresa, we must do our part, and suffer
with patience the crosses which God sends us, that we
may be like our head, Jesus Christ, according to what
the Apostle writes to the Romans: *Whom He foreknew,
them He also predestinated to be conformed to the image of His
Son, that He might be the first-born among many brethren.*²
Still we must ever remember, as the Angelic Doctor
warns us, that all the virtue of our good works, satisfactions, and penances, is communicated to them by the
satisfaction of Jesus Christ: *The satisfaction of man has
its efficacy from the satisfaction of Christ.*³ And thus we
reply to the Protestants, who call our penances injurious
to the Passion of Jesus Christ, as if it were not sufficient
to satisfy for our sins.

What we say is, that in order that we may be partakers in the merits of Jesus Christ, it is necessary that
we labor to fulfil the divine precepts, even by doing
violence to ourselves, in order that we may not yield to
the temptations of hell. And this is what our Lord
meant when he said, *The kingdom of heaven suffereth violence, and the violent seize upon it.*⁴ It is necessary, when
occasions occur, that we do violence to ourselves by con-

¹ "Adimpleo ea quæ desunt passionum Christi in carne mea."—
Col. i. 24.
² "Nam quos præscivit, et prædestinavit conformes fieri Imaginis
Filii sui, ut sit ipse primogenitus in multis fratribus."—*Rom.* viii. 29.
³ "Hominis satisfactio efficaciam habet a satisfactione Christi."
⁴ "Regnum cœlorum vim patitur, et violenti rapiunt illud."—*Matt.*
xi. 12.

tinence, by the mortification of our senses, that we may
not be conquered by our enemies. And when we find
ourselves guilty through the sins we have committed,
we must do violence to God with our tears, says St.
Ambrose, in order to obtain pardon.[1] And then, to
console us, the saint adds, " O blessed violence, which is
not punished with the wrath of God, but is welcomed
and rewarded with mercy !"[2] The more violent any
man is with Christ, the more religious is he accounted
by Christ. For we must first rule over ourselves by
conquering our passions, that we may one day seize
upon heaven, which our Saviour has merited for us.[3]
And therefore we must do violence to ourselves by suffering contradictions and persecutions, and by conquering the temptations and passions which, without violence, are never conquered.

God teaches us that, in order not to lose our souls, we
must be prepared to suffer the agonies of death, and to
die; but, at the same time, he says that for him who is
thus prepared he himself will fight, and will destroy his
enemies.[4] St. John saw before the throne of God a
great multitude of saints clothed in white garments (because into heaven nothing defiled can enter), and he
beheld that every one of them bore in his hand a palm,
the token of martyrdom.[5] What, then, are all the saints

[1] " Vim faciamus Domino, non compellendo, sed lacrymis exoran-
do."

[2] " O beata violentia, quæ, non indignatione percutitur, sed misericordia condonatur !"

[3] " Quisquis enim violentior Christo fuerit, religiosior habebitur a
Christo. Prius enim ipsi regnare debemus in nobis, ut regnum pos-
simus diripere Salvatoris."—*Serm.* 15.

[4] " Pro justitia agonizare pro anima tua, et usque ad mortem certa
pro justitia; et Deus expugnabit pro te inimicos tuos."—*Ecclus.* iv.
33.

[5] " Vidi turbam magnam . . . . , stantes ante thronum in conspectu
Agni amicti stolis albis ; et palmæ in manibus eorum."—*Apoc.* vii. 9.

martyrs? Yes, Lord, all grown-up persons who are saved must either be martyrs in blood or martyrs in patience, in conquering the assaults of hell and the inordinate desires of the flesh. Bodily pleasures send innumerable souls to hell, and, therefore, we must resolve with courage to despise them. Let us be assured that either the soul must tread the body under foot, or the body the soul.

We must, then (I repeat), do ourselves violence in order to be saved. But this violence is such (it will be said by some one) that I cannot do it of myself, if God does not give it me through his grace. To such a one St. Ambrose says, "If you look to yourself, you can do nothing; but if you trust in God, strength will be given you."[1] But, in doing this, we must suffer, and it is impossible to avoid it; if we would enter into the glory of the Blessed, says the Scripture, we must, through much tribulation, enter into the kingdom of God.[2] Thus St. John, beholding the glory of the saints in heaven, heard a voice saying, *These are they who have come out of great tribulation, and have washed their garments, and have made them white in the blood of the Lamb.*[3] It is true that they all attained heaven by being washed in the blood of the Lamb, but they all went there after suffering great tribulation.

Be assured, St. Paul wrote to his disciples, that God is faithful, who will not suffer you to be tempted above what you are able.[4] God has promised to give us sufficient help to conquer every temptation, if only we ask

---

[1] "Si te respicis, nihil poteris; sed, si in Domino confidis, dabitur tibi fortitudo."

[2] "Per multas tribulationes oportet nos intrare in regnum Dei."— *Acts,* xiv. 21.

[3] "Hi sunt qui venerunt de tribulatione magna, et laverunt stolas suas et dealbaverunt eas in sanguine Agni."—*Apoc.* vii. 14.

[4] "Fidelis autem Deus est, qui non patietur vos tentari supra id quod potestis."—1 *Cor.* x. 13.

him. *Ask, and it shall be given you; seek, and ye shall find.*[1]
He cannot, therefore, fail of his promise. It is a fatal
error of the heretics to say that God commands things
which it is impossible for us to observe. The Council of
Trent says: *God does not command impossible things; but when
He commands, He bids us do what we can, and seek help for
what we cannot do, and He will help us.*[2] St. Ephrem writes,
"If men do not put upon their beasts a greater burden
than they can bear, much less does God lay greater temptations upon men than they can endure."[3]

Thomas à Kempis writes, "The cross everywhere
awaits thee; it is needful for thee everywhere to preserve
patience, if thou wouldst have peace. If thou willingly
bearest the cross, it will bear thee to thy desired end."[4]
In this world, we all of us go about seeking peace; and
would find it without suffering; but this is not possible
in our present state; we must suffer; the cross awaits us
wherever we turn. How, then, can we find peace in the
midst of these crosses? By patience, by embracing the
cross, which presents itself to us. St. Teresa says "that
he who drags the cross along with ill-will feels its weight,
however small it is; but he who willingly embraces it,
however great it is, does not feel it."

The same Thomas à Kempis says, "Which of the
saints is without a cross? The whole life of Christ was
a cross and a martyrdom, and dost thou seek for pleas-

---

[1] "Petite, et dabitur vobis; quærite, et invenietis."—*Matt.* vii. 7.
[2] "Deus impossibilia non jubet; sed jubendo monet, et facere quod possis, et petere quod non possis; et adjuvat ut possis."—*Sess.* vi. c. 11.
[3] "Si homines suis jumentis non plus oneris imponunt, quam ferre possint, multo minus hominibus plus tentationum imponet Deus, quam ferre queant."—*De Patientia.*
[4] "Crux ubique te exspectat; necesse est te ubique tenere patientiam, si internam vis habere pacem. Si libenter crucem portas, portabit te ad desideratum finem."—*Imit. Chr.* l. 2, c. 12.

ure?"[1] Jesus, innocent, holy, and the Son of God, was
willing to suffer through his whole life, and shall we go
about seeking pleasures and comforts? To give us an
example of patience, he chose a life full of ignominies
and pains within and without; and shall we wish to be
saved without suffering, or to suffer without patience,
which is a double suffering, and without fruit, and with
increase of pain? How can we think to be lovers of
Jesus Christ, if we will not suffer for love of him who
has so much suffered for love of us? How can he glory
in being a follower of the Crucified who refuses or receives with ill-will the fruits of the cross, which are sufferings, contempt, poverty, pains, infirmities, and all
things that are contrary to our self-love?

II.

The Sight of Jesus Crucified consoles us and sustains us in Sufferings.

Let us not lose courage, but keep our eyes ever fixed
on the crucified one, because from him we shall draw
strength to endure the evils of this life not only with patience, but even with joy and gladness, as the saints have
done: *Ye shall draw waters in joy from the fountains of the
Saviour;*[2] that is, says St. Bonaventure, from the wounds
of Jesus Christ.[3] Therefore, the saint exhorts us ever to
keep our eyes fixed on Jesus dying upon the cross, if we
would live always united to God.[4] "Devotion," says
St. Thomas, "consists in being ready to accomplish in
ourselves whatever God demands of us."[5]

[1] "Quis Sanctorum sine cruce fuit? Tota vita Christi crux fuit et
martyrium; et tu tibi quæris gaudium?"

[2] "Haurietis aquas in gaudio de fontibus Salvatoris."—*Isa.* xii. 3.

[3] "'De fontibus Salvatoris,' hoc est, de vulneribus Jesu Christi."

[4] "Semper oculis cordis sui Christum in cruce tamquam morientem
videat, qui devotionem in se vult conservare."—*De Perf. vit.* c. 6.

[5] 2. 2, q. 82, a. 1.

Observe the excellent advice which St. Paul gives us, that we may live ever united with God, and may patiently endure the troubles of this present life : *Think diligently upon Him who endured contradiction against Himself for sinners, that ye be not weary and faint in your minds.*[1] He says, *think diligently;* for in order to suffer with resignation and peace present troubles, it is not enough to give a hasty glance, a few times in the year, at the Passion of Jesus Christ; we must often think of it, and every day turn our eyes to the pain which the Lord suffered for love of us. And what were the pains he suffered ? The Apostle says, *He endured such contradiction.* The contradiction which Jesus Christ endured from his enemies was such as to make him, as it had been foretold by the Prophet, the vilest of men, and the man of sorrows,[2] until he died of agony, and overwhelmed with insults, upon a gibbet belonging to the most reprobate. And why did Jesus Christ embrace this load of pains and insults? *That ye might not be weary and faint in your minds;* that seeing how much a God has been willing to endure, in order to give us an example of patience, we might be patient, and endure all to be delivered from our sins.

Thus the Apostle goes on to encourage us, saying, *Ye have not yet resisted unto blood, striving against sin.*[3] Think, he says, that Christ poured forth for you all his blood in his Passion through torments, and that the holy martyrs, after the example of him, their king, have courageously endured hot plates, and iron nails, which have torn open their very bowels ; but you have not shed a single drop of blood for Jesus Christ, while we ought to be ready to

---

[1] " Recogitate enim eum qui talem sustinuit a peccatoribus adversus semetipsum contradictionem, ut ne fatigemini, animis vestris deficientes."—*Heb.* xii. 3.

[2] "Novissimum virorum, virum dolorum."—*Isa.* liii. 3.

[3] " Nondum enim usque ad sanguinem restitistis, adversus peccatum repugnantes."—*Heb.* xii. 4.

give our life rather than offend God, as St. Edmund said,
" I would rather leap into a burning pile than commit a
sin against my God." [1]   And thus St. Anselm, Arch-
bishop of Canterbury, said, " If I must either endure all
the bodily pains of hell, or else commit a sin, rather than
commit it I would choose hell." [2]

The infernal lion ceases not through all our life to go
about seeking to devour us; therefore St. Peter tells us
that, by thinking of the Passion of Christ, we ought to
arm ourselves against his attacks.[3]   St. Thomas says
that the mere recollection of the Passion is a great defence against all the temptations of hell.[4]   And St. Ambrose, or some other saint, says, " If there had been any
better way of salvation for men than the way of suffering, Christ would have shown it to us both by word and
example;[5] but now, going before us with the cross upon
his shoulders, he has shown us that there is no better
way of obtaining salvation than suffering with patience
and resignation; and he himself has given us the example in his own person.

St. Bernard says that when we look upon the afflictions of the Lord, we will find our own lighter to bear.[6]
And in another place, " What more can be given to thee,
since thou hast the bitternesses of thy Lord ?" [7]   St.

---

[1] " Malim insilire in rogum ardentissimum, quam peccatum ullum
admittere in Deum meum."—*Vit.* c. 19, *ap. Sur.* 16 *Nov.*

[2] *Simil.* c. 190.

[3] " Christo igitur passo in carne, et vos eadem cogitatione armamini."—1 *Pet.* iv. 1.

[4] " 'Armamini,' quia memoria passionis contra tentationes munit et
roborat."

[5] " Si quid melius saluti hominum quam pati fuisset, Christus utique
verbo et exemplo ostendisset."

[6] " Videntes angustias Domini, levius vestras portabitis."—*In Cant.*
s. 43.

[7] " Quid non suave tibi esse poterit, cum tibi collegeris omnes
amaritudines Domini ?"—*De Divers.* s. 22.

Eleazar, being one day asked by his good wife, Delphina,
how he bore so many injuries with a calm mind, replied,
" When I see myself injured, I think on the injuries of
my crucified Saviour, and cease not to think of them
until I am calmed." [1] " Sweet is the ignominy of the cross
to him who is not ungrateful to the Crucified," says St.
Bernard.

To souls that desire to be grateful to Jesus Christ,
the contempt they receive is not displeasing, but welcome.[2] Who will not gladly embrace opprobrium and
ill-treatment when he thinks of the ill-treatment which
Jesus endured in the commencement of his Passion,
when, in the house of Caiphas, he was on that night
struck with blows and stripes, spit upon in the face, and,
with a cloth spread before his eyes, derided as a false
prophet ?[3]

And how did it ever happen that the martyrs endured
with such patience the torments of executioners ? They
were torn with iron, they were burned upon hot grat-
ings. Were they not made of flesh and blood, or had
they lost all sense ? No; when the martyr sees his blood,
he thinks not of his own wounds, but of those of his
Redeemer ; he does not feel pain ; not that there is no
pain, but that for Christ's sake it is contemned. There
is nothing so bitter, even to death, which is not sweetened by the death of Christ.[4]

The Apostle writes that through the merits of Jesus

[1] *Vit.* c. 23, *ap. Sur,* 27 *Sept.*

[2] " Grata ignominia crucis ei qui Crucifixo ingratus non est."—*In Cant.* s. 25.

[3] " Tunc exspuerunt in faciem ejus, et colaphis eum ceciderunt; alii autem palmas in faciem ejus dederunt, dicentes : Prophetiza nobis, Christe, quis est qui te percussit ?"—*Matt.* xxvi. 67.

[4] " Martyr, videns sanguinem suum, non sua, sed Redemptoris vulnera attendit, dolores non sentit; nec deest dolor, sed pro Christo contemnitur. Nihil enim tam amarum ad mortem est, quod morte Christi non sanetur."

Christ we are all made rich.[1] But Jesus Christ chooses that, in order to obtain the graces we desire, we should ever have recourse to God with prayer, and beseech him to hear us through the merits of his Son; and Jesus himself promises that whatever we ask the Father in his name, he will give it us. Thus did the martyrs; when the pain of their torments was too sharp and bitter, they went to God, and God gave them patience to endure. The martyr St. Theodore, in the midst of all the cruelties inflicted on him, feeling at one time a most terrible torture from the balls of hot chalk which the tyrant had put upon the wounds they had caused him, besought Jesus Christ to give him strength to suffer, and thus remained conqueror, ending his life in the torments.

We need not fear the attacks we must endure from the world and from hell; if we take heed ever to have recourse to Jesus Christ with prayer, he will obtain for us every blessing;[2] he will obtain for us patience in all our labors, perseverance, and, in the end, will grant us a good death.

III.

The Passion of our Saviour will give us Strength when at the Point of Death.

Great is the bitterness we endure at the point of death; Jesus Christ only can give us constancy to suffer with patience and meritoriously. Especially great are then the temptations of hell, which vehemently strive to destroy us, seeing us near our end. Rinaldus relates that St. Eleazar, at the point of death, endured horrible attacks from the devils, after leading a most holy life, so that he said, "Great are the temptations of hell at this

---

[1] "In omnibus divites facti estis in illo."—1 *Cor.* i. 5.
[2] "Amen, amen, dico vobis: si quid petieritis Patrem in nomine meo, dabit vobis."—*John*, xvi. 23.

moment, but Jesus Christ, by the merits of his Passion, destroys all their power." [1] St. Francis desired that at the hour of his death the Passion should be read to him. In like manner, St. Charles Borromeo, seeing himself near death, had himself taken near the images of the Passion, that in sight of these he might breathe out his blessed soul.

St. Paul writes that Jesus Christ chose to endure death, that through death he might destroy him who had the power of death ; that is, the devil ; and might deliver those who, through fear of death, were through their whole life subject to bondage.[2] And he adds, *Wherefore it was necessary that He should be in all things like His brethren, that He might be merciful. For in that He Himself suffered, and was tempted, He is able to succor those who are tempted.*[3] He chose to take on him all the circumstances and passions of human nature (except ignorance, concupiscence, and sin); and wherefore? That he might be merciful, that by taking on himself our miseries, he might be more compassionate to us, because misery is much better known by experience than by reflection ; and thus he became more ready to help us when we are tempted during life, and especially at the hour of death. To this the saying of St. Augustine refers, "If you are disturbed at the time of death, do not think yourself a reprobate, nor give yourself up to despair ; for Christ himself was thus disturbed at the prospect of his own death."[4]

---

[1] *Ann.* 1323, n. 68.

[2] "Ut per mortem destrueret eum qui habebat mortis imperium, id est, diabolum, et liberaret eos qui, timore mortis, per totam vitam obnoxii erant servituti."—*Heb.* ii. 14, 15.

[3] "Unde debuit per omnia fratribus similari, ut misericors fieret . . .; in eo enim in quo passus est ipse et tentatus, potens est et eis, qui tentantur, auxiliari."—*Ibid.* 17.

[4] "Si imminente morte turbaris, non te existimes reprobum, nec desperationi te abjicias; ideo enim Christus turbatus est in conspectu suæ mortis."

Hell, therefore, at the time of our death, will put forth
all its strength to make us distrust the divine mercy, by
placing before our eyes all the sins of our life ; but the
memory of the death of Jesus Christ will give us courage
to trust in his merits, and not to fear death.   St. Thomas
remarks on St. Paul's words, *Christ, by death, took away
the fear of death:* "When a man reflects that the Son of
God chose to die, he does not fear death."[1]   To the
Gentiles death was an object of the greatest terror, because they thought that with death every blessing ceased ;
but the death of Jesus Christ gives us a firm hope that,
dying in the grace of God, we shall pass from death to
eternal life.   Of this hope St. Paul gives us a sure confidence, saying that the Eternal Father did not spare his
own Son, but delivered him up for us all ; and how
has he not with him given us all things?[2]   For giving
us Jesus Christ, he gives us pardon, final perseverance, his love, a good death, eternal life, and every
blessing.

Thus, when the devil frightens us in life or in death,
by representing to us the sins of our youth, let us answer
him with St. Bernard, "What is wanting to me of myself, I take to myself from the bowels of my Lord."[3]   St.
Paul writes, *It is God who justifieth; who is He that shall
condemn?   It is Jesus Christ who died, and who also is risen
again, who is at the right hand of God, who also intercedes for
us.*[4]   These words of the Apostle are of great comfort to

[1] "Christus, per mortem suam, abstulit timorem mortis; quando
enim considerat homo quod Filius Dei mori voluit, non timet mori."
—*In Heb.* ii. *lect.* 4.

[2] "Proprio Filio suo non pepercit, sed pro nobis omnibus tradidit
illum; quomodo non etiam cum illo omnia nobis donavit ?"—*Rom.*
viii. 32.

[3] "Quod ex me mihi deest, usurpo mihi ex visceribus Domini."—
In Cant. s. 61.

[4] "Deus qui justificat, quis est qui condemnet?   Christus Jesus,
qui mortuus est, imo qui et resurrexit, qui est ad dexteram Dei, qui
etiam interpellat pro nobis."—*Rom.* viii. 34.

us sinners; it is God who justifies us sinners, and pardons us with his grace ; and if God makes us just, who can condemn us as guilty. Will Jesus Christ, who died for us, and gave himself for our sins, that he might redeem us from the present evil world?[1]

He burdened himself with our sins, and gave himself to death to deliver us from this wicked world, and to bring us with himself to his kingdom, where (as St. Paul goes on to say) he performs the office of our advocate, and intercedes for us with the Father. St. Thomas explains this, saying that Jesus Christ intercedes for us in heaven, by presenting to his Father his wounds which he endured for love of us. And St. Gregory does not hesitate to assert (in opposition to what some say) that the Redeemer, as truly man, ever after his death, prays for the Church militant, that we may be faithful to him: "Christ daily prays for his Church."[2] And St. Gregory Nazianzen before had said, "He intercedes, that is, he prays for us in the way of meditation."[3] And St. Augustine,[4] on the thirty-ninth Psalm, says that Jesus prays for us in heaven, not that he may now obtain for us any fresh grace, for during his life he obtained all that he could obtain; but he prays, inasmuch as he begs of the Father, through his merits, the salvation already obtained and promised to us. And though to Christ all power is committed by the Father, yet, as man, he only possesses this power as depending upon God. For the rest, the Church is not accustomed to ask him to intercede for us, because she regards that which is most exalted in him, that is, his divinity; and therefore she prays to him as God to grant her what she asks.

[1] "Qui dedit semetipsum pro peccatis nostris, ut eriperet nos de præsenti sæculo nequam."—*Gal.* i. 4.

[2] "Quotidie orat Christus pro Ecclesia."—*In Ps. pœn.* v.

[3] "'Interpellat,' id est, pro nobis mediationis ratione supplicat." —*De Theol. or.* 4.

[4] *In Ps.* xxix. *en.* 2.

IV.

Confidence in Jesus Christ, and Love for Him.

But let us return to the confidence we ought to have
in Jesus Christ for our salvation. St. Augustine encourages us, saying that this Lord, who has delivered
us from death by shedding all his blood, desires not
that we should perish; and that if our sins separate us
from God, and make us worthy of being rejected, our
Saviour, on the other hand, cannot reject the price of
the blood which he has shed for us.[1] Let us, then, follow with boldness the counsel of St. Paul, who says,
*Let us run with patience the race that is put before us, looking
to Jesus, the author and finisher of faith; who, for the joy
that was set before Him, endured the cross and despised the
shame.*[2] He says, "Let us run with patience the race
before us," because it profits little to begin, if we do not
struggle to the end; while patience in enduring labor
will obtain for us the victory, and the crown that is
promised to him who conquers.

This patience will be the cuirass which will defend us
from the swords of our foes; but how shall we obtain it?
"By looking," says the Apostle, "to Jesus, the author and
finisher of the faith," who, says St. Augustine, despised
all earthly goods, that he might show that they are to
be despised; who endured all earthly evils, which he
taught us were to be endured, that in these we might
neither seek happiness nor fear unhappiness.[3] Then

[1] "Qui nos tanto pretio redemit, non vult perire quos emit . . . ;
si peccata nostra superant nos, pretium suum non contemnit Deus."
—*Serm.* 22, E. B.

[2] "Per patientiam curramus ad propositum nobis certamen, aspicientes in Auctorem fidei et Consummatorem Jesum, qui, proposito
sibi gaudio, sustinuit crucem, confusione contempta."—*Heb.* xii. 1.

[3] "Omnia bona terrena contempsit Christus, ut contemnenda
demonstraret; omnia terrena sustinuit mala, quæ sustinenda præci-
piebat: ut neque in illis quæreretur felicitas, neque in istis infelicitas
timeretur."—*De catech. rud.* c. 22.

with his glorious resurrection he animated us not to fear
death; because, if we are faithful to him even to death,
after it we shall obtain eternal life, which is free from
all evil, and full of every good thing. This is signified
by the Apostle's words, "Jesus, the author and finisher
of faith;" for Jesus Christ is the author of the faith, in
teaching us what to believe, and giving us grace to believe it; and so also is he the finisher of faith, by prom-
ising that we shall one day enjoy that blessed life which
now he teaches us to believe in. And that we may be
sure of the love which this Saviour bears to us, and of
the will he has that we should be saved, St. Paul adds,
"Who for the joy set before Him, endured the cross;"
on which words St. John Chrysostom remarks that
Jesus might have saved us by leading a life of joy upon
earth; but that to make us more certain of the love he
bears to us, he chose a life of pain, and a death of shame,
dying as a malefactor upon a cross.

Let us, then, give ourselves, O souls that love the
Crucified, for the life that remains to us, to love this loving Redeemer, so worthy of love, to our utmost power;
and also to suffer for him, because he has been willing
to suffer for love of us; and let us not cease to ask him
continually to grant us the gift of his holy love. Happy
are we if we attain to a great love for Jesus Christ!
The Venerable Father Vincent Carafa, an eminent servant of God, in a letter which he wrote to some studious
and devout young men, said as follows: "To reform
ourselves in our whole life, we must give all our study
to the exercise of the divine love; the love of God alone,
when it enters a heart, and obtains possession of it, pu-
rifies it from all inordinate love, and makes it at once
obedient and pure." St. Augustine says, a pure heart is
a heart emptied of every desire; and St. Bernard, he
that loves, loves and desires nothing more; meaning
that he who loves God desires nothing but to love him,

and banishes from his heart everything which is not
God. And thus it is that, from being empty, the heart
becomes full, that is, full of God, who brings with himself every good thing ; and then earthly blessings, finding no place in such a heart, have no power to move it.
What power can earthly pleasures have over us if we
enjoy divine consolations? What power is there in
ambition for vain honors, and the desire of earthly
riches, if we have the honor of being loved by God,
and begin to possess in part the riches of paradise?
To measure, therefore, the advance we have made in the
ways of God, let us observe what advance we have made
in loving him ; whether we often during the day make
acts of love towards God; often speak of the love of God;
whether we take pains to produce it in others; whether
we perform our devotions solely to please God; whether
we suffer with full resignation all adversities, infirmities,
pains, poverty, slights, and persecutions, in order to
please God. The saints say that a soul that truly loves
God ought not more to breathe than to love, since the
life of the soul, both in time and eternity, consists in the
love of our sovereign good, which is God.

But let us be sure that we shall never attain to a great
love for God, except through Jesus Christ, and unless
we have a special devotion to his Passion, by which he
procured the divine grace for us. The Apostle writes,
Through Him we have access to the Father.[1] The way to
ask for grace would be closed to us sinners, were it not
for Jesus Christ. He opens the gate to us, he introduces
us to the Father, and, by the merits of his Passion, he obtains for us from the Father pardon for our sins, and all
the graces that we receive from God. Miserable we
should be if we did not possess Jesus Christ. And who
can ever sufficiently praise and thank the love and good-

---

[1] "Per ipsum habemus accessum . . . ad Patrem."—*Eph.* ii. 18.

ness which this merciful Redeemer has shown to us poor sinners, in being willing to die to deliver us from eternal death? *Scarcely*, says the Apostle, *will any die for a just man, but for a good man perhaps some would dare to die; but when we were sinners, Christ died for us.*[1]

Wherefore the Apostle teaches us that if we are resolved to seek the love of Jesus Christ at all costs, we ought to expect from him every help and favor; and he thus reasons, *For if when we were enemies we were reconciled to God by the death of His Son, much more, being reconciled, we shall be saved by His life.* He thus warns those who love Jesus Christ, that they do injustice to the love which this our merciful Saviour bears to us, if they fear that he will deny them any of the graces necessary to salvation and to make them holy. And that our sins may not not cause us to fail in trusting him, St. Paul goes on to say, *For not according to the fault so is the gift; for if by the fault of one man many have died, much more has the grace and gift of God abounded by the grace of one man, Jesus Christ, to many more;*[2] giving us to understand that the gift of grace obtained by the Redeemer through his Passion brings us blessings far greater than the loss we sustained in the sin of Adam; for the merits of Christ have a greater power to cause us to be loved by God than the sin of Adam had to make him hate us. "We obtained," say St. Leo, "greater things by the unspeakable grace of Christ than we lost by the malice of the devil."[3]

[1] "Vix enim pro justo quis moritur; nam pro bono forsitan quis audeat mori.—Cum adhuc peccatores essemus, secundum tempus, Christus pro nobis mortuus est.—Si enim, cum inimici essemus, reconciliati sumus Deo per mortem Filii ejus, multo magis, reconciliati, salvi erimus in vita ipsius."—*Rom.* v. 7-10.

[2] "Sed non sicut delictum, ita et donum; si enim unius delicto multi mortui sunt, multo magis gratia Dei et donum in gratia unius hominis Jesu Christi in plures abundavit."—*Ibid.* 15.

[3] "Ampliora adepti per ineffabilem Christi gratiam, quam per diaboli amiseramus invidiam."—*De Asc. Dom.* s. 1.

Let us, then, conclude. O devout souls, let us love
Jesus Christ; let us love this Redeemer who is so worthy
of being loved, and has so loved us that it seems as if
he could not have done more to gain our love. It is
enough for us to know that, for love of us he has been
willing to die, consumed by griefs upon a cross; and,
not satisfied with this, has left us himself in the sacrament of the Eucharist, where he gives us for food the
very same body which he sacrificed for us, and gives us
to drink the very same blood that he poured forth for us
in his Passion. Most ungrateful shall we be to him, not
merely if we offend him, but if we love him little, and do
not consecrate to him all our love.

O my Jesus, may I be all consumed with love for Thee,
as Thou wast all consumed for me! And since Thou
hast so much loved me, and bound me to love Thee, help
me now not to be ungrateful to Thee; and most ungrateful should I be if I loved anything apart from Thee.
Thou hast loved me without reserve; without reserve I
also would love Thee. I leave all, I renounce all, to give
myself wholly to Thee, and to have in my heart no love
but Thine. Accept my love in pity, without taking account of the offences that I have committed against Thee
during the time past. Behold, I am one of the sheep for
whom Thou hast shed Thy blood; we therefore pray
Thee, help Thy servants, whom Thou hast redeemed with
Thy precious blood.[1] Forget, O my dear Saviour, the
many offences that I have committed against Thee.
Chastise me as Thou wilt, deliver me only from the
punishment of not being able to love Thee, and then do
with me whatever pleases Thee. Deprive me of everything. O my Jesus, but deprive me not of Thyself, my
only good. Teach me to know what Thou wilt have
from me, that, by Thy grace, I may fulfil all Thy will.

[1] " Te ergo quæsumus, tuis famulis subveni, quos pretioso sanguine redemisti."

Make me forget everything, that I may remember Thee alone, and all the pains Thou hast suffered for me. Grant that I may think of nothing but of pleasing Thee, and loving Thee. Look upon me with that love with which Thou didst look upon me at Calvary, when dying for me upon the cross, and hear me. In Thee I place all my hopes, O my Jesus, my God, and my all.[1]

O holy Virgin Mary, my mother and my hope, recommend me to thy Son, and obtain for me faithfulness to love him until my death.

[1] " Jesus meus, Deus meus, et omnia !"

Meditations on the Passion of Jesus Christ for each Day of the Week.*

MEDITATION FOR SUNDAY.

The Love of Jesus in suffering for Us.

I.

The time since the coming of Jesus Christ is no longer a time of fear, but a time of love, as the prophet foretold: *Thy time is a time of lovers,*[1] because a God has been seen to die for us: *Christ hath loved us, and hath given Himself up for us.*[2] Under the old law, before the Word was made flesh, man might, so to speak, have doubted whether God loved him with a tender love; but after having seen him suffer a bloody and ignominious death for us on a cross of infamy, we can no longer possibly doubt that he loves us with the utmost tenderness. And who will ever arrive at comprehending what was the excess of the love of the Son of God in being willing to pay the penalty of our sins? And yet this is "of faith." *Truly He hath borne our griefs and carried our sorrows. He was wounded for our iniquities; He was bruised for our sins.*[3] All this was the work of the great love which he

[1] "Tempus tuum, tempus amantium."—*Ezech.* xvi. 8.

[2] "Christus dilexit nos, et tradidit semetipsum pro nobis."—*Eph.* v. 2.

[3] "Vere languores nostros ipse tulit, et dolores nostros ipse portavit . . . ; vulneratus est propter iniquitates nostras, attritus est propter scelera nostra."—*Isa.* liii. 4, 5.

---

* The Meditations on the Passion collected in this volume are thirty in number; thirteen others are found among the Meditations suitable for all times in the year (see Vol. II.); and two of them among those that make up the Meditations for a Retreat in Vol. III. —ED.

bears us: *He hath loved us, and hath washed us in His blood.*[1] In order to wash us from the defilements of our sins, he was willing to empty his veins of all his blood, to make of it for us, as it were, a bath of salvation. O infinite mercy! O infinite love of a God!

Ah, my Redeemer, too surely hast Thou obliged me to love Thee; too surely should I be ungrateful to Thee, if I did not love Thee with my whole heart. My Jesus, I have despised Thee, because I have lived in forgetfulness of Thy love; but Thou hast not forgotten me. I have turned my back on Thee; but Thou hast come near to me. I have offended Thee, and Thou hast so many times forgiven me. I have returned to offend Thee; Thou hast returned to pardon me. Ah, my Lord, by that affection with which Thou didst love me on the cross, bind me tightly to Thee by the sweet chains of Thy love; but bind me in such wise that I may nevermore see myself separated from Thee. I love Thee, O my chief good, and I desire to love Thee ever for the time to come.

II.

That which ought most to inflame our love for Jesus Christ is not so much the death, the sorrows, and the ignominies which he suffered for us, as the end which he had in view in suffering for us so many and so great pains; and that was, to show us his love and to win our hearts: *In this have we known the charity of God, because He hath laid down His life for us.*[2] For it was not absolutely necessary in order to save us that Jesus should suffer so much and die for us; it were enough that he should pour forth but one drop of blood, should shed but

---

[1] " Dilexit nos, et lavit nos a peccatis nostris in sanguine suo."—*Apoc.* i. 5.

[2] " In hoc cognovimus charitatem Dei, quoniam ille animam suam pro nobis posuit."—*1 John*, iii. 16.

one tear only for our salvation; this drop of blood, this tear shed by a Man-God, were sufficient to save a thousand worlds: but he willed to pour out all his blood, he willed to lose his life in a sea of sorrows and contempt, to make us understand the great love which he has for us, and to oblige us to love him. *The charity of Christ urgeth us,* says St. Paul.[1] He says not the Passion or the death, but the love of Jesus Christ constrains us to love him.

And what were we that Thou, O Lord, wert willing at so great a price to purchase our love? *Christ died for all, that they too who live should not now live to themselves, but to Him who died for them.*[2] Hast Thou, then, my Jesus, died for us, that we might live wholly for Thee alone, and for Thy love? But, my poor Lord (permit me so to call Thee), Thou art so full of love that Thou hast suffered so much in order to be loved by men. But, after all, what is the number of those who love Thee? I see all these intent on loving,—some their riches, some honors, some pleasures, some their relatives, some their friends, some, in fine, the beasts; but of those who truly love Thee, who alone art worthy of love, oh, how few such do I see! O God, how few they are! Among these few, nevertheless, I too desire to be, who at one time, just like the rest, offended Thee by loving filth; now, however, I love Thee above every other good. O my Jesus! the pain which Thou hast suffered for me urgently obliges me to love Thee; but that which the more binds me to Thee and enkindles me to love Thee, is hearing of the love which Thou hast shown in suffering so much, to the end that Thou mayest be loved by me. Yes, O my Lord, most worthy of love; Thou, through love, hast given Thyself wholly to me; I, through love,

---

[1] "Charitas enim Christi urget nos."—2 *Cor.* v. 14.

[2] "Pro omnibus mortuus est Christus, ut et qui vivunt, jam non sibi vivant, sed ei qui pro ipsis mortuus est."—*Ibid.* 15.

give myself wholly to Thee. Thou for love of me didst die ; I for love of Thee am willing to die when and as it shall please Thee. Accept of my loving Thee, and help me by Thy grace to do so worthily.

III.

There is no means which can more surely kindle in us divine love than to consider the Passion of Jesus Christ. St. Bonaventure says that the wounds of Jesus Christ, because they are wounds of love, are darts which wound hearts the most hard, are flames which set on fire souls the most cold: "O wounds, wounding stony hearts, and inflaming frozen minds !"[1] It is impossible that a soul which believes and thinks on the Passion of the Lord should offend him and not love him, nay, rather that it should not run into a holy madness of love, at seeing a God, as it were, mad for love of us: "We have seen," says St. Laurence Justinian, "Wisdom infatuated by too much love."[2] Hence it is that the Gentiles, as the Apostle says, when hearing him preach the Passion of Jesus crucified, thought it a folly: *We preach Christ crucified, to the Jews indeed a scandal, but to the Gentiles foolishness.*[3] How is it possible (said they) that a God, almighty and most happy, such as he who is preached to us, could have been willing to die for his creatures ?

Ah, God enamoured of men! how is it possible (let us say this who by faith believe that he really died for love of us),—how is it possible that a goodness so great, that such a love, should remain so badly corresponded to by men ? It is wont to be said that love is repaid with love ;

[1] "O vulnera, corda saxea vulnerantia, et mentes congelatas inflammantia !"—*Stim. div. am.* p. 1, c. 1.

[2] " Vidimus Sapientiam amoris nimietate infatuatam."—*S. de Nat. D.*

[3] " Prædicamus Christum crucifixum, Judæis quidem scandalum, Gentibus autem stultitiam."—1 *Cor.* i. 23.

but Thy love—with what manner of love can it be ever repaid? It would be necessary that another God should die for Thee, to make recompense for the love which Thou hast borne towards us in dying for us. O cross, O wounds, O death of Jesus! you bind me closely to love him. O God, eternal and infinitely worthy of love, I love Thee, I desire to live only for Thee, only to please Thee; tell me what Thou willest of me, and I will wholly to do it. Mary, my hope, pray to Jesus for me.

MEDITATION FOR MONDAY.

The Sweat of Blood, and the Agony of Jesus in the Garden.

I.

Our loving Redeemer, as the hour of his death was approaching, went away into the garden of Gethsemani, in which of his own self he made a beginning of his own most bitter Passion, by giving free way to fear and weariness and sorrow, which came to torment him: *He began to fear, and to be heavy; to grow sorrowful, and to be sad.*[1] He began, then, to feel a great fear and weariness of death, and of the pains which must accompany it. At that moment there were represented to his mind most vividly the scourges, the thorns, the nails, the cross, which then, not one after the other, but all together, came to afflict him ; and specially there stood before him that desolate death which he must endure, abannoned by every comfort, human and divine ; so that, terrified by the sight of the horrid apparatus of such torments and ignominies, he besought his Eternal Father to be freed from them : *My Father, if it be possible let this chalice pass from Me.*[2] But how is this? Was it not this

---

[1] " Cœpit pavere et tædere,—contristari et mœstus esse."—*Mark*, xiv. 33: *Matt.* xxvi. 37.

[2] "Pater mi ! si possibile est, transeat a me calix iste."—*Matt.* xxvi. 39.

same Jesus who had so much desired to suffer and die for men, saying, *I have a baptism to be baptised with, and how am I straitened until it be accomplished?*[1] How, then, does he fear these pains and this death? Nay, it was with good-will he was going to die for us : but to the end, we might not suppose that through any virtue of his divinity he could die without pain, for this it was he made this prayer to his Father, to make us know that he not only died for love of us, but that the death he died was so tormenting as to terrify him greatly.

II.

And then to torment the Lord thus afflicted was added a great sorrowfulness—such that, as he said, it was enough to cause death : *My soul is sorrowful even unto death.*[2] But, Lord, to deliver Thyself from the death which men are preparing for Thee is in Thy hands, if it so please Thee ; why, then, afflict Thyself? Ah, it was not so much the torments of his Passion as our sins which afflicted the heart of our loving Saviour. He had come on earth to take away our sins ; but then, seeing that, after all his Passion, there would yet be committed such iniquities in the world, this was the pang which before dying reduced him to death, and made him sweat living blood in such abundance that the ground all round about him was bathed therewith : *And His sweat became as drops of blood running down on the earth.*[3] Yes, this precisely it was,—because Jesus then saw before him all the sins which men were going to commit after his death, all the hatred, the impurities, thefts, blasphemies, sacrileges ; and because then each

[1] " Baptismo habeo baptizari; et quomodo coarctor usque dum perficiatur ! "—*Luke*, xii. 50.

[2] " Tristis est anima mea usque ad mortem."—*Matt.* xxvi. 38.

[3] " Et factus est sudor ejus sicut guttæ sanguinis decurrentis in terram."—*Luke*, xxii. 44.

sin, with its own malice, came like a cruel wild beast to rend his heart. So that he seemed to be saying, Is this, then, O men, the recompense which you make to my love? Ah, if I could see you grateful to me, with what gladness should I now go to die; but to see, after so many pains of mine, so many sins; after so great love, so great ingratitude,—this it is which causes me to sweat blood.

Were they then my sins, my beloved Jesus, which in that hour so greatly afflicted Thee? If, then, I had sinned less, Thou wouldst have suffered less. The more pleasure I have taken in offending Thee, so much the more horror I then caused Thee. How is it that I do not die of grief in thinking that I have repaid Thy love by increasing Thy pain and sorrow? Have I, then, afflicted that heart which has so much loved me? With creatures I have been grateful enough ; with Thee only have I been ungrateful. My Jesus, pardon me; I repent with all my heart.

III.

At seeing himself burdened with our sins, Jesus *fell down on His face.*[1] He prostrated himself with his face on the earth, as ashamed to lift up his eyes to heaven, and lying in the agony of death he prayed a long time : *Being in an agony, He prayed.*[2]

At that time, my Lord, Thou didst pray for me to the Eternal Father to pardon me, offering Thyself to die in satisfaction for my sins. O my soul, how is it that thou dost not surrender thyself to such great love? How, believing this, canst thou love aught else than Jesus ? Come! cast thyself at the feet of thy Saviour in his agony, and say to him, my dear Redeemer, how is it that Thou couldst love one who had so offended Thee? How

[1] " Procidit in faciem suam."—*Matt.* xxvi. 39.
[2] " Et factus in agonia, prolixius orabat."—*Luke*, xxii. 43.

couldst Thou suffer death for me, seeing my ingratitude?
Make me, I pray Thee, partaker of this sorrow which
Thou didst feel in the garden. Now I abhor all my
sins, and unite this abhorrence to that which Thou then
hadst for them. O love of my Jesus, Thou art my love!
Lord, I love Thee, and for love of Thee I offer myself to
suffer every pain, any death. Ah, by the merits of the
agony which Thou didst suffer in the garden, give me
holy perseverance! Mary, my hope, pray to Jesus for
me.

MEDITATION FOR TUESDAY.

Jesus is made Prisoner, and is led away to the Jews.

I.

Judas arrives at the garden, and when he had betrayed
his master with a kiss, there fell on Jesus those insolent
servants, and bound him as a malefactor: *They took
Jesus and bound Him.*[1] A God bound? and wherefore?
and by whom? By his own very creatures. Angels of
heaven, what say you to this?

And Thou, my Jesus, why cause Thyself to be bound?
"O King of kings" (mourns St. Bernard), "what hast
Thou to do with chains?"[2] What can the bonds of slaves
and of the guilty have to do with Thee, the King of
kings, and the Saint of saints? But if men dare to bind
Thee, Thou who art Almighty, why dost Thou not
deliver and free Thyself from the torments which these
barbarous men provide for Thee? Ah, but it is not
these ropes which tie Thee. Thy love towards us it is
which binds Thee and condemns Thee to death.

---

[1] "Comprehenderunt Jesum, et ligaverunt eum."—*John*, xviii. 12.
[2] "O Rex regum! quid tibi et vinculis?"—*De Pass.* c. 4.

II.

Look, O man, says St. Bonaventure,[1] how these dogs illtreat Jesus: one drags him, another pushes him, another binds him, another smites him. And look how Jesus, like to a gentle lamb, without resistance suffers himself to be led to the sacrifice. And you, disciples, what are you doing? Why do you not run up to rescue him out of the hands of his enemies? Why at least do you not accompany him to defend his innocence before his judges? Ah, my God, even his disciples too, at seeing him taken and bound, take to flight and abandon him: *Then His disciples leaving Him all fled.*[2]

O my Jesus, thus abandoned, who shall ever undertake Thy defence, if these Thy most dear disciples forsake Thee? But, alas! to think that this injury ended not with Thy Passion! How many souls after having consecrated themselves to follow Thee, and after having received from Thee many special graces, have through some passion of vile interest, or human respect, or defiling pleasure, abandoned Thee! Unhappy me, of the number of these ungrateful ones am I. My Jesus, pardon me, for I wish nevermore to leave Thee. I love Thee, and desire sooner to lose my life than ever again to lose Thy grace.

III.

When brought before Caiphas, Jesus was questioned by him about his disciples and his doctrine. Jesus answered that he had not spoken in private but in public, and that those very persons who were standing round him well knew what he had taught: *I spoke openly to the*

---

[1] *Med. vit. Chr.* c. 74, 75.

[2] "Tunc discipuli ejus, relinquentes eum, omnes fugerunt."—*Mark,* xiv. 50.

world: . . . lo, these know what I said.[1] But at this answer one of the servants, treating him as if too bold,
gave him a horrible blow on the cheek, saying to him,
Dost Thou answer the high-priest so?[2] O the patience of
my Lord ! How did an answer so gentle deserve an insult so great in the presence of so many people and of
the high-priest himself, who, instead of reproving this
insolent servant, rather by his silence applauds him ?

Ah, my Jesus, Thou didst suffer all this to pay the
penalty for those affronts which I in my rashness have
done to Thee. My Love, I thank Thee for it. O Eternal Father, pardon me through the merits of Jesus. My
Redeemer, I love Thee more than myself.

IV.

Next, the iniquitous high-priest asked him whether
he were truly the Son of God. Jesus, through respect
for the divine name, affirmed that this was the truth; and
then Caiphas rent his clothes, saying that Jesus had
blasphemed, and they all cried out that he was worthy of
death: *But they answering said, He is guilty of death.*[3]

Yes, my Saviour, truly art Thou guilty of death, since
Thou art bound to make satisfaction for me who am
guilty of eternal death. But because Thou by Thy
death hast acquired life for me, it is but just that I
should spend my life wholly for Thee. I love Thee, and
desire nothing else than to love Thee. And since Thou,
who art the greatest of all kings, wert willing, through
love of me, to be despised more than all men, I, for love
of Thee, am willing to suffer every affront which can befall me. Give me, I pray Thee, strength to bear them
through the merits of the insults done to Thee.

[1] " Ego palam locutus sum mundo . . . ; ecce hi sciunt quæ dize-
rim ego."—*John*, xviii. 20, 21.

[2] " Sic respondes Pontifici ?"—*Ibid.* 22.

[3] " At illi respondentes, dixerunt: Reus est mortis."—*Matt.* xxvi.
66.

v.

The council of priests having declared Jesus Christ guilty of death, the rabble set itself to illtreat him all the night through with blows and kicks, and spitting on him as a man already declared infamous: *Then did they spit in His face, and buffeted Him.*[1] And then they mocked Him, saying, *Prophesy to us, O Christ, who it is that struck Thee.*[2]

Ah, my dear Jesus, these buffet Thee, and spit in Thy face, and Thou art silent; and as a lamb without complaining Thou sufferest all for us: *As a lamb before the shearer He shall be dumb, and shall not open His mouth.*[3] But if these know Thee not, I confess Thee for my God and Lord, and protest that I well understand that how much soever Thou innocently sufferest, it is all for love of me. I thank Thee for it, my Jesus, and love Thee with all my heart.

VI.

When day was come they led Jesus Christ to Pilate to have him condemned. Pilate, nevertheless, declared him innocent; but to rid himself of the Jews, who followed to make a tumult, he sent him to Herod, who, desiring to see some miracle through mere curiosity, began to question him about divers things. But Jesus, not deigning to answer this wicked one, was silent and gave him no answer. Wherefore this proud one offered him many insults, and especially made them clothe him as a madman in a white robe.

O eternal wisdom! O my Jesus! there lacked only this other injury, that Thou shouldst be treated as a fool. O

[1] "Tunc exspuerunt in faciem ejus, et colaphis eum ceciderunt."—*Matt.* xxvi. 67.

[2] "Prophetiza nobis, Christe, quis est qui te percussit?"—*Ibid.* 68.

[3] "Quasi agnus coram tondente se, obmutescet, et non aperuit os suum."—*Isa.* liii. 7

God! that even I in time past should have, like Herod,
thus despised Thee! Do not, I pray Thee, chastise me,
as Thou didst Herod, by depriving me of Thy voice.
Herod knew Thee not for what Thou art; but I confess
Thee for my God: Herod repented not of having injured
Thee; but I repent of it with all my heart: Herod loved
Thee not; but I love Thee above everything. Ah, deny
me not the voice of Thy inspirations. Tell me what
Thou wouldst have of me, for by Thy grace I am willing
to do all. Mary, my hope, pray to Jesus for me.

MEDITATION FOR WEDNESDAY.

The Scourging of Jesus Christ.

I.

Pilate, seeing that the Jews ceased not to demand the
death of Jesus, condemned him to be scourged: *Then
therefore Pilate took Jesus and scourged Him.*[1] The unjust
judge thought by this to quiet his enemies; but this re-
source turned out the more grievous for Jesus Christ.
The Jews, however, discovering that Pilate after thus
punishing him wished to let him go free,—as indeed he
had already sufficiently indicated, *I will chastise Him
therefore, and release Him; I will chastise Him therefore,
and let Him go,*[2]—they bribed the executioners to scourge
him to such a degree that he might die under the torment. Enter, O my soul, into the judgment-hall of
Pilate, made on this day the horrible theatre of the pain
and ignominies of thy Redeemer, and see how Jesus,
when he had arrived there, of his own accord strips himself of his clothes (as was revealed to St. Bridget)[3] and

[1] "Tune ergo apprehendit Pilatus Jesum, et flagellavit."—*John,* xix. 1.
[2] "Emendatum ergo illum dimittam;—corripiam ergo illum, et di-mittam."—*Luke* xxiii. 16, 22.
[3] *Rev.* l. 4, c. 70

embraces the column; thereby giving to men a most clear testimony how voluntarily he submitted for their sake to pains the most unmerciful, and how much he loved them. Look how this innocent Lamb goes with head bent down, and, as if all blushing through modesty, awaits this great torment. Lo, how these barbarians, like rabid dogs, already fly at him! Behold there these pitiless executioners; look how among them one strikes his breast, another his shoulders, another his thighs, and another other parts of his body; even his sacred head and beautiful face escape not from the blows. Alas! already flows that divine blood from every part; already are the scourges saturated with blood, and the hands of the executioners, the column, and even the earth. O God! the smiters, no longer finding any whole part to strike, add wound to wound, and lacerate all over that most holy Flesh; *And they have added to the grief of My wounds.*[1] O my soul! how couldst thou offend a God who was scourged for thee? And Thou, my Jesus, how couldst Thou suffer so much for one so ungrateful? O wounds of Jesus! you are my hope. O my Jesus! Thou art the only love of my soul.

II.

Exceedingly tormenting was this scourging for Jesus Christ, because there were sixty executioners (as was revealed to St. Mary Magdalen of Pazzi) succeeding one another. The scourges chosen for this work were the most severe, and every blow made a wound. The strokes, besides, reached to many thousand ; so that even the very bones of the sides of our Lord were laid bare, as was revealed to St. Bridget.[2] In a word, such was the havoc they made that Pilate thought to be able to move

---

[1] "Et super dolorem vulnerum meorum addiderunt."—*Ps.* lxviii. 27.

[2] *Rev.* l. 1, c. 10.

even his enemies to compassion ; wherefore he showed
him to them on the balcony, saying, *Behold the man.*[1] And
well did the prophet Isaias foretell to us the pitiful state
to which our Saviour was to be reduced by His scourging, saying that his flesh was to be all rent: *He was
bruised for our sins ;*[2] and his blessed body to become
like the body of one leprous—all sores: *And we accounted
Him one leprous.*[3]

Ah, my Jesus, I thank Thee for Thy great love. It
grieves me that I too joined in scourging Thee. I curse
all my sinful pleasures which cost Thee so much pain.
Make me often remember, O Lord, the love which Thou
hast borne me, to the end that I may love Thee, and
never offend Thee any more. Alas, what a special hell
should there be for me if, after having known Thy love,
and after Thou hast so often forgiven me, I should mis-
erably offend Thee afresh, and damn myself! Ah! this
very love and pity would be for me another hell still
more tormenting. No, my love, permit it not. I love
Thee, O my highest Good. I love Thee with all my
heart, and will love Thee forever.

III.

To pay the penalty, then for our crimes, and specially
of impurity, Jesus was willing to suffer this great torment in his innocent flesh: *He was wounded for our iniquities.*[4]

Is it we, then, O Lord, who have offended God, and
Thou who hast been willing to pay the penalty? Forever blessed be Thine infinite charity. What would have
been my lot, my Jesus, if Thou hadst not made satisfaction for me? Oh that I had never offended Thee! But

[1] "Ecce Homo!"—*John*, xix. 5.
[2] "Attritus est propter scelera nostra."—*Isa.* liii. 5.
[3] "Et nos putavimus eum quasi leprosum."—*Ibid.* 4.
[4] "Ipse autem vulneratus est propter iniquitates nostras."—*Ibid.* 5.

if by sinning I have despised Thy love, now I have no other desire than to love Thee and to be loved by Thee. Thou hast said that Thou lovest him who loveth Thee. I love Thee above everything; I love Thee with my whole soul : do Thou make me worthy of Thy love. Yes, I hope that Thou hast already pardoned me, and that at present Thou of Thy goodness lovest me. Ah, my dear Redeemer, bind me ever more indissolubly to Thy love: suffer me not to separate myself ever from Thee. Lo, I am all Thine; chastise me as Thou willest, but per-mit me not to remain deprived of Thy love. Make me to love Thee, and then dispose of me as pleaseth Thee. Mary, my hope, pray to Jesus for me.

MEDITATION FOR THURSDAY.

The Crowning with Thorns, and the Words " Ecce Homo" (" Behold the Man ").

I.

Not content with having horribly torn the flesh of the sacred body of Jesus Christ with the scourging, these barbarous servants, instigated by devils and by the Jews, wished to treat him as a mock king, and put upon his back a ragged scarlet robe to imitate a royal mantle, a reed in his hand by way of sceptre, and on his head a bundle of thorns plaited together instead of a crown: and in order that this crown might be not only for a mockery, but also cause him great pain, with that same reed (as St. Matthew says, *And they took the reed and struck His head*)[1] they struck the thorns till they pierced far into his head ; insomuch that the thorns, as says St. Peter Damian,[2] penetrated to the very brain, and so copious was the blood which flowed from the wounds that, as it was revealed to St. Bridget,[3] it filled the beard, the eyes,

---

[1] " Acceperunt arundinem, et percutiebant caput ejus."—*Matt.* xxvii. 30.

[2] *Serm.* 47.

[3] *Rev.* l. 4, c. 70.

and all the hair of Jesus Christ. This torment of the crowning was very painful to him, and was also the longest, since the pain of it was prolonged even till his death: and every time that the crown on his head came to be touched, the torture was always renewed.

Ah, ungrateful thorns, what are you doing? Is it thus that you torment your Creator? But what thorns? O my soul! it was thou, with thy depraved consenting to sin, who didst wound the head of thy Lord.

My dear Jesus, Thou art the king of heaven; but now Thou art become the king of reproaches and sufferings. Behold whither the love of Thy little sheep has brought Thee. O my God! I love Thee; but, alas! as long as I live I stand in peril of forsaking and denying Thee, my love, as I have done in time past. My Jesus, if Thou seest that I would ever turn to offend Thee, let me, I pray Thee, die now, since I hope to die in Thy grace. Suffer me not, I beseech Thee, ever to lose Thee again; by my faults I should worthily deserve this misfortune, but of a surety Thou deservest not to be abandoned anew by me. No, my Jesus, I desire nevermore to lose Thee.

II.

This vile crowd, not content with having so barbarously crowned Jesus Christ, wished to mock him, and to multiply fresh insults and torments; and so they bent the knee before him, and deridingly saluted him, "Hail, King of the Jews;" they spat in his face, they struck him with the palms of their hands; with cries and ridicule and contempt they vilely insult him: *And bending the knee before Him, they mocked Him, saying, Hail, King of the Jews; and spitting on Him, they gave Him blows.*[1] Ah, my Lord,

---

[1] "Et genu flexo ant: eum, illudebant ei, dicentes: Ave, Rex Judæorum! Et exspuentes in eum,—dabant ei alapas."—*Matt.* xxvii. 29; *John*, xix. 3.

to what art Thou reduced? O God, if any one had chanced to pass that way, and had seen this man thus disfigured, covered with these purple rags, with this sceptre in his hand, with this crown on his head, thus derided and illtreated by this rabble, for what could he ever have accounted him but for a man the most infamous and wicked in all the world. Behold, then, the Son of God become the mockery of Jerusalem !

Ah, my Jesus, if I look on Thy body without, I see nothing but wounds and blood. If within, in Thy heart, I find nothing else but bitterness and anguish, which make Thee suffer the agonies of death. Ah, my God, who but infinite goodness, such as Thou art, could ever have humbled himself to suffer so much for his creatures? —but creatures beloved of God, because Thou art God. These wounds which I see in Thee are all tokens of the love which Thou bearest to us. Oh, if all men could have contemplated Thee in the condition in which on that day Thou wast a spectacle of sorrow and reproach to all Jerusalem, who would not have been seized by love of Thee ? Lord, I love Thee, and give myself wholly to Thee. Behold, my blood, my life, all I offer Thee. Behold me ready to suffer and die as it pleaseth Thee. And what can I deny to Thee who hast not denied to me Thy blood and life? Deign to accept the sacrifice which a miserable sinner makes of himself, who now loves Thee with all his heart.

III.

Pilate, when Jesus was brought back to him, showed him from a balcony to the people, saying, *Behold the man.*[1] As though he would say, Behold that man whom you have brought before my tribunal, accusing him of having pretended to make himself a king; behold, this fear is at an end. Now that you have reduced him, as you see, to

[1] "Ecce Homo !"—*John*, xix. 5.

such a state that but little life can remain in him, suffer him to go and die in his own house ; oblige me not to condemn one innocent. But the Jews, being infuriated, as they had at first cried out in their frenzy, *His blood be upon us,*[1] so now they cried out, *Crucify Him, crucify Him. . . . Away, away with Him; crucify Him.*[2] But just as then Pilate was from the balcony showing Jesus to the people, so the Eternal Father from heaven was pointing out to us his Son, saying in like manner, Behold the man ! He who was promised by me as your Redeemer, and was by you so much desired; he who is my only Son, beloved by me even as myself. Behold him, for the love of you, become man, the most afflicted and despised among all men. Ah, meditate, on him, and love him.

Ah, my God ! be it so that I look upon Thy Son, and love him; but do Thou, too, look on him, and, by the merit of his sorrows and insults, pardon me all the offences which I have done against Thee. *His blood be upon us.* Let the blood of this Man-God, who is Thy Son, descend upon our souls, and obtain for us Thy mercy. I repent, O infinite goodness, of having offended Thee, and I love Thee with all my heart. But Thou knowest my weakness ; help me ; O Lord, have pity on me. Mary, my hope, pray to Jesus for me.

MEDITATION FOR FRIDAY.

The Condemnation of Jesus, and the Journey to Calvary.

I.

Pilate at length, through fear of losing the favor of Cæsar, after having so many times declared Jesus inno-cent, condemns him to die on the cross. O my most inno-cent Saviour ! (laments St. Bernard) and what crime hast

[1] "Sanguis ejus super nos."—*Matt.* xxvii. 25.
[2] "Crucifige, crucifige eum ! . . . Tolle, tolle, crucifige eum!"—*John,* xix. 6, 15.

Thou committed, that Thou must be condemned to death?
"What hast Thou done, O most innocent Saviour, that
Thou shouldst be thus judged?"[1] But I well understand (replies the saint) the sin which Thou hast committed: "Thy sin is Thy love."[2] Thy crime is the too
great love which Thou hast borne to us. This, rather
than Pilate, condemns Thee to death.

The unjust sentence is read; Jesus hears it, and altogether resigned accepts it, submitting himself to the will
of the Eternal Father, which wills him to die, and to die
on the cross, for our sins: *He humbled Himself, made obedient unto death, even the death of the cross.*[3]

Ah, my Jesus, if Thou who wast innocent didst accept
death for love of me, I, a sinner, for love of Thee, accept my death in such time and manner as it shall please
Thee.

II.

When the sentence had been read, they drag off with
fury this innocent divine Lamb; they put his own garments on him again, and, taking the cross, composed of
two rough beams, present it to him. Jesus waits not for
them to lay it on him, but of himself embraces it, kisses
and lays it upon his wounded shoulders, saying, Come,
my beloved cross, three-and-thirty years I have been going about seeking thee; on thee I desire to die for the
love of my little flock.

Ah, my Jesus! what more couldst Thou possibly have
done to lay on me the necessity of loving Thee? If one
of my servants only had offered himself to die for me,
surely he would have won my love; and how, then, can I
have lived so long a time without having loved Thee,

[1] "Quid fecisti, innocentissime Salvator, quod sic condemnareris?"
[2] "Peccatum tuum est amor tuus!"
[3] "Humiliavit semetipsum, factus obediens usque ad mortem, mortem autem crucis."—*Phil.* ii. 8.

knowing that Thou, my sovereign and only Lord, didst die to pardon me? I love Thee, O my chief Good, and because I love Thee I repent of having offended Thee.

III.

Those who had been condemned issued from the tribunal and go on the way to the place of punishment; amongst them goes also the King of heaven, with his cross on his shoulders: *And bearing His cross, He went forth to the place which is called Calvary.*[1] Go forth also, ye seraphim, from paradise, and come to accompany your Lord, who is going to the mount, to be there crucified. What a sight! A God who goes to be crucified for men! My soul, look, I pray thee, on thy Saviour, who goes to die for thee. Look on him, how he goes with head bent down, with trembling knees, all torn with wounds and dropping with live blood, with that bundle of thorns on his head, and with that load of wood on his shoulders. God! he walks with such difficulty that it seems as if at every step he would breathe forth his soul. O Lamb of God! (say thou to him) whither goest Thou? I go (he answers) to die for thee. When thou shalt see me now dead, remember (he says to thee) the love I bore to thee; remember it and love me. Ah, my Redeemer, how can I have lived for the past so forgetful of Thy love? O my sins! you have caused bitterness to the heart of my Lord, the heart which has loved me so much. My Jesus, I repent of the wrong which I have done Thee; I thank Thee for the patience which Thou hast shown me, and I love Thee. I love Thee with all my soul, and desire to love Thee alone. Remind me ever, I pray Thee, of the love Thou hast borne me, so that I may nevermore forget to love Thee.

[1] "Et bajulans sibi crucem exivit in eum, qui dicitur Calvariæ, locum."—*John*, xix. 17.

III.

Jesus Christ goes up Calvary, and invites us to follow him.

Yes, my Lord, Thou who art innocent goest before me with Thy cross. Walk on, for I will not leave Thee. Give me that cross which Thou willest, that I may embrace it, and with it I am willing to follow Thee even unto death. I wish to die together with Thee, who hast died for me. Thou commandest me to love Thee and I desire nothing else than to love Thee. My Jesus, Thou art, and shalt ever be, my only Love. Assist me to be faithful to Thee. Mary, my hope, pray to Jesus for me.

MEDITATION FOR SATURDAY.

The Crucifixion and Death of Jesus.

I.

Lo, we are on Calvary! made the theatre of divine love, where a God dies for us in a sea of sorrows. When Jesus had arrived there, they violently strip off his garments cleaving to his torn flesh, and cast him on the cross. The divine Lamb stretches himself out on this bed of death, presents his hands to the executioners, and offers to the Eternal Father the great sacrifice of his life for the salvation of men. Behold, now they nail him to the cross and raise him on it. Look, my soul, on thy Saviour, who, fastened by three hard nails, hangs from the cross, where he can find neither room nor rest. At one time he leans on his hands, at another on his feet; but where he leans, there the pain is increased.

O my Jesus! and what a bitter death is this which Thou diest? I see written over the cross, *Jesus of Nazareth, King of the Jews.*[1] But except this title of scorn, what

---

[1] "Jesus Nazarenus, Rex Judæorum."— *John,* xix. 19.

token dost Thou show of being a king? Ah, indeed, this throne of tortures, these hands pierced with nails, this head transfixed, this flesh all torn, may well make Thee known for a king, but a king of love. I draw near, then, with tenderness, to kiss these wounded feet. I embrace this cross, where Thou, made a victim of love, wouldst die a sacrifice for me. Ah, my Jesus, what would have become of me if Thou hadst not satisfied the divine justice? I thank Thee, and I love Thee.

II.

Whilst hanging on the cross, Jesus has no one who can console him. Among those who stand around him, some are blaspheming, some are deriding him; some say, *If Thou art the Son of God, descend from the cross;*[1] others, *He saved others, Himself He cannot save.*[2] And he receives no compassion even from those who are his very companions in punishment; nay, rather, one of them joins those others in blaspheming him: *One of the thieves who were hanging with Him, blasphemed Him.*[3] There stood, it is trne, below the cross, Mary assisting with love her dying Son. But the sight of this mother in her sorrows, so far from consoling Jesus, afflicted him so much the more, at seeing the pain which she endured for love of him. So, then, our Redeemer, finding no comfort here on earth, turned himself to the Eternal Father in heaven above. But the Father, seeing him covered with all the sins of mankind, for which he was making satisfaction, said, No, my Son, I cannot console Thee. It is meet that even I too should abandon Thee to Thy pains, and leave Thee to die without comfort. And then

---

[1] "Si filius Dei es, descende de cruce."—*Matt.* xxvii. 40.
[2] "Alios salvos fecit, seipsum non potest salvum facere."—*Ibid.* 42.
[3] "Unus autem de his, qui pendebant, latronibus, blasphemabat eum."—*Luke*, xxiii. 39.

i t was that Jesus cried out, *My God, My God, why hast Thou forsaken me ?* [1]

Ah, my Jesus, how do I see Thee in pains and sorrow ? Ah, too good reason hast Thou for Thy grief, to think that Thou art suffering in order to be loved by men, and yet that there should be found so few to love Thee. O sweet flames of love, which are consuming the life of a God, consume in me, I pray you, all earthly affections, and make me burn only with love for that Lord who was willing for love of me to lay down his life on an infamous gibbet. But Thou, O Lord, how couldst Thou die for me, foreseeing the injuries which I should afterwards do to Thee ? Avenge Thyself, I pray Thee, now on me, but avenge Thyself for my salvation; grant to me such a sorrow that it shall always make me sorry for the vexations which I have given Thee. Come, scourges, thorns, nails, and cross, which are so grievously tormenting my Lord, come and wound my heart, and ever remind me of the love which he has borne to me. Save me, my Jesus, and let this saving be to give me the grace of loving Thee,— to love Thee and my own salvation.

III.

The Redeemer, now nigh to expiring, with dying breath said, *It is consummated.* [2] As if he had said, O men, all has been completed and done for your redemption. Love me, then, since I have nothing more that I can do to make you love me. My soul, look up at thy Jesus who is now going to die. Look at those eyes growing dim, that face grown pale, that heart which is beating with languid pulse, that body which is now abandoning itself to death; and look at that beautiful soul which is just on the point of forsaking that sacred body. The heavens

[1] "Deus meus! Deus meus ! ut quid dereliquisti me ?"—*Matt.* xxvii. 46.

[2] "Consummatum est !"—*John,* xix. 30.

are darkened, the earth trembles, the sepulchres are opened; signs that now the maker of the world is about to die. Lo, at last Jesus, after having commended his blessed soul to his Father, first giving a deep sigh from his afflicted heart, and then bowing his head in sign of the offering of his life which at this moment he renewed for our salvation, at length, by the violence of his sorrow, expires and renders up his spirit into the hand of his beloved Father. Approach up hither, my soul, to this cross. Embrace the feet of thy dead Saviour, and think that he is dead through the love which he bore to thee.

Ah, my Jesus, to what has Thy affection towards me reduced Thee? And who, more than I, has enjoyed the fruits of Thy death? Make me, I beseech Thee, understand what love that must have been that a God should die for me, to the end that from this day forth I may love none other than Thee. I love Thee, O greatest Good; O true lover of my soul, into Thy hands I here commend it. I beseech Thee, by the merits of Thy death, make me to die to all earthly loves, in order that I may love Thee alone, who art alone worthy of all my love. Mary, my hope, pray to Jesus for me.

Hail, Jesus, our Love, and Mary, our hope!

"O riven Heart! O Love for me now crucified!
Give to my soul repose within Thy wounded side."

Eight Meditations Drawn from the Considerations on the Passion of Jesus Christ.*

FIRST MEDITATION.

The Passion of Jesus Christ is our Consolation.

Who can ever give us so much consolation in this valley of tears as Jesus crucified? What can sweeten the punctures of remorse, arising from the remembrance of our past sins, better than the consideration that Jesus Christ has voluntarily suffered death in order to atone for our sins? *He*, says the Apostle, *gave Himself for our sins.*[1]

In all the persecutions, calumnies, insults, spoliations of property and honors, which happen to us in this life, who is better able to give us strength to bear them with patience and resignation than Jesus Christ, who was despised, calumniated, and poor; who died on a cross, naked, and abandoned by all?

What more consoling in infirmities than the sight of Jesus crucified? In our sickness we find ourselves on a comfortable bed; but when Jesus was sick on the cross on which he died, he had no other bed than a hard tree, to which he was fastened by three nails; no other pillow on which to rest his head than the crown of thorns, which continued to torment him till he expired.

In our sickness, we have around our bed friends and relatives to sympathize with us and to divert us. Jesus

---

[1] " Dedit semetipsum pro peccatis nostris."—*Gal.* i. 4.

* Page 221.

died in the midst of enemies, who insulted and mocked him as a malefactor and seducer, even when he was in the very agony of death. Certainly, there is nothing so well calculated as the life of Jesus crucified to console a sick man in his sufferings, particularly if he finds himself abandoned by others. Ah, to unite, in his infirmity, his own pains to the pains of Jesus Christ is the greatest comfort that a poor sick man can enjoy.

In the anguish caused at death by the assaults of hell, the sight of past sins, and the account to be rendered in a short time at the divine tribunal, the only consolation which a dying Christian, combating with death, can have consists in embracing the crucifix, saying, My Jesus and my Redeemer, Thou art my love and my hope.

In a word, all the graces, lights, inspirations, holy desires, devout affections, sorrow for sins, good resolutions, divine love, hope of paradise, that God bestows upon us, are fruits and gifts which come to us through the Passion of Jesus Christ.

Ah, my Jesus, if Thou, my Saviour, hadst not died for me, what hope could I, who have so often turned my back upon Thee and so often deserved hell, entertain of going to behold Thy beautiful countenance in the land of bliss, among so many innocent virgins, among so many holy martyrs, among the apostles and seraphs? It is Thy Passion, then, that makes me hope, in spite of my sins, that I too will one day reach the society of the saints and of Thy holy mother, to sing Thy mercies, and to thank and love Thee forever in paradise. Such, O Jesus, my hope. "*The mercies of the Lord I will sing forever.*"[1] Mary, mother of God, pray to Jesus for me.

---

[1] "Misericordias Domini in æternum cantabo."—*Ps.* lxxxviii. 2.

SECOND MEDITATION.

The Great Obligations by which we are Bound to Love Jesus Christ.

Forget not the kindness of thy surety; for He hath given His life for thee.[1] By this surety, commentators commonly understand Jesus Christ, who, seeing that we were unable to atone to the divine justice, *offered Himself because it was His own will.*[2] He offered to make satisfaction for us, and he actually paid our debts by his blood and by his death. *He hath given His life for thee.*

To repair the insults which we offered to the divine majesty, the sacrifice of the life of all men was not sufficient: God alone could atone for an injury done to a God; and this Jesus Christ has accomplished. *By so much*, says St. Paul, *is Jesus made a surety of a better testament.*[3] By making satisfaction, as his surety, in behalf of man, our Redeemer, says the Apostle, obtained by his merits a new compact,—that if man should observe the law, God would grant him grace and eternal life. This is precisely what Jesus Christ himself expressed in the institution of the Eucharist when he said, *This chalice is the new testament in my blood.*[4] By these words he meant, that the chalice of his blood was the instrument or written security by which was established the new covenant between God and Jesus Christ, that to men who were faithful to him should be given the gift of grace and of eternal life.

[1] "Gratiam fidejussoris ne obliviscaris; dedit enim pro te animam suam."—*Ecclus.* xxix. 20.

[2] "Oblatus est, quia ipse voluit."—*Isa.* liii. 7.

[3] "In tantum melioris testamenti sponsor factus est Jesus."—*Heb.* vii. 22.

[4] "Hic calix novum testamentum est in meo sanguine."—1 *Cor.* xi. 25.

Hence, by suffering the penalties due to us, the Redeemer, through the love which he bore us, made in our behalf a rigorous atonement to the divine justice. *Surely,* says the Prophet, *He hath borne our infirmities, and carried our sorrows.*[1] And all this was the fruit of his love. *Christ hath loved us, and hath delivered Himself for us.*[2] St. Bernard says that to pardon us, Jesus Christ has not pardoned himself. "To redeem a slave he spared not himself."[3] O miserable Jews, why do you wait for the Messiah promised by the Prophets? He has already come: you have murdered him; but, in spite of your guilt, your Redeemer is ready to pardon you; for he has come to save the lost sheep of the house of Israel: *The Son of Man came to save that which was lost.*[4]

St. Paul has written that, to deliver us from the malediction due to our sins, Jesus Christ has charged himself with all the maledictions which we merited; and therefore he wished to suffer the death of the accursed, that is, the death of the cross: *Christ hath redeemed us from the curse of the law, being made a curse for us; for it is written, Cursed is every one that hangeth on a tree.*[5]

What a source of glory would it be to a poor peasant, captured by pirates, and reduced to slavery, to be ransomed by his sovereign at the cost of a kingdom! But how much greater glory do we derive from having been redeemed by Jesus Christ at the expense of his own blood, a single drop of which is worth more than a

[1] "Vere languores nostros ipse tulit, et dolores nostros ipse portavit."—*Isa.* liii. 4.

[2] "Dilexit nos, et tradidit semetipsum pro nobis."—*Eph.* v. 2.

[3] "Ut servum redimeret, sibi Filius ipse non pepercit."—*S. de Pass. D.*

[4] "Venit enim Filius hominis salvare quod perierat."—*Matt.* xviii. 11.

[5] "Christus nos redemit de maledicto legis, factus pro nobis maledictum; quia scriptum est: Maledictus omnis qui pendet in ligno."—*Gal.* iii. 13.

thousand worlds! *You were not redeemed with corruptible things as gold or silver, . . . but with the precious blood of Christ, as of a lamb unspotted and undefiled.*[1] Hence, St. Paul tells us that we commit an act of injustice against our Saviour if we dispose of ourselves according to our own, and not according to his, will, or if we reserve anything to ourselves, or, what is worse, if we indulge our inclinations so as to offend our God. For we belong not to ourselves, but to Jesus Christ who has purchased us with a great price. *Know you not that . . . you are not your own? For you are bought with a great price.*[2]

Ah, my Redeemer, if I had shed all my blood for Thee, and even given for Thee a thousand lives, what compensation would it be for the love of Thee, who hast given Thy blood and Thy life for me? Give me strength, O my Jesus, to be entirely Thine during the remainder of my life.

THIRD MEDITATION.

Jesus a Man of Sorrows.

The Prophet Isaias called our Saviour *a man of sorrows, and acquainted with infirmity.*[3] Contemplating the sorrows of Jesus Christ, Salvian exclaimed, " O love, I know not whether to call Thee sweet or severe : Thou dost appear to be both."[4] O love of my Jesus, I know not what to call Thee. Thou hast indeed been sweet towards us in loving us after so much ingratitude; but to

---

[1] " Non corruptibilibus auro vel argento redempti estis . . . , sed pretioso sanguine quasi Agni Immaculati Christi."—1 *Pet.* i. 18, 19.

[2] " An nescitis quoniam . . . non estis vestri? Empti enim estis pretio magno."—1 *Cor.* vi. 19, 20.

[3] " Virum dolorum et scientem infirmitatem."—*Isa.* liii. 3.

[4] " O Amor ! quid te appellem nescio, dulcem an asperum, utrumque esse videris."—*Ep.* 1.

Thyself Thou has been cruel to excess, in choosing a life so full of pains, and in suffering a death so full of bitterness, for the purpose of atoning for our sins.

St. Thomas, the Angelic Doctor, writes that, to save us from hell, Jesus Christ assumed extreme pain and extreme ignominy.[1] To satisfy the divine justice, it would be enough for him to have suffered any pain; but no, he wished to submit to the most galling insults and to the sharpest pains, in order to make us comprehend the malice of our sins, and the love with which his heart was inflamed for us.

He assumed extreme pain; hence, as we read in the Epistle of St. Paul to the Hebrews, he said, *A body Thou hast fitted to me.*[2] The body which God gave to Jesus Christ was made on purpose for suffering, and therefore his flesh was most sensitive and delicate. *Sensitive,* or capable of feeling pain in the most lively manner ; *delicate,* or so tender that every stroke which it received left a wound: in a word, his sacred body was made on purpose for suffering.

Besides, all the sorrows that Jesus Christ suffered till he expired on the cross were always present to his mind from the first moment of his incarnation. He saw them all, and cheerfully embraced them, in order to accomplish the will of his Father, who wished that he should be offered in sacrifice for our salvation. *Then, I said, Behold, I come: in the head of the book it is written of Me that I should do Thy will, O God.*[3] As if he said: Behold me, O my God; I cheerfully offer myself to Thee without reserve. This, according to the Apostle, was the oblation which obtained for us the divine grace. *In the which*

[1] "Assumpsit dolorem in summum, vituperationem in summum."
[2] "Corpus autem aptasti mihi."—*Heb.* x. 5.
[3] "Tunc dixi : Ecce venio, ut faciam, Deus, voluntatem tuam."—*Heb.* x. 9

will we are sanctified by the oblation of the body of Jesus Christ once.[1]

But what, O my Redeemer, induces Thee to sacrifice Thy life amid so many sorrows for our salvation. St. Paul answers: to this he was led by the love which he bore us: *Christ hath loved us, and hath delivered Himself for us.*[2] *He hath delivered Himself:* love has induced him to give up his back to the scourges, his head to the thorns, his face to the spittle and buffets, his hands and feet to the nails, and his life to death.

Let him who wishes to see a man of sorrows look at Jesus Christ. Behold him hanging on three nails; behold the entire weight of his body sustained by the wounds in his hands and feet; each member suffers its proper torment without any mitigation of pain. The three hours during which Jesus remained on the cross are justly called the three hours of the Saviour's agony; for during these three hours he suffered a continual agony and sorrow, which gradually brought him to death, and in the end took away his life; this man of sorrows died of pure pain.

And what Christian, O my Jesus, can believe that Thou hast died for him on the cross, and not love Thee? And how have I been able to live so many years in such forgetfulness of Thee, as to offend so often and so grievously a God who has loved me so intensely? Oh that I had died before I had ever offended Thee! O love of my soul! O my Redeemer! Oh that I could die for Thee, who hast died for me! I love Thee, O my Jesus, and I wish to love nothing but Thee.

[1] "In qua voluntate sanctificati sumus per oblationem corporis Jesu Christi semel."—*Heb.* x. 10.

[2] "Dilexit nos, et tradidit semetipsum pro nobis."—*Eph.* v. 2.

FOURTH MEDITATION.

Jesus Treated as the Last of Men.

We have seen Him, says the Prophet Isaias, *despised and the most abject of men, a man of sorrows.*[1] This great prodigy was once seen on earth; the Son of God, the king of heaven, the Lord of the whole world, despised as the most abject of all men.

St. Anselm[2] says that Jesus Christ wished to be humbled and despised in such a manner that it would be impossible for him to endure greater humiliations or contempt. He was treated as a person of mean condition. *Is not this,* said the Jews, *the carpenter's son?*[3] He was despised on account of his country: *Can anything good come from Nazareth?*[4] He was held up as a madman: *He is mad; why hear you Him.*[5] He was considered to be a glutton and a friend of wine: *Behold a man that is a glutton and a drinker of wine.*[6] He was called a sorcerer: *By the prince of devils He casteth out devils.*[7] And also a heretic: *Do we not say well that Thou art a Samaritan?*[8]

But during his Passion he suffered still greater insults. He was treated as a blasphemer: when he declared that he was the Son of God, Caiphas said to the other priests, *Behold, now you have heard the blasphemy: what think you?   But they answering said, He is guilty of*

---

[1] "Vidimus eum . . . despectum, et novissimum virorum, virum dolorum."—*Isa.* liii. 2, 3.

[2] *In Phil.* 2.

[3] "Nonne hic est fabri filius?"—*Matt.* xiii. 55.

[4] "A Nazareth potest aliquid boni esse?"—*John,* i. 46.

[5] "Insanit; quid eum auditis?"—*John,* x. 20.

[6] "Ecce homo devorator et bibens vinum."—*Luke,* vii. 34.

[7] "In principe dæmoniorum ejicit dæmones."—*Matt.* ix. 34.

[8] "Nonne bene dicimus, quia Samaritanus es tu?"—*John,* viii. 48.

death.[1] As soon as he was declared guilty of blasphemy, some began to spit in his face, and others to buffet him.[2] Then, indeed, was fulfilled the prediction of Isaias : *I have given My body to the strikers, and My cheeks to them that plucked them ; I have not turned away My face from them that rebuked Me and spit upon Me.*[3] He was next treated as a false prophet: *Prophesy unto us, O Christ ; who is he that struck Thee ?*[4] The injury done him by his disciple Peter, who denied him three times, and swore that he had never known him, added to the pain which our Saviour suffered from the ignominies of that night.

Let us, O devout souls, go to our afflicted Lord, in that prison in which he is abandoned by all, and accompanied only by his enemies, who contend with each other in insulting and maltreating him. Let us thank him for all that he suffers for us with so much patience : and let us console him by acts of sorrow for the insults that we have offered to him ; for, we too have treated him with contempt, and by our sins we have denied him, and declared that we knew him not.

Ah, my amiable Redeemer, I would wish to die of grief at the thought of having given so much pain to Thy heart, which has loved me so ardently. Ah, forget the great offences I have offered Thee, and look at me with that loving look which Thou didst cast on Peter after he denied Thee, and which made him bewail his sins unceasingly till death. O great Son of God, O infinite love, who dost suffer for the very men that hate

---

[1] "Ecce nunc audistis blasphemiam; quid vobis videtur? At illi respondentes dixerunt: Reus est mortis."—*Matt.* xxvi. 65, 66.

[2] "Tunc exspuerunt in faciem ejus, et colaphis eum ceciderunt; alii autem palmas in faciem ejus dederunt."—*Ibid.* 67.

[3] "Corpus meum dedi percutientibus, et genas meas vellentibus; faciem meam non averti ab increpantibus et conspuentibus in me."—*Isa.* l. 6.

[4] "Prophetiza nobis, Christe, quis est qui te percussit?"—*Matt.* xxvi. 68.

27

and maltreat Thee, Thou art adored by the angels
Thou art infinite majesty ; Thou wouldst confer a great
honor on men by permitting them to kiss Thy feet.
But, O God, how hast Thou borne on that night to be
made an object of mockery to so vile a rabble ? My despised Jesus, make me suffer contempt for Thy sake.
How can I refuse insults, when I see that Thou, my
God, hast borne so many for the love of me ? Ah, my
crucified Jesus, make me know Thee and love Thee.

Alas ! what a pity to see the contempt with which men
treat the Passion of Jesus Christ ! How few are there,
even among Christians, who reflect on the sorrows and
ignominies which this Redeemer has endured for our
sake. We barely remember in a passing way the Passion of Jesus Christ, during the last days of Holy Week,
when the Church renews the remembrance of his death
by its mournful chant, by the nakedness of its altars,
the darkness of its temples, and by the silence of its
bells. But, during the rest of the year, we think as little
of the Passion of the Redeemer as if it were a fable, or
as if he had died for others and not for us. O God !
how great must be the torture of the damned in hell
when they see all that a God has suffered for their salvation, and that they have voluntarily brought themselves to perdition !

My Jesus, do not permit me to be among the number
of the unhappy damned. No; I will never cease to
think of the love which Thou hast shown me in bearing
so many torments and ignominies for me. Help me to
love Thee, and always to remember the love that Thou
hast borne me.

FIFTH MEDITATION.
The Desolate Life of Jesus Christ.

The life of our loving Redeemer was all full of desolation, and bereft of every comfort. The life of Jesus was

that great ocean which was all bitter, without a single drop of sweetness or consolation : *For great as the sea is thy destruction.*[1] This is what was revealed by our Lord to St. Margaret of Cortona, when he said to her that in his whole life he never experienced sensible con-solation.

The sadness which he felt in the garden of Gethsem-ani was so great that it was sufficient to take away his life. *My soul,* he said, *is sorrowful even unto death.*[2] This sadness afflicted him not only in the garden, but it always filled his soul with desolation, from the first moment of his conception : for, all the pains and igno-minies which he was to suffer until death were always present to him.

But the extreme affliction which he suffered during his whole life arose not so much from the knowledge of all the sufferings he was to endure in his life, and espe-cially at death, as from the sight of all the sins which men would commit after his death. He came to abolish sin, and to save souls from hell by his death ; but, after all his cruel sufferings, he saw all the sins which men would commit ; and the sight of each sin, being clearly before his mind while he lived here below, was to him, as St. Bernadine of Sienna writes, a source of immense affliction.[3] This was the sorrow which was always be-fore his eyes, and kept him always in desolation : *My sorrow is continually before me.*[4] St. Thomas teaches that the sight of the sins of men, and of the multitude of souls that would bring themselves to perdition, excited in Jesus Christ a sorrow which surpassed the sorrow of all penitents, even of those who died of pure grief. The

[1] "Magna est enim velut mare contritio tua."—*Lam.* ii. 13.
[2] "Tristis est anima mea usque ad mortem."—*Matt.* xxvi. 38.
[3] "Ad quamlibet culpam singularem habuit aspectum."—T. 2 s. 56, a. 1, c. 1.
[4] "Dolor meus in conspectu meo semper."—*Ps.* xxxvii. 18

holy martyrs have suffered great torments; they have borne to be tortured with iron hooks, and nails, and red-hot plates: but God always sweetened their pains by interior consolations. But no martyrdom has been more painful than that of Jesus Christ; for his pain and sadness were pure, unmitigated pain and sorrow, without the smallest comfort. " The greatness of Christ's suffering," says the Angelic Doctor, "is estimated from the pureness of his pain and sadness." [1]

Such was the life of our Redeemer, and such his death, all full of desolation. Dying on the cross bereft of all comfort, he sought some one to console him, but he found none. *I looked for one . . . that would comfort Me, and I found none.* [2] He found only scoffers and blasphemers, who said to him: *If Thou be the Son of God, come down from the cross. He saved others, Himself He cannot save.* [3] Hence, our afflicted Lord, finding himself abandoned by all, turned to his Eternal Father: but seeing that his Father too had abandoned him, he cried out with a loud voice, and sweetly complained of his Father's abandonment, saying, *My God, my God, why hast Thou forsaken me ?*

Thus our Saviour terminated his life, dying, as David had foretold, immersed in a tempest of ignominies and sorrows : *I am come into the depth of the sea, and a tempest hath overwhelmed Me.* [4]

When we are in desolation, let us console ourselves by the desolate death of Jesus Christ : let us offer him our

[1] " Magnitudo doloris Christi potest considerari ex doloris et tristitiæ puritate."—P. 3, q. 46, a. 6.

[2] "Sustinui . . . qui consolaretur, et non inveni."—*Ps.* lxviii. 21.

[3] " Si Filius Dei es, descende de cruce ! . . . Alios salvos fecit, seipsum non potest salvum facere."—*Matt.* xxvii. 40–42.

[4] "Clamavit Jesus voce magna, dicens . . . Deus meus ! Deus meus ! ut quid dereliquisti me ?"—*Ibid.* 46.

[5] " Veni in altitudinem maris, et tempestas demersit me."—*Ps.* lxviii. 3.

desolation in union with that which he, an innocent
God, suffered on Calvary for the love of us.

Ah, my Jesus! who will not love Thee when he sees
Thee die in such desolation, consumed by sorrows, in
order to pay our debts? Behold me: I am one of the
executioners, who have, by my sins, so grievously
afflicted Thee during Thy whole life. But, since Thou
dost invite me to repentance, grant that I may feel at
least a part of that sorrow which Thou didst feel during
Thy Passion, for my sins. How can I, who have, by my
sins, so much afflicted Thee during Thy life, seek after
pleasures? No, I do not ask for pleasures and delights;
I ask of Thee tears and sorrow: make me, during the
remainder of my life, weep continually for the offences
that I have given Thee. I embrace Thy feet, O my
crucified and desolate Jesus: in embracing them, I wish
to die. O afflicted Mary, pray to Jesus for me.

SIXTH MEDITATION.

The Ignominies which Jesus Christ suffered in His Passion.

The greatest ignominies that Jesus Christ suffered
were those which were offered to him in his Passion.
In the first place, he then bore to see himself abandoned
by his beloved disciples; one of them betrayed him,
another denied him, and when he was captured in the
garden, all fled and abandoned him: *Then His disciples
leaving Him, all fled away.*[1] Afterwards the Jews presented him to Pilate as a malefactor who deserved to be
crucified. *If*, said they, *He were not a malefactor, we
would not have delivered Him up to thee.*[2] Herod treated
him as a fool: *Herod*, says St. Luke, *with his army, set*

---

[1] "Tunc discipuli ejus, relinquentes eum, omnes fugerunt."—*Mark*,
xiv. 50.

[2] "Si non esset hic malefactor, non tibi tradidissemus eum."—
John, xviii. 30.

Him at nought and mocked Him, putting on Him a white garment.[1]

Barabbas, a robber and murderer, was preferred before him. When Pilate gave the Jews the choice of rescuing Jesus Christ or Barabbas from death, they exclaimed, *Not this man, but Barabbas.*[2] He was chastised with the lash, a punishment inflicted only on slaves : *Then, therefore,* says John, *Pilate took Jesus and scourged Him.*[3] He was treated as a mock king; for after having through mockery crowned him with thorns, they salute him as king and spit in his face : *They mocked Him, saying, Hail, King of the Jews. And spitting upon Him, they took the reed, and struck His head.*[4] He was afterwards, as Isaias had foretold, condemned to die between two malefactors : *He was reputed with the wicked.*[5]

Finally, he died on the cross : that is the most opprobrious death which was then inflicted on malefactors, for the man whom the Jews condemned to the death of the cross was, as we read in Deuteronomy,[6] said to be an object of malediction to God and man. Hence, St. Paul has said, *Being made a curse for us* (that is, a mere curse), *for it is written, Cursed is every one that hangeth on a tree.*[7] Our Redeemer, says the same Apostle, renouncing the life of splendor and happiness which he might enjoy

[1] "Sprevit autem illum Herodes cum exercitu suo, et illusit indutum veste alba."—*Luke,* xxiii. 11.

[2] "Clamaverunt ergo rursum omnes, dicentes: Non hunc, sed Barabbam."—*John,* xviii. 40.

[3] "Tunc ergo apprehendit Pilatus Jesum, et flagellavit."—*John,* xix. 1.

[4] "Illudebant ei, dicentes: Ave Rex Judæorum! Et exspuentes in eum, acceperunt arundinem, et percutiebant caput ejus."—*Matt.* xxvii. 29, 30.

[5] "Et cum sceleratis reputatus est."—*Isa.* liii. 12.

[6] *Deut.* xxi. 23.

[7] "Factus pro nobis maledictum; quia scriptum est: Maledictus omnis qui pendet in ligno."—*Gal.* iii. 13

on this earth, chose for himself a life full of tribulations, and a death accompanied with so much shame : *Who, having joy set before Him, endured the cross, despising the shame.*[1]

Thus in Jesus Christ was fulfilled the prediction of Jeremias, that he should live and die saturated with opprobrium. *He shall give His cheek to him that striketh Him, He shall be filled with reproaches.*[2] Hence St. Bernard exclaims, O grandeur! O abasement![3] Behold the Lord, who is exalted above all, become the most contemptible of all. The holy Doctor then concludes that all this proceeded from the love which Jesus Christ bore us.[4]

O my Jesus! save me ; do not permit me, after being redeemed by Thee with so much pain and so much love, to lose my soul and go to hell, there to hate and curse the very love which Thou hast borne me. This hell I have indeed so often deserved ; for, though Thou couldst do nothing more than Thou hast done to oblige me to love Thee, I have done everything in my power to compel Thee to chastise me. But since, in Thy goodness, Thou hast waited for me, and even still dost continue to ask me to love Thee, I wish to love Thee: I wish henceforth to love Thee with my whole heart and without reserve. Give me strength to make this wish effective. O Mary, mother of God, assist me by thy prayers.

[1] "Qui, proposito sibi gaudio, sustinuit crucem, confusione contempta."—*Heb.* xii. 2.

[2] "Dabit percutienti se maxillam, saturabitur opprobriis."—*Lam.* iii. 30.

[3] "O novissimum et altissimum ! Opprobrium hominum et gloriam Angelorum."—*S. de Pass. D.*

[4] "Itane summus omnium imus factus est omnium? O Amoris vim ! quis hoc fecit ? Amor !"—*In Cant.* s. 64.

SEVENTH MEDITATION.

Jesus on the Cross.

Jesus on the cross! What a spectacle to the angels in heaven to see a God crucified! And what sentiments should we conceive at the sight of the king of heaven hanging on a gibbet, covered with wounds, agonizing, and dying of pure unmitigated pain!

O God! why does this divine Saviour, this innocent and saint, suffer such torments? Ah, he suffers them to expiate the sins of men. And who has ever seen such an example: the Lord suffering for his slaves, the shepherd dying for his sheep, the Creator immolated and offered as a holocaust for his creatures.

Jesus on the cross! Behold the man of sorrows[1] foretold by Isaias. Behold him on that infamous tree, full of exterior and interior sorrows. In his body he is torn with scourges, thorns, and nails: blood flows from every wound, and each member suffers its proper torment. In his soul he is afflicted with sadness and desolation; he is abandoned by all, even by his very Father. But what tormented him most severely was the horrid sight of all the sins that the very men, redeemed by his blood, would commit after his death.

Ah, my Redeemer, among these ungratful men Thou didst see me, and all my sins. Then I too had a great part in all Thy afflictions on the cross, when Thou wast dying for me. Oh that I had been dead, and had never offended Thee!

My Jesus and my hope! death terrifies me, because I know that I shall then have to render an account of all the insults that I have offered to the love which Thou hast borne me. But Thy death encourages me, and makes me hope for pardon. I am sorry with my whole

[1] "Virum dolorum."—*Isa.* liii. 3.

heart for having insulted Thee. If I have not hitherto
loved Thee, I now wish to love Thee during all the remaining days of my life, and I wish to do and suffer all
things in order to please Thee. O my Redeemer, who
died on a cross for me, assist me.

Lord Thou hast said that when Thou wouldst be exalted on the cross, Thou wouldst draw all hearts to Thee.
*And I, if I be lifted up from the earth, will draw all things
to myself.*[1] By dying on the cross for us, Thou hast already drawn to Thy love so many who, for Thy sake,
have forsaken all things, their goods, their country, their
relatives, and their life. Ah, draw also my poor heart,
which, through Thy grace, now pants to love Thee; do
not permit me to love mire, as I have hitherto done. O
my Redeemer, that I could see myself stripped of every
wordly affection, so as to forget all things, to remember
only Thee, and to love Thee alone! I hope for all things
from Thy grace. Thou knowest my inability to do any
good: through the love which made Thee submit to so
cruel a death on Calvary for my sake, I pray Thee to
assist me. O death of Jesus, O love of Jesus, take possession of all my thoughts and affections, and grant that,
for the future, to please Thee, O Jesus, may be the sole
object of all my thoughts and desires. O most amiable
Lord, hear my prayer, through the merits of Thy death.

Do thou too, O Mary, who art the mother of mercy,
hear me: pray to Jesus for me. Thy prayers can make me
a saint. Such my hope.

EIGHTH MEDITATION.

Jesus Dead on the Cross.

O Christian, lift up your eyes, and behold Jesus dead
on that gibbet: look at his body full of wounds, stream-

[1] "Et ego, si exaltatus fuero a terra, omnia traham ad meipsum."—
John, xii. 32.

ing blood. Faith teaches you that he is your Creator, your Saviour, your life, your deliverer; and that he, whose love for you exceeds the love of all others, is the only being that can make you happy.

Yes, my Jesus, I believe it; Thou hast loved me from eternity, without any merit of mine; and even with the foreknowledge of my frequent ingratitude, Thou hast, through Thy own goodnes, given me existence. Thou art my Saviour, who, by Thy death, hast delivered me from hell, which I have so often deserved. Thou art my life, by the grace which Thou hast given me, without which I should have remained dead in hell. Thou art my Father, and a loving Father, who hast pardoned me with so much mercy the many insults that I have offered Thee. Thou art my treasure, enriching me with so many lights and favors, instead of chastising me as I deserved. Thou art my hope; for I can hope for no good from any one but from Thee. Thou art my true and only lover: it is enough to say that Thou hast even died for me. In fine, Thou art my God, my sovereign good, my all.

O men, O men, let us love Jesus Christ, let us love a God who sacrificed himself entirely for the love of us. He has sacrificed the honors which were due to him on this earth, he has sacrificed all the riches and pleasures that he could have enjoyed, and was content to lead an abject life in poverty and tribulations; and finally in order to atone by his sufferings for our sins, he has voluntarily sacrificed his blood and his life, dying in an ocean of sorrows and ignominies.

Son, exclaims the Redeemer from the cross to each of us,—son, what more could I do than die for you, in order to gain your love? See if any one in this world has loved you more than I, your Lord and God, have loved you. Love me, then, at least in return for the love which I have borne you.

Ah, my Jesus, how can I remember that my sins have

made Thee die through pain on an infamous gibbet, and
not weep unceasingly for having thus despised Thy love?
And how can I behold Thee hanging on this cross for
my sake, and not love Thee with all my strength?

But, O Lord, how does it happen that Thou hast died
for all, that no one might live any longer to himself, and
that afterwards, instead of living, only to love Thee and
give Thee glory, I have lived only to afflict and dishonor
Thee? *Christ died for all, that they also who live may not
now live to themselves, but unto him who died for them and
rose again.*[1]

Ah, my crucified Lord, forget the insults that I have
given Thee; I am sincerely sorry for them: draw me, by
Thy grace, entirely to Thyself. I wish to live no longer to
myself, but only to Thee, who hast loved me so tenderly,
and who dost merit all my love. I give Thee myself and
all that I possess, without reserve. I renounce all the
honors and pleasures of this life, and I offer myself to
suffer for Thy sake whatsoever Thou pleasest. I entreat
Thee, who dost give me this good will, to grant me
strength to execute it. O Lamb of God, immolated on
the cross, O victim of love, O enamoured God, that I
could die for Thee as Thou hast died for me!

O Mary, mother of God! obtain for me the grace to
sacrifice all the remaining moments of my life to the love
of Thy most amiable Son.

[1] "Pro omnibus mortuus est Christus, ut et qui vivunt, jam non
sibi vivant, sed ei qui pro ipsis mortuus est et resurrexit."—2 *Cor.*
v. 15.

Fifteen Meditations on the Passion of Jesus Christ,

TO BE MADE DURING THE FIFTEEN DAYS BEGINNING ON THE SATURDAY BEFORE PASSION SUNDAY, AND ENDING ON HOLY SATURDAY.

MEDITATION I.

FOR SATURDAY BEFORE PASSION SUNDAY.

Jesus makes His Triumphant Entry into Jerusalem.

I.

The time of his Passion being now at hand, our Redeemer departs from Bethany to go to Jerusalem. On drawing nigh to that ungrateful city, he beheld it, and wept: *Beholding the city, He wept over it.*[1] He wept because he foresaw its ruin, which would be the consequence of the stupendous crime of taking away the life of the Son of God, of which that people would shortly become guilty. Ah, my Jesus, when Thou wert then weeping over that city Thou wert weeping also over my soul, beholding the ruin which I have brought upon myself by my sins, constraining Thee to condemn me to hell, even after Thy having died to save me. Oh, leave it to me to weep over the great evil of which I have been guilty in despising Thee, the greatest of all good, and do Thou have mercy upon me.

II.

Jesus Christ enters the city : the people go forth to meet him ; they receive him with acclamations and rejoicings ; and, in order to do him honor, some of them strew branches of palms along the road, whilst others

---

[1] "Videns civitatem, plevit super illam."—*Luke*, xix. 41.

spread out their garments for him to pass over. Oh, who would ever then have said that that Lord, now recognized as the Messias, and welcomed with so many demonstrations of respect, the next time that he appeared along the self-same ways would be under sentence of death, and with a cross upon his shoulders? Ah, my beloved Jesus, these people now receive Thee with acclamations, saying, *Hosanna to the Son of David! Blessed is he that cometh in the name of the Lord!*[1] Glory to the Son of David! Blessed be he who cometh in the name of God for our salvation! And then they will raise their voices insultingly to Pilate to take Thee out of the world, and cause Thee to die upon a cross: *Away with Him! away with Him! crucify Him!*[2] Go, my soul, and do Thou too lovingly say to him, *Blessed is he that cometh in the name of the Lord!* Blessed forever be Thou that art come, O Saviour of the world! for, otherwise, we had all been lost. O my Saviour, save me!

III.

When the evening, however, was come, after all those acclamations, there was no one found who would invite him to lodge in his house; so that he was obliged to retrace his steps to Bethany.

O my beloved Redeemer, if others will not give Thee a welcome, I desire to welcome Thee into my poor heart. At one time, I, unhappily, expelled Thee from my soul; but I now prize to have Thee with me more than the possession of all the treasures of earth. I love Thee, O my Saviour; what power shall ever be able to separate me from my love of Thee? Sin only; but from this sin it is Thine to deliver me, by Thy help, O my Jesus; and thine too, by thy intercession, O Mary, my Mother.

[1] "Hosanna Filio David! benedictus qui venit in nomine Domini!"—*Matt.* xxi. 9.

[2] "Tolle, tolle, crucifige eum!"—*John,* xix. 15.

MEDITATION II.

FOR PASSION SUNDAY.

Jesus prays in the Garden.

I.

Jesus, knowing that the hour of his Passion had now come, after having washed the feet of his disciples and instituted the most Holy Sacrament of the Altar,— wherein he left us his whole self,—goes to the Garden of Gethsemani, whither he knew already that his enemies would come to take him. He there betakes himself to prayer, and lo! he finds himself assailed by a great dread, by a great repugnance, and by a great sadness: *He began to be afraid, to be weary, and sorrowful.*[1] There came upon him, first, a great dread of the bitter death which he would have to suffer on Calvary, and of all the anguish and desolations by which it would be accompanied. During the actual course of his Passion, the scourges, the thorns, the nails, and the rest of his tortures came upon him but one at a time ; whereas, in the garden, they all came upon him together at once, crowding into his memory in order to torment him. For his love of us he embraced them all ; but in embracing them, he trembles and is in agony: *Being in an agony, He prayed the longer.*[2]

II.

There comes upon him, moreover, a great repugnance to that which he has to suffer ; so that he prays his Father to deliver him from it: *My Father, if it be possible, let this chalice pass away from Me.*[3] He prayed thus to teach

---

[1] "Cœpit pavere et tædere,—contristari et mœstus esse."—*Mark,* xiv. 33 ; *Matt.* xxvi. 37.

[2] "Factus in agonia, prolixius orabat."—*Luke,* xxii. 43.

[3] "Pater mi ! si possibile est, transeat a me calix iste."—*Matt.* xxvi. 39.

us that in our tribulations we may indeed beg of God to
deliver us from them ; but we ought at the same time to
refer ourselves to his will, and to say, as Jesus then
said, *Not, however, as I will, but as Thou wilt.*[1] Yes, my
Jesus, Thy will, not mine, be done. I embrace all the
crosses that Thou wilt send me. Thou, innocent as
Thou art, hast suffered so much for love of me ; it is
but just that I, who am a sinner, and deserving of hell,
should suffer for love of Thee that which Thou dost
ordain.

III.

There came upon him, likewise, a sadness so great
that it would have been enough to cause him to die, had
he not, of himself, kept death away, in order to die for
us after having suffered more : *My soul is sorrowful even
unto death.*[2] This great sadness was occasioned by the
sight of the future ungratefulness of men, who, instead
of corresponding to so great a love on his part, would
offend him by so many sins, the sight of which caused
him to sweat in streams of blood: *And his sweat became as
drops of blood trickling down upon the ground.*[3]

So, then, O my Jesus, it is not the executioners, the
scourges, the thorns, or the cross that have been so
cruel : the cruelty lies in my sins, which afflicted Thee
so much in the garden. Do Thou give me, then, a share
of that sorrow and abhorrence which Thou didst experience in the garden, that so, even to my death, I may
bitterly weep for the offences that I have given Thee.
I love Thee, O my Jesus : do Thou receive with kindness a sinner who wishes to love Thee. Recommend
me, O Mary, to this thy Son, who is in affliction and
sadness for love of me.

[1] " Verumtamen, non sicut ego volo, sed sicut tu."—*Matt.* xxvi. 39.
[2] " Tristis est anima mea usque ad mortem."—*Mark,* xiv. 34.
[3] " Et factus est sudor ejus sicut guttæ sanguinis decurrentis in terram.'·—*Luke,* xxii. 44.

MEDITATION III.

Jesus is apprehended, and led before Caiphas.

I.

The Lord, knowing that the Jews who were coming to take him were now at hand, rose up from prayer, and went to meet them ; and so, without reluctance, he lets them take him and bind him : *They apprehended Jesus, and bound Him.*[1] O amazement ! A God bound as a criminal by his own creatures ! Behold, my soul, how some of them seize hold of his hands ; others put the handcuffs on him ; and others smite him ; and the innocent Lamb lets himself be bound and struck at their will, and says not a word: *He was offered because it was His own will, and opened not his mouth. He is led as a sheep to the slaughter.*[2] He neither speaks nor utters complaint, since he had himself already offered himself up to die for us ; and, therefore, did that Lamb let himself be bound and led to death without opening his mouth.

II.

Jesus enters Jerusalem bound. Those who were asleep in their beds, at the noise of the crowd passing by, awake, and inquire who that might be whom they are taking along in custody ; and they are told in reply, " It is Jesus of Nazareth, who has been found out to be an impostor and seducer." They bring him up before Caiphas, who is pleased at seeing him, and asks him about his disciples, and about his doctrine. Jesus replies that he has spoken openly ; so that he calls upon the Jews themselves, who were standing around him, to bear their tes-

---

[1] "Comprehenderunt Jesum, et ligaverunt eum."—*John,* xviii. 12.
[2] "Oblatus est, quia ipse voluit, et non aperuit os suum ; sicut ovis ad occisionem ducetur."—*Isa.* liii. 7.

28

timony as to what he has said : *Behold, these know what I have said.*[1] But upon this reply, one of the officials of the court gives him a blow in the face, saying, *Dost Thou answer the high-priest so?*[2] But, O God, how does a reply, so humble and gentle, deserve so great an insult?

Ah, my Jesus, Thou dost suffer it all in order to pay the penalty of the insults that I have offered to Thy heavenly Father.

III.

The high-priest, in the next place, conjures him, in the name of God, to say whether he be truly the Son of God. Jesus answered in the affirmative, that such he was; and Caiphas, on hearing this, instead of prostrating himself upon the floor to adore his God, rends his garments, and, turning to the other priests, says, *What more need have we of witnesses? Behold, ye have now heard His blasphemy: what is your opinion?* And they unanimously replied, *He is guilty of death.*[3] And then, as the Evangelists relate, they all began to spit in his face, and to abuse him, and slapping him with their hands, and striking him with their fists; and then, tying a piece of cloth over his face, they turned him into ridicule, saying, *Prophesy to us, Thou Christ; who is it that smote Thee?* Thus writes St. Matthew. And St. Mark writes, *And some began to spit upon Him, and to cover His face, and to deal upon Him blows, and to say to Him, Prophesy. And the officers did smite Him with the palms of their hands.*[4]

[1] "Ecce hi sciunt quæ dixerim ego."—*John*, xviii. 21.
[2] "Sic respondes Pontifici?—*Ibid.* 22.
[3] "Quid adhuc egemus testibus? Ecce, nunc audistis blasphemiam! Quid vobis videtur? At illi respondentes, dixerunt: Reus est mortis!"—*Matt.* xxvi. 65, 66.
[4] "Prophetiza nobis, Christe, quis est qui te percussit?—Tunc cœperunt quidam conspuere eum, et velare faciem ejus, et colaphis eum cædere, et dicere ei : Prophetiza. Et ministri alapis eum cædebant."—*Matt.* xxvi. 68; *Mark*, xiv. 65.

Behold Thyself, O my Jesus, become, upon this night, the butt of the rabble. And how can men see Thee in such humiliation for love of them, and not love Thee? And how have I been able to go so far as to outrage Thee by so many sins, after that Thou hast suffered so much for me? Forgive me, O my love, for I will not displease Thee more. I love Thee, my supreme Good, and I repent above every other evil of having despised Thee. O Mary, my Mother, pray thy ill-treated Son to pardon me.

MEDITATION IV.

FOR PASSION TUESDAY.

Jesus is led before Pilate and Herod, and then has Barabbas preferred before Him.

I.

The morning being come, they lead Jesus to Pilate, that he may pronounce upon him the sentence of death. But Pilate is aware that Jesus is innocent, and, therefore, he tells the Jews that he can find no reason why he should condemn him. However, on seeing them obstinate in their desire for his death, he referred him to the court of Herod. Herod, on seeing Jesus before him, desired to see some one of the Lord's great miracles, of which he had heard accounts, wrought in his presence, The Lord would not vouchsafe so much as an answer to the questions of that audacious man. Alas for that poor soul to which God speaks no more!

O my Redeemer, such, too, were my deserts, for not having obeyed so many calls of Thine; I deserved that Thou shouldst not speak to me more, and that Thou shouldst leave me to myself: but no, my Jesus, Thou hast not abandoned me yet. Speak to me, then: *Speak, Lord, for Thy servant heareth;*[1] tell me what Thou desirest of me, for I will do all to please Thee.

[1] "Loquere, Domine, quia audit servus tuus."—1 *Reg.* iii. 10.

II.

Herod, seeing that Jesus gave him no **answer**, drove him away from his house with scorn, turning him into ridicule with all the persons of his court; and in order to load him with the greater contempt, he had him clothed in a white garment, so treating him like a fool; and thus he sent him back again to Pilate : *He despised and mocked Him, putting on Him a white garment, and sent Him again to Pilate.*[1] Behold how Jesus, clad in that robe which makes him a laughing-stock, is borne on along the streets of Jerusalem. O my despised Saviour, this additional wrong, of being treated as a fool, was still wanting to Thee ! If, then, the divine wisdom is so treated by the world, happy is he who cares nothing for the world's approbation, and desires nothing but to know Jesus crucified, and to love sufferings and con-tempt, saying, with the Apostle: *For I judged not myself to know anything among you, but Jesus Christ, and Him cruci-fied.*[2]

III.

The Jews had the right of demanding from the Roman Governor the liberation of a criminal on the feast of the Passover. Pilate, therefore, asked the peo-ple which of the two they would wish to have liberated, Jesus or Barabbas: *Whom will you that I release to you, Barabbas or Jesus?*[3] Barabbas was a wicked wretch, a murderer, a thief, and held in abhorrence by all : Jesus was innocent ; but the Jews cry aloud for Barabbas to to live, and for Jesus to die.

[1] "Illusit indutum veste alba, et remisit ad Pilatum."—*Luke*, xxiii. 11.

[2] "Non enim judicavi me scire aliquid inter vos, nisi Jesum Chris-tum, et hunc crucifixum."—1 *Cor.* ii. 2.

[3] "Quem vultis dimittam vobis, Barabbam an Jesum?"—*Matt.* xxvii. 17.

Ah, my Jesus, so too have I said, whenever I have deliberately offended Thee for some satisfaction of my own, preferring before Thee that miserable pleasure of mine, and, in order not to lose it, contenting myself to lose Thee, O infinite Good. But now I love Thee above every other good, and more than my life itself. Have compassion upon me, O God of mercy. And do thou, O Mary, be my advocate.

MEDITATION V.

FOR PASSION WEDNESDAY.

Jesus is scourged at the Pillar.

I.

Then, Pilate, therefore, took Jesus and scourged Him.[1] O thou unjust judge, thou hast declared him innocent, and then thou dost condemn him to so cruel and so ignominious a punishment! Behold, now, my soul, how, after this unjust decree, the executioners seize hold of the divine Lamb ; they take him to the pretorium, and bind him with ropes to the pillar.

O ye blessed ropes that bound the hands of my sweet Redeemer to that pillar, bind likewise this wretched heart of mine to his divine heart, that so I may, from this day forth, neither seek for, nor desire, anything but what he doth wish.

II.

Behold how they now lay hold of the scourges, and, at a given sign, begin to strike, in every part, that sacred flesh, which at first assumes a livid appearance, and then is covered all over with blood, that flows from every pore. Alas, the scourges and the executioners' hands

---

[1] "Tunc ergo apprehendit Pilatus Jesum, et flagellavit."—*John,* xix. 1.

are all now dyed in blood ; and with blood is the ground all drenched. But, O God, through the violence of the blows, not only does the blood, but pieces of the very flesh, of Jesus Christ go flying through the air. That divine body is already but one mass of wounds ; and yet do those barbarians continue to add blow to blow and pain to pain. And all this while, what is Jesus doing? He speaks not ; he complains not ; but patiently endures that great torture in order to appease the divine justice, that was wroth against us : *As a lamb before the shearer is dumb, so opened He not His mouth.*[1] Go quickly, O my soul, go and wash thyself in that divine blood.

My beloved Saviour, I behold Thee all torn in pieces for me; no longer, therefore, can I doubt that Thou dost love me, and love me greatly, too. Every wound of Thine is a sure token on Thy part of Thy love, which with too much reason demands my love. Thou, O my Jesus, dost, without reserve, give me Thy blood; it is but just that I, without reserve, should give Thee all my heart. Do Thou, then, accept of it, and make it to be ever faithful.

III.

O my God, had Jesus Christ not suffered more than a single blow for love of me, I ought yet to have been burning with love for him, saying, A God hath been willing to be struck for me! But no: he contented not himself with a single blow ; but, to pay the penalty due to my sins, he was willing to have his whole body torn to shreds, as Isaias had already foretold : *He was bruised for our iniquities;*[2] and that even until he looked like a leper covered with wounds from head to foot: *And we thought Him to be, as it were, a leper.*[3] While, then, O my

---

[1] "Sicut agnus coram tondente se sine voce, sic non aperuit os suum."—*Acts*, viii. 32.

[2] "Attritus est propter scelera nostra."—*Isa.* liii. 5.

[3] "Et nos putavimus eum quasi leprosum."—*Ibid.* 4.

soul, Jesus was being scourged, he was thinking of thee, and offering to God those bitter sufferings of his, in order to deliver thee from the eternal scourges of hell. O God of love, how have I been able to live so many years, in time past, without loving Thee? O ye wounds of Jesus, wound me with love towards a God who has loved me so much! O Mary, O Mother of graces, do thou gain for me this love!

MEDITATION VI.

FOR PASSION THURSDAY.

Jesus is crowned with Thorns, and treated as a Mock King.

I.

When the soldiers had finished the scourging of Jesus Christ, they all assembled together in the pretorium, and, stripping his own clothes off him again, in order to turn him into ridicule, and to make him into a mock king, they put upon him an old ragged mantle, of a reddish color, to represent the royal purple; in his hand a reed, to represent a sceptre; and upon his head a bundle of thorns, to represent a crown, but fashioned like a helmet, so as to fit close upon the whole of his sacred head. *Stripping Him, they put a scarlet cloak about Him, and plaiting a crown of thorns they put it upon His head, and a reed in His right hand.*[1] And when the thorns, by the pressure of their hands alone, could not be made to penetrate deeper into that divine head which they were piercing, with the self-same reed, and with all their might, they battered down that barbarous crown: *And spitting upon Him, they took the reed, and struck His head.*[2] O ungrate-

---

[1] "Exuentes eum, chlamydem coccineam circumdederunt ei; et plectentes coronam de spinis, posuerunt super caput ejus, et arundinem in dextera ejus."—*Matt.* xxvii. 28, 29.

[2] "Et exspuentes in eum, acceperunt arundinem, et percutiebant caput ejus."—*Ibid.* 30.

ful thorns, do you thus torture your Creator? But
what thorns? what thorns? You, ye wicked thoughts
of mine; it is you that have pierced the head of my
Redeemer.

I detest, O my Jesus, and I abhor, more than I do
death itself, the evil consent by which I have so often
grieved Thee, my God, who art so good. But since
Thou dost make me know how much Thou hast loved me,
Thee alone will I love, Thee alone.

II.

O my God! how the blood is now streaming down
from that pierced head over the face and the breast of
Jesus!

And Thou, my Saviour, dost not even utter a complaint of such unjust cruelties! Thou art the King of
heaven and of earth; but now. my Jesus, Thou art
brought down so low as to appear before us a king of
derision and of sorrows, being made the laughing-stock
of all Jerusalem. But the prophecy of Jeremias had to
be fulfilled, that Thou wouldst one day have Thy fill of
sorrows and shame: *He will give His cheek to the smiter,
He will be satiated with reproaches.*[1] O Jesus, my love! in
time past I have despised Thee; but now I prize Thee,
and I love Thee with all my heart, and I desire to die
for love of Thee.

III.

But no; these men for whom Thou art suffering have
not yet their fill of torturing and making game of Thee.
After having thus tortured Thee, and dressed Thee up
as a mock king, they bend their knee before Thee, and
scornfully address Thee: *Hail to Thee, O King of the
Jews.* And then, with shouts of laughter, they deal out

[1] "Dabit percutienti se maxillam, saturabitur opprobriis."—*Lam.*
iii. 30.

more blows upon Thee, thus rendering twofold the anguish of the head already pierced by the thorns : *And bowing the knee before Him, they derided Him, saying, Hail, King of the Jews; and they gave Him blows.*[1] Do thou at least go, O my soul, and recognize Jesus for what he is, the King of kings, and Lord of lords; and return thanks to him, and love him, now that thou beholdest him become, for love of Thee, the king of sorrows. O my Lord, keep not in Thy remembrance the griefs which I have caused Thee. I now love Thee more than myself. Thou only dost deserve all my love, and, therefore, Thee only do I wish to love. I fear, on account of my weaknesses ; but it is for Thee to give me the strength to execute my desire. And thou, too, O Mary, must help me by thy prayers.

MEDITATION VII.

For Passion Friday.

Pilate exhibits Jesus to the People, saying, "Behold the Man!"

I.

Jesus having again been brought and set before Pilate, he beheld him so wounded and disfigured by the scourges and the thorns that he thought, by showing him to them, to move the people to compassion. He therefore went out into the portico, bringing with him the afflicted Lord, and said, *Behold the Man!*[2] As though he would say, Go now, and rest content with that which this poor innocent one has already suffered. Behold him brought to so low a state that he cannot long survive. Go your way, and leave him, for he can but have

[1] "Et genu flexo ante eum, illudebant ei, dicentes : Ave, Rex judæorum !—et dabant ei alapas."—*Matt.* xxvii. 29; *John,* xix. 3.

[2] "Ecce homo !"—*John,* xix. 5.

a short time to live. Do thou too, my soul, behold thy Lord in that portico, bound and half naked, covered only with wounds and blood; and consider to what thy Shepherd has reduced himself, in order to save thee, a sheep that was lost.

II.

At the same time that Pilate is exhibiting the wounded Jesus to the Jews, the Eternal Father is from heaven inviting us to turn our eyes to behold Jesus Christ in such a condition, and in like manner says to us, *Behold the Man!* O men, this man whom you behold thus wounded and set at naught, he is my beloved Son, who is suffering all this in order to pay the penalty of your sins; behold him, and love him. O my God and my Father, I do behold Thy Son, and I thank him, and love him, and hope to love him always; but do Thou, I pray Thee, behold him also, and for love of this Thy Son have mercy upon me; pardon me, and give me the grace never to love anything apart from Thee.

III.

But what is it that the Jews reply, on their beholding that king of sorrows? They raise a shout and say, *Crucify, crucify Him!*[1] And seeing that Pilate, notwithstanding their clamor, was seeking a means to release him, they worked upon his fears by telling him: *If thou release this Man, thou art not Cæsar's friend.*[2] Pilate still makes resistance, and replies, *Shall I crucify your King?* And their answer was, *We have no king but Cæsar.*[3]

Ah, my adorable Jesus, these men will not recognize Thee for their King, and tell Thee that they wish for no other king but Cæsar. I acknowledge Thee to be my

[1] "Crucifige, crucifige eum!"—*John*, xix. 6.
[2] "Si hunc dimittis, non es amicus Cæsaris."—*Ibid.* 12.
[3] "Non habemus regem, nisi Cæsarem."—*Ibid.* 15.

King and God; and I protest that I wish for no other king of my heart but Thee, my love, and my one and only good. Wretch that I am! I at one time refused Thee for my King, and declared that I did not wish to serve Thee; but now I wish Thee alone to have dominion over my will. Do Thou make it obey Thee in all that Thou dost ordain. O will of God, thou art my love. Do thou, O Mary, pray for me. Thy prayers are not rejected.

MEDITATION VIII.

FOR PASSION SATURDAY.

Jesus is condemned by Pilate.

I.

Behold, at last, how Pilate, after having so often declared the innocence of Jesus, declares it now anew, and, protesting that he is innocent of the blood of that just man,—*I am innocent of the Blood of this Just Man*,[1] after all this he pronounces the sentence, and condemns him to death. Oh, what injustice—such as the world has never seen! At the very time that the judge declares the accused one to be innocent, he condemns him. Ah, my Jesus, Thou dost not deserve death; but it is I that deserve it. Since, then, it is Thy will to make satisfaction for me, it is not Pilate, but Thy Father himself, who justly condemns Thee to pay the penalty that was my due. I love Thee, O Eternal Father, who dost condemn Thine innocent Son in order to liberate me, who am the guilty one. I love Thee, O Eternal Son, who dost accept of the death which I, a sinner, have deserved.

II.

Pilate, after having pronounced sentence upon Jesus, delivers him over to the hands of the Jews, to the end

---

[1] "Innocens ego sum a sanguine justi hujus."—*Matt.* xxvii. 24.

that they may do with him whatsoever they please : *He delivered Jesus up to their will.*[1] Such truly is the course of things. When an innocent one is condemned, there are no limits to the punishment ; but he is left in the hands of his enemies, that they may make him suffer and die according to their own pleasure. Poor Jews ! you then imprecated chastisement upon yourselves in saying, *His Blood be upon us, and upon our children;*[2] and the chastisement has come: you now endure, you miserable men, and will endure, even to the end of the world, the penalty of that innocent blood.

Do Thou, O my Jesus, have mercy upon me, who by my sins have also been a cause of Thy death. But I do not wish to be obstinate, and like the Jews ; I wish to bewail the evil treatment that I have given Thee, and I wish to love Thee—always, always, always !

III.

Behold, the unjust sentence of death upon a cross is read over in the presence of the condemned Lord. He listens to it ; and, all-submissive to the will of the Father, be obediently and humbly accepts it : *He humbled Himself, becoming obedient unto death, and that the death of the cross.*[3] Pilate says on earth, "Let Jesus die ;" and the Eternal Father, in like manner, says from heaven, "Let my Son die ;" and the Son himself makes answer, "Behold me ! I obey ; I accept of death, and death upon a cross."

O my beloved Redeemer ! Thou dost accept of the death that was my due. Blessed for evermore be Thy mercy: I return Thee my most hearty thanks for it.

---

[1] "Jesum vero tradidit voluntati eorum."—*Luke*, xxiii. 25.

[2] "Sanguis ejus super nos, et super filios nostros."—*Matt.* xxvii. 25.

[3] ' Humiliavit semetipsum, factus obediens usque ad mortem, mortem autem crucis."—*Phil.* ii. 8.

But since Thou who art innocent dost accept of the death of the cross for me, I, who am a sinner, accept of that death which Thou dost destine to be mine, together with all the pains that shall accompany it ; and from this time forth I unite it to Thy death, and offer it up to Thy Eternal Father.   Thou hast died for love of me, and I wish to die for love of Thee.   Ah, by the merits of Thy holy death, make me die in Thy grace, and burning with holy love for Thee.   Mary, my hope, be mindful of me.

MEDITATION IX.

FOR PALM SUNDAY.

Jesus carries the Cross to Calvary.

I.

The sentence upon our Saviour having been published, they straightway seize hold of him in their fury: they strip him anew of that purple rag, and put his own raiment upon him, to lead him away to be crucified on Calvary,—the place appropriated for the execution of criminals : *They took off the cloak from Him, and put on Him His own garments, and led Him away to crucify Him.*[1] They then lay hold of two rough beams, and quickly make them into a cross, and order him to carry it on his shoulders to the place of his punishment.   What cruelty, to lay upon the criminal the gibbet on which he has to die !

But this is Thy lot, O my Jesus, because Thou hast taken my sins upon Thyself.

II.

Jesus refuses not the cross ; with love he embraces it, as being the altar whereon is destined to be completed

[1] " Exuerunt eum chlamyde, et induerunt eum vestimentis ejus, et duxerunt eum ut crucifigerent."—*Matt.* xxvii. 31.

the sacrifice of his life for the salvation of men : *And, bearing His own Cross, He went forth to that place which is called Calvary.*[1] The condemned criminals now come forth from Pilate's residence, and in the midst of them there goes also our condemned Lord. O that sight, which filled both heaven and earth with amazement! To see the Son of God going to die for the sake of those very men from whose hands he is receiving his death! Behold the prophecy fulfilled : *And I was as a meek lamb, that is carried to be a victim.*[2] The appearance that Jesus made on this journey was so pitiable that the Jewish women, on beholding him, followed him in tears : *They bewailed and lamented Him.*[3]

O my Redeemer! by the merits of this sorrowful journey of Thine, give me strength to bear my cross with patience. I accept of all the sufferings and contempts which Thou dost destine for me to undergo. Thou hast rendered them lovely and sweet by embracing them for love of us: give me strength to endure them with calmness.

III.

Behold, my soul, now that thy condemned Saviour is passing, behold how he moves along, dripping with blood that keeps flowing from his still fresh wounds, crowned with thorns, and laden with the cross. Alas, how at every motion is the pain of all his wounds renewed! The cross, from the first moment, begins its torture, pressing heavily upon his wounded shoulders, and cruelly acting like a hammer upon the thorns of the crown. O God! at every step, how great are the suffer-

---

[1] " Et bajulans sibi crucem, exivit in eum, qui dicitur Calvariæ, locum."—*John*, xix. 17.

[2] " Ego quasi agnus mansuetus qui portatur ad victimam."—*Jer.* xl. 19.

[3] " Plangebant et lamentabantur eum."—*Luke*, xxiii. 27.

ings! Let us meditate upon the sentiments of love wherewith Jesus, in this journey, is drawing nigh to Calvary, where death stands awaiting him.

Ah, my Jesus, Thou art going to die for us. In time past I have turned my back upon Thee, and would that I could die of grief on this account! but for the future I have not the heart any more to leave Thee, O my Redeemer, my God, my love, my all! O Mary, my Mother, do thou obtain for me strength to bear my cross in peace.

MEDITATION X.

FOR HOLY MONDAY.

Jesus is placed upon the Cross.

L

No sooner had the Redeemer arrived, all suffering and wearied out, at Calvary, than they strip him of his clothes,—that now stick to his wounded flesh,—and then cast him down upon the cross. Jesus stretches forth his holy hands, and at the same time offers up the sacrifice of his life to the Eternal Father, and prays of him to accept it for the salvation of mankind. In the next place, the executioners savagely lay hold of the nails and hammers, and, nailing his hands and his feet, they fasten him to the cross. O ye sacred hands, which by a mere touch have so often healed the sick, wherefore are they now nailing you upon this cross? O holy feet, which have encountered so much fatigue in your search after us lost sheep, wherefore do they now transfix you with so much pain? When a nerve is wounded in the human body, so great is the suffering, that it occasions convulsions and fits of fainting: what, then, must not the suffering of Jesus have been, in having nails driven through his hands and feet, parts which are most full of nerves and muscles!

O my sweet Saviour! so much did the desire of seeing
me saved and of gaining my love cost Thee! And I
have so often ungratefully despised Thy love for nothing;
but now I prize it above every good.

II.

The cross is now raised up, together with the Crucified, and they let it fall with a shock into the hole that
had been made for it in the rock.. It is then made firm
by means of stones and pieces of wood; and Jesus remains hanging upon it, to leave his life thereon. The
afflicted Saviour, now about to die upon that bed of
pain, and finding himself in such desolation and misery,
seeks for some one to console him, but finds none.
Surely, my Lord, those men will at least compassionate
Thee, now that Thou art dying! But no; I hear some
outraging Thee, some ridiculing Thee, and others blaspheming Thee, saying to Thee, "Come down from the
cross if Thou art the Son of God. He has saved others,
and now he cannot save himself."[1] Alas, you barbarians,
he is now about to die, according as you desire; at least
torment him not with your revilings.

III.

See how much thy dying Redeemer is suffering. upon
that gibbet! Each member suffers its own pain, and the
one cannot come to the help of the other. Alas, how
does he experience in every moment the pains of death!
Well may it be said that in those three hours during
which Jesus was suffering his agony upon the cross he
suffered as many deaths as were the moments that he
remained there. He finds not there even the slightest
relief or repose, whether he lean his weight upon his
hands or upon his feet; wheresoever he leans the pain

[1] *Matt.* xxvii. 40.

is increased, his most holy body hanging suspended, as it does, from his very wounds themselves. Go, my soul, and tenderly draw nigh to that cross, and kiss that altar, whereon thy Lord is dying a victim of love for thee. Place thyself beneath his feet, and let that divine blood trickle down upon thee.

Yes, my dear Jesus, let this blood wash me from all my sins, and set me all on fire with love towards Thee, my God, who hast been willing to die for love of me. Do thou, O suffering Mother, who dost stand at the foot of the cross, pray to Jesus for me.

MEDITATION XI.

FOR HOLY TUESDAY.

Jesus upon the Cross.

I.

Jesus on the cross! Behold the proof of the love of a God; behold the final manifestation of himself, which the Word Incarnate makes upon this earth,—a manifestation of suffering indeed, but, still more, a manifestation of love. St. Francis of Paola, as he was one day meditating upon the divine Love in the person of Jesus Crucified, rapt in ecstasy, exclaimed aloud three times, in these words, "O God—Love! O God—Love! O God —Love!" wishing hereby to signify that we shall never be able to comprehend how great has been the divine love towards us, in willing to die for love of us.

II.

O my beloved Jesus! if I behold Thy body upon this cross, nothing do I see but wounds and blood; and then, if I turn my attention to Thy heart, I find it to be all afflicted and in sorrow. Upon this cross I see it written that Thou art a king; but what tokens of majesty dost Thou retain? I see not any royal throne save that of this tree of infamy ; no other purple do I behold save Thy wounded and bloody flesh ; no other crown save this band of thorns that tortures Thee. Ah, how it all declares Thee to be king of love ! yes, for this cross, these nails, this crown, and these wounds are, all of them, tokens of love.

III.

Jesus, from the cross, asks us not so much for our compassion as for our love ; and, if even he does ask our compassion, he asks it solely in order that the compassion may move us to love him. As being infinite goodness, he already merits all our love ; but when placed upon the cross, it seems as if he sought for us to love him, at least out of compassion.

Ah, my Jesus, and who is there that will not love Thee, while confessing Thee to be the God that Thou art, and contemplating Thee upon the cross ? Oh, what arrows of fire dost Thou not dart at souls from that throne of love ! Oh, how many hearts hast Thou not drawn to Thyself from that cross of Thine ! O wounds of my Jesus ! O beautiful furnaces of love ! admit me, too, amongst yourselves to burn, not indeed with that fire of hell which I have deserved, but with holy flames of love for that God who has been willing to die for me, consumed by torments. O my dear Redeemer ! receive back a sinner, who, sorrowing for having offended Thee, is now earnestly longing to love Thee. I love Thee, I love Thee, O infinite goodness, O infinite love. O Mary, O Mother of beautiful love ! obtain for me a greater measure of love, to consume me for that God who has died consumed of love for me.

MEDITATION XII.

FOR HOLY WEDNESDAY.

The Words spoken by Jesus upon the Cross.

I.

While Jesus upon the cross is being outraged by that barbarous populace, what is it that he is doing? He is praying for them, and saying, *O My Father, forgive them; for they know not what they do.*[1] O Eternal Father, hearken to this Thy beloved Son, who, in dying, prays Thee to forgive me too, who have outraged Thee so much. Then Jesus, turning to the good thief, who prays him to have mercy upon him, replies: *To-day shalt thou be with Me in paradise.* Oh, how true is that which the Lord spake by the mouth of Ezechiel, that when a sinner repents of his faults, he, as it were, blots out from his memory all the offences of which he has been guilty : *But if the wicked do penance . . . I will not remember all his iniquities.*[2]

Oh, would that it were true, my Jesus, that I had never offended Thee! But, since the evil is done, remember no more, I pray Thee, the displeasures that I have given Thee; and, by that bitter death which Thou hast suffered for me, take me to Thy kingdom after my death ; and, while I live, let Thy love ever reign within my soul.

II.

Jesus, in his agony upon the cross, with every part of his body full of torture, and deluged with affliction in his soul, seeks for some one to console him. He looks towards Mary ; but that sorrowing Mother only adds by

[1] " Pater, dimitte illis ! Non enim sciunt, quid faciunt."—*Luke*, xxiii. 34.

[2] " Si autem impius egerit poenitentiam . . . , omnium iniquitatum ejus . . . non recordabor."—*Ezech.* xviii. 21, 22.

her grief to his affliction. He casts his eyes around him and there is no one that gives him comfort. He asks his Father for consolation ; but the Father, beholding him covered with all the sins of men, even he too abandons him ; and then it was that Jesus cried out with a loud voice: *Jesus cried out with a loud voice, saying, My God, My God, why hast Thou forsaken Me ?*[1] My God, my God, and why hast Thou also abandoned me ? This abandonment by the Eternal Father caused the death of Jesus Christ to be more bitter than any that has ever fallen to the lot of either penitent or martyr; for it was a death of perfect desolation, and bereft of every kind of relief.

O my Jesus ! how is it that I have been able to live so long a time in forgetfulness of Thee ? I return Thee thanks that Thou hast not been unmindful of me. Oh, I pray Thee ever to keep me in mind of the bitter death which Thou hast embraced for love of me, that so I may never be unmindful of the love which Thou hast borne me !

III.

Jesus then, knowing that his sacrifice was now completed, said that he was thirsty: *He said, I thirst.*[2] And the executioners then reached up to his mouth a sponge, filled with vinegar and gall.

But, Lord, how is it that Thou dost make no complaint of those many pains which are taking away Thy life, but complainest only of Thy thirst ? Ah, I understand Thee, my Jesus; Thy thirst is a thirst of love ; because Thou lovest us, Thou dost desire to be beloved by us. Oh, help me to drive away from my heart all affections which are not for Thee; make me to love none other but Thee, and to have no other desire save that of doing Thy will.

---

[1] "Clamavit Jesus voce magna, dicens : . . . Deus meus ! Deus meus ! ut quid dereliquisti me ?"—*Matt.* xxvii. 46.

[2] "Dixit: Sitio !"—*John*, xix. 28.

O will of God ! Thou art my love. O Mary, my Mother!
obtain for me the grace to wish for nothing but that
which God doth will. ·

MEDITATION XIII.

For Holy Thursday.

Jesus dies upon the Cross.

I.

Behold how the loving Saviour is now drawing nigh
unto death. Behold, O my soul, those beautiful eyes
growing dim, that face become all pallid, that heart all
but ceasing to beat, and that sacred body now disposing
itself to the final surrender of its life. After Jesus had
received the vinegar, he said, *It is consummated.*[1] He
then passed over in review before his eyes all the sufferings that he had undergone during his life, in the shape
of poverty, contempt, and pain ; and then offering them
all up to the Eternal Father, he turned to him and said,
It is finished. My Father, behold by the sacrifice of my
death, the work of the world's redemption, which Thou
hast laid upon me, is now completed. And it seems as
though, turning himself again to us, he repeated, *It is
finished;* as if he would have said, O men, O men, love
me, for I have done all; there is nothing more that I can
do in order to gain your love.

II.

Behold now, lastly, Jesus dies. Come, ye angels of
heaven, come and assist at the death of your King. And
thou, O sorrowing Mother Mary, do thou draw nearer
to the cross, and fix thine eyes yet more attentively on
thy Son, for he is now on the point of death. Behold
him, how, after having commended his spirit to his

---

[1] "Consummatum est !"—*John,* xix. 30.

Eternal Father, he calls upon death, giving it permission
to come to take away his life. Come, O death, says he
to it, be quick and perform thine office; slay me, and
save my flock. The earth now trembles, the graves open,
the veil of the temple is rent in twain. The strength of
the dying Saviour is failing through the violence of the
sufferings; the warmth of his body is gradually dimin-
ishing; he gives up his body to death: he bows his head
down upon his breast, he opens his mouth and dies:
And bowing His head, He gave up the ghost.[1] The people
behold him expire, and, observing that he no longer
moves, they say, he is dead, he is dead; and to them the
voice of Mary makes echo, while she too says, "Ah, my
Son, Thou art, then, dead."

III.

He is dead! O God! who is it that is dead? The
author of life, the only-begotten Son of God, the Lord
of the world,—he is dead. O death! thou wert the
amazement of heaven and of all nature. O infinite
love! A God to sacrifice his blood and his life! And
for whom? For his ungrateful creatures; dying in an
ocean of sufferings and shame, in order to pay the
penalty due to their sins. Ah, infinite goodness! O infinite love!

O my Jesus! Thou art, then, dead, on account of the love
which Thou hast borne me! Oh, let me never again
live, even for a single moment, without loving Thee! I
love Thee, my chief and only good; I love Thee, my
Jesus,—dead for me! O my sorrowing Mother Mary!
do thou help a servant of thine, who desires to love
Jesus.

[1] " Et inclinato capite, tradidit spiritum."—*John*, xix. 30.

MEDITATION XIV.

FOR GOOD FRIDAY.

Jesus hanging Dead upon the Cross.

I.

Raise up thine eyes, my soul, and behold that crucified man. Behold the divine Lamb now sacrificed upon that altar of pain. Consider that he is the beloved Son of the Eternal Father ; and consider that he is dead for the love that he has borne thee. See how he holds his arms stretched out to embrace thee ; his head bent down to give the kiss of peace ; his side open to receive thee into his heart. What dost thou say? Does not a God so loving deserve to be loved ? Listen to the words he addresses to thee from that cross : " Look, my son, and see whether there be any one in the world who has loved thee more than I have."

No, my God, there is none that has loved me more than Thou. But what return shall I ever be able to make to a God who has been willing to die for me? what love from a creature will ever be able to recompense the love of his Creator, who died to gain his love ?

II.

O God ! had the vilest one of mankind suffered for me what Jesus Christ has suffered, could I ever refrain from loving him ? Were I to see any man torn to pieces with scourges and fastened to a cross in order to save my life, could I ever bear it in mind without feeling a tender emotion of love ? And were there to be brought to me the portrait of him, as he lay dead upon the cross, could I behold it with an eye of indifference, when I considered : "This man is dead, tortured thus, for love of me. Had he not loved me, he would not so have died."

Ah, my Redeemer, O love of my soul! How shall I
ever again be able to forget Thee? How shall I ever be
able to think that my sins have reduced Thee so low,
and not always bewail the wrongs that I have done to
Thy goodness? How shall I ever be able to see Thee
dead of pain on this cross for love of me, and not love
Thee to the uttermost of my power?

III.

O my dear Redeemer! well do I recognize in these Thy
wounds, and in Thy lacerated body, as it were through
so many lattices, the tender affection which Thou dost
retain for me. Since, then. in order to pardon me, Thou
hast not pardoned Thyself, oh, look upon me now with
the same love wherewith Thou didst one day look upon
me from the cross, whilst Thou wert dying for me.
Look upon me and enlighten me, and draw my whole
heart to Thyself, that so, from this day forth, I may love
none else but Thee. Let me not ever be unmindful of
Thy death. Thou didst promise that, when raised up
upon the cross, Thou wouldst draw all our hearts to
Thee. Behold this heart of mine, which, made tender
by Thy death, and enamoured of Thee, desires to offer
no further resistance to Thy calls. Oh, do Thou draw
it to Thyself, and make it all Thine own! Thou hast
died for me, and I desire to die for Thee; and if I continue to live, I will live for Thee alone. O pains of
Jesus, O ignominies of Jesus, O death of Jesus, O love of
Jesus! fix yourselves within my heart, and let the remembrance of you abide there always, to be continually
smiting me, and inflaming me with love. I love Thee.
O infinite goodness; I love Thee, O infinite love. Thou
art, and shalt ever be, my one and only love. O Mary,
Mother of love, do thou obtain me love.

MEDITATION XV.

FOR HOLY SATURDAY.

Mary Present on Calvary at the Death of Jesus.

I.

There stood by the cross of Jesus His Mother.[1] We observe in this the Queen of Martyrs, a sort of martydom more cruel than any other martyrdom,—that of a mother so placed as to behold an innocent Son executed upon a gibbet of infamy: "she stood." Ever since Jesus was apprehended in the garden, he has been abandoned by his disciples; but Mary abandons him not. She stays with him till she sees him expire before her eyes: "she stood close by." Mothers, in general, flee away from the presence of their sons when they see them suffer, and cannot render them any assistance : content enough would they be themselves to endure their sons' sufferings ; and, therefore, when they see them suffering without the power of succoring them, they have not the strength to endure so great a pain, and consequently flee away, and go to a distance. Not so Mary. She sees her Son in torments ; she sees that the pains are taking his life away ; but she flees not, nor moves to a distance. On the contrary, she draws near to the cross whereon her Son is dying.

O sorrowing Mary! disdain me not for a companion to assist at the death of thy Jesus and mine.

II.

She stood near to the cross. The cross, then, is the bed whereon Jesus leaves his life ; a bed of suffering, where this afflicted Mother is watching Jesus, all wounded as he is with scourges and with thorns. Mary observes how this her poor Son, suspended from those three iron nails, finds neither a position nor repose. She would wish to

[1] "Stabant autem juxta crucem Jesu Mater ejus. . . ."—*John*, xix. 25.

give him some relief ; she would wish, at least, since he
has to die, to have him die in her arms. But nothing of
all this is allowed her. Ah, cross! she says, give me
back my Son ! Thou art a malefactor's gibbet ; whereas
my Son is innocent.

But grieve not thyself, O Mother. It is the will of
the Eternal Father that the cross should not give Jesus
back to thee until after he has died and breathed his
last. O Queen of Sorrows ! obtain for me sorrow for my
sins.

III.

There stood by the cross His Mother ! Meditate, my soul,
upon Mary, as she stands at the foot of the cross watching her Son. Her Son ! but, O God, what a Son ! a Son
who was, at one and the same time, her Son and her
God ! a Son who had from all eternity chosen her to be
his Mother, and had given her a preference in his love
before all mankind and all the angels ! A Son so beautiful, so holy, and so lovely ; a Son who had been ever
obedient unto her ; a Son who was her one and only
love, being as he was both her Son and God. And this
Mother had to see such a Son die of pain before her very
eyes !

O Mary, O Mother, most afflicted of all mothers! I
compassionate thy heart, more especially when thou
didst behold thy Jesus surrender himself up upon the
cross, open his mouth, and expire ; and, for love of this
thy Son, now dead for my salvation, do thou recommend
unto him my soul.

And do Thou, my Jesus, for the sake of the merits of
Mary's sorrows, have mercy upon me, and grant me the
grace of dying for Thee, as Thou hast died for me :
" May I die, O my Lord " (will I say unto Thee, with St.
Francis of Assisi), "for love of the love of Thee, who
hast vouchsafed to die for love of the love of me."

Three Meditations on Paradise, for the Easter Festival.

MEDITATION I.

FOR EASTER SUNDAY.

The Joys of Heaven.

I.

Oh, happy are we if we suffer with patience on earth the troubles of this present life! Distress of circumstances, fears, bodily infirmities, persecutions, and crosses of every kind, will one day all come to an end; and if we be saved, they will all become for us subjects of joy and glory in paradise: *Your sorrow* (says the Saviour, to encourage us) *shall be turned into joy.*[1] So great are the delights of paradise, that they can neither be explained nor understood by us mortals: *Eye hath not seen* (says the Apostle), *nor ear heard, neither hath it entered into the heart of man, what things God hath prepared for those who love Him.*[2] Beauties like the beauties of paradise, eye hath never seen; harmonies like unto the harmonies of paradise, ear hath never heard; nor hath ever human heart gained the comprehension of the joys which God hath prepared for those that love him. Beautiful is the sight of a landscape adorned with hills, plains, woods, and views of the sea. Beautiful is the sight of a garden abounding with fruit, flowers, and fountains. Oh, how much more beautiful is paradise!

[1] "Tristitia vestra vertetur in gaudium."—*John*, xvi. 20.

[2] "Oculus non vidit, nec auris audivit, nec in cor hominis ascendit, quæ præparavit Deus iis qui diligunt illum."—1 *Cor.* ii. 9.

II.

To understand how great the joys of paradise are, it
is enough to know that in that blessed realm resides a
God omnipotent, whose care is to render happy his
beloved souls. St. Bernard says that paradise is a place
where " there is nothing that thou wouldst not, and
everything that thou wouldst." There shalt thou not
find anything displeasing to Thyself, and everything
thou dost desire thoû shalt find: " There is nothing that
thou wouldst not." In paradise there is no night ; no
seasons of winter and summer; but one perpetual day of
unvaried serenity, and one perpetual spring of unvaried
delight. No more persecutions, no jealousies are there;
for there do all in sincerity love one another, and each
rejoices in each other's good, as if it were his own. No
more bodily infirmities, no pains are there, for the body
is no longer subject to suffering; no poverty is there, for
every one is rich to the full, not having anything more
to desire ; no more fears are there, for the soul being
confirmed in grace can sin no more, nor lose that supreme good which it possesses.

III.

"There is everything that thou wouldst." ¹ In paradise thou shalt have whatsoever thou desirest. There the
sight is satisfied in beholding that city so beautiful, and
its citizens all clothed in royal apparel, for they are all
kings of that everlasting kingdom. There shall we see
the beauty of Mary, whose appearance will be more
beautiful than that of all the angels and saints together.
We shall see the beauty of Jesus, which will immeasur-
ably surpass the beauty of Mary. The smell will be satisfied with the perfumes of paradise. The hearing will
be satisfied with the harmonies of heaven and the can-

¹ " Nihil est quod nolis, totum est quod velis."

ticles of the blessed, who will all with ravishing sweetness sing the divine praises for all eternity.

Ah, my God, I deserve not paradise, but hell; yet Thy death gives me a hope of obtaining it. I desire and ask paradise of Thee, not so much in order to enjoy, as in order to love Thee everlastingly, secure that it will never more be possible for me to lose Thee. O Mary, my Mother, O Star of the Sea, it is for thee, by thy prayers, to conduct me to paradise.

MEDITATION II.

For Easter Monday

The Soul that leaves this Life in the State of Grace.

I.

Let us imagine to ourselves a soul that, on departing out of this world, enters eternity in the grace of God. All full of humility and of confidence, it presents itself before Jesus, its judge and Saviour. Jesus embraces it, gives it his benediction, and causes it to hear those words of sweetness : *Come, my spouse, come, thou shalt be crowned.*[1] If the soul have need of being purified, he sends it to purgatory, and, all resigned, it embraces the chastisement, because itself wishes not to enter into heaven, that land of purity, if it is not wholly purified. The Guardian Angel comes to conduct it to purgatory; it first returns him thanks for the assistance he has rendered it in its lifetime, and then obediently follows him.

Ah, my God, when will that day arrive on which I shall see myself out of this world of perils, secure of never being able to lose Thee more ? Yes, willingly will I go to the purgatory which shall be mine ; joyfully will I embrace all its pains; sufficient will it be for me in that

---

[1] "Veni de Libano, sponsa mea, veni; coronaberis."—*Cant.* iv. 3.

fire to love Thee with all my heart, since there I shall love none else but Thee.

II.

The purgation over, the angel will return and say to it, Come along, beautiful soul, the punishment is at an end; come, and enjoy the presence of thy God, who is awaiting thee in paradise. Behold, the soul now passes beyond the clouds, passes beyond the spheres and the stars, and enters into heaven. O God, what will it say on entering into that beautiful country, and casting its first glance on that city of delights? The angels and saints, and especially its own holy advocates, will go to meet it, and with jubilation will they welcome it, saying, Welcome, O companion of our own; welcome!

Ah, my Jesus, do Thou make me worthy of it.

III.

What consolation will it not feel in meeting there with relatives and friends of its own who have previously entered into heaven! But greater by far will be its joy in beholding Mary its Queen, and in kissing her feet, while it will thank her for the many kindnesses she has done it. The Queen will embrace it, and will herself present it unto Jesus, who will receive it as a spouse. And Jesus will then present it to his divine Father, who will embrace and bless it, saying, *Enter thou into the joy of thy Lord.*[1] And thus will he beatify it with the same beatitude that he himself enjoys. Ah, my God, make me love Thee exceedingly in this life, that I may love Thee exceedingly in eternity. Thou art the object most worthy of being loved; Thou dost deserve all my love; I will love none but Thee. Do Thou help me by Thy grace. And Mary, my Mother, be thou my protectress.

[1] " Intra in gaudium Domini tui."—*Matt.* xxv. 21.

MEDITATION III.

FOR EASTER TUESDAY.

The Sight of God is that in which the Happiness of the Elect consists.

I.

The beauties of the saints, the heavenly music, and all the other delights of paradise, form but the lesser portion of its treasures. The possession which gives to the soul its fulness of bliss is that of seeing a loving God face to face. St. Augustine says that were God to let his beautiful face be seen by the damned, hell with all its torments would become to them a paradise. Even in this world, when God gives a soul in prayer a taste of his sweet presence, and by a ray of light discovers to it his goodness and the love which he bears it, so great is the contentment that the soul feels itself dissolve and melt away in love ; and yet, in this life, it is not possible for us to see God as he is ; we behold him obscured, as if through a thick veil. What, then, will it be, when God shall take away that veil from before us, and shall cause us to behold him face to face openly?

O Lord! for having turned my back upon Thee, no more should I be worthy to behold Thee ; but, relying on Thy goodness, I hope to see Thee, and to love Thee in paradise forever. I speak thus, because I am speaking with a God who has died in order to give paradise to me.

II.

Although the souls that love God are the most happy in this world, yet they cannot, here below, enjoy a happiness full and complete ; that fear, which arises from not knowing whether they be deserving of the love or the hatred of their beloved Saviour, keeps them, as it were, in perpetual suffering. But in paradise the soul is certain that it loves God, and is loved by God; and it sees that that sweet tie of love which holds it united with God will never be loosened throughout all eternity. The flames of its love will be increased by the clearer knowledge which the soul will then possess of what the love of God has been in being made man, and having willed to die for it; and in having, moreover, given himself to it in the sacrament of the Eucharist. Its love will be increased by then beholding, in all their distinctness, the graces which he has given it, in order to lead it to heaven; it will see that the crosses sent to it in lifetime have all been artifices of his love to render it happy. It will see, besides, the mercies he has granted it, the many lights and calls to penance. From the summit of that blessed Mount will it behold the many lost souls now in hell for sins less than its own, and it will behold itself now saved, possessed of God, and certain that it can nevermore lose him throughout all eternity.

My Jesus, my Jesus, when will that too happy day for me arrive?

III.

The happiness of the blessed soul will be perfected by knowing with absolute certainty that that God whom it then enjoys it will have to enjoy for all eternity. Were there to be any fear in the blessed that they might lose that God whom they now enjoy, paradise would no more be paradise. But no; the blessed soul is certain, with the certainty which it has of the existence of God, that that supreme good which it enjoys, it will enjoy forever. That joy, moreover, will not grow less with time; it will be ever new. The blessed one will be ever happy, and ever thirsting for that happiness; and, on the other hand, while ever thirsting, will be ever satiated. When, therefore, we see ourselves afflicted with the troubles of this life, let us lift up our eyes unto heaven, and console ourselves by saying, Paradise. The sufferings will one day come to an end; nay, they will themselves become objects over which to rejoice. The saints await us; the angels await us; Mary awaits us; and Jesus stands with the crown in his hand wherewith to crown us if we shall be faithful to him.

Ah, my God, when will come that day on which I shall arrive at possessing Thee, and be able to say unto Thee, My love, I cannot lose Thee more? O Mary, my hope, never cease from praying for me, until thou dost see me safe at thy feet in paradise!

30

Various Exercises for the Use of Persons devoted to the Passion of our Lord.

The Clock of the Passion.

P.M.

5 to 7	Jesus, having taken leave of Mary, celebrates his last supper.
8	Jesus washes the feet of the apostles, and institutes the Most Holy Sacrament.
9	Discourse of Jesus; he goes to the Garden of Olives.
10	Prayer of Jesus in the garden.
11	Agony.
MIDNIGHT.	The sweating of blood.
1	Jesus is betrayed by Judas, and is bound.
2	Jesus is led before Annas.
3	Jesus is taken before Caiphas, and receives a blow in the face.
4	Jesus is blindfolded, struck, and scoffed at.
5	Jesus is led to the council, and declared guilty of death.
6	Jesus is taken to Pilate, and accused.
7	Jesus is mocked by Herod.
8	Jesus is conducted to Pilate, and Baraboas is preferred to him.
9	Jesus is scourged at the pillar.
10	Jesus is crowned with thorns, and exhibited to the people.
11	Jesus is condemned to death, and goes to Calvary.
MIDDAY.	Jesus is stripped and crucified.
1	Jesus prays for his murderers.
2	Jesus recommends his spirit to his Father.
3	Jesus dies.
4	Jesus is pierced with a lance.
5	Jesus is taken down from the cross, and delivered over to his Mother,
6	Jesus is buried, and left in the sepulchre.

GRADUS PASSIONIS D. N. JESU CHRISTI.

I. *Jesu dulcissime, in horto mæste Patrem orans et in agonia posite, sanguineum sudorem effundens: miserere nobis.*

R. *Miserere nostri, Domine, miserere nostri.*

(*Sic respondetur ad omnes ceteros gradus.*)

II. *Jesu dulcissime, osculo traditoris in manus impiorum tra dite et tanquam latro capte et ligate, et a discipulis derelicte: miserere nobis.*

III. *Jesu dulcissime, ab iniquo Judæorum concilio reus mortis acclamate, ad Pilatum tamquam malefactor ducte, ab iniquo Herode sprete et deluse: miserere nobis.*

IV. *Jesu dulcissime, vestibus denudate, et in columna crudelissime flagellate: miserere nobis.*

V. *Jesu dulcissime, spinis coronate, colaphis cæse, arundine percusse, facie velate, veste purpurea circumdate, multipliciter derise et opprobriis saturate: miserere nobis.*

VI. *Jesu dulcissime, latroni Barabbæ postposite, a Judæis reprobate, et ad mortem crucis injuste condemnate: miserere nobis.*

VII. *Jesu dulcissime, ligno crucis onerate, et ad locum supplicii tamquam ovis ad occisionem ducte: miserere nobis.*

VIII. *Jesu dulcissime, inter latrones deputate, blasphemate et derise, felle et aceto potate, et horribilibus tormentis ab hora sexta usque ad horam nonam in ligno cruciate: miserere nobis.*

IX. *Jesu dulcissime, in patibulo crucis mortue, et coram tua sancta Matre lancea perforate, simul sanguinem et aquam emittens: miserere nobis.*

X. *Jesu dulcissime, de cruce deposite et lacrymis mæstissimæ Virginis Matris tuæ perfuse: miserere nobis.*

XI. *Jesu dulcissime, plagis circumdate, quinque vulneribus signate, aromatibus condite et in sepulcro reposite: miserere nobis.*

V. *Vere languores nostros ipse tulit.*

R. *Et dolores nostros ipse portavit.*

OREMUS.

Deus, qui pro redemptione mundi nasci voluisti, circumcidi, a Judæis reprobari, a Juda traditore osculo tradi, vinculis alligari, sicut agnus innocens ad victimam duci, atque conspectibus Annæ. Caiphæ. Pilati et Herodis indecenter offerri; a falsis tes-

tibus accusari, flagellis et colaphis cædi, opprobriis vexari, con-spui, spinis coronari, arundine percuti, facie velari, vestibus spoliari, cruci clavis affigi, in cruce levari, inter latrones depu-tari, felle et aceto potari et lancea vulnerari. Tu, Domine, per has sanctissimas pœnas, quas ego indignus recolo, et per sanctis-simam crucem et mortem tuam, libera me a pœnis inferni, et per-ducere digneris, quo perduxisti latronem tecum crucifixum. Qui , cum Patre et Spiritu Sancto vivis et regnas in sæcula sæculorum. Amen.

[Translation.]

Steps of the Passion.

My sweetest Jesus, who, while praying in the garden, didst sweat blood, wast in agony, and didst suffer a sor-row so great as to suffice to cause Thee death, have mercy on us.

R. Mercy on us, O Lord, have mercy on us.

My sweetest Jesus, who wast betrayed by Judas with a kiss, and delivered over into the hands of Thine enemies, and then wast taken prisoner by them and bound, and abandoned by Thy disciples, have mercy on us.

R. Mercy on us, O Lord, etc.

My sweetest Jesus, declared by the council of the Jews guilty of death, and in the house of Caiphas blindfolded with a piece of cloth, and then buffeted, spit at, and derided, have mercy on us.

R. Mercy on us, O Lord, etc.

My sweetest Jesus, led away as a malefactor to Pilate, and then turned by Herod into ridicule, and treated as a mádman, have mercy on us.

R. Mercy on us, O Lord, etc.

My sweetest Jesus, stripped of Thy garments, and bound to the pillar, and so cruelly scourged, have mercy on us.

R. Mercy on us, O Lord, etc.

My sweetest Jesus, crowned with thorns, covered with

a red mantle, buffeted, and in mockery saluted as King
of the Jews, have mercy on us.

R. Mercy on us, O Lord, etc.

My sweetest Jesus, rejected by the Jews, and placed
after Barabbas, and then unjustly condemned by Pilate
to die upon a cross, have mercy on us.

R. Mercy on us, O Lord, etc.

My sweetest Jesus, laden with the wood of the cross,
and as an innocent Lamb led away unto death, have
mercy on us.

R. Mercy on us, O Lord, etc.

My sweetest Jesus, nailed upon the cross, placed between two thieves, ridiculed and blasphemed, and for
three hours in an agony of the most horrible torments,
have mercy on us.

R. Mercy on us, O Lord, etc.

My sweetest Jesus, dead upon the cross, and in sight
of Thy holy Mother, transfixed in Thy side with the
spear, from whence there issued forth blood and water,
have mercy on us.

R. Mercy on us, O Lord, etc.

My sweetest Jesus, taken down from the cross, and
placed in the bosom of Thine afflicted Mother, have
mercy on us.

R. Mercy on us, O Lord, etc.

My sweetest Jesus, who, torn with stripes and stamped
with Thy five wounds, wast laid in the sepulchre, have
mercy on us.

R. Mercy on us, O Lord, etc.

V. Surely he hath borne our infirmities.

R. And he hath carried our sorrows.

Let us pray.

O God, who, for the redemption of the world, didst
will to be born, to be circumcised, rejected by the Jews,
betrayed by the traitor Judas with a kiss, bound with

cords, led as an innocent Lamb to the sacrifice, and with so many insults taken before Annas, Caiphas, Pilate, and Herod, accused by false witnesses, beaten with scourges and buffetings, overwhelmed with ignominies, spit upon, crowned with thorns, smitten with the reed, blindfolded, stripped of Thy raiment, fastened with nails to the cross lifted up on the cross, numbered amongst thieves, with gall and vinegar given Thee to drink, and wounded with the spear,—do Thou, Lord, by these sacred pains, which I, unworthy, venerate, and by Thy holy cross and death, deliver me from hell, and vouchsafe to conduct me whither Thou didst conduct the thief that was crucified with Thee: Thou, who livest and reignest with the Father and the Holy Spirit for ever and ever. Amen. So do I hope; and so may it be.

Little Chaplet of the Five Wounds of Jesus Crucified.

I.

O my Lord Jesus Christ, I adore the wound in Thy left foot. I thank Thee for having suffered it for me with so much sorrow and with so much love. I compassionate Thy pain, and that of Thine afflicted Mother. And, by the merit of this sacred wound, I pray Thee to grant me the pardon of my sins, of which I repent with all my heart, because they have offended Thine infinite goodness. O sorrowing Mary, pray to Jesus for me.

Our Father, Hail Mary, Glory, etc.

> By all the wounds which Thou didst bear
> With so much love and so much pain,
> Oh, let a sinner's prayer
> Thy mercy, Lord, obtain!

II.

O my Lord Jesus Christ, I adore the wound in Thy right foot. I thank Thee for having suffered it for me with so much sorrow and with so much love. I compassionate Thy pain, and that of Thine afflicted Mother. And, by the merit of this sacred wound, I pray Thee to give me the strength not to fall into mortal sin for the future, but to persevere in Thy grace unto my death. O sorrowing Mary, pray to Jesus for me.

Our Father, etc.

> By all the wounds which Thou didst bear
> With so much love and so much pain,
> Oh, let a sinner's prayer
> Thy mercy, Lord, obtain!

III.

O my Lord Jesus Christ, I adore the wound in Thy left hand. I thank Thee for having suffered it for me with so much sorrow and with so much love. I compassionate Thy pain, and that of Thine afflicted Mother. And, by the merit of this sacred wound, I pray Thee to deliver me from hell, which I have so often deserved, where I could never love Thee more. O sorrowing Mary, pray to Jesus for me.

Our Father, etc.

> By all the wounds which Thou didst bear
> With so much love and so much pain,
> Oh, let a sinner's prayer
> Thy mercy, Lord, obtain!

IV.

O my Lord Jesus Christ! I adore the wound in Thy right hand. I thank Thee for having suffered it for me with so much sorrow and with so much love. I compassionate Thy pain, and that of Thy most afflicted Mother. And, by the merit of this sacred wound, I pray Thee to give me the glory of paradise, where I shall love Thee perfectly, and with all my strength. O sorrowing Mary! pray to Jesus for me.

Our Father, etc.

> By all the wounds which Thou didst bear
> With so much love and so much pain,
> Oh, let a sinner's prayer
> Thy mercy, Lord, obtain!

V.

O my Lord Jesus Christ! I adore the wound in Thy side. I thank Thee for having willed, even after Thy death, to suffer this additional injury, without pain indeed, yet with consummate love. I compassionate Thine afflicted Mother, who alone felt all its pain. And, by the merit of this sacred wound, I pray Thee to bestow upon me the gift of holy love for Thee, that so I may ever love Thee in this life, and in the other, face to face, for all eternity, in paradise. O sorrowing Mary, pray to Jesus for me.

Our Father, etc.

> By all the wounds which Thou didst bear
>   With so much love and so much pain,
> Oh, let a sinner's prayer
>   Thy mercy, Lord, obtain!

Prayer to Jesus Crucified, to be said Every Day to obtain His Holy Love.

My crucified love, and my most sweet Jesus, I believe in Thee, and confess Thee to be true Son of God and Saviour of the world! I adore Thee from the abyss of my misery, and thank Thee for the death which Thou didst suffer, to obtain for me the life of divine grace. O most faithful of all friends! O most loving of all fathers! O kindest of all masters! my beloved Redeemer, to Thee I am indebted for my salvation, for my soul, my body, and my whole self. Thou hast delivered me from hell; through Thee I have received the pardon of my sins; through Thee do I hope for paradise. But my ingratitude is so great that, instead of loving Thee, after so many mercies and special endearments of love, I have only offended Thee afresh. I confess that I deserve not to be allowed to love Thee any more. But no, my Jesus, choose some other punishment for me, and not this. If I have despised Thee up to this time, now I love Thee, and I desire to love Thee with all my heart. Thou knowest very well that without Thy help I can do nothing. Since, then, Thou dost command me to love Thee, and dost offer me Thy grace, provided I ask it in

Thy name, confiding in Thy goodness, and in the promise Thou hast made me, saying, *Whatsoever you shall ask the Father in My name, that I will do,*[1]—I present myself, poor as I am, before the throne of Thy mercy; and by the merits of Thy Passion, I ask Thee first to pardon all my sins, of which I repent with all my soul, because by them I have offended Thee, who art infinite goodness. Pardon me, then, and at the same time, give me holy perseverance till death; grant me also the gift of Thy holy love.

Ah, my Jesus, my hope, and my only love! my life, my treasure, my all! shed over my soul that light of truth and that fire of love which Thou didst come to bring into the world. Enlighten me to know every day better why Thou shouldst be loved, and to see the immense love Thou hast shown me in suffering and dying for me. Ah, grant that the same love may be in me as that with which Thy eternal Father loves Thee. And as he is in Thee, and is one with Thee, so may I, by means of a true love, be in Thee, and, by a perfect union of will, become one with Thee. Grant me, then, O my Jesus, the grace of loving Thee with all my affections, that I may love Thee always, and ever beg the grace to love Thee; so that, ending my life in Thy love, I may come to love Thee in heaven with a purer and more perfect love, never to cease loving Thee, and to possess Thee for all eternity!

O Mother of beautiful love, most blessed Virgin, my advocate, my mother, my hope after Jesus,—who art of all creatures the most loving towards God, and desirest nothing but that he should be loved by all,—ah, for the love of this Son dying before thine eyes for my salvation, pray for me, and obtain for me the grace to love him always, and with all my heart! I ask it of thee, and from thee do I hope to obtain it. Amen.

[1] "Si quid petieritis me in nomine meo, hoc faciam."—*John*, xiv. 14.

Prayers to Jesus.

By the Merit of each Particular Pain which He suffered in His Passion.

O my Jesus! by that humiliation which Thou didst practise in washing the feet of Thy disciples, I pray Thee to bestow upon me the grace of true humility, that I may humble myself to all, especially to such as treat me with contempt.

My Jesus, by that sorrow which Thou didst suffer in the garden, sufficient, as it was, to cause Thy death, I pray Thee to deliver me from the sorrow of hell, from living for evermore at a distance from Thee, and without the power of ever loving Thee again.

My Jesus, by that horror which Thou hadst of my sins, which were then present to Thy sight, give me a true sorrow for all the offences which I have committed against Thee.

My Jesus, by that pain which Thou didst experience at seeing Thyself betrayed by Judas with a kiss, give me the grace to be ever faithful unto Thee, and nevermore to betray Thee, as I have done in time past.

My Jesus, by that pain which Thou didst feel at seeing Thyself bound like a culprit to be taken before the judges, I pray Thee to bind me to Thyself by the sweet chains of holy love, that so I may nevermore see myself separated from Thee, my only good.

My Jesus, by all those insults, buffetings, and spittings which Thou didst on that night suffer in the house of Caiphas, give me the strength to suffer in peace, for love of Thee, all the affronts which I shall meet with from men.

My Jesus, by that ridicule which Thou didst receive

from Herodin being treated as a fool, give me the grace to endure with patience all that men shall say of me, treating me as base, senseless, or wicked.

My Jesus, by that outrage which Thou didst receive from the Jews in seeing Thyself placed after Barabbas, give me the grace to suffer with patience the dishonor of seeing myself placed after others.

My Jesus, by that pain which Thou didst suffer in Thy most holy body when Thou wast so cruelly scourged, give me the grace to suffer with patience all the pains of my sicknesses, and especially those of my death.

My Jesus, by that pain which Thou didst suffer in Thy most sacred head when it was pierced with the thorns, give me the grace never to consent to thoughts displeasing unto Thee.

My Jesus, by that act of Thine by which Thou didst accept of the death of the cross, to which Pilate condemned Thee, give me the grace to accept of my death with resignation, together with all the other pains which shall accompany it.

My Jesus, by the pain which Thou didst suffer in carrying Thy cross on Thy journey to Calvary, give me the grace to suffer with patience all my crosses in this life.

My Jesus, by that pain which Thou didst suffer in having the nails driven through Thy hands and Thy feet, I pray Thee to nail my will unto Thy feet, that so I may will nothing save that which Thou dost will.

My Jesus, by the affliction which Thou didst suffer in having gall given Thee to drink, give me the grace not to offend Thee by intemperance in eating and drinking.

My Jesus, by that pain which Thou didst experience in taking leave of Thy holy Mother upon the cross, deliver me from an inordinate love for my relatives, or for any other creature, that so my heart may be wholly and always Thine.

My Jesus, by that desolation which Thou didst suffer in Thy death in seeing Thyself abandoned by Thy Eternal Father, give me the grace to suffer all my desolations with patience, without ever losing my confidence in Thy goodness.

My Jesus, by those three hours of affliction and agony which Thou didst suffer when dying upon the cross, give me the grace to suffer with resignation, for love of Thee, the pains of my agony at the hour of death.

My Jesus, by that great sorrow which Thou didst feel when Thy most holy soul, when Thou wast expiring, separated itself from Thy most sacred body, give me the grace to breathe forth my soul in the hour of my death, offering up my sorrow then to Thee, together with an act of perfect love, that so I may go to love Thee in heaven, face to face, with all my strength, and for all eternity.

And thee, most holy Virgin, and my Mother Mary, by that sword which pierced thine heart when thou didst behold thy Son bow down his head and expire, do I pray to assist me in the hour of my death, that so I may come to praise thee and to thank thee in paradise for all the graces that thou hast obtained for me from God.

Way of the Cross.

Among the devotional exercises which have for their object meditation on the Passion, the cross, and the death of our Lord and Saviour Jesus Christ, the sovereign means for the conversion of sinners, for the renovation of the tepid, and for the sanctification of the just, one of the chief has ever been the exercise of the Way of Calvary, commonly called the Way of the Cross. This devotion, continued in an unbroken tradition from the time Jesus Christ ascended into heaven, arose, first in Jerusalem, amongst the Christians who dwelt there, out of veneration for those sacred spots which were sanctified by the sufferings of our divine Redeemer. •From that time, as we learn from St. Jerome, Christians were wont to visit the holy places in crowds; and the gathering of the faithful, he says, even from the farthest corners of the earth, to visit the holy places, continued to his own times.

•From Jerusalem this devout exercise began to be introduced into Europe by various pious and holy persons who had travelled to the Holy Land to satisfy their devotion. Amongst others, we read of the Blessed Alvarez, of the Order of Friars Preachers, who, after he returned to his own convent of St. Dominic, in Cordova, built several little chapels, in which he represented, station by station, the principal events which took place on our Lord's way to Mount Calvary. Afterward, more formally, the Fathers Minorite Observants of the Order of St. Francis, as soon as ever, on the foundation of their Order, they were introduced into the Holy Land, and more especially from the time when, in the year 1342, they had their house in Jerusalem, and the custody of the sacred places, began, both in Italy and elsewhere, in short, throughout the whole Catholic world, to spread the devotion of the Way of the Cross. This they effected by erecting, in all their own churches, fourteen separate stations, in visiting which the faithful, like the devout pilgrims who go in person to visit the holy places in Jerusalem, do themselves also make this journey in spirit, whilst they meditate on all that our Lord Jesus Christ vouchsafed to suffer for our eternal salvation at those holy places, in the last hours of his life.

This excellent devotion has met with the repeated approvals of the holy Church ; in the Constitutions, for instance, of the venerable pontiff Innocent XI.; Innocent XII.; of the two Benedicts, XIII. and XIV.; and of Clement XII. By this last Pope it was extended to the whole Catholic world; and it is now in constant use with persons of every condition, being, moreover, enriched with most numerous indulgences. For instance, those who perform devoutly the Way of the Cross may gain all the indulgences which have been granted by the Popes to the faithful who visit in person the sacred places in Jerusalem. All, however, who wish to gain these indulgences by means of this devotion must bear in mind that it is indispensably required of them to meditate, according to their ability, on the Passion of our Lord and Saviour Jesus Christ, and to go from one station to the other, so far as the number of persons engaged in the devotion, and the confined space where the fourteen stations are erected, will admit. This is evident from the Apostolical Constitutions above named. And from this it follows that the recitation at each of the stations of the words " We adore Thee, Christ," etc., the *Our Father*, the *Hail Mary*, and " Have mercy on us, O Lord," is nothing more than a pious and praiseworthy custom, introduced by devout persons into the devotion of the Way of the Cross. This the Sacred Congregation of Indulgences declared, in the instructions for performing the exercises of the Way of the Cross, Nos. VI. and IX., published by the order and with the approbation of Clement XII., April 3. 1731, and Benedict XIV., May 10, 1742.

All, however, who are sick, all who are in prison or at sea, or *in partibus infidelium*, or are prevented in any other way from visiting the stations of the Way of the Cross erected in churches or public oratories, may gain these indulgences by saying, with at least contrite heart and devotion, the *Our Father*, the *Hail Mary*, and the *Glory be to the Father*, each fourteen times; and at the end of these the *Our Father*, the *Hail Mary* and the *Glory be to the Father* each five time ; and again one *Our Father*, one *Hail Mary*, and one *Glory be the Father* for the Sovereign Pontiff, holding in their hands the while a crucifix of brass, or of any other solid substance, which has been blessed by the Father-General of the Order of the Friars Minor Observants, or else by the Father-Provincial or by any Father-Guardian, subject to the said Father General, or by a priest who has the faculties to bless such a crucifix. This favor was granted by Pope Clement XIV., Jan. 26, 1773. at the prayer of the Reformed Minorites of the Retreat of St. Bonaventure, in Rome, who keep this decree in their archives.

It is also to be observed that these crucifixes, thus indulgenced, after they have been blessed, cannot be sold, or given away, or lent to any one for the purpose of enabling them to gain the indulgences of the Way of the Cross, as appears from the decrees to this effect of the Sacred Congregation of Indulgences. ED.

MANNER OF PRACTISING THE EXERCISE OF THE WAY OF THE CROSS.

Let each one, kneeling before the high altar, make an act of contrition, and form the intention of gaining the indulgences, whether for himself or for the souls in purgatory. Then say: My Lord Jesus Christ, Thou hast made this journey to die for me with love unutterable, and I have so many times unworthily abandoned Thee ; but now I love Thee with my whole heart, and because I love Thee I repent sincerely for having ever offended Thee. Pardon me, my God, and permit me to accompany Thee on this journey. Thou goest to die for love of me ; I wish also, my beloved Redeemer, to die for love of Thee. My Jesus, I will live and die always united to Thee.

> Dear Jesus, Thou dost go to die
> For very love of me :
> Ah ! let me bear Thee company,
> I wish to die with Thee.

FIRST STATION.

Jesus is condemned to Death.

V. We adore Thee, O Christ, and praise Thee.

R. Because by Thy holy cross Thou hast redeemed the world.

Consider that Jesus, after having been scourged and crowned with thorns, was unjustly condemned by Pilate to die on the cross.

My adorable Jesus, it was not Pilate, no, it was my sins, that condemned Thee to die. I beseech Thee, by the merits of this sorrowful journey, to assist my soul in its journey towards eternity. I love Thee, my beloved

Jesus; I love Thee more than myself; I repent with my whole heart of having offended Thee. Never permit me to separate myself from Thee again. Grant that I may love Thee always; and then do with me what Thou wilt.

Our Father. Hail Mary. Glory be, etc.

> Dear Jesus, Thou dost go to die
> For very love of me :
> Ah ! let me bear Thee company,
> I wish to die with Thee.

SECOND STATION.

Jesus is made to bear His Cross.

V. We adore Thee, O Christ, and praise Thee.

R. Because by Thy holy cross Thou hast redeemed the world.

Consider that Jesus, in making this journey with the cross on his shoulders, thought of us, and offered for us to his Father the death that he was about to undergo.

My most beloved Jesus, I embrace all the tribulations that Thou hast destined for me until death. I beseech Thee, by the merits of the pain Thou didst suffer in carrying Thy cross, to give me the necessary help to carry mine with perfect patience and resignation. I love Thee, Jesus, my love; I repent of having offended Thee. Never permit me to separate myself from Thee again. Grant that I may love Thee always, and then do with me what Thou wilt.

Our Father. Hail Mary. Glory be, etc.

> Dear Jesus, Thou dost go to die
> For very love of me:
> Ah! let me bear Thee company,
> I wish to die with Thee.

THIRD STATION.

Jesus falls the First Time under His Cross.

V. We adore Thee, O Christ, and praise Thee.

R. Because by Thy holy cross Thou hast redeemed the world.

Consider this first fall of Jesus under his cross. His flesh was torn by the scourges, his head crowned with thorns, and he had lost a great quantity of blood. He was so weakened that he could scarcely walk, and yet he had to carry this great load upon his shoulders. The soldiers struck him rudely, and thus he fell several times in his journey.

My beloved Jesus, it is not the weight of the cross, but of my sins which has made Thee suffer so much pain. Ah, by the merits of this first fall, deliver me from the misfortune of falling into mortal sin. I love Thee, O my Jesus, with my whole heart; I repent of having offended Thee. Never permit me to offend Thee again. Grant that I may love Thee always; and then do with me what Thou wilt.

Our Father. Hail Mary. Glory be, etc.

> Dear Jesus, Thou dost go to die
> For very love of me :
> Ah ! let me bear Thee company.
> I wish to die with Thee.

FOURTH STATION.

Jesus meets His Afflicted Mother.

V. We adore Thee, O Christ, and praise Thee.

R. Because by Thy holy cross Thou hast redeemed the world.

Consider the meeting of the Son and the Mother, which took place on this journey. Jesus and Mary looked at each other, and their looks became as so many arrows to wound those hearts which loved each other so tenderly.

My most loving Jesus, by the sorrow Thou didst experience in this meeting, grant me the grace of a truly devoted love for Thy most holy Mother. And thou, my Queen, who wast overwhelmed with sorrow, obtain for me by thy intercession a continual and tender remembrance of the Passion of thy Son. I love Thee, Jesus, my love; I repent of ever having offended Thee. Never permit me to offend Thee again. Grant that I may love Thee, and then do with me what Thou wilt.

Our Father. Hail Mary. Glory be, etc.

Dear Jesus, Thou dost go to die
For very love of me :
Ah ! let me bear Thee company,
I wish to die with Thee.

FIFTH STATION.

The Cyrenian helps Jesus to carry His Cross.

V. We adore Thee, O Christ, and praise Thee.

R. Because by Thy holy cross Thou hast redeemed the world.

Consider that the Jews, seeing that at each step Jesus, from weakness, was on the point of expiring, and fearing that he would die on the way, when they wished him to die the ignominious death of the cross, constrained Simon the Cyrenian to carry the cross behind our Lord.

My most sweet Jesus, I will not refuse the cross as the Cyrenian did; I accept it, I embrace it. I accept in particular the death that Thou hast destined for me, with all the pains which may accompany it; I unite it to Thy death, I offer it to Thee. Thou hast died for love of me ; I will die for love of Thee, and to please Thee.

Help me by Thy grace. I love Thee, Jesus, my love; I repent of having offended Thee. Never permit me to offend Thee again. Grant that I may love Thee ; and then do with me what Thou wilt.

Our Father. Hail Mary. Glory be, etc.

> Dear Jesus Thou dost go to die
> For very love of me :
> Ah! let me bear Thee company,
> I wish to die with Thee.

SIXTH STATION.

Veronica wipes the Face of Jesus.

V. We adore Thee, O Christ, and praise Thee.

R. Because by Thy holy cross Thou hast redeemed the world.

Consider that the holy woman named Veronica, seeing Jesus so afflicted, and his face bathed in sweat and blood, presented him with a towel, with which he wiped his adorable face, leaving on it the impression of his holy countenance.

My most beloved Jesus, Thy face was beautiful before, but in this journey it has lost all its beauty, and wounds and blood have disfigured it. Alas ! my soul also was once beautiful, when it received Thy grace in baptism ; but I have disfigured it since by my sins; Thou alone, my Redeemer, canst restore it to its former beauty. Do this by Thy Passion, and then do with me what Thou wilt.

Our Father. Hail Mary. Glory be, etc.

> Dear Jesus, Thou dost go to die
> For very love of me :
> Ah ! let me bear Thee company,
> I wish to die with Thee.

SEVENTH STATION.

Jesus falls the Second Time.

V. We adore Thee, O Christ, and praise Thee.

R. Because by Thy holy cross Thou hast redeemed the world.

Consider the second fall of Jesus under the cross,—a fall which renews the pain of all the wounds of the head and members of our afflicted Lord.

My most gentle Jesus, how many times Thou hast pardoned me, and how many times have I fallen again, and begun again to offend Thee ! Oh, by the merits of this new fall, give me the necessary helps to persevere in Thy grace until death. Grant that in all temptations which assail me I may always commend myself to Thee. I love Thee, Jesus, my love, with my whole heart ; I repent of having offended Thee. Never permit me to offend Thee again. Grant that I may love Thee always ; and then do with me what Thou wilt.

Our Father. Hail Mary. Glory be, etc.

> Dear Jesus, Thou dost go to die
> For very love of me :
> Ah ! let me bear Thee company,
> I wish to die with Thee.

EIGHTH STATION.

Jesus speaks to the Daughters of Jerusalem.

V. We adore Thee, O Christ, and praise Thee.

R. Because by Thy holy cross Thou hast redeemed the world.

Consider that those women wept with compassion at seeing Jesus in so pitiable a state, streaming with blood, as he walked along. But Jesus said to them, " Weep not for me, but for your children."

My Jesus, laden with sorrows, I weep for the offences

that I have committed against Thee, because of the pains which they have deserved, and still more because of the displeasure which they have caused Thee, who hast loved me so much.   It is Thy love, more than the fear of hell, which causes me to weep for my sins.   My Jesus, I love Thee more than myself; I repent of having offended Thee.   Never permit me to offend Thee again.   Grant that I may love Thee always; and then do with me what Thou wilt.

Our Father. Hail Mary. Glory be, etc.

> Dear Jesus, Thou dost go to die
> For very love of me :
> Ah ! let me bear Thee company,
> I wish to die with Thee.

NINTH STATION.
Jesus falls the Third Time.

V. We adore Thee, O Christ, and praise Thee.

R. Because by Thy holy cross Thou hast redeemed the world.

Consider the third fall of Jesus Christ.   His weakness was extreme, and the cruelty of his executioners excessive, who tried to hasten his steps when he had scarcely strength to move.

Ah, my outraged Jesus, by the merits of the weakness that Thou didst suffer in going to Calvary, give me strength sufficient to conquer all human respect and all my wicked passions, which have led me to despise Thy friendship.   I love Thee, Jesus, my love, with my whole heart; I repent of having offended Thee.   Never permit me to offend Thee again.   Grant that I may love Thee always; and then do with me what Thou wilt.

Our Father. Hail Mary. Glory be, etc.

> Dear Jesus, Thou dost go to die
> For very love of me :
> Ah ! let me bear Thee company,
> I wish to die with Thee.

TENTH STATION.

Jesus is stripped of His Garments.

V. We adore Thee, O Christ, and praise Thee.

R. Because by Thy holy cross Thou hast redeemed the world.

Consider the violence with which the executioners stripped Jesus. His inner garments adhered to his torn flesh, and they dragged them off so roughly that the skin came with them. Compassionate your Saviour thus cruelly treated, and say to him: My innocent Jesus, by the merits of the torment that Thou hast felt, help me to strip myself of all affection to things of earth, in order that I may place all my love in Thee, who art so worthy of my love. I love Thee, O Jesus, with my whole heart; I repent of having offended Thee. Never permit me to offend Thee again. Grant that I may love Thee always; and then do with me what Thou wilt.

Our Father.   Hail Mary.   Glory be, etc.

> Dear Jesus, Thou dost go to die
> For very love of me :
> Ah ! let me bear Thee company,
> I wish to die with Thee.

ELEVENTH STATION.

Jesus is nailed to the Cross.

V. We adore Thee, O Christ, and praise Thee.

R. Because by Thy holy cross Thou hast redeemed the world.

Consider that Jesus, after being thrown on the cross, extended his hands, and offered to his Eternal Father the sacrifice of his life for our salvation. These barbarians fastened him with nails ; and then, raising the cross, leave him to die with anguish on this infamous gibbet.

My Jesus, loaded with contempt, nail my heart to Thy feet, that it may ever remain there to love Thee, and never quit Thee again. I love Thee more than myself; I repent of having offended Thee. Never permit me to offend Thee again. Grant that I may love Thee always; and then do with me what Thou wilt.

Our Father. Hail Mary. Glory be, etc.

> Dear Jesus, Thou dost go to die
> For very love of me :
> Ah ! let me bear Thee company,
> I wish to die with Thee.

TWELFTH STATION.

Jesus dies on the Cross.

V. We adore Thee, O Christ, and praise Thee.

R. Because by Thy holy cross Thou hast redeemed the world.

Consider that thy Jesus, after three hours' agony on the cross, consumed at length with anguish, abandons himself to the weight of his body, bows his head, and dies.

O my dying Jesus, I kiss devoutly the cross on which Thou didst die for love of me. I have merited by my sins to die a miserable death; but Thy death is my hope. Ah, by the merits of Thy death, give me grace to die, embracing Thy feet and burning with love to Thee. I commit my soul into Thy hands. I love Thee with my whole heart; I repent of ever having offended Thee. Permit not that I ever offend Thee again. Grant that I may love Thee always; and then do with me what Thou wilt.

Our Father. Hail Mary. Glory be, etc.

> Dear Jesus, Thou dost go to die
> For very love of me :
> Ah ! let me bear Thee company,
> I wish to die with Thee.

THIRTEENTH STATION.

Jesus is taken down from the Cross.

V. We adore Thee, O Christ, and praise Thee.

R. Because by Thy holy cross Thou hast redeemed the world.

Consider that, our Lord having expired, two of his disciples, Joseph and Nicodemus, took him down from the cross, and placed him in the arms of his afflicted mother, who received him with unutterable tenderness, and pressed him to her bosom.

O Mother of sorrow, for the love of this Son, accept me for thy servant, and pray to him for me. And Thou, my Redeemer, since Thou hast died for me, permit me to love Thee; for I wish but Thee, and nothing more. I love Thee, my Jesus, and I repent of ever having offended Thee. Never permit me to offend Thee again. Grant that I may love Thee always; and then do with me what Thou wilt.

Our Father. Hail Mary. Glory be, etc.

> Dear Jesus, Thou dost go to die
> For very love of me :
> Ah ! let me bear Thee company,
> I wish to die with Thee.

FOURTEENTH STATION.

Jesus is placed in the Sepulchre.

V. We adore Thee, O Christ, and praise Thee.

R. Because by Thy holy cross Thou hast redeemed the world.

Consider that the disciples carried the body of Jesus to bury it, accompanied by his holy Mother, who arranged it in the sepulchre with her own hands. They then closed the tomb, and all withdrew.

Ah, my buried Jesus, I kiss the stone that encloses Thee. But Thou didst rise again the third day. I beseech Thee, by Thy resurrection, make me rise glorious with Thee at the last day, to be always united with Thee in heaven, to praise Thee, and love Thee forever. I love Thee, and I repent of ever having offended Thee. Permit not that I ever offend Thee again. Grant that I may love Thee; and then do with me what Thou wilt.

Our Father. Hail Mary. Glory be, etc.

> Dear Jesus, Thou dost go to die
> For very love of me :
> Ah ! let me bear Thee company,
> I wish to die with Thee.

After this, return to the high altar, and say, *Our Father, Hail Mary*, and *Glory be*, etc., five times, in honor of the Passion of Jesus Christ, to gain the other indulgences granted to those who recite them.*

---

* At the end, the *Our Father*, the *Hail Mary*, and the *Glory be to the Father* may be said to the intention of the Sovereign Pontiff.

Hymns.

I.

THE PASSION OF JESUS CHRIST.

O ruthless scourges, with what pain you tear
My Saviour's flesh, so innocent and fair!
Oh, cease to rend that flesh divine,
 My loving Lord torment no more;
Wound rather, wound this heart of mine,
 The guilty cause of all he bore.

Ye cruel thorns, in mocking wreath entwin'd
My Saviour's brow in agony to bind,
Oh, cease to rend that flesh divine,
 My loving Lord torment no more;
Wound rather, wound this heart of mine,
 The guilty cause of all he bore.

Unpitying nails, whose points, with anguish fierce,
The hands and feet of my Redeemer pierce!
Oh, cease to rend that flesh divine,
 My loving Lord torment no more;
Wound rather, wound this heart of mine,
 The guilty cause of all he bore.

Unfeeling lance, that dar'st to open wide
The sacred temple of my Saviour's side!
Oh, cease to wound that flesh divine,
 My loving Lord insult no more;
Pierce rather, pierce this heart of mine,
 The guilty cause of all he bore.

II.

TO JESUS IN HIS PASSION.

My Jesus! say, what wretch has dar'd
 Thy sacred hands to bind?
And who has dar'd to buffet so
 Thy face so meek and kind?

'Tis I have thus ungrateful been,
  Yet, Jesus, pity take!
Oh, spare and pardon me, my Lord,
  For Thy sweet mercy's sake!

My Jesus! who with spittle vile
  Profan'd Thy sacred brow?
Or whose unpitying scourge has made
  Thy precious blood to flow?

'Tis I have thus ungrateful been;
  Yet, Jesus, pity take!
Oh, spare and pardon me, my Lord,
  For Thy sweet mercy's sake!

My Jesus! whose the hand that wove
  That cruel thorny crown?
Who made that hard and heavy cross
  That weighs Thy shoulders down?

'Tis I have thus ungrateful been,
  Yet, Jesus, pity take!
Oh, spare and pardon me, my Lord,
  For Thy sweet mercy's sake!

My Jesus! who has mock'd Thy thirst
  With vinegar and gall!
Who held the nails that pierc'd Thy hands,
  And made the hammer fall?

'Tis I have thus ungrateful been,
  Yet, Jesus, pity take!
Oh, spare and pardon me, my Lord,
  For Thy sweet mercy's sake?

My Jesus! say, who dar'd to nail
  Those tender feet of Thine?
And whose the arm that rais'd the lance
  To pierce that heart divine?

'Tis I have thus ungrateful been,
   Yet, Jesus, pity take!
Oh, spare and pardon me, my Lord,
   For Thy sweet mercy's sake!

And, Mary! who has murder'd thus
   Thy lov'd and only One?
Canst thou forgive the blood-stain'd hand
   That robb'd thee of thy Son?

'Tis I have thus ungrateful been
   To Jesus and to thee;
Forgive me for thy Jesus' sake,
   And pray to him for me.

Cantata on the Passion.

THE SOUL AND THE REDEEMER.

The Soul.

Tell me, thou judge iniquitous, ah! tell me why
Thou didst so oft my Saviour's innocence proclaim,
And yet, at length, condemn him to a death of shame,
Like vilest criminal upon a cross to die?
Of what avail the barb'rous scourges, cruel blows,
If, in thy heart, thou didst his future death decree?
Why not at once have doom'd him to the bitter tree
When the first cry of hate from surging crowds arose?
Since well thou knewest thou wouldst sentence him to die,
Why not at once make known his cruel destiny?
But what do I behold? an angry crowd draws near,
Confused cries are heard, and threat'ning groans resound;
Nearer still and nearer there comes a thrilling sound.
What is this clam'rous music breaking on mine ear?
Ah! it is the trumpet, whose shrill discordant breath
Proclaims aloud the sentence of my Saviour's death.
Now, alas! I see him: along the rugged road
Painfully he's toiling with tott'ring step and slow,
Wounded, sore, and bleeding, he bears the heavy load
Laid upon his shoulder by his relentless foe.

At ev'ry painful step he makes
Fresh blood-drops mark the way he takes.
 A cross of wood
Upon his wounded shoulder rests ;
His bruised flesh ·is staining it with blood:
His venerable head a mocking crown adorns ;
His aching brows are pierc'd with long and cruel thorns.
'Tis Thy unfathom'd love, my dearest Lord,
That makes Thee wear this crown of mockery.
Where goest Thou, my God ador'd ?

The Redeemer.

I go to die for thee.

The Soul.

Dear Lord, it is for me
Thou goest forth to die ?
How gladly, then, would I
Lay down my life for Thee !

The Redeemer.

Peace ! till thy dying breath
Think on My love for thee ;
After My bitter death
Forever love thou Me.
Remain, my turtle dove !
For My Heart give me thine;
My faithful one ! be Mine,
And pledge Me all thy love.

The Soul.

My Lord ! I Thee adore,
To Thee my heart I bring.
I'm Thine, my treasur'd King,
I'm Thine for evermore !

The original text of this cantata was discovered in London in the
year 1859, the words and music being by St. Alphonsus, who, we are
assured, composed them in 1760, with corrections made with his own
hand. We here give the entire text, such as has been published in
London by M. J. Philip.—Ed.

L' Anima e il Redentore.

ANIMA.

Giudice ingiusto e iniquo !
Dopo che tu più volte
Dichiaravi innocente il mio Signore,
Or così lo condanni
A morir da ribaldo in una croce !
Barbaro ! a che serviva
Condannarlo a flagelli,
Se condannarlo a morte poscia volevi ?
Meglio, alle prime voci
De' suoi nemici,
Condannato l'avresti a quella morte
A cui, malvagio, lo destini e mandi.

Ma oimè ! qual misto
D'armi, di grida e pianti,
Rumor confuso io sento !
E quale mai è questo
Suono ferale e mesto ?
Ahimè ! quest' è la tromba
Che forse publicando
Va la condanna
Del mio Signore a morte !

Ma, oh Dio ! ecco, ahi dolore !
Il mio Gesù afflitto,
Versando sangue e con tremante passo,
Appena, ahimè ! può camminare ! e intanto
Del suo divino sangue
Segna la terra dov' ei posa il piede !
Una pesante croce preme
Le sue piagate e tormentate spalle ;
E barbara corona,
D'acute spine intesta,
Il venerando capo
Circonda !—Ah ! mio Signore ! l'amore
Rè ti fecè di scherno e di dolore !
Dove, Gesù, ten vai ?

REDENTORE.
Vado per te a morir.

ANIMA.
Dunque per me a morire
Ten vai, mio caro Dio!
Voglio venire anch' io,
Voglio morir con te.

REDENTORE.

Tu resta in pace, e intendi
L' amor che io ti porto ;
E quando sarò morto,
Ricordati di me.

Restane dunque, o cara !
E in segno dell' amore,
Donami tutto il core
E serbami la fè.

ANIMA.

Sì, mio Tesor, mio Bene !
Tutto il mio cor ti dono ;
E tutta quant' io sono,
Tutta son tua, mio Rè !

INDEX.

G.

God, love that he has shown us in giving us his Son, 142, 232, 322. The sight of God constitutes the happiness of the elect, 463.
Giacopone, Blessed, his love for Jesus Christ, 39.

H.

Herod interrogates the Saviour and insults him, 76.
Hope that the death of the Son of God for us gives to us, 129, 234, 254, 300, 313, 336.
Heart of Jesus, opened after his death, 318.

I.

Insults offered to Jesus while he was hanging on the cross, 271.

J.

Jerusalem: Jesus enters it in triumph, 164, 429; he enters it as a prisoner, 179, 433.
Jesus Christ, Pontiff of future blessings and Mediator of the New Testament, 311, 346, 359; eternal Priest according to the order of Melchisedech, 350; love that he has shown us in wishing to atone for our sins, 23, 233, 345; in suffering so much for us, 32, 385; in wishing to die for us, 149, 324; in instituting the Eucharist, 52, 171. He loves each one of us in particular as much as all, 28, 327. Desire that He had to suffer for us, 43. He wished to suffer during his whole life, 41, 418; and what sufferings, 45, 120, 239, 271, 413; and what humiliations, 69, 242, 272, 416, 421. Jesus on the cross teaches patience, 115, 364; and charity, 118; he gains hearts, 116. Consideration of Jesus on the cross, 267, 303, 424, 425, 449, 455. He has brought us more good than the devil brought us evil, 138. Thanks that we owe to him, 233, 330; confidence and love, 378, 411.
John, St., at the foot of the cross, 284.
Judas, his treachery, 71, 167.

L.

Love, divine, the consideration of the Passion of Christ is a great means to obtain it, 17, 159.

T.

W.

www.ingramcontent.com/pod-product-compliance
Lightning Source LLC
Chambersburg PA
CBHW020449270326
41926CB00008B/542